Fury of Past Time

A LIFE OF
GWYN THOMAS

DARYL LEEWORTHY

PARTHIAN

Parthian, Cardigan SA43 1ED
www.parthianbooks.com
© Daryl Leeworthy 2022 2023
ISBN 9781913640101
Edited by Dai Smith
Typeset by Elaine Sharples
Index by Non Lowri Evans
Printed by 4edge Limited
Published with the financial support of the Welsh Books CouncilThe
Modern Wales series receives support from the Rhys Davies Trust

the Rhys Davies Trust

British Library Cataloguing in Publication Data
A cataloguing record for this book is available from the British Library.
Every attempt has been made to secure the permission of copyright
holders to reproduce archival and printed material.

For Dad

CONTENTS

ABBREVIATIONS

AFSE	*A Few Selected Exits*
AWE	*A Welsh Eye*
BBC	British Broadcasting Corporation
BBC WAC	BBC Written Archives Centre, Caversham, Reading
BL	British Library, London
DH	*Daily Herald*
DM	*Daily Mail*
GTP	Gwyn Thomas Papers, National Library of Wales
HTV	Harlech Television
ITV	Independent Television
LFD	*Laughter from the Dark* by Michael Parnell
NLW	National Library of Wales, Aberystwyth
OULC	Oxford University Labour Club
RBA	Richard Burton Archives, Swansea University
RMP	Reginald Moore Papers, British Library
RT	*Radio Times*
SEH	St Edmund Hall, Oxford
SWML	South Wales Miners' Library, Swansea University
TLS	*Times Literary Supplement*
TNA	The National Archives, Kew
TW	*Television Weekly*
TWW	Television Wales and the West
WM	*Western Mail*

PROLOGUE

In 1974, Gwyn Thomas sat down with the HTV arts programme, *Nails*, to discuss his life and his creative work in fiction, for the stage, for television and for radio.[1] Filmed in Gwyn's favourite pub, the Sportsman's Rest, near his house in the village of Peterston-super-Ely in the Vale of Glamorgan, the interview was a generally light-hearted portrait, mixing comedy with sweeping suggestions about the writer's self-declared 'wings of significance.' There was a darker tone at times, too. At one point, staring askance at the camera, his head tilted and index finger pointing, as if instructing the viewer like a chapel minister or university lecturer, Gwyn spoke with the imagined voice of his mother telling him to 'abuse them, my friend, level them, give them a black eye, this life is not worth living.' And then, as if the sermon/lecture had been delivered, the writer snapped out of his character, his voice raised to its normal pitch, and with a smile on his face, returned to his reflective mood. 'That's what I've tried to do you know,' he said, 'in a quiet way. In my novels, in my plays, there is no love of life at all.' To which the interviewer interjected, confused by the observation, 'plenty of love of people?' Gwyn responded: 'love of people, yes, yes, but deep down always the voice of the mother, the marvellous contralto voice ... who said, "there is a trap here Gwyn, we are not going to be happy here, I'm bringing you out into this world and I pity you."'

Throughout his adult life, with fame assured first by his pen and then by his on-screen personality, Gwyn sought to balance the light of his comedy with the darkness of his collective and individual reality. His books, especially those in their bright

1

yellow dust jackets published by Victor Gollancz in the 1950s, were splashed with endorsements from reviewers, each attesting to a 'uniquely satisfying' novelist, one who was widely regarded in post-war Britain as a 'comic genius.' Gwyn, it was said, wrote in 'magic prose' and 'passionate poetry.' His 'wild humour' was the essence of a 'most stimulating, vigorous, biting [and] exuberant novelist.' His work, which revelled in the 'sheer beauty of language,' was the product of a man 'full of raging, brilliant, entirely idiosyncratic fun.' He was compared to the French satirist François Rabelais; to the worldly creator of *The Canterbury Tales*, Geoffrey Chaucer; and to the distinctive twentieth-century American short-story writer and hard-boiled journalist, Damon Runyon. 'Mr Thomas's inspiration is rich and inexhaustible,' observed the marketing voice on the dust jacket of *Now Lead Us Home* in 1952, the second of the novels released by Gollancz, 'the style, the poetry, the wit, the vivid setting peopled with its fascinating, individual characters ... are unique in modern fiction.'

This comedic quality was much prized by radio and television producers, newspaper columnists, documentary makers, and magazine editors, all keen for a memorable but revelatory soundbite. Gwyn happily obliged. Prompted by Michael Parkinson to ponder the magnetism of the Rhondda and its people, in an interview broadcast on the BBC in November 1971, Gwyn observed that his native valley pulled on him because it was 'really one of the most entertaining parts of the world, you know' and home to a marvellous 'set of comedians, liars [and] thinkers.'[2] Yet, for a writer of Gwyn's calibre and character, comedy always had a deliberate purpose: it was the means of passing judgement on awful circumstances in a manner palatable to audiences. Laughter was, as the American songwriters Richard and Robert Sherman famously suggested in the 1964 film, *Mary Poppins*, the spoonful of sugar. The darker roots of Gwyn's humour lay in the collective traumas experienced by the people of the South Wales Valleys in the 1920s and 1930s such as mass unemployment, poverty, and emigration; and in the personal traumas of losing his mother in 1919 when he was just six years old, and a life-threatening illness of his own. It was as if Gwyn was 'crouched there in the darkness of my childhood, my beginning, my growing up, and out there in the dark are the people who are waiting to hear what I'm saying.'

Understanding why Gwyn articulated his thoughts through comedy, his laughter from the dark, whether in print or in verbal anecdote, is not enough to fully understand the man. Too much is left out. He used conversations and interviews as a performance, never really listening to what others were saying but always waiting for the opportune moment to seize the limelight and become the centre of attention. His personality on screen was thus carefully constructed. There was the voice and insistent accent, neither of which were easy to replicate; there was the command of the rhythm and metre of language; the physical gesturing; and even the trademark mackintosh and trilby hat. These elements were all fundamental to a character which Gwyn was playing. For he was as oral in intent as he was verbal in approach. Harsher critics labelled it 'windbaggery' or a 'Welsh style of speaking,' barbs thrown variously at Aneurin Bevan and Neil Kinnock, or worse. As though the performance of these men was untrustworthy or the act of a jester hoping to amuse a colonial master.[3] And yet, such artistry provided audiences with a means of comprehension, of showing that they too understood 'the joke.' It was never allowed to distract from 'a pattern of thought at once clear and complex,' as Dai Smith has observed. This was a method of emotive persuasion through an appeal to shared experiences, showing a clear understanding that 'it was language alone which allowed ... listeners to comprehend reality as something which could be fashioned in its plasticity not just endured in its materiality.'[4]

Gwyn, like Bevan, recoiled from and aspired to the removal of the ugly, neglectful capitalist society which had created the coal mining industry and exploited generation after generation of working-class people. Mining was a form of labour which removed from most of either man's contemporaries the opportunities to enjoy the full creative potential of human existence. 'To go down into the pit,' Gwyn explained,

> was to go down into the grave socially; some of the lads they really loved the idea of following their mates down into the hole, earning money at fourteen or fifteen or whatever it was; and they used to wear ... the white ducks, the trousers they used to wear – virgin white. And this was one of the great things, to watch these lads going for the first time down into the pit with these marvellous trousers glowing in the pre-dawn dark. And, of course, the whiteness and virginity would go out of their lives almost as fast as it went out of their trousers.

To escape this fate, Gwyn reasoned, one had to use language. 'Words are, after all, weapons,' he told Michael Parkinson in 1971, 'and the weapons we had to use to get out.'

Gwyn did not mean emigration but something more complex: the getting out of the mindset of the doldrums which exploitation and poverty had occasioned. 'Had the Rhondda evolved one great anthem to itself,' he wrote in 1974 in an essay to accompany a collection of old photographs gathered together by Cyril Batstone, 'it would have been a unique salute to the cruelty and greatness of life among the common folk. The Rhondda mind grew bright over the task of sorting the ecstasy from the outrage.'[5] What had been the economic, social and industrial dynamism of the South Wales Valleys of the late

Victorian and Edwardian years, which did not survive much beyond Gwyn's early childhood, a fact which always weighed upon him and gave purpose to his writing, gave way first to the austerity of the interwar years and then to the affluence of post-war Britain. It was this 'vulgar' and 'meretricious society' in which 'priorities have gone all wrong,' as Aneurin Bevan put it in his final speech to the Labour Party's annual conference in 1959, which Gwyn tackled in his comedy novels for Victor Gollancz. Set against the backdrop of Harold MacMillan's 'never had it so good' prosperity, Gwyn pointed to the contradictions of the 1950s and to the malice and ugliness which had survived the War and the Depression intact. His plots illustrated the challenge of remaining honest in a dishonest age and the need to hold onto the values of a collective society as it fragmented.

In other words, here was a deeply political writer whose purpose can be entirely misunderstood if his politics are not recognised and set at the heart of the biographical portrait, alongside humour and melancholy. The best of Gwyn's reviewers and readers, whether fellow Welshmen such as Raymond Williams or Richard Burton, or Englishmen such as Alan Plater and Sid Chaplin, or Americans such as Studs Terkel, Norman Rosten, and Nelson Algren, all appreciated the political foundations of his work and the complexity of his creative voice. As did the historian Eric Hobsbawm.[6] They realised, as some of Gwyn's biographers and more recent critics have not, that the laughter was individual and collective, that the darkness was individual and collective, that the politics were individual and collective, and that this interwoven trinity of mood and motivation set down more fully in fiction what others have come to understand through the partial vision of the historical lens. Hence Gwyn's insistence in the interview with *Nails* that his interest was not life (and thus the 'systems' into which life can be organised) but people, and especially those of the Rhondda. As he put it in his foreword for *Old Rhondda*:

> The people who lived between the Rhondda hills were infinitely more interesting and precious than the stuff they hauled out of the rich seams and exported to any part of the earth in need of power. Singularly little of the wealth they produced stuck to the valley people's fingers. They generated a unique humour, fortitude and goodness, a currency not recognised at the bank. They worked, worshipped, sang and laughed at record levels. It was a place gifted and deprived, glorious and absurd, in equal measure ... created by a world mad for steam, warmth and money.

Foregrounding the political facets of Gwyn's character and creative output offers a necessary counterpoint – and, at times, an insistent corrective – to the understandings of the writer which may be found in other studies, not least in Michael Parnell's influential biography *Laughter From The Dark* which was first published in 1988.[7] Therein and elsewhere, Parnell argued that social comedy was the key to understanding Gwyn, and the writer's political enthusiasms, which could hardly be avoided in the private correspondence to which Parnell had wide-ranging access, were cast as youthful forays into ideology. Those forays were eventually cast aside as the writer matured and gained a more sober disposition (or at least a comportment palatable to the biographer).[8] Parnell's prioritising of laughter at the expense of politics has been rejected in turn by a nationalist school of literary criticism identified with M. Wynn Thomas, Stephen Knight, Daniel Williams, and Barbara Prys-Williams. These critics collectively stress what they see as the negative consequences of 'spoiled' Welshness – an identity as much defined by the Edwardian Liberal institutions of chapel, language, and nation, as by its modern devolved variant – and the internal darkness of mood which such a spoilation occasioned.[9] What these understandings have in common – and which enables their casting aside here in favour of a more holistic portrait of Gwyn Thomas – is their mutual discomfort with the collective nature and reality of South Walian society after the First World War, its individual and collective traumas, and the political rhythms of that place which were orientated towards (and around) social class, not nation and language. Yet, without each of these elements there would be no writer to analyse.

There are attendant risks in recasting Gwyn as a political writer, of course, even as such a presentation reveals the truth of the man and the artist. The 'normal' facets of his life such as his teaching career, his long marriage to Lyn, his numerous friendships, his wider family, and even the literary functions of his writing, can easily be overshadowed by the worlds of interwar communism and anti-fascism and post-war Bevanite social democracy, the Cold War, or the African American civil rights movement. A more typical literary biographer might well have sought to provide an answer to the debate about whether Gwyn was an expressionist, modernist, fabulist, or realist; a writer of comedy, of fable, or of something along the lines of socialist realism. The truth is, he was all those things, when it suited him. He was influenced on the one hand, as Gareth Williams has noted, by nineteenth-century French and Italian opera and, on the other, as Victor Golightly identified, by the cinema, peppering his writing with synaesthetic cues intended to evoke the aural and visual world of the coalfield.[10] And literary influences ran from the theatre of the Spanish Golden Age to the English social comedies of Aldous Huxley to the autobiographical narratives of Maxim Gorky and Leo Tolstoy to the hard-boiled crime stories imported from the United States and which were a life-long passion for Gwyn.

*

This book is the first full-length biography of Gwyn Thomas to appear in more than three decades. The facts of Gwyn's life, personal and professional, are relatively well-known and have been established by previous biographers, albeit with varying degrees of accuracy which I have corrected where necessary. Dai Smith's recovery of Gwyn's literary ambitions has been instructive, too.[11] Consequently, readers will not necessarily find new biographical insights or literary criticism here so much as a major historical expansion in our understanding of Gwyn's global reach, which was quite extraordinary. I have taken full advantage of digitised sources to bring together, for the first time, the response to Gwyn's work in multiple languages. It has long been known that novels such as *The Dark Philosophers* and *All Things Betray Thee* were translated into several European tongues including Russian and German, but little attempt has been made to understand the reaction in those countries. Recognising *why* Gwyn Thomas was translated and published and discussed, and by whom, is both a revelation and a justification of a political approach to the writer. Out of necessity, therefore, this biography is an interpretation of a life and a career, this is not a literary biography but a political and historical one. Put straightforwardly, the joker was always a judge.[12]

A further motivation in writing this book has been to rescue the totality of Gwyn's career from the condescension of posterity. In the years since his death in 1981, at the comparatively young age of sixty-seven, Gwyn has faded somewhat from public consciousness and is now best known to those older generations who remember him from television in the 1970s. The consequent neglect of his writing is significant: every novel and short-story collection written for Victor

Gollancz in the 1950s is now out of print and increasingly hard to find in that form. The books originally published by Hutchinson, such as *A Welsh Eye* in 1964 and *A Few Selected Exits* in 1968, as well as the Punch compilation *The Lust Lobby* in 1971, have fared a little better. Hutchinson were also responsible for collecting the short stories *Oscar* and *Simeon* and the novella *The Dark Philosophers* in the repackaged *The Sky of our Lives*. Released in hardback in the autumn of 1972, with a paperback following a year later, reviewers embraced the book as a development of 'the macabre and poetic side of [Thomas's] basically comic imagination,' failing to notice that each story had been originally published in the mid-1940s at the start, not the end, of a career.[13]

During the 1980s and 1990s, except for Lawrence and Wishart's release of three of Gwyn's novels, two of which had not previously been published, most republications of the writer's work were undertaken by Welsh publishers.[14] In 1985, the Bridgend-based Seren issued a new edition of Gwyn's memoir *A Few Selected Exits* and followed this with a tie-in edition linked to the television adaptation starring Anthony Hopkins in 1993. Seren also released two volumes of short stories and, in 1990, one volume of plays, each of which was steered to publication by Michael Parnell. *Selected Short Stories* first appeared in 1984 with an expanded edition released in 1988 (itself reprinted in 1995). *Meadow Prospect Revisited*, a compilation largely drawing on Gwyn's work for Punch, arrived in 1992. The Carmarthen-based Golden Grove released an edition of *The Dark Philosophers* coupled with *The Alone to the Alone* and an afterword from Michael Parnell, also in 1988. This trend has continued in recent years with the arrival of the Library of Wales, itself edited by Gwyn's former pupil and long-term champion, Dai Smith, published by Parthian.[15]

The Dark Philosophers was released as the third volume in

the Library of Wales in 2006 (a compilation mirroring the Hutchinson *The Sky of our Lives* release from 1972) with a foreword by the television dramatist Elaine Morgan. *The Alone to the Alone* and *All Things Betray Three* followed in 2008 and 2011 (respectively), the former with a new foreword by the playwright Ian Rowlands, the latter with its 1986 Lawrence and Wishart foreword by Raymond Williams. The Library of Wales has arrested the decline in knowledge and understanding of Gwyn's writing, somewhat, asserting the political vitality of his 1940s breakthrough over the social comedies of the 1950s, although it remains the case that he is regarded by many of his critics as much a figure of the past as a voice current to Wales as it exists in the early twenty-first century. Not so his contemporaries on the Victor Gollancz lists, all of whom had a hand in presenting Wales on the page: Alexander Cordell, whose entire catalogue of work was reprinted in 2014; A. J. Cronin, whose 1937 novel *The Citadel* is now hailed as the literary inspiration for the National Health Service; or Kingsley Amis, whose *Lucky Jim* (1954) and *That Uncertain Feeling* (1955) enjoy the status of a Penguin modern classic. 'Artists are like politicians,' as Gwyn might have observed, using one of Bevan's barbed asides, 'they don't flourish without audiences.'[16]

One of Gwyn's leading champions, Raymond Williams, felt that the novelist was attempting to find the 'voice of the history' of industrial South Wales and, as a consequence, a literary language which went beyond 'either the flattened representations or the applied ideological phrases.'[17] Gwyn thus strove to find the right 'composition of voices.' In a lecture on the 'industrial novel' given at Aberystwyth in September 1977, a preview of the more famous version given as the Gwyn Jones Lecture at University College Cardiff on 21 April 1978, Williams reflected on this problem and the novelist's confrontation with it.[18] It was, Williams thought, fundamentally a matter of form and the need to reconcile literary expectations with the realisation that the South Walian milieu was 'a total transforming social experience.' Williams explained:

> If you are attempting in fiction to respond to the industrial experience, that is, then you are forced into kinds of exploration, kinds of description, kinds of action, which that form can't contain; and which the traditional and received form of the novel seems almost to eject from itself as unmanageable. So that much that is genuinely historically informing in a moving way of a more general kind than the experience of individuals and families becomes difficult to assimilate into the novel form and all the keepers of the form – of the conventional form – will tell the writer that that is not material for fiction. But the more they tell him that is not material for fiction, the more impossible they are making it for him to break through to a form which could comprehend the general experience. What he then usually does is to respond by the change of mood.

Gwyn's response, Williams concluded, was a complete shift in tone; a tone which in some cases conveyed a certain contempt for the situations he was describing, 'but which I see as the humour of a man who has suffered and seen others suffering so much that really is nothing to say but that kind of bitter commentary. At least within the available fictional mode.' His writing,

> revealed the sudden alteration of dimension between formal thought and the experience of suffering, which is concealed inside the joke and the joke, in a way, is the way of communicating it that avoids exposing yourself to yet more suffering in the very patronage of suffering or the consumption of suffering, all the things that in a sense that people have got

used to in those modes. It's a self-protective bitterness, in one way, but it is protective of a community.

Raymond Williams began to grapple seriously with Gwyn's writing in the early 1970s as his attention turned towards Wales once more. He noted in a television review for *The Listener* in 1974, for example, almost as an aside in a discussion otherwise about the drama serial *Perils of Pendragon* which was broadcast on BBC 2 in January and February that year, that 'I prefer both Dylan Thomas and Gwyn Thomas straight.'[19] That is, without fable or fantasy. Hence the status afforded by Raymond Williams to *All Things Betray Thee* as 'the most important novel of this whole phase' of Welsh writing from the 1930s to the 1950s.[20]

A similar line of analysis has been taken by Dai Smith, who noted Gwyn's 'distancing' and suggested that it was the product of using 'a comic irony to open our minds to fresh possibilities. He gave us detached observers whose discursive abilities stemmed from their recognition that they were trapped *as* individuals within a shaping social history.' And this, argued Smith, begins to explain the evident shift in tone and mood from *Sorrow For Thy Sons*, which was written in the second half of the 1930s but went unpublished until the 1980s, to an episodic caper like *The Stranger At My Side*, which was written and published a decade and a half later. Smith concluded: 'In a one-class, one-industry-dominated, geographically isolated area, full of mass actions, collective institutions and self-confidence, it would prove difficult to write anything that did not appear to be overcharged melodrama.'[21] Once that world began to disappear, as it did in earnest in the 1950s and 1960s, leaving just a trio of pits in the Rhondda by 1970, younger novelists such as Alun Richards (1929–2004) and Ron Berry (1920–1997) were free to write in a different but related way about the experience of being South Walian. Albeit not without expressing, in public and in private to each other, their own frustrations about the cultural scene they had entered.

In an article for the literary magazine, *Wales*, published in the autumn of 1959, Alun Richards complained about the artistic quality and breadth of social presentation to be found, in his view, in contemporary 'Anglo-Welsh' literature. Gwyn himself came in for some of Richards's scorn, although the purpose of Richards's intervention was to point, in essence, to the gap in quality between the best of English–English literature and the best of Welsh–English literature, as identified in the literary criticism of figures such as Gwyn Jones, rather than necessarily to attack Gwyn.[22] 'Even given that Mr Thomas is a well-known humorist as well as a chronicler of the times,' Richards began, 'it could scarcely be held that either he or his contemporaries compare as interpreters of economic depression and personal tragedy with such writers as, say, George Orwell or Henry Miller.'[23] The article earned a rebuke from Glyn Jones, himself leading figure in the Anglo-Welsh literary world and the author of *The Dragon Has Two Tongues* (1968), who failed to land his return blows.[24] It took Richards many years to warm to Gwyn's writing, and then only partially. In a letter to Dai Smith sent from Tokyo in 1984, Richards confessed that 'I wish I had read that book of Gwyn's [*The Dark Philosophers*] when he was alive. I don't quite agree with you on him. Maybe I'm deaf still. I think he gave up too early.'[25]

Ron Berry was much more enthusiastic an admirer taking enjoyment from the 'nagging resentment of Welsh people who saw him on the box,' which he felt was the 'proof of Gwyn.' He added, in a letter to Dai Smith, that 'my mother despised Gwyn's TV persona.'[26] This admiration was partly because of an existing friendship and partly because of shared Rhondda roots. Richards was from Pontypridd, the metropolis of the

Rhondda, and from the town's high-on-the-hillside shopocracy, which made all the difference.[27] Berry famously observed that Gwyn was 'the greatest aesthete of all of us,' an observation as accurate as it is odd.[28] Certainly, he was appreciative of and sensitive to art and beauty, as the Oxford English Dictionary defines the term, but perhaps behind Berry's appellation also lies a reference to the aesthetic movement of the nineteenth century: artists, writers, poets, and dramatists, such as Edward Carpenter, William Morris, James Whistler, Walt Whitman, and Oscar Wilde. Of these five, the most obvious influence on Gwyn was Morris who believed in the intimate connection between art and politics, especially socialist politics.[29] It is not a surprise, therefore, that one of the oldest surviving books found in Gwyn's personal library is a copy of *News From Nowhere*, Morris's novel fusing science fiction and utopian socialism, which was first published in 1890.[30]

*

But who was Gwyn Thomas? Or rather, who did he imagine himself to be? In the spring of 1945, presenting his work for publication in the *Modern Reading* series, Gwyn gave the following answer to the series editor Reginald Moore (1914–1990), himself a novelist and writer of short stories.

Gwyn Thomas. Born in the Rhondda Valley, 1913. Son of a miner, whose dislike of mining, if properly expressed and if anyone had bothered to listen, might have opened a new chapter in labour relations – there would have been no more labour. Youngest of a large family who taught him to like large families, radical opinions, invective as a sport and singing songs of a sad flavour in close harmony. Elementary and County schools. Collected some scholarships from county and state authorities and went to Oxford where he felt lost, and then the University of Madrid in the days before its destruction by fascism. Has worked since as an organiser of adult education, lecturer on social and political themes and teacher. Likes walking on and looking at mountains. Thinks himself lucky to have survived as well-thronged a lash of strikes, slumps and major wars as ever caused a man to jump around and feel baffled. Tried to express what he feels when he stares at the roots of discomfort and disorder among his fellows and what he says when those same roots trip him up. Regards the corruption by poverty and depression of the great, crudely artistic, militant life of the Glamorgan valleys as one of the bitterest tragedies in the domestic history of Britain.[31]

To understand these words is to comprehend a writer whose life's work was committed to exposing the corruption of the South Wales Coalfield and its people by economic disaster, and the decay of its political and cultural institutions. The biography was sent to Moore as an accompaniment to a set of short stories. 'These stories,' Gwyn explained,

> though completely presentable as single units, are fragments, in style and conception, of a larger attempt to interpret in terms of tranquil humour the often horrifying emotions of those early years spent in the curious atmospheric blending of lyrical regret and sheer physical disintegration which marked the derelict mining areas of South Wales before the war.

He added:

> I have made no effort to stand away from the things I relate and get the details impeccably straight. The old 'naturalistic' idiom which still holds the fort in proletarian fiction would have

conveyed nothing of the essence of what I felt and wanted to say. The whole period was so richly fantastic I simply planted my own anger and compassion upon it as soil from which to force my harvest of private myths. In this way, to my thinking, can the meaning of individual experience be given a full literary expression in periods of great historical confusion and pain.[32]

Had this letter been written in 1975, say, in the twilight of a career, it would now read as a summation of three decades of creative output garlanded with awards and accolades, albeit without the financial success which might have been expected of post-war Wales' most prolific and globally significant writer of fiction. But no. This was Gwyn, at the very beginning of his career, establishing a literary purpose rarely understood by those who have since offered critique, whether sympathetic or hostile.

Gwyn's letters to Reginald Moore, published here for the first time, establish the precise chronology of his arrival as a writer in the second half of the 1940s, as well as opportunities missed because of the chaos of post-war recovery. First and foremost, Gwyn was not launched as a writer, as his previous biographers have described, by his wife Lyn's haphazard interventions. Thus, in Parnell's rendition,

> One day early in 1946 [Lyn] found in the library a copy of a useful-looking directory called *The Writers' & Artists' Year Book* and thumbed through its pages seeking advice. ... Seized with enthusiasm she sorted through the stories she had already typed, made up three parcels and, unaware of matters like contract and copyright, addressed them to three different publishing houses.[33]

Although a nice tale, it is entirely false. In fact, as the Moore letters conclusively demonstrate, Gwyn designed his own destiny, deliberately choosing London publishers and editors for his work based not on the pages of the *Writers' & Artists' Year Book*, although there is no reason to think that he did not consult directories of that kind, but on his own reading choices and his obvious ambition to be part of a new, post-war literary left.

An obscure figure by contemporary standards, in the middle of the twentieth century Reginald Moore was well known as a collector and editor of shorter fiction. His journal *Modern Reading*, which launched in 1941, and the armed services anthology series *Bugle Blast*, which he edited with the novelist Jack Aistrop (1916–1995), provided novice, often working-class writers with their first break. The cohort of discoveries and promotions made by Aistrop and Moore, and their friend John Lehmann who edited the journal *New Writing*, included Sid Chaplin, B. L. Coombes, and the poet Alun Lewis.[34] Reading Gwyn's submissions, Moore was quickly convinced that, with a careful nurturing of style and creative image, and a reining in of Gwyn's tendency to disregard plot, they were the work of a promising talent. Moore wrote back in effusive terms, agreeing to publish two of the stories – 'The Limp in My Longing' and 'The Pot of Gold at Fear's End' – in forthcoming volumes of *Modern Reading* and to find outlets for the other three.[35] He told Gwyn,

> I like these stories of yours very much. Here and there your writing needs a little trimming but on the whole yours is a refreshing and unusual talent, and I find myself in full agreement with your views on writing up South Wales material: it is certainly time this was approached with something more than the all too earnest, 'realistic' method with which we are all so familiar.[36]

Gwyn's reaction to Moore's letter, which arrived in Barry a week after the war ended in Europe, was jubilant:

Thank you for the most delightful brace of letters I have ever received. I have written in an obstinate darkness for so long, trying to breathe life into a humour that wanted to give up the ghost, I sometimes thought my efforts would meet the same wasted, ravaged destiny as the valley communities of which I write. I knew from the very first word of yours I read in the preface to an anthology that you would understand what kind of fish that they were that were swimming around in my pool.[37]

Gwyn had been writing for more than a decade: his earliest short stories, written when he was still a schoolboy at Rhondda County School in Porth, had been a personal salve. At Oxford, especially, they were a means of soothing his depression and the profound alienation he felt towards the city, the university, and his fellow students. Returning to the Rhondda in the middle of the 1930s, his writing took on a sharper edge offering a critique of the economics and politics laying waste to his home. But this was raw and oftentimes scarcely fictionalised autobiography. The products of those years were a series of theatrical sketches, short stories, complete and incomplete novels, some of which survived, some of which did not, which were as much contemporary history as they were the continuation and development of a literary canon already containing the work of Merthyr-born playwright J. O. Francis, novelists and short-story writers such as Gwyn Jones, Glyn Jones, Jack Jones, Rhys Davies, and Gwyn's friend and erstwhile mentor Lewis Jones, the Rhondda-born author of *Cwmardy* (1937) and *We Live* (1939) and one of the coalfield's leading communists.

For a time, Reginald Moore took Gwyn under his wing, offering to use his own extensive contacts in London to foster publishing contracts and to establish a steady, albeit carefully cultivated, series of appearances in anthologies and magazines. This strategy might have worked but for the effects of paper shortages which delayed the appearance of *Modern Reading* volumes fifteen and sixteen, wherein 'The Limp in My Longing' and 'The Pot of Gold at Fear's End' were to be published, and Gwyn's own youthful exuberance. Parallel with his correspondence to Reginald Moore, Gwyn had been in discussions with Daniel George Bunting, the chief reader at Jonathan Cape, about publishing a novel.[38] Gwyn explained the enterprise to Moore as taking the form of two interconnected 'contes,' or tales. Although well received, the novel was eventually turned down for publication as a single volume. Bunting suggested instead that the stronger of the two stories might be better suited to a magazine such as *Windmill*, which was edited by Reginald Moore. So, in mid-September 1945, Gwyn sent the story on to Moore with an explanation of its sudden appearance, the link to Bunting and Jonathan Cape, and the suggestion that it might fit into an edition of *Windmill*.[39] The title of the short story: 'The Dark Philosophers.'

As with the earlier batch of short stories Gwyn had sent in, Moore immediately recognised in 'The Dark Philosophers' a powerful piece of contemporary writing and showed it to Jack Aistrop, who happened to be staying with him.[40] The latter had already been contracted by the publisher Dennis Dobson to edit a new series to be called *Triad* – the premise being that each volume would contain the work of three new writers: a poet, a short-story writer, and a novelist. Explaining his actions to Gwyn, Moore remarked 'I recommended him to take it, which I believe he did.' Aistrop duly wrote to Gwyn in the autumn of 1945, explaining how he had come to read the manuscript of 'The Dark Philosophers,' and offering to publish the work in the debut volume of *Triad*, which was due to appear the following year, for a fee of 'thirty quid.'[41] In August 1946, alongside short stories by James Gordon and poems by Moore's wife, Elizabeth Berridge (1919–2009), 'The Dark Philosophers' became the first of Gwyn's major writings to be published.[42] The novella was quickly followed by 'My Fist Upon the Stone,' a reworked excerpt from an unpublished novel titled 'Abel,' which Gwyn had written at the end of the 1930s. It appeared in John Singer's anthology *New Short Stories* in September 1946.[43]

By any stretch of the imagination, Gwyn's burst onto the literary scene was as remarkable as it was successful. He had chosen wisely seeking out those magazines and anthologies which were identified as the heirs to the popular front cultural politics of the 1930s, and which thus fitted with his creative intent.[44] Singer had signalled the spirit of this renewed leftist creativity in his essay 'Literature and War' published early in 1944. 'The true artists, the real writers,' he wrote, 'all the people in whom there flows a passionate and joyous and positive vitality are anti-fascist to the depths of their soul. And they will recognise and combat Fascism wherever it may be and whatever it may call itself. Creative art is life's greatest ally.'[45] Gwyn agreed with the sentiment. But he also had a dilemma. He knew that his personal politics lay to the left of Aistrop, Moore, and Singer. To that end, he also offered his work to publishers and creative outlets aligned to the Communist Party, most notably the Progress Publishing Company. Gwyn's first published short story, 'The Hands of Chris,' about anti-fascism in 1930s Rhondda, appeared in the anthology *Saturday Saga* in January 1946.[46] Progress subsequently released Gwyn's inaugural collection – *Where Did I Put My Pity?* – in the autumn of 1946, capping a year which confirmed not only Gwyn's tremendous potential but also his political convictions.

Unfortunately, Gwyn's determination to be published got the better of him, or 'obtaining work' as Alun Richards put it, and he was soon faced with multiple offers and contracts, and a very confused set of editors and publishers in London. Seeking to get a grip on the situation, Reginald Moore wrote to Gwyn in early January 1947 expressing his concern about the future. 'At the risk of your telling me to mind my own business,' Moore said, candidly, 'I must ask you if you really think it the best thing for you to have given your first three books to three separate publishers?'[47] No less honestly, Gwyn responded:

> I quite agree with you that the arrangement is untidy, but it was not of my choosing for the acceptances came fast one after the other at a time when I simply did not appreciate objectively the enormous importance of a consistent and sympathetic presentation of one's works. I thought only that to be published was the be all and end all.

The third book, the second of the two interconnected tales Gwyn had originally offered to Jonathan Cape, was *The Alone to the Alone*, then forthcoming with Nicholson and Watson. For Moore, it seems, the sticking point was not the mainstream publishers but one whose communist associations were concerning and might well put off more lucrative opportunities, particularly as the wartime alliance with the Soviet Union soured. Gwyn explained,

> it is true that this latest work of mine *Where Did I Put My Pity?* could have been dressed up more attractively than Progress Publishing has done it, but I temper my slight impatience with the reminder that the particular standpoint expressed in this work would be found acceptable by only a tiny minority of publishing houses and I am grateful to the firm for that reason.[48]

Moore persisted:

> Think long about who shall handle your stories. And don't be too grateful to any publisher who appears interested in you. You

have already made a reputation with *The Dark Philosophers*. Say to yourself, I <u>can</u> write, and I deserved to be published and published <u>well</u>. For publishers as a tribe are cunning and often unscrupulous – remember that.[49]

It was a lesson Gwyn was to learn the hard way.

*

Gwyn was just thirty-three when *The Dark Philosophers* was published in the summer of 1946. Hs life had been marked already by frustration, illness, depression, and grief, as well as by academic brilliance and remarkable creative potential. Born in the Rhondda on 6 July 1913, in the twilight of the social and economic dynamism of the South Wales Coalfield, he grew up alongside the industrial turbulence and economic dereliction of the interwar years; he spent the Second World War variously in Manchester, Cardigan, and Barry; and in a writing career spanning more than three decades he published no fewer than twenty books comprising novels, short-story collections, plays, essays, and an autobiography 'of sorts.' His popularity was not limited to Wales, nor even to Britain, but led to demands for his work in the United States, Australia and Canada, and to translation into several European languages including Dutch, German, Italian, Norwegian, and Russian. He was one of very few contemporary British writers to have an audience on both sides of the Cold War divide (and the only Welsh writer of note until the détente of the 1970s, when Eastern Europeans rediscovered Dylan Thomas and were introduced to Alun Richards), a status which saw his work placed on the bookshelves of New York, Chicago and Los Angeles as well as Berlin, Moscow, Prague, and Warsaw.[50]

Gwyn's traverse of the Cold War was by no means accidental:

it reflected his own intense political convictions, his ambition to be a 'revolutionary artist,' and the way his writing was interpreted at home and abroad. Gwyn involved himself in the anti-apartheid campaign (joining the cultural boycott of South Africa in June 1963), in the peace movement, in the African American civil rights movement, in the battle against the death penalty, and in the anti-McCarthyite politics of post-war America.[51] Reference was even made to his writing in the United States Congress, at the height of the House of Representatives' Un-American Activities Committee (HUAC) investigations of the 1950s.[52] But why? Chiefly because of Gwyn's leftist politics. From the moment he became fully aware of the world around him in the 1920s and 1930s, Gwyn was a socialist. He remained a socialist for the rest of his life. This was, argued Dai Smith, 'from the very beginning ... one of the things that you can see infusing his work.' Adding that

I think this is what gave him a universal appeal to fellow writers, if you like, both in New York and in Europe. ... This is a Welsh writer whose socialism, a faith which he had early, is there, I think, right to the very end with Gwyn and we ignore the political content of his sardonic humour at the cost of misunderstanding the man and the writer.[53]

Like many young men and women in the interwar years, particularly students or the unemployed, and those most opposed to fascism, Gwyn swayed between the left wing of the Labour Party and the Communist Party, although he was never openly a card-carrying member of the latter, and was an enthusiastic supporter of the popular front – a position intended to bring unity to the entire labour movement in the second half of the 1930s.[54] In March 1933, he returned home from Oxford to support Arthur Horner in the Rhondda East by-election against the Labour candidate, W. H. Mainwaring. Likewise, when Gwyn was able to vote in a general election for the first time in 1935, he joined more than thirteen and a half thousand people in the constituency in voting for Harry Pollitt, the general secretary of the Communist Party. W. H. Mainwaring won for Labour on both occasions. Living in Barry in 1945, Gwyn did not hesitate in voting for Labour's Lynn Ungoed-Thomas against the incumbent, Cyril Lakin.[55] Gwyn supported Labour in every subsequent election, despite misgivings about aspects of the party's post-war direction. Those concerns were played out in the literary comedy of the 1950s and the developed television persona of the 1960s and 1970s. By then, he had become a Bevanite and was firmly within the Labour tent.[56]

Gwyn's turn towards communism began when he was a student at Oxford in the early 1930s, a period marked by sharp divergences between, and occasional overlaps of, members of the university's Labour Club, its communist-orientated October Club, the aristocratic New Party (which collapsed into the British Union of Fascists), and the traditional Liberals and Conservatives.[57] In this way, he pre-empted student communists such as Iris Murdoch, Kingsley Amis, and Denis Healey, who were at Oxford a few years later.[58] Gwyn rarely wrote or spoke about university with enthusiasm, in fact he frequently expressed his regret at having gone to Oxford, but his three years as an undergraduate had a profound impact on his life. He carried with him a palpable sense of having been in the wrong place, at the wrong time, amongst the wrong kind of people, and possessed of the wrong kind of temperament for a college full of the grandeur entirely absent from the 'Rhondda hutch' which he had left. He suffered from a deep and long-lasting but undiagnosed and untreated depression. Later he turned the dislocation into one of his best jokes. 'How did you get to Oxford, Gwyn?' Answer: 'I got on the wrong bus in

Bargoed.'[59] For the political activists whom he admired, notably Lewis Jones, the very fact Gwyn was a student was itself a form of social separation from his own class and the social classes which normally filled out the undergraduate ranks. In 1933, Jones was interviewed by *This Unrest*, a left-wing newsletter published by students at Ruskin College, Oxford, and was asked his opinion of the university. Jones replied:

By the time you receive this I shall probably be commencing a further spell in prison for no specific charge, but for refusing to enter into £400 or £500 sureties to keep a peace the authorities fear I may break. Such is the democratic 'freedom' of the bourgeoisie. The people you ask me to write an opinion of are the puppies of the bourgeoisie.

Now, obviously, I cannot give you an article upon what the workers think about the university student. I suppose they don't think of them at all except in those cases where they should come in contact with some of the breed. When this latter occurs the worker ceases to think. But if you ask me what a worker thinks of the university student, then perhaps I can help you from experiences I have had of them under many conditions and in various circumstances.

I would divide the species into two. That rare phenomenon who diligently tries to intelligently cope with the tremendous problems confronting himself and society. This pugnacious specimen (made so by the nature of his curio) has a hard and thankless task to perform, and represents about one in two hundred of the species. The remaining one hundred and ninety-nine make up a social stratum of demoralized and degenerate nonentities. Of course, each of them thinks otherwise. Each thinks the world exists merely to move around himself, the centre of perpetually admiring mass. This idea arises from the fact that the whole training of the university student during his life in the institution, is concentrated upon removing the medium of his reflections and perspectives to a point somewhere between his navel and his knees. His brain is treated as an inconvenient adjunct to his body, much as the gourmet regards his posterior as an unfortunate addition to his food.

The greatest mental strain upon the student arises from the need for a progressively increasing tempo of erotic imaginings as a necessary prerequisite for satisfactory masturbation.[60]

At the time, Gwyn might well have written something similar, or said it. He certainly shared the sentiments, although Jones's language was far more direct than Gwyn's – it was blunt. Angry, even.

What Lewis Jones failed to articulate, and perhaps could not, was the profound jest involved in being a South Walian, in those years and in the decades since. An 'absurd thing had happened to this proud, intelligent people,' to borrow Dai Smith's characterisation, they had been thrust 'into ugliness, into poverty, into neglect.' Lewis Jones responded, in speech and story, with ideological anger and proletarian melodrama which forced a confrontation between raw emotion and external disinterest, with trade unions and radical political parties as the vehicle for expressing that conflict and the means to a remedy (i.e. a worker's revolution). To respond with a form of comedy was to speak with a more universal voice. It was a gesture towards the absurdity of the situation faced by South Walians rather than a direct confrontation with its realistic foundations. 'For Gwyn, of course,' Smith added, 'the joke was one of the ways in which the dispossessed in this world, the disempowered, could actually indicate their human worth and their human destiny.' Or, as the writer himself observed in his letters to Reginald Moore,

I thought that for all the lack of action and frequent dilations of the dialogue, I was adding another shade here and there to the total portrait of the humour produced by the misfortunes of the community which gives me my background.[61]

He added later,

I suppose every art is largely a matter of the artist's confidence in his own resources and that confidence may be quicker to weaken and gutter into silence in the case of writing ... With me, that tendency was made chronic by a humility of approach to the task of helping create a light of special penetration for the nightmare world of the valleys I come from, where the young see the whole heritage of life that has been dumped into their arms as a spoiled and rotten thing.[62]

In the totality of his artistic vision, Gwyn was unique. His politics were considerably sharper than those of his nearest comparator, Dylan Thomas, although not all that different in form and worldview. Gwyn came to believe that his contemporary was not 'politically up to it' and lacked the critical edge which might have been gained had he spent 'five years in the miners' federation being butchered and badgered around by [Arthur] Horner and Will Paynter.'[63] In other words, had Dylan Thomas, the schoolmaster's son, come from a background more like Gwyn's own. His pessimism was more carefully shrouded by comedy than was the case in Ron Berry's novels and radioplays of the 1960s, which had more in common with the kitchen sink dramas produced by Alan Sillitoe (1928–2010), Sid Chaplin (1916–1986), and Stan Barstow (1928–2011). And, by remaining in South Wales, rather than leaving for a life in the academic cloisters of southern England, he retained the perspective of the insider which eluded Raymond Williams. The

27

divergence between the two was never more apparent than in the 1970s when Gwyn became an antagonist of the revived linguistic nationalist movement and Raymond Williams – who temporarily joined Plaid Cymru in 1969 and increasingly spoke of Welsh Europeanism in the latter stages of his life – 'felt close to the arguments being put forward by nationalists leading up to and during the devolution debate.'[64] Gwyn never did.[65]

Given the continued salience of the debate between cultural nationalism and the politics of social class, to say nothing of the insistent presence of the material foundations of the joke, there has never been a better time to recover the life and literary-political purpose of Gwyn Thomas and to show, just as he did, the intellectual and cultural necessity and vitality of the valleys of a capitalised South Wales. Gwyn's voice is by no means a comfortable one in devolved, post-Brexit Wales: he was profoundly hostile to the imposition of the Welsh language in areas which were overwhelmingly Anglophone; he was profoundly hostile, too, to political and cultural nationalism and its proponents which he believed to be the politics of the puddle; and he rejected the folkish amateurism of the National Eisteddfod and literary, artistic, and political cultures which spoke only to Wales – in whatever language. Many will find such views unpalatable, but they are unavoidable. In other ways, Gwyn's perspectives and interests are strikingly contemporary: his close engagement with the African American civil rights movement in the United States, for example, and the anti-Apartheid campaign in South Africa, his willingness to express support for Israel in the aftermath of the Six-Day War in 1967, or his reading of the *Quran* decades before it was fashionable to do so in the West.[66] At his best, he embraced the fusion of American and European cultural inheritance which lay at the heart of twentieth-century modernity and worked it into the mix of his real and imaginary American Wales.

Gwyn could also be contradictory, even on matters such as nationalism, which makes him a difficult subject for a biographer – and for a reader. Throughout his writing he sprinkled a kind of 'Celtic fairy dust,' presenting a land full of male voice choirs, amateur sportsmen, and other similar relics of the Edwardian age, which struck some readers even half a century ago as false – perhaps even fustian – and has often confused literary critics.[67] Kingsley Amis, for instance, who shared Gwyn's dislike of Welsh nationalism and called it 'an entirely peripheral movement,' thought that whereas 'some will enjoy the oddness of Welsh village life' in Gwyn's writing, 'others will find it a "cloud-cuckoo-town" described in a "vein of irresponsible logorrhea."'[68] Amis nevertheless excluded Gwyn from the pantheon of Anglo-Welsh writers who filled their plots with a 'stage Welshman,' and who did such damage to the development of a more exciting literature.[69] Given a tendency to use conversations as performances, some of Gwyn's private correspondence, particularly with friends on the American left in the 1950s such as Howard Fast and Norman Rosten, was undoubtedly overblown. It was as if Gwyn was gesturing and performing, going along with the rhetoric, in which he had some belief, to please his friends, but generally avoiding taking too active a role in what was going on. This gap between what Gwyn said and wrote and what he physically did was – and remains – one of the more problematic aspects of his biography and is not easily or neatly resolved.

*

In researching this book, I have gone back to voluminous published and unpublished writings, to hundreds of surviving letters (including a tranche of original letters given to Dai Smith by Gwyn's late nephew, David), to radio and television broadcasts, and to global archival holdings which were either closed to previous biographers or about which they were unaware or were in languages which they could not read. Where possible I have quoted at length to ensure that Gwyn's voice is fully heard, as it deserves to be. I share some of the frustrations expressed by those who have previously endeavoured to make sense of Gwyn's life: he was a master of obfuscation and comedic dislocation who believed, as he put it in a diary entry in 1970, that 'for the humorous writer, the fantasist, writing straight autobiography is a cyanide trip.'[70] Lyn Thomas explained to Michael Parnell in the 1980s that her husband found 'the truth was boring.' Gwyn was not particularly interested in organisation, either. His life is not easily reduced to a year by year or even decade by decade account. Simultaneously he could be teaching, writing for broadcast, writing for magazines, preparing a script for the London stage, trying to work on a novel, and presenting on radio and television. That defies straightforward, chronological delineation of a career or a life which passes from moment to moment, as others have found. My solution in this book has been to adopt a thematic mode, even though this inevitably means sharing the burden of exploration with the reader and demands greater concentration on their part – this is the best way of understanding our subject.

Moreover, this is what Gwyn did in his own description of his life, *A Few Selected Exits*, which he described as an 'autobiography of sorts.' Therein, he said almost nothing about his novels nor anything of note about how he first came to the notice of publishers in London in the mid-1940s. Absent, too, at least in the British edition, was any significant discussion of the first eighteen years of his life – the book began *in media res* in 1931, just as he was about to go to Oxford for the first time. Even Oxford passed by in 'one stupor and four and a half suits.' Lyn herself was absent from the narrative. All the same, behind the jokes and the distraction, behind the invention of character and scenario, lay the truth. That is, if you understand that to view the world through Gwyn's eyes was akin to looking through a kaleidoscope. Although one must always keep in mind, as Gwyn told his London editor, Harold Harris, 'the book was chiselled out of vast unwillingness. The literal facts of my life are so loathsome to my mind I get a withering shock right up my arm whenever I set them down.'[71] Gwyn was forced by his American publisher, the Boston-based Little, Brown, to fill in some of the gaps, especially about his early years, which he did, and as such the two editions differed both in form and length.[72] The American edition was nearly twenty pages longer and had more of the character of a memoir, rather than a series of connected quasi-autobiographical tales. It began with a portrait of Gwyn's grandparents.[73]

I have also brought my own experience to bear on certain matters. Gwyn's previous biographer Michael Parnell, like the present author, was a graduate of Oriel College, Oxford, and so had a personal sense of what it was like to study amongst the dreaming spires. Consequently, Parnell felt unable to 'accept that Oxford rejected so totally and so injudiciously a man of Gwyn's potential' and that the traumatic experiences he had there must have been brought 'at least partly upon himself.'[74] I do not, however, share that view. Oxford University can be utterly alienating, as I discovered when I went up in 2004, most especially for those making a social leap as unthinkably large as Gwyn himself made in 1931. As he told Michael Parkinson forty years later, and the deliberate wandering around the question and the landing of a joke was typical of Gwyn's anxiety, Oxford was

not very pleasant because, you know, when a boy comes from a mining valley – this is a kind of Emlyn Williams thing, you know, but actually Emlyn was far luckier than I because he came not from South Wales, which is a very separate territory, but from the North, where sensibilities are very different. But the effect of Oxford on me, you know, the son of an unemployed: I mean, there were thousands of people at Oxford whose fathers were unemployed, but I was the only one whose father was officially unemployed, he was on the books. And instead of being surrounded by these dark, squat, passionate men, who sort of frequent the valleys, who are the miners; suddenly to be surrounded by men who are sad with height, you know, they were all sort of looking down on me and I'm still neurotic about the top of my head because of this; and, you know, people who sort of lived in a sort of world that I could not have been more alien to. And you say that I set myself up as a target, I did and they all hit the mark too, the people who wanted to shoot me.

It seems to me that Parnell misunderstood and misdiagnosed the reasons for Gwyn's alienation, as well as the personal price which was paid. Oxford pushed Gwyn into a period of mental ill health which persisted and from which he recovered only by leaving the Rhondda for stable employment at the end of the thirties. He was never to return to the valley to live. The implications of that depressive trauma have been little understood but had a profound bearing on Gwyn. His departure was the great watershed of his life and although a certain regret can be detected in family letters back and forth, his exile provided the necessary distance for his writing to develop and for his health to improve. Leaving enabled the setting aside of the 'haste, immaturity and over-earnestness' which Gwyn later recognised for himself in the novels and short stories written whilst living in the poverty and misery of the Depression. The Rhondda never truly left him, of course; it was always there, in the 'only landscape that matters to a writer, which is the landscape of the mind, the remembering mind.' It indubitably marked his every creative output whether conceived as a novel, a play, a radio drama, or a television documentary. It was, Gwyn confessed, at the end of *A Few Selected Exits*, 'the land of my emotions.' And it was the source of his politics. But it was no longer his home.

There was a final, social trauma which surfaced in Gwyn: the rupture which created American Wales, real and imagined. Gwyn felt himself to be akin to an American who never got on the boat, or rather who got stuck in Wales because his father, who was an American by birth, had come back to the old world. I share Dai Smith's view that Gwyn, like Richard Burton or Dylan Thomas, 'was one of those in [South] Wales who suffered a "Welsh" death to live an "American" life,' who rejected the particular to belong to the universal.[75] The construction of this new life, made up from an addiction to the cinema of the 1930s, to the writings of Damon Runyon, Dashiell Hammett, and Raymond Chandler, on the one hand, and Thomas Wolfe on the other, and the adoption of a slouch-brimmed hat and trench coat, which made Gwyn look uncannily like Edward G. Robinson, was both personal and professional. Gwyn wrote for *Punch* as if he were writing for the *New Yorker*, he wrote about Tasso's Tavern on the Windy Way as if it were Mindy's Restaurant on Broadway, and even satirised the newspaper magnate William Randolph Hearst (who bought St Donat's Castle in the Vale of Glamorgan in 1925). In so doing he created, for the first time in Welsh literature, a recognisably modern body of writing capable of conveying the full extent of the coalfield milieu, its society, and its culture. 'Rhondda Runyonism' was Gwyn's greatest literary innovation.

If, as Anthony Hopkins, who portrayed Gwyn in Alan Plater's 1993 adaptation of *A Few Selected Exits* for television, has suggested, the writer 'seemed to me to be a rather confused man searching for something in himself ... he looked like a man, to me, [who] was really struggling to find himself, you know,' then it was a search for answers to those profound questions of identity and purpose which lay at the heart of his personal struggle. How did one resolve the dialectical battle of beauty and ugliness side-by-side, each trying to put each other out of business? How did one resolve, in oneself, as much as in society, the matter of a 'Welsh' death in order to live an 'American' life? How did one come to terms with the trauma of losing one's mother as a young child; a bitter, scarring undergraduate experience at a university which ought to have afforded every opportunity but failed; and a decade of unemployment and underemployment which wiped out one's twenties? And all of it packed in before reaching one's thirtieth birthday? In later life, Gwyn reflected, in lamenting tone, that

> to be a kind of humorous writer. A maker of laughter out of the most unlikely circumstances, out of the most unlikely contexts, that would occasion no injury – no pain. Whether I succeeded, I do not know. I don't think that I succeeded because you cannot be consciously aware of life's strange jokes without feeling somebody's flesh, somewhere or another, wince, resent, and hate.

It is too easy to swallow that lament whole and to think of a career which crossed into failure when it did no such thing. Alan Plater believed that Gwyn had a wonderful ability to convey 'the ultimate failure of any of us to actually achieve our aspirations' and to come to terms with the necessary compromises that follow. As for Gwyn's love of history, the Birmingham *Daily Post* opined following the publication of *A Welsh Eye* that 'the future will be able to reconstruct much of the effect of the Depression on South Wales from Gwyn

Thomas's writings alone.'[76] If we step back and look at what
lay beneath Gwyn's creative aspirations, it is possible to observe
a writer and a broadcaster who spent his entire adult life trying
to bring South Walian politics and South Walian culture together
in a universal way. That he was someone who endeavoured to
forge an encompassing body of work which was both art and
history; opera and cinema; belly-aching comedy and dramatic
epic. That, in the end, Gwyn's commitment to the unique social
dynamics and creativity of South Wales, of Labour Country, and
to its modernity and cultural potential, mark him out as the
most significant Welsh writer of the twentieth century.

[1] *Nails* (episode first broadcast: 5 November 1974).

[2] *Parkinson* (series one, episode twenty; episode first broadcast: 28 November
1971).

[3] This is the line of argument taken by literary critic Stephen Knight in his
analysis of Gwyn Thomas's writing. Knight, 'The Voices of Glamorgan: Gwyn
Thomas's Colonial Fiction', *Welsh Writing in English: A Yearbook of Critical
Essays* 7 (2001–2), 16–34; and Knight, *A Hundred Years of Fiction: From Colony
to Independence* (Cardiff, 2004). For Knight, Gwyn 'was a colonized person, as
the Welsh still are' who used 'the language of the colonizer against itself in the
context of inherently imperialist publishing' (p. 32). He did no such thing!
Indeed, as the present biography makes clear, Knight's argument is based on a
profound misreading of Gwyn's intentions, his context, and rooted humanism. As
Alun Richards observed, somewhat caustically, if no less correctly, this line of
argument is full of 'mumbo-jumbo' and is a misreading of 'historical
perspectives, even what happened at any given time'. Richards's comments are
made in a letter to Dai Smith written in November 2002 and reprinted in Dai
Smith, *In The Frame: Memory in Society, Wales 1910–2010* (Cardigan, 2010),
281–284.

[4] Dai Smith, *Aneurin Bevan and the World of South Wales* (Cardiff, 1993), 183–5.

[5] Gwyn Thomas, 'Foreword', in Cyril Batstone (ed), *Old Rhondda* (Cowbridge,
1974).

[6] Eric Hobsbawm, *Primitive Rebels* (Manchester, 1959), 133; Francis Newton [i.e.
Eric Hobsbawm], 'Young Men With Guitars', *New Statesman*, 27 December 1958,
914.

[7] Michael Parnell, *Laughter from the Dark: A Life of Gwyn Thomas* (London,
1988). Ian Michael's biography of Gwyn Thomas which appeared in the Writers of
Wales series in 1977, sought an objective understanding of the writer and his
work, and benefitted from the biographer's considerable personal knowledge. Ian
Michael, *Gwyn Thomas* (Cardiff, 1977).

[8] The point is made most overtly in Michael Parnell, 'Years of apprenticeship: the early life of Gwyn Thomas', *Planet* 59 (1986), 64–70.

[9] Knight, *A Hundred Years*; M. Wynn Thomas, *In The Shadow of the Pulpit: Literature and Nonconformist Wales* (Cardiff, 2010); Barbara Prys-Williams, *Twentieth-Century Autobiography* (Cardiff, 2004).

[10] Gareth Williams, 'Then Came We, Singing: Gwyn Thomas's World of Music', *History From The Forest: University of South Wales Student History Journal* 2, no. 2 (August 2014). The article was revised and republished in *Llafur* in 2017; Victor Golightly, 'Gwyn Thomas's American "Oscar"', *New Welsh Review* 22 (Autumn 1993).

[11] Dai Smith, 'Breaking Silence: Gwyn Thomas and the pre-history of Welsh working-class fiction', in Clive Emsley and James Walvin (eds), *Artisans, Peasants and Proletarians, 1760-1860: essays presented to Gwyn A. Williams* (London, 1985), 104–123; 'The Early Gwyn Thomas', *Transactions of the Honourable Society of Cymmrodorion* (1985), 71–89; 'Satellite Pictures and Close-Ups: The Welsh Working-Class Novel', *Planet* 101 (1993), 88–92. Smith's entry in the Welsh Arts Council's 'Writer's World' series provides useful illustrative material. See: Dai Smith, *Gwyn Thomas, 1913–1981* (Cardiff, 1986).

[12] A point Gwyn himself made to an audience at the Cheltenham Literature Festival in 1969. His session was called 'The Novelist as Judge and Joker'. *Birmingham Daily Post*, 1 November 1969.

[13] *Birmingham Daily Post*, 10 February 1973.

[14] *Sorrow For Thy Sons* (edited by Dai Smith) and *All Things Betray Thee* (with a new foreword by Raymond Williams) appeared in 1986, *The Thinker and the Thrush* (edited by Michael Parnell) in 1988.

[15] Dai Smith, 'The Library of Wales', *Welsh Book Studies* 6 (2005), 72–79.

[16] *Wales* 39 (April 1959), 54.

[17] Raymond Williams, *The Welsh Industrial Novel: The Inaugural Gwyn Jones Lecture* (Cardiff, 1979). Williams returned to these themes in his introduction to the Lawrence and Wishart edition of *All Things Betray Thee* in 1986 and in his essay 'Working-class, proletarian, socialist: problems in some Welsh novels', in H. Gustav Klaus (ed.), *The Socialist Novel in Britain: Towards the Recovery of a Tradition* (Brighton, 1982), 110–121.

[18] The recording was digitised by the Raymond Williams Society in 2020 and made available here: https://soundcloud.com/user-902721807-400345305/the-welsh-industrial-novel [Accessed 15 April 2021].

[19] Raymond Williams, 'Television: Isaac's Urges', *The Listener*, 31 January 1974.

[20] Raymond Williams, 'Region and Class in the Novel', in Douglas Jefferson and Martin Graham (eds), *The Uses of Fiction: Essays on the Modern Novel in Honour of Arnold Kettle* (Milton Keynes, 1982), 67; reprinted in Raymond Williams, *Writing in Society* (London, 1984), 237.

[21] David Smith [i.e. Dai Smith], 'Myth and Meaning in the Literature of the South Wales Coalfield: The 1930s', *Anglo-Welsh Review* 25 (1976), 26.

[22] Gwyn Jones, 'Language, Style and the Anglo-Welsh', *Essays and Studies* (1953). Jones focused on four writers whom he thought offered 'highly distinctive facets of our Welsh stylistic diamond' (p. 102), namely Caradoc Evans, Gwyn Thomas, Dylan Thomas, and Glyn Jones.

²³ Alun Richards, 'The Never-Never Land', *Wales* 45 (October 1959), 27–29.

²⁴ Glyn Jones, 'The Literary Scene', *Wales* 47 (New Year 1959), 15–17; Alun Richards, 'The Literary Scene', *Wales* 47 (New Year 1959), 17–18.

²⁵ Alun Richards to Dai Smith, 2 May 1984, published in Smith, *In the Frame*, 221–225.

²⁶ Ron Berry to Dai Smith, undated but 1993. In Smith, *In The Frame*, 235–236.

²⁷ A background revealed in his memoir. Alun Richards, *Days of Absence* (London, 1986).

²⁸ Dai Smith, 'Introduction' in Ron Berry, *History Is What You Live* (Llandysul, 1998), 9–10.

²⁹ Ruth Livesey, 'Morris, Carpenter, Wilde, and the Political Aesthetics of Labor', *Victorian Literature and Culture* (2004), 601–616; E. P. Thompson, *William Morris: Romantic to Revolutionary* (London, 1955).

³⁰ The copy, now held at the South Wales Miners' Library, dates from 1928.

³¹ British Library, Reginald Moore Papers (hereafter BL RMP), Volume 38, Add MS 79448: biography of Gwyn Thomas enclosed with letter from Gwyn Thomas to Reginald Moore, 15 May 1945.

³² BL RMP: Letter from Gwyn Thomas to Reginald Moore, 30 April 1945.

³³ *LFD*, 89; similar wording is apparent in Ian Michael, *Gwyn Thomas*, 2–3, which is the likely origin.

³⁴ Jack Aistrop's relationship with Alun Lewis is evident from the letters sent back and forth between Aistrop and Reginald Moore in the 1940s. These are held at the British Library: BL RMP, Volume 19, Add MS 79429. Elements of the relationship between Aistrop, Lehmann, and Lewis are noted in John Pikoulis, *Alun Lewis: A Life* (Bridgend, 1984) and *Alun, Gweno & Freda* (Bridgend 2015). Aistrop first met Alun Lewis during training at Longmoor Military Camp. Alun Lewis (ed. Gweno Lewis), *Letters To My Wife* (Bridgend, 1989), 329, no. 2.

³⁵ Namely, 'Grief Comes Again to Gaza', 'Shudder in Sunlight', and 'Little Tempest'.

³⁶ BL RMP: Letter from Reginald Moore to Gwyn Thomas, 14 May 1945.

³⁷ BL RMP: Letter from Gwyn Thomas to Reginald Moore, 15 May 1945.

³⁸ Bunting (1890–1967) had joined Jonathan Cape in 1940 and was the publisher's reader for George Orwell's *Animal Farm*. In addition to his editorial duties, Bunting regularly wrote book reviews for Aneurin Bevan's *Tribune* newspaper under the pseudonym Daniel George.

³⁹ BL RMP: Letter from Gwyn Thomas to Reginald Moore, 19 September 1945.

⁴⁰ BL RMP: Letter from Reginald Moore to Gwyn Thomas, 10 December 1945; Letter from Gwyn Thomas to Reginald Moore, 12 December 1945.

⁴¹ BL RMP: Letter from Jack Aistrop to Reginald Moore, 29 December 1945. The letters from Aistrop to Gwyn (and vice versa) do not appear to have survived, however. There is a hint in Aistrop's own correspondence that the relationship between the two soured slightly. 'He doesn't write to me now', Aistrop complained to Elizabeth Berridge in 1947, 'I wrote months ago to say how pleased I was to see his reviews, but he ignored the letter. Ah well'. BL RMP: Letter from Jack Aistrop to Elizabeth Berridge, undated but 1947.

[42] *TLS*, 31 August 1946; Gwyn Thomas, 'The Dark Philosophers', in Jack Aistrop (ed.), *Triad One* (London, 1946). A negative review of the Triad enterprise by the novelist Gerald Kersh (1912–1968) convinced Aistrop that 'Triad is under an unlucky star', although he felt that 'that bastard Kersh ... obviously hadn't read Gwyn Thomas's novel'. BL RMP: 'Letter from Jack Aistrop to Lisa [i.e. Elizabeth] Berridge, undated but 1946'. Kersh's review appeared in the London *Evening Standard*.

[43] John Singer (ed.), *New Short Stories, 1945–1946* (Glasgow, William MacLellan, 1946); *TLS*, 7 September 1946. Singer was the left-leaning editor of the magazine *Million: New Left Writing*, first published in Glasgow in late 1943. Its first issue included writing by Reginald Moore, Langston Hughes, and Sean O'Casey, as well as Soviet cartoons and adverts for *Tribune* and Alun Lewis's *The Last Inspection*. A second collection appeared in 1945. For its third and final issue, published in 1946, *Million* gained the subtitle *People's Review*. Writers included Sid Chaplin and W. Glynne-Jones.

[44] The 'popular front' literary and creative scene has been widely discussed. On the immediate description of the 'heirs': Christopher Hilliard, *To Exercise Our Talents: The Democratization of Writing in Britain* (Cambridge, Mass., 2006), 167–168. For elements of the scene itself, Andy Croft, *Red Letter Days: British Fiction in the 1930s* (London, 1990) and his *The Years of Anger: The Life of Randall Swingler* (London, 2020); the essays in Andy Croft (ed.), *A Weapon in the Struggle: The Cultural History of the Communist Party in Britain* (London, 1998); Jim Fyrth (ed.), *Britain, Fascism and the Popular Front* (London, 1985); Eleanor Taylor, *The Popular Front Novel in Britain, 1934–1940* (Leiden, 2017); and Daryl Leeworthy 'A Chorus of Greek Poignancy: Communism, Class and Pageantry in Interwar South Wales', in Angela Bartie, Linda Fleming, Mark Freeman, Alexander Hutton, and Paul Readman (eds), *Restaging the Past: Historical Pageants, Culture and Society in Modern Britain* (London, 2020), 180–200.

[45] John Singer, 'Literature and War', in John Singer (ed.), *Million: New Left Writing* (Glasgow, 1944), 57–62, p. 62.

[46] *TLS*, 26 January 1946.

[47] BL RMP: Letter from Reginald Moore to Gwyn Thomas, 3 January 1947.

[48] BL RMP: Letter from Gwyn Thomas to Reginald Moore, 10 January 1947.

[49] BL RMP: Letter from Reginald Moore to Gwyn Thomas, 14 January 1947.

[50] Lewis Jones was also translated into German for readers in the German Democratic Republic. Lewis Jones, *Im Tal der Schlagenden Wetter* (Berlin, 1969). This aspect of Gwyn's career is discussed in Daryl Leeworthy, 'The World Cannot Hear You: Gwyn Thomas (1913–1981), Communism and the Cold War', *Welsh History Review* 28, no. 2 (2016), 335–362. The wider appropriation of western 'radical' literature in the Soviet sphere of influence is a growing field of scholarship. Especially useful studies include Eleonory Gilburd, *To See Paris and Die: The Soviet Lives of Western Culture* (Cambridge, Mass., 2018); Alexei Yurchak, *Everything Was Forever, Until It Was No More: The Last Soviet Generation* (Princeton, 2005); Juliane Fürst, *Stalin's Last Generation: Soviet Post-War Youth and the Emergence of Mature Socialism* (Oxford, 2010).

[51] The cultural boycott of South Africa involved a range of leading playwrights and writers including Samuel Beckett, Daphne du Maurier, Graham Greene, Arthur Miller, and Tennessee Williams. Gwyn was one of the original group of fifty-four

writers to sign the 25 June 1963 declaration, which was made in conjunction with the Anti-Apartheid Movement in London.

[52] United States Senate Judiciary Committee, *Strategies and Tactics of World Communism: The Significance of the Matusow Case* (Washington DC, 1955), 1209–1210.

[53] Dai Smith speaking in *A Sad But Beautiful Joke* (BBC Wales, 1993).

[54] For instance, Raymond Williams. Dai Smith, *Raymond Williams: A Warrior's Tale* (Cardigan, 2008). The relationship between anti-fascism and membership of (or sympathy with) the Communist Party in the 1930s is effectively discussed in Geoff Andrews, *Agent Molière: The Life of John Cairncross, the Fifth Man of the Cambridge Spy Circle* (London, 2020).

[55] Geoff Andrews, *Smooth Operator: The Life and Times of Cyril Lakin, Editor, Broadcaster and Politician* (Cardigan, 2021).

[56] Joining in during what Mark Jenkins has called 'Labour's high tide'. Mark Jenkins, *Bevanism: Labour's High Tide* (London, 1979).

[57] M. P. Ashley and C. T. Saunders, *Red Oxford: A History of the Growth of Socialism in the University of Oxford* (Oxford, [1930] 1933 edn).

[58] Peter J. Conradi, *Iris Murdoch: A Life* (London, 2001); Zachary Leader, *The Life of Kingsley Amis* (London, 2006); Denis Healey, *The Time of My Life* (London, 1989).

[59] *The Colliers' Crusade, Episode One: How the Red Road Began* (Dir. John Ormond: BBC 2, 16 May 1980). Although Elaine Morgan's reference to the joke in her 1960 serial *A Matter of Degree* illustrates that it was well established in Gwyn's repertoire by the time the documentary was recorded. Daryl Leeworthy, *Elaine Morgan: A Life Behind The Screen* (Bridgend, 2020).

[60] *This Unrest* 1 (1933), 5–6.

[61] BL RMP: Gwyn Thomas to Reginald Moore, 19 September 1945.

[62] BL RMP: Gwyn Thomas to Reginald Moore, 30 December 1945.

[63] Gwyn Thomas speaking on *Nails* (HTV, 1974). Dylan Thomas's politics are set out in Victor Golightly, '"Writing with Dreams and Blood": Dylan Thomas, Marxism and 1930s Swansea', *Welsh Writing in English: A Yearbook of Critical Essays* 8 (2003).

[64] Smith, *Raymond Williams*, 478–9, fn. 12.

[65] Nor, for that matter, did Alun Richards or Ron Berry.

[66] Gwyn's copy of the *Quran* remains in his library now housed at the South Wales Miners' Library. His support for Israel was elicited by the novelist Alan Sillitoe, who was involved in the Committee for Israel in the 1970s. See Richard Bradford, *The Life of a Long-Distance Writer: The Biography of Alan Sillitoe* (London, 2008), 267–268. For an indication of Gwyn's anti-apartheid views see British Library, Add MS 80776, f.123, 'Letter from Gwyn Thomas to Freda Levson', 1963.

[67] Note Stephen Knight's rather misguided – and misleading – pondering as to whether Gwyn might 'even have made peace with his Welsh-language familial demons'. Knight, 'Voices', 32. He would not have done.

[68] Kingsley Amis, 'New Novels', *The Spectator*, 23 July 1954, 126. Amis's view of Welsh nationalism is taken from his *Memoirs* (London, 1991).

[69] Kingsley Amis, 'Waving the Leek', *The Spectator*, 6 July 1956, 33. An earlier blast was delivered in chapter nine of Amis's *That Uncertain Feeling* (London, 1955), in which he lamented 'all those boring myths about the wonder and the glory and the terror of life in the valley towns'.

[70] NLW, GTP, N2, Extracts from Gwyn Thomas Journals/Notebooks compiled by Michael Parnell, entry for 31 March 1970 (Notebook 21).

[71] NLW, GTP, J57/19, Letter to Gwyn Thomas from Harold Harris, 28 June 1967; Gwyn Thomas draft reply to Harold Harris.

[72] NLW, GTP, J66/7, Letter from Harry Sions to Gwyn Thomas, 21 August 1967.

[73] Gwyn recycled the American material for his contribution to Meic Stephens's *Artists in Wales* series, published in 1971. The material had previously been published as an article for the London *Evening Standard*. Gwyn Thomas, 'The Incomparable Cradle', *London Evening Standard*, 13 February 1965. It was included in the American edition following a plea from the editor at Little, Brown for a more conventional start to the memoir. NLW, GTP, J66/11, Letter from Harry Sions to Gwyn Thomas, 29 March 1968.

[74] *LFD*, 33.

[75] Smith, *Aneurin Bevan*, 14.

[76] *Birmingham Daily Post*, 31 October 1964.

CHAPTER ONE

A Masterpiece of Absurdity

During the 'long, idle, beautifully lit summer of 1926,' with its 'illusion of paradise,' Gwyn celebrated his thirteenth birthday. The pit wheels were silent, the great pit-head chimneys no longer belched their fumes into the air, and there was no longer the ever-present danger of death or injury underground. 'The silence was sweet,' he recalled half a century later, 'people sang in ways they'd never sang before and it was, in a way, to the mind of the wondering child the beginning of a new age.' Two months earlier, at the start of May, all work had ceased in the valley in support of the General Strike. After nine days, only the miners were left carrying the banner of industrial action: they remained locked out of the collieries until the autumn. Out of this 'enchanted moment,' he continued, 'came this incredible phenomenon, one of the strangest things that I have ever seen happen on this earth: the bands.' He meant the marching jazz bands of men, women and children dressed up in often outlandish home-made costumes, tea cosies on their heads, with their music played on marching drums and the gazooka. Its sound, like air blown across a comb, wispy but insistent. It had all 'emerged from one of the most sombre, dangerous moments in our past ... [and] one of the most decisive wounds in our social experience.'[1]

Porth held its first major carnival of the summer on 8 July, two days after Gwyn's birthday. Thousands of people were in attendance at Bronwydd Park, drawn in part by the exhibition game of baseball by two visiting teams from Cardiff, with jazz bands and other carnival contests all judged by a panel chaired by the wife of the local Labour MP, David Watts Morgan.[2] The events grew in size throughout July and August so that by September there were even bigger crowds, even bigger sporting events (including a game between Cardiff City and a Pick of the Rhondda XI), and substantial contests featuring dozens of bands: sixty in Porth Carnival alone.[3] The purpose of the community carnivals was not simply to entertain, nor even were they designed to defuse the potentially violent situation as anger mixed with frustration, although they did just that, but rather they were the best, collective way of raising money for the community's distress fund. There was a fund for each township of the Rhondda. Collectively their resources paid for the food and drink at the communal soup kitchens, paid for the supplies to sustain the boot repair centres, paid for children's clothes and other essential items, and kept debt and rent collectors at bay – at least for a time.

The industrial conflict which had sparked the General Strike and the miners' lockout was accompanied by a social conflict whose battlegrounds were everywhere. In school 'every class witnessed a bijou but solemnly bitter civil war.' On the one side, the sons of miners like Gwyn himself; on the other, 'the sons of tradesmen and other people not affected by the fight' who were 'malignantly opposed to the whole business.' Nor was this 'civil war' entirely limited to the schoolboys themselves, as Gwyn recalled in a series of articles entitled 'Growing Up in Meadow Prospect' written for *Punch* in the early 1960s. This was a quasi-fictional representation of Gwyn's childhood, with events and locations pulled out of Porth and Cymmer and into the world of Meadow Prospect and the Windy Way. Part four, 'Explosion Point,' was set during 1926 and explored one of Gwyn's scholastic nemeses: 'Mr Thurlow,' the junior chemistry master at Rhondda County School, 'a High Churchman [and] an austere traditionalist.' Hardly the sort of figure who would take kindly to Gwyn's joining in with the processions and demonstrations where 'the banners were infinite' and international as well as local in their messages of solidarity. 'There were demands for the release of imprisoned Radicals the world over and we had a long list. Some would be well-known like Tom Mooney, Sacco, Vanzetti. Others might be local boys currently in the County Keep for railing at some or other aspect of the Establishment in public.'[4]

The 1926 General Strike and lockout was the second of the two great strikes of the 1920s which Gwyn lived through as a child, and which brought the curtain down on the old Rhondda. The lockout of 1921 began in mid-April and ended a matter of days before Gwyn's eighth birthday. 'We were idle until the beginning of July,' recalled Will Paynter, at the time a young miner employed at Cymmer Colliery, 'then went back into the pits having accepted big reductions in wages.' The experience was to 'lead to a decisive change' in Paynter's life.[5] Money was already becoming scarce. 'The restraint upon progress which the present economic conditions have imposed has been most severely felt,' recorded the Rhondda's medical officer of health, Dr J. D. Jenkins, in the spring of 1921.[6] By the end of December 1925, more than seven thousand families across the Rhondda were being sustained by welfare payments from the Board of Guardians, at an annual cost of nearly three hundred and fifty thousand pounds.[7] The good times which were the hallmark of Edwardian Rhondda, when front rooms of terraced houses had been decked with family photographs and doily-covered pianos, the objects of pride and prosperity and status, were over.

Gwyn admitted in a BBC documentary broadcast in 1976 to mark the fiftieth anniversary of the events of 1926 that, as a child, he may not have fully understood the implications of the strikes and struggles over wages and working conditions which were going on around him. But he did appreciate the social consequences and the creation of a new type of collective culture in which 'our imagination [was left] with a perpetual tilt towards the sardonic.' Poverty and misery, Gwyn had previously explained to viewers of *Return to Rhondda* in 1965, were the making of the total human being. There *was* something to laugh about in the contest over who got the middle cutlet of the sardine. As he got older, he was better able to understand what had happened and what its real meaning was. In a lecture given to an audience at University College Cardiff in 1979, he lamented that he had been 'denied the sight of a society that was economically sure of itself, confident that we had got hold of a productive system that was on the make, on the way, glad to be making things it was making, devoutly proud of its money.'[8] In the absence of such a society, the Rhondda of the interwar years was full of stories of past glories, of wealth lost, and of once and future possibility. It was a valley both monstrous and beautiful. A masterpiece of absurdity.

*

The Rhondda reached its economic peak in the year that Gwyn was born: 1913. At midsummer that year, the population stood at more than one hundred and sixty thousand. Twenty years earlier, at the time of the decennial census of 1891, it had been under ninety thousand, and in 1881 not much more than fifty-five thousand. Those men, women and children lived in, and were crammed into, a district twelve miles long and less than five miles wide at its greatest extent. This was a landscape of narrow, terraced, winding, hill-strewn gulches. For all its apparent uniformity, the Rhondda was not a single place. There were two valleys: the Fawr and the Fach, with Porth at the confluence of the two. There were two parliamentary constituencies (from 1918), ten electoral wards and more than thirty distinct communities. Gwyn grew up in ward eight: Cymmer and Porth. In his annual survey for 1913, the district's medical officer, Dr Jenkins, noted that if the Rhondda were regarded as a single town it would stand at twenty-first in the league table of the largest urban centres in Britain. But a unique town where coal was king. As Dr Jenkins put it, the 'prosperity of the district is entirely dependent upon its coal, which in its steam-raising properties, is reputed to be inferior to none.' More than fifty collieries produced more black gold than they ever had before, or ever would again, providing a vast proportion of the world's energy supply; over forty thousand miners worked in those pits, itself a quarter of the entire coal mining workforce of South Wales.

By the time Gwyn was in secondary school, it was all over. The pits stopped, the money vanished, those who could leave did so, and those who could not leave found themselves living in social and economic conditions which worsened year after year after year. When the government ordered a hurried census of the district's population on the outbreak of war in 1939, fewer than one hundred and twenty thousand people were found to be living in the Rhondda – for the first time the majority were women. An entire generation of people had disappeared. At the end of the 1930s more than forty per cent of Rhondda's workforce were unemployed. 'It is obvious,' recorded Dr Jenkins in 1938, 'that the majority of the population in the district were living under financial conditions which only provided for the bare necessities of life.' Insoles Cymmer Colliery, the community's 'dark heart,' as Gwyn put it in 1969, indicatively suffered terminal decline between the two world wars. In 1914 almost two and a half thousand men and boys were employed at the pit; the figure slumped to fewer than

45

fifteen hundred by 1938. Two years earlier the company recorded a twenty-five thousand pound loss on the year's trading.[9] Such financial haemorrhage heralded closure, which happened in March 1939. The pit and its people were left to decay.

Gwyn's father, Walter Morgan Thomas, was an American. He was born in Youngstown, a burgeoning coal and steel community south-east of Cleveland, Ohio, on 26 September 1873. His parents, John and Jane Thomas, together with their eldest son, David, who was born in Aberdare in 1864, had emigrated to the United States, which was then rebuilding itself in the aftermath of the Civil War, seeking a more comfortable life. Youngstown was a recent move, however; for much of their time in America, the Thomases had lived in Cleveland itself. In August 1870, when called upon to give their details to the census enumerator, they were living in the city's seventh ward not far from the banks of Lake Erie. John was working as a carpenter, Jane looked after their young children: David, then aged six, and the infant Mary, who had been born in Cleveland ten months earlier.[10] A second daughter, Minnie, followed two years later, in 1872. But then the family came back, first to Aberdare where a third daughter, Annie, was born in 1877, and then to the Rhondda. In 1881, the family lived at 93 Rheola Row, Porth, a short walk from the house in which Gwyn himself grew up.

The reasons for the family's return from the United States are not immediately obvious. Perhaps the primary motivation was the sudden death of Mary, who was no more than seven years old when she passed away. Another reason may have been the associated difficulty of settling in the United States as monoglot Welsh speakers, especially outside of the main areas of Welsh settlement in Pennsylvania and south-eastern Ohio.[11] On their arrival in Cleveland, the Thomas family lived in an industrial district in the east of the city which was assuredly multicultural but Anglophone out of necessity. Their neighbours came from all over Britain and Ireland, as well as France, Germany, the Netherlands, and elsewhere in the United States. Some of them were fellow Welsh people who earned their living as puddlers in the burgeoning iron and steel works. It does not seem to have been enough to develop roots, however. Searching for a Welsh cultural enclave may well have precipitated the move from Cleveland to Youngstown, which had its own Welsh congregational chapel and was the focus for the eisteddfodic tradition in Ohio. Biannual eisteddfodau began there in 1860 before becoming annual events by the mid-1880s.[12] This is not to discount the material context for such a move: Youngstown had its own coal mines and iron and steel works, which readily offered work for a carpenter such as John Thomas. But Youngstown was culturally different from Cleveland: it seemed to be more Welsh.

John Thomas, Gwyn's paternal grandfather, was born in Llanddarog in rural Carmarthenshire in 1834. He left the village to settle in Aberdare, drawn there by the mining industry. By 1861, he was living in lodgings and working as a joiner. There he met Jane, who was a few years younger and also from Llanddarog. Within a few years, they were married. But they were also restless. Even on their return from America, John and Jane were itinerant, moving back and forth from the Cynon Valley to the Rhondda before finally settling in Mountain Ash. In the years before his death shortly before the First World War, John Thomas built a successful carpentry and building business in the town and, as Gwyn was later to remark, 'when he wanted the odd laugh [John] did a little undertaking.' The business was maintained as a family concern by John William Thomas, the eldest grandson.[13] At no stage did John or Jane learn English – unlike Walter, who remained in Porth, and picked up the language sometime in the 1890s. It was always his second language. Learning English was the main distinction between the Rhondda Thomases and those parts of the family who lived in Mountain Ash.

Given John Thomas's relatively prosperous joinery business, Walter could have easily avoided going into the mines. His brother, David, followed the family line and became a carpenter; his sister, Minnie, turned to school teaching. In fact, the reason Walter learned English in the first place is because by the census of 1891, he was working as a telegraph clerk – a job which suited his bookish, musical instincts. One portrait Gwyn wrote of his father many years later pointed to this bookishness and the ability to quote from Charles Dickens, Friedrich Engels, Leo Tolstoy, Eugene Debs, and Pierre-Joseph Proudhon.[14] But Walter Thomas was also a man who loved sex, and this proved his undoing. To be able to sustain his family, after marriage and the start of a family which grew to twelve children, Walter left the office and went underground where he could make more money. He was not a natural manual labourer and so tried to escape the 'poignant ironies of his life' through alcohol, thereby becoming 'a lost man, unutterably sad when wholly sober [and] consciously out on some cold ironic margin of his own. The laughing, happy side of his life was turned away from us.' And especially from Gwyn, who felt that he was utterly unwanted as a child. No wonder Gwyn was ambivalent to sexual intimacy and described his own desires as having brought on 'more tears than hayfever.'[15]

Gwyn's mother, Ziphorah Thomas (née Davies) came from the Rhondda. She was born into a mining family in Porth in 1875. Her father, Thomas, a monoglot Welsh speaker, came from Kenfig near Bridgend but had moved with his family a few years after he was born in 1840. He began work underground at George Insole's brand new Cymmer Pit when he was just seven years old, surviving the series of disasters which plagued the underground workings including the powerful and deadly explosion of 1856, which claimed the lives of one hundred and fourteen people. Hannah Davies, Ziphorah's mother, also had roots in Kenfig, where she was born in 1842. It was she who taught her children English. Together Thomas and Hannah Davies had six children including Ziphorah. The eldest, Julia, was born in 1863; she was followed by Thomas (1866), Gwilym (1872), Mary (1874), and Hannah (1877). The family lived in various rented houses in Porth's Taff Street before finally settling at 68 High Street, Cymmer. Exactly when Ziphorah met Walter is not clear, but they were married in 1893, when she was just seventeen and already pregnant with the couple's eldest child, Caroline. As was common, Caroline, or Carrie as she was known to the family, was sent to live with her grandparents in Mountain Ash to be raised as their child; Walter and Ziphorah were given a second chance.

They lived alone, for a short time, in a small house in York Terrace, Porth. With sex never far from Walter's mind, it was not long before a second daughter, Jennie, was born. Her arrival in the autumn of 1894 was followed by Emlyn (1897) and Minnie (1898). When Ziphorah discovered that she was pregnant with her fifth child in the autumn of 1900, Walter was compelled to seek a larger house. With financial support from his father, John, and the additional income from his recently widowed father-in-law, Thomas, who moved in with them as a lodger, Walter was able to put down a deposit on 196 High Street, Cymmer. Hannah, Gwyn's beloved older sister, was born there in the summer of 1901, as was the rest of the younger half of the family: twins Gwilym and Arthur (1904), John (1905), Walter (1907), Dilwyn (1909), Eddie (1911), and Gwyn last of all in 1913. The house was soon a 'busy, bilingual bomb of a place' commanded by Ziphorah.

Gwyn's mother was, as he affectionately observed years later, 'a woman of enormous creative power, whose kindliness must have embraced half the world.' But giving birth to twelve children, raising eleven of them, and maintaining a household always at risk of financial ruin, was mentally and physically exhausting. Ziphorah died of 'sheer weariness,' as Gwyn put it, in 1919. She was forty-four.

Gwyn never truly got over the death of his mother. Her absence, and the often-tense relationship with his father, Walter, indelibly marked his life. As he observed knowingly in the preface to the published edition of *The Keep* in 1962:

> We do not see her in this play. She is a lustrous portrait on the wall of the Morton's parlour. Yet such a woman throbs and booms through a vast area of our South Welsh life. Creative, handsome, very often a contralto with the vocal impact of a herd of Jerseys, she will become the magnetic core of her home, exercising a pull upon her brood which will keep one side of their being vibrant and joyful. The other side, denied free communion with the rough and inconsiderate world without, will slide into the most terrible atrophy and regret. But from the outside the citadel seems firm and well.

Into the gap left by Ziphorah's early death stepped Hannah Thomas, known always to Gwyn as Nan. It was a reluctant surrogacy. Nan had just turned eighteen and dreamed of an independent career in music. Singing was her greatest talent. As the *Rhondda Leader* enthused in the autumn of 1920, 'Miss Nana Thomas, Cymmer, a lovely contralto, sang solo at a concert by the Rhondda Cymric Orpheus Concert Party. There is a successful future for Miss Thomas, coming as she does from a very musical family.'[16] Nan had already been offered a scholarship to study music at the university college in Cardiff but was never able to take it up. Her older sisters put their own interests first, escaping the duty which might otherwise have been their own. Jennie was a trained nurse and worked at Porth Cottage Hospital. Caroline, the eldest, had spent much of the previous decade caring for her ailing grandmother, Jane, and was little interested in leaving Mountain Ash for Porth. Minnie was pregnant and soon to be married to her sweetheart, Emlyn Jones. Walter pressured Nan into accepting the role of mother – as the last of the Thomas girls to be asked, what choice did she have but to say yes?

Ziphorah Thomas's death amplified the social and cultural distance between Walter and his youngest children. 'I entered late boyhood in complete ignorance of the language my father spoke as his first choice if he wanted to say anything really significant,' Gwyn wrote, 'whenever that happened I was usually the only person around, and this led to plenty of strain. It frustrated him and tired me.'[17] The divide split the top half of the family and the bottom half. 'Politics in English, gossip in Welsh, and downright lies in both,' as Gwyn put it in 1969. He added, in a separate setting, that he 'simply had to make the best of this.' Eddie, two years older than Gwyn, similarly recalled that Welsh disappeared from the family, despite Walter's own preferences. 'We were never encouraged,' Eddie said, in an interview for HTV after his brother's death, 'and that was the whole farce of the situation.'[18] Welsh was to be the language of a religious world to which neither Gwyn nor Eddie had access. The family were taken three times every Sunday to Cymmer Chapel, one of the oldest nonconformist centres in the Rhondda. There, the younger Thomas children were compelled to listen to sermons 'which lasted anything up to two hours,' as Eddie recalled, and which they could not understand. Or in Gwyn's view,

51

The preachers of the period were all of the classic cut and any one of them who preached for less than ninety minutes at a stretch was considered to be less than frank. The rhetoric from the start was hot, and the sermon would end in a spurt of howling shamanism, an ecstatic lycanthropic baying at the nonconformist moon.[19]

Compulsion and loyalty to the family traditions ensured that the boys kept going to services, despite their obvious alienation. 'We resented it because obviously we wished to understand' – Eddie's voice once more – 'we were of an age when we wanted to know. And there were these preachers pouring out this endless stream of sermonising and we didn't understand a single word of what was happening. Not a word.'

In his own reflections on this farcical situation, Gwyn ranged from the comedic to the ideologically serious and sociologically analytical. 'Theologically, as a child,' I had a tangled time of it,' he explained in *A Welsh Eye* in the mid-1960s, 'I was one of the Rhondda generation whose language, with an almost malignant ease, had changed from Welsh to English. But the chapel's teaching had remained in Welsh.' On television in the same period, he frequently made light of the situation telling Michael Parkinson, for instance, that he was a 'theological virgin.' But it was the more resolute position, which enabled Gwyn to observe the linguistic and cultural forces to which he had been subject, seemingly with no autonomy or agency, as a child. As Gwyn put it in *The Colliers' Crusade* in 1979, the South Wales of the early twentieth century

had been lit up by this great evangelical belief that things by the exchange of a few sermons and hymns were going to be transformed, changed in shape and flavour, and that had happened all of a sudden and it changed all of a sudden. The

52

first world war saw the end of the great preachers. Nobody would listen to them again with a grain of belief.

Unable to follow the Welsh sermons, those 'world-slapping phrases of which we did not understand a single word,' Gwyn found a more comfortable environment in the Band of Hope where the musical proceedings were conducted in English.[20] He was never tempted by Rhys Davies's solution to the same linguistic-cultural quandary, namely 'defection' to Anglicanism. As Davies explained shortly before his death in 1978,

> I used to be forced to go to chapel, which was Welsh-speaking, which I didn't understand – even three times on Sundays – and I got my own way about that first by going to the Anglican Church, in English, with a magnificent vicar whose sermons were very beautiful. He was an actor really, rather than a vicar. ... I didn't fight, it was passive resistance, and I achieved it.

Entering the world of Anglophone religious service, neither writer entirely fell under the spell of Welsh nonconformity and the legacy of nineteenth-century cultural practice. Neither preachers nor deacons nor the milieu embodied by the *capelwyr*, the chapel-goers, either. Gwyn was not 'crusadingly anti-chapel' for the sake of it, his was an expression of alienation and of sheer boredom.[21] That brought childhood resistance. Gwyn later claimed to have been 'expelled from the Sunday School under an arch of frowning deacons.' He also boasted of having been 'mentioned in dispatches' for his activities at the Band of Hope.[22] Either way he wriggled free of religious domination.

In fact, the best descriptions of Gwyn's involvement with the Band of Hope relate to music rather than to religion. The group in Cymmer staged operettas and cantatas and occasionally full-scale operas. These captured the young man's imagination. He recalled that 'when I was about eleven the nip of autumn was mitigated by the Band of Hope. We had been drafted into the chorus of a junior operetta of the "Merry Widow" type that involved a lot of fondling, waltzing and bussing.' Never one to miss an opportunity to poke at religious hypocrisy, he continued, 'Deacons would appear briefly at the door of the vestry and say it was nothing more than bland sensuality. We warmed to this tale of Viennese smooching, and as the melodies and words slipped into our bloodstream, we could hear the laces of our moral stays go snapping.'[23] It was the Italian, Giuseppe Verdi, who appealed most. At the age of nine, Gwyn recalled, he had been a child rioter in a production of *Les Vêpres Siciliennes* 'and everyone agreed that my loud voice and the perpetual indignation of my face had given the sense of trouble a tangible edge.'[24] He appeared as a monk and as the Conte di Luna in *Il Trovatore*, too. With its famous 'Anvil Chorus' sung by Spanish gypsies, wandering troubadours, and swashbuckling themes, it readily appealed, particularly in a household and a community where such music abounded. As Gwyn put it, 'the valley where I was born was one vast choral impulse. If you had anything more than a fag end of a voice, and there happened to be room for one more on the stage, you were just whipped into the nearest choral unit.'[25]

Most of the Thomas family was involved in the musical life of Cymmer and Porth. Gwyn's older siblings, Emlyn and Dilwyn, both trained in music college in London. Eddie, the best of the family of singers, was a member of the Covent Garden Chorus. There he met his wife, the later radio and television personality and women's columnist, Irene (née Ready). The pair married in 1950. Music was the one enthusiasm which the entire family shared with Walter. He sang in a male voice choir and maintained a fine collection of gramophone records. They were mostly of operatic tenors, notably the great Italian Enrico Caruso, whose voice was amongst the most widely recorded and recognisable of the early twentieth century. Little wonder that in 1954, Gwyn revelled in the opportunity to work with Treorchy Male Voice Choir. He wrote up the experience for the choir's magazine, *Excelsior*:

> We made our way up the valley. We were to attend a rehearsal of the Treorchy Male Voice Choir. We had some time in hand. The driver of the bus took us up the great switchback road to the top of the Bwlch. We got out of the bus. ... We looked down over Cwmparc and Treorchy. It was a bowl of green and amber evening light, the sort of prospect that brings out in all the children of the valleys a sense of their beauty and pathos that is almost beyond expression. Down we went. The Treorchy choristers were waiting, as brilliant and merry a band of carolling meibion as will ever shame the silence that is supposed to be of gold. ... John Davies led the choir into the first notes of Cherubini's *Sanctus*. A great column of silver sound. The bodies of the people around me shot up, and in their eyes was the sort of expression that must have been in Ali Baba's when he caught his first glimpse of that cave.[26]

As an adult, Gwyn had developed a rich musical appreciation ranging from the popular oratorios of George Frederick Handel and the comic operas of Gilbert and Sullivan, to the nineteenth and twentieth century Romanticism of Carl Maria von Weber, Jean Sibelius and Sergei Rachmaninov, to the darker operatic complexities of Richard Wagner. He enjoyed American folk music and spirituals, particularly those performed by Paul Robeson, and shared a love of popular singers such as Bing Crosby with his sister, Nan. But opera was the great constant of his life. For if *Il Trovatore* and Verdi's other great works had a rival for Gwyn's affection, then it was *Carmen* – George Bizet's 1875 masterpiece with its sultry *Habanera* and addictive *March of the Toreadors*. Rather than the cheap Argentine tobacco and 'sensuality kept on a looser rein,' or indeed the idea that 'Buenos Aires was top of the league for sin, sex and sun,' both of which Gwyn offered as an explanation for his passion for Spain and the Spanish language, it was this proletarian love-story-cum-tragedy which captured and held Gwyn's imagination and gave him a model for his stories. As he put it in *Gazooka*, his most famous short story, in which *Carmen* featured prominently, 'there are strong affinities between Iberian music and our own and I don't see why we shouldn't exploit this.'

*

Gwyn began his schooling at Cymmer Elementary, a short walk up the hill from 196 High Street, just as the First World War was coming to an end. 'I was an eager learner,' he remembered, 'literacy was regarded as a kind of scrubbing brush and our faces shone.'[27] His teachers were 'some of the grimmest taskmasters ever let loose on the young.'[28] Little detail survives about this period of Gwyn's life, in part because he seldom wrote about it himself. These years were overshadowed by the death of his mother, Ziphorah, and by the economic and social turbulence apparent in the community at large. In the summer of 1925, not 1926 as he often claimed, Gwyn sat the eleven-plus examination for entry to the prestigious Rhondda County School. He came seventh in the all-Rhondda race for a scholarship – the golden ticket out of the mines. [29] The County School had an unusually rich academic atmosphere at that time, sustained by a dedicated teaching staff led by Evan Thomas Griffiths (1886–1967), the headmaster.[30] Griffiths was born in Cardiganshire, educated at Aberystwyth, where he proved himself a gifted linguist, and then undertook postgraduate

56

research in Italian literature. For a time, he taught at various European universities, including the Sorbonne in Paris, and even taught Welsh for London County Council, before lecturing at Victoria University, Manchester, between 1912 and 1916.[31]

After the First World War, Griffiths returned to Europe, earning his *licence ès lettres* (or Bachelor of Arts) from the University of Geneva in 1922.[32] Then he turned away from the academy to enter the teaching profession, arriving at Porth in January 1926 to replace the retiring Richard David Chalke (1869–1960), who had been the headmaster at Rhondda County School since 1913.[33] Having begun his career as a science teacher, Chalke embodied the technocratic mindset from which Gwyn readily recoiled. The distinction was also political: Chalke was a prominent member of the Liberal Party and stood as the party's parliamentary candidate in Rhondda East in the 1929 General Election; Griffiths, by contrast, was a member of the Labour Party and had been involved in the foundation of the party in Cardiganshire.[34] Gwyn never discussed Chalke in his writing. Perhaps, because in comparison with Griffiths, the older man had comparatively little impact on Gwyn's life – a single term.[35] Griffiths was headmaster at Rhondda County School for the remainder of Gwyn's time as a pupil and from 1933 until retirement in 1948 served as headmaster of Barry County School for Boys, where Gwyn also taught for two decades. The two men came to know and admire each other. In 1968, in one of his last articles for *Punch*, Gwyn penned a warm and reflective obituary to 'Ev' which he titled 'The Improver':

His career, through the eyes of a nation of fanatical auto-didacts and book-worshippers, had been nothing short of remarkable. Indeed the movements of his body, jerky beyond prediction, seemed to suggest that he was still reacting to the spinning miracles of his race through time. [...] As for Ev himself ... his life [was charged] with what he called a creative mistrust and he passed it on to the large majority of those he taught.[36]

Griffiths's influence on Gwyn was second only to that of Georges-Henry Louis Rochat (1901–1992). A Swiss-born émigré, Rochat arrived to teach modern languages (chiefly French, German and Spanish) at Rhondda County School in 1928, having been coaxed from the continent by Griffiths. The two men had met whilst studying at the University of Geneva and had already collaborated on a textbook on the teaching of French in British secondary schools.[37] Such was the lasting influence of the Swiss that he appeared, albeit heavily disguised by comedic exaggeration, in the first story Gwyn ever wrote for *Punch* – 'On Leaving a Lover' – which was published in the magazine in July 1953. It was a sympathetic portrait of a man Gwyn labelled a 'refugee from the bleakest ice caps of Calvinism' and the 'first teacher at school to tackle European literature with me.' Gwyn continued:

> for the first five minutes of each lesson he would shiver and be reticent, then his body would grow calm as he drew the blazing torches of the Romantics across the frozen surfaces of his old acceptances. His voice would rise as he savoured the grieving runes of Musset and the orgiastic shouts of Byron and Espronceda. He was in full flight from bowlers, seed-cake and penny-a-week death policies.[38]

Throughout his time at Rhondda County School, Gwyn demonstrated a tremendous facility with language, a talent recognised and nurtured by Griffiths and Rochat. A testimonial sent by the latter to St Edmund Hall in support of Gwyn's application to study at Oxford noted that the young man has remarkable proficiency in Spanish; not only has he displayed an uncommon aptitude for the assimilation of the purely linguistic side of French and Spanish studies but made, under my guidance, a study both comprehensive and penetrative of the literature and general culture of the countries concerned; in this respect, he has shown a maturity of mind rarely found in boys of his age.[39]

Gwyn's fluency in both French and Spanish was apparent in his higher certificate results in which he achieved a distinction with special commendation for conversational power.[40] He had had similar success in his school certificate examinations in 1929, winning merit for his proficiency in French, although at that age his best results were history rather than in languages – he earned a distinction.[41] It was not enough to dissuade him from a linguistic focus in the Sixth Form, but Gwyn's interest in history never left him. In place of history, and with university entry in mind, he elected to study Latin for his higher certificate.[42]

As a dedicated student of the humanities, Gwyn never had much enthusiasm for the sciences or mathematics – nor for the masters at Rhondda County School who taught those subjects, such as the chemist 'Mr Thurlow' or the mathematician 'Mr Glenn.' The latter 'was the man who kept bowling sums at me for most of the time in the County School, and consciously I never left the pavilion.' In Gwyn's portrait, 'Glenn' was a former member of the Royal Flying Corps who regarded the teaching of mathematics rather like an aerial engagement between Sopworth Camels and Fokker triplanes. 'If, as it well might, a wild hatred of mathematics will one day qualify as a damnable heresy, I will walk gently and proudly as Latimer to the stake,' Gwyn wrote later.[43] To prove his point, and with the flexibility afforded by fiction, Gwyn concluded his *Punch* article about

59

'Mr Glenn' with a set of observations about E. T. Griffiths's replacement as headmaster at Rhondda County School, W. J. Howells.[44] Formerly the senior chemistry master at Quakers Yard, Howells was 'porous to any suggestion that came from Mr Glenn,' and the result was a compulsory two periods a week of mathematics even for the arts stream. Gwyn added, 'this was a definite manoeuvre by Mr Glenn to counter the markedly left-wing flavour of the teaching done in the Literature and History Departments.' It was a view of the technocratic flavour of the sciences and mathematics which Gwyn kept all his life.

In Sixth Form, Gwyn was a model student. He was hard-working, dedicated to the pursuit of knowledge, and academically successful. He had also begun to write, publishing several pieces in the school magazine. This reality contrasts with the portrait of a wayward child who took up smoking Woodbines at the age of ten and became the 'first smoker to have permanent drifts of ash on both knee caps' which was Gwyn's presentation of his early years in secondary school.[45] As he put it in the 1970s, 'once a boy got into the secondary school, if he had any sense at all, he really set himself to winning the scholarships that would take him out of the valley into another place.' That was Gwyn's ambition, and his determination to succeed was readily apparent in truth, if not on the page. The first article which Gwyn wrote for the school magazine was published in July 1927, at the end of his year in the second form. It was a description of his cohort and their experiences since September 1926. His wise-cracking humour was already apparent, of course, but this was the annual report on the top set in the school – hardly the words of a slouch hiding behind the bike sheds delinquently smoking his way through the day.

No event of great interest has broken in upon the school year in IIa. There are now various changes in our form, owing to the changing of certain boys at the end of each term. A notable addition to our form is L. Evans, who has shown exceptional ability throughout the year and deserved promotion. This fear of relegation has added zest to our studies and has been a large factor in making the boys of IIa into very studious youths. Some of the boys have suddenly become aged owing to the addition of Latin to the timetable, and Horace and Cicero have become part of our existence. The boys have done well in sport, and last winter we became staunch Rugbyites, J. R. Jones being a very capable captain to our team. We also had a representative in the Junior Rugby Team. G. V. Cadogan did his part in the sports on behalf of IIa, and gained a few points. The form has done well in cricket, the most conspicuous exponents being White and M. Rees, who should do well in the noble sport at a later date. There are also two members of our form to whom the rest should be thankful for their infectious humour throughout the year.

G. Thomas, IIa.[46]

Gwyn's next article was written a year or so later, when he was in the fourth form. Entitled, 'An Hour in a Children's Library,' it was a consideration of the types of books young people might read and gave a clear insight into the studious and dedicated scholar which he had become – or, in fact, had always been. He wrote:

To spend an hour in a children's library is to be taken back to those early days of your life, which you loved so dearly. Memories, awakened by the sight of those books which you once read with youthful eagerness, flash upon that inward eye, and you are for the moment a child once more.

You grasp a children's encyclopaedia, and the reading is refreshingly light after the more ponderous and deep works of the masters. You note the familiar stains of toffee-smeared fingers on an interesting page dealing with the stories of Drake and Raleigh which children love so dearly.

You pass along to the department of books dealing with the fundamental facts of natural history. These books give at once the type of literature children appreciate, for, in contrast with the dirty, stained books in the other cases, these books are unsoiled and clean.

The interesting study of animal life has evidently no fascination for the youthful mind.

The cases containing the Greek mythology books apparently have an irresistible attraction for children, for the illustrations of the usually lily-white statues of the Greek gods are reduced to little more than black smudges. One can easily imagine the youthful admirers of Apollo or Mercury gazing in rapt admiration at his idol, sighing dolefully as he thinks of the glorious times the object of his thoughts used to live in, compared with the present era of coal dust and strikes.

You pass on to the nursery rhyme department for the youngest element, and the thing which first strikes your eye is a lurid painting of the well-known scene, – Miss Bo-peep receiving her cattle, minus their tails.

For the more serious-minded of the coming generation are a few books of simple verse, the lightest of the classics, apparently looked upon with disdain by the uncultured element.

The latter's Arcadia is the next department we see. It is full of blood-curdling stories, which fire their unruly blood to such a degree that it would be advisable to put some of them away.

Hark! I hear the tramp of thousands. Our hour has drawn to a close, and the approaching multitude is the children coming to pick the book of their choice.

Gwyn Thomas, IVa.[47]

As a teenager, Gwyn expressed himself through a mixture of humour and political righteousness. 'I recall, one day,' he wrote in *A Welsh Eye* in the 1960s, 'trying to explain to the son of a draper, a torpid, powerful boy, the content of a speech I had heard the night before in the concert room of the Library and Institute. The speaker had given us the exact shade and time of arrival of the Red Dawn.' Such a memory might seem made up but for the fact that, when he was in Sixth Form, Gwyn was one of those who established the literary and debating society at Rhondda County School. He spoke at the society's first ever debate on 20 November 1929, six months after Arthur Horner had stood as a communist candidate in the Rhondda East constituency. Chaired by the headmaster, E. T. Griffiths, the debate considered the motion that 'civilisation is a failure.' Gwyn spoke in favour of the motion and, as the school magazine recorded, 'in a distinctly witty and spirited manner struck a novel note, condemning, amid general laughter, the whole industrial system which has grown up during the last two hundred years.'[48]

Gwyn's socialist leanings emerged no less clearly in his first published short stories, which appeared in the *Rhondda County Magazine* when he was in the Sixth Form. The first was called 'The Meeting.' A compelling piece of juvenilia, it prefigured some of Gwyn's later writing, both for its politics and the chatter of the dark philosophers. The central scene ran as follows,

> By far the most interesting characters in the meeting belonged to the audience. One sat immediately in front of me, the other, immediately behind. Totally oblivious of this handicap, they talked to each other throughout the whole period. The one in front was a bemuffled, demure specimen called Alec. The other was a robust, domineering fellow who had mastered the

supreme art of expectorating with deadly accuracy, and who rejoiced in the name of George. To record the whole of their conversation would be a sheer impossibility, but I will here endeavour to give a fair sample of it:-

George (expectorating over my shoulder with a grunt of intense satisfaction at his prowess): Hey, Alec, gimme a monkeynut.

Alec: I suppose you want me to shell it, do you? (Aside) You're a lazy tyke, that's what you are.

George (grasping the fruit): Righto-o, thanks. But, look here, Alec, what do you think of this speaker chap? He's giving me a bit of fright with his jumping about.

Alec (with a grunt of disdain): Same here, too. He'll be jumping off the stage before long. His luck can't last for ever, and, what's another thing, I can't understand half those words he's using. Now, look here, what does he mean by 'pro borno publico?' I don't know why he can't speak plain English.

George (grandly): Pro borno publico? Why, Alec, my boy, your ignorance is quite appalling, but then you never was a lad for reading, so I might as well tell you what it means. It's French, see, and it means 'Down with capitalism.'

Alec (bowing to superior wisdom): Oh! Quite right, too.

The leaping orator would reappear decades later in another story, which Gwyn told to the television producer and interviewer, Denis Mitchell:

My father had this kind of residual desire to be in touch with beauty by planting a few flowers and his favourite flowers were nasturtium. And then for about five years running when the crocuses and the nasturtiums were just bringing to flaunt their little bit of beauty, Arthur Cook would start to make a speech and he would come up into our front garden to make it. He was the most restless orator that I've ever seen. He was like Nijinsky. He would leap in the middle of a phrase ... And he would land on a nasturtium, and he would land on a crocus, with infallible accuracy.

Whether or not the speaker jumping about on stage in Gwyn's teenage story was modelled after A. J. Cook, the miner's leader from nearby Porth, is not clear. The echo merely tantalises. That same sensation can be felt reading the second of Gwyn's teenage short stories, 'Decadence.' Its links are to 'Gazooka' and are made through an evocation of the American singer Al Jolson. The story merits repeating in full.

There is an old tradition in this country which entitles adult folks to titter derisively at the opinions of the youthful element, whose startling views so often scorch the ceilings of the Form VI rooms throughout our secondary schools. These adults, upon hearing some youth expressing himself rather strongly upon the state of the universe at large, close their eyes and say, in sepulchral tones: "Tush, tush; O! callous youth. By you, the well of life is still untasted; so, hold your peace, I crave?" To sage aphorism, my reply is: "Bunk".

Everything around us savours of decay, and if these intellectual grown-ups titter until they collapse, they will not be able to deny the fact. But, personally, I am not the type who goes off into the wilderness and chews grass like a demented donkey, just because the world happens to be showing the very distinct signs of the "latter days". There are two reasons which stop me from taking this rash course. Firstly, because one can obtain plenty of fun looking at the different aspects of this moral and physical degeneration; and, secondly, because there is a fine selection of coal-tips covering the wilderness, which reason obviates the necessity of emulating Nebuchadnezzar.

For example: our politics and everything else connected with them have been degraded and debased so much that they hardly reach the level of a third-class music-hall turn; the countries of the world organise magnificent peace conferences, the only object of which is to show the ordinary people how many typists and private secretaries are really to be had when one has the necessary money to engage them; and the nations, with a unity, which is really admirable, are all doing their utmost to make the next war bigger and better than ever.

After which unnecessary perambulation I am going to air my principal grievance, namely, the utter contempt which most people have for good music. Many are the hours I have spent in trying to convince some people that a good piece of music contains four times as much moral uplift as twelve fanatical evangelists. But, it was in vain that I cried! The accursed Alphonse Jolson and his horde of Broadway Babies have the country in a stranglehold, and while the minority applaud and revere the masterpieces of Wagner, Schubert, Beethoven, and their immortal companions, the wooden-headed majority is lapping up with gleaming eyes, the syncopated stuff-and-nonsense called, impudently enough, low-brow music. If that is low-brow music, the brows of those that appreciate it must be floating around somewhere near their ankles.

It has penetrated even into the schools, and it is really alarming the way these crazy little "song-hits" are perpetually in the mouths of one's class-mates. One day, while bent over my work, some songster approached me and outlined, in song, some plan which he had formed. He proposed that we should go out to the West, and there built a nest, at which, however humble, we would never grumble. Then, in a last line of tremendous poetic imagery, he compared us to Darby and Joan. That, I confess, was too much for me, so I hurled a book at him; but it was as futile as old Canute's orders to Neptune; another musical student approached and told me another charming story in song. He was sobbing too much for me to catch the first half of his dirge, but after gaining courage from striking a beautiful top C., he lost his shyness and his mumblings became coherent, and I discovered that he was addressing me as Sonny Boy, and chat, although the angels should grow lonely, they were vested with full permission to take me into their loving arms, because he, as my loving father, would make it his duty to slip from his earthly chains and join his own little Sonny Boy. Without commenting that it would be rather a joke if the angels did not take him. I got ready to swing in a terrible left at the songster's head, but, seeing that he was, by now, overwrought by the intense pathos of his song, and that he was causing universal havoc with his bitter tears, I swam out of the danger line and left him to his fate.

So then, we have descended to this! We, the boys of the bull-dog breed, are on a level with the snivelling Pekinese! But there will come a day when all this tension which is around us will break and we shall come back to our normal senses. There will be a tremendous reaction, and we will all bring harps to school and will hasten up to the field and sing psalms and hymns, and we shall, in short, provide a very sharp contrast to the Jolsonian school which now holds sway. Instead of hearing incessant declarations that 'Yes, sir, you're my baby,' and 'Give yourself a pat on the back,' and tearful confessions that 'I'll always be Mother's Boy,' the schoolboys of the next generation will be listening all day to pure oratorio. They will walk about the corridors with saintly features and New Testaments and soap and water in buckets, with which to erase from the walls any obscene expression of art; the School Dramatic Society will be doing Passion plays every Friday afternoon, and on St David's Day, one of the Junior School will ascend the platform and sing his way manfully through the 'Messiah' unaccompanied.

As a last word I might say that when any one of these things starts happening, the Millennium will be about a fortnight distant.

G. Thomas, VI. Arts

For all the earnestness on display in this piece, Gwyn was never actually hostile to popular music. He later claimed that his singing voice 'owed much to Bing Crosby,' who was one of Nan's favourite artists. He wove into 'Gazooka' references to Al Jolson's 1920 hit, *Swanee*, which had been written by George Gershwin for a New York revue the previous year. Gwyn's story opened, famously,

> Somewhere outside my window a child is whistling. He is walking fast down the hill and whistling. The tune on his lips is 'Swanee.' I go to the window and watch him. He is moving through a fan of light from a street lamp. His head is thrown back, his lips protrude strongly and his body moves briskly. 'D. I. X. I. – Even Mamee, How I love you, how I love you, my dear old Swanee...'

Swanee was one of the most popular tunes of the 1920s, on either side of the Atlantic.[49] Al Jolson himself was well-known in Britain. In 1927 he starred in the *Jazz Singer*, the first full-length motion picture to feature synchronised sound, which was subsequently credited for launching the talkie age. The film arrived in Britain in the autumn of 1928. But it was *Swanee* which made Jolson and Gershwin famous; it was, as one London newspaper put it in 1928, 'sung everywhere.'[50] Even to the point of distracting Gwyn from his Sixth Form studies.

Gwyn's final contribution to the school magazine as a pupil was the annual review of life in Form VI Arts, 'a deep, dark, den of learning,' published in 1931. On the reading list that year was R. C. Sherriff's *Journey's End*, a 'masterpiece' of which they gave 'candid criticism.' 'Each boy,' Gwyn wrote, 'has a peculiar art of his own in our form ... there is one who has such a host of yarns, jokes, and stories, that I am sure he could keep us in our doubles.' That was surely him. Gwyn would subsequently write that that summer of 1931 was 'a bonanza time for me.' He sailed through his higher certificate examinations bringing scholarship offers for study at university. 'They were,' he said, 'going to spend more on me than on the roads.' He added:

I became a notable figure. I had my name mentioned in a newspaper for the first time. My father was interviewed and congratulated on having given a new sheen to the poverty belt. Four neighbours tried to touch the hem of my coat as a healing tactic but were later found to be after my coat.

Gwyn kept his coat. He wrote to several Oxford colleges seeking entry to study modern languages. One of those which wrote back was St Edmund Hall with an invitation from the Principal, the historian Alfred Emden (1888–1979), to come up for an interview. Travelling on the long-distance Red and White coach which wound its way from South Wales to Gloucester and then on to Oxford, Gwyn came close enough to the Severn 'to kiss, if the bus company had allowed such emotional antics.' In a letter to his brother Walt, who was by then living and working in Neath, Gwyn described what happened. 'I set out to Oxford at 8 o'clock on Tuesday morning, arrived at 3pm, had interview with principal at 3.30; I was the guest of the Hall for the night and got back to Porth at 8pm on Wednesday.'[51] For *Punch* in the late 1960s, Gwyn added that 'I occupied the aisle-side seat next to a man who had been in the bus from the journey's beginning. Every time I moved my head to peer at some strange town or unfamiliar vegetation the man would put his head forward and obstruct my view.'[52] Of his interview, Gwyn recalled,

I grew to feel more and more like a Martian as [it] went on. The Principal had been a distinguished submarine commander in the First World War, and in the sort of glance he kept giving me, lowering his head and gazing upwards at me, there was the suggestion of a man looking through a periscope, a person studying another from another medium of experience altogether. He said he would be delighted to see me at the beginning of term … he added that he was sure I would be happy in my new community.[53]

Discombobulated after his interview, Gwyn used the free evening to wander around the centre of Oxford and found solace in a transport café on the High Street, where pies and strong tea provided a welcome respite from the more luxurious and alien repast offered in the college dining hall.[54] In the back of his mind, despite the assurances from Principal Emden, Gwyn was uncertain as to whether Oxford was the right choice, but since no university college in Wales taught Spanish and it was the language he wanted most to study, he had few options. He told Walt that the 'worst I have to fear is a nervous breakdown and I have been so near that particular treat for the past year that I now treat it like an old friend.' The words would prove prophetic. Three months later, Gwyn made the same journey from the Rhondda to Oxford, and settled into his lodgings at 27 Minster Road, a modern house situated in the east end of the city. His landlord and landlady, he wrote, were 'traditionalists to within a breath of coma. Their heads were stuffed with old *Daily Mails* and every time they turned an ear to the quick, subversive tumble of my words you could hear the Mafeking headlines rustle.' At one end of the street was Oriel College's cricket ground, Bartlemas, at the other end was Oxford's workhouse, by then known as Cowley Road Hospital. Gwyn could hardly fail to notice the ironic juxtaposition of privilege and poverty into which he had now been thrust.

[1] The quotes in this paragraph draw on Gwyn's contributions to two television documentaries: *Return to Rhondda* for TWW in 1965 and *Gazooka Summer* for BBC One (Wales) in 1976.

[2] *WM*, 9 July 1926.

[3] *WM*, 20 September 1926.

[4] Gwyn Thomas, 'Growing Up in Meadow Prospect, Part 4: Explosion Point', *Punch*, 3 May 1961. Tom Mooney (1882–1942) was an American labour union official imprisoned, on falsified evidence, for the 1916 Preparedness Day Bombing in San Francisco. He served twenty-two years before his release in 1939. Nicolo Sacco (1891–1927) and Bartolomeo Vanzetti (1888–1927) were Italian anarchists convicted of murder following an armed robbery at a shoe factory in Massachusetts in 1920. They were executed by electric chair on 23 August 1927. Sacco and Vanzetti were a cause célèbre for the global communist movement with protests held all over the world.

[5] Will Paynter, *My Generation* (London, 1972).

[6] J. D. Jenkins, *Annual Report of the Medical Officer of Health for 1920* (Tonypandy, 1921), 13–14.

[7] J. D. Jenkins, *Annual Report of the Medical Officer of Health for 1925* (Tonypandy, 1926), 24.

[8] Gwyn Thomas, *The Subsidence Factor* (Cardiff, 1979).

[9] *WM*, 26 August 1936.

[10] National Archives and Records Administration, Washington D. C., United States Census for Cuyahoga County, Cleveland Ward 7, Enumeration date 17 August 1870. Available on microfilm: M593, roll 1190.

[11] Cuyahoga County was not like the emigrant world of Pennsylvania, which sustained a rich Welsh-speaking community – a community recovered and considered by Bill Jones in his *Wales in America: Scranton and the Welsh, 1860–1920* (Cardiff, 1993) and by Richard Lewis in his *Welsh Americans: A History of Assimilation in the Coalfields* (Chapel Hill, NC, 2008). Iowa similarly appealed to Welsh migrants. Cherilyn A. Walley, *The Welsh in Iowa* (Cardiff, 2009).

[12] William Osborn, *Music in Ohio* (Kent, OH, 2004), 363.

[13] *Aberdare Leader*, 17 February 1906. The workshop was in Pryce Street, Mountain Ash; the quote is taken from Dai Smith, *Writer's World: Gwyn Thomas, 1913–1981* (Cardiff, 1986), 4.

[14] Gwyn Thomas, 'The Touch', *Punch*, 22 January 1964.

[15] Gwyn Thomas, 'Ace Writer', *TW*, 24 August 1962.

[16] *Rhondda Leader*, 4 November 1920.

[17] Gwyn Thomas, 'Growing Up in Meadow Prospect, Part 2: Change Here for Strangeness', *Punch*, 19 April 1961.

[18] *Wings of Significance* (HTV, 1988).

[19] 'Change here for strangeness', *Punch*, 19 April 1961.

[20] *Artists in Wales*, 69.

[21] The phrase belongs to M. Wynn Thomas, *In the Shadow of the Pulpit*, 166.

[22] *Artists in Wales*, 70.

[23] Gwyn Thomas, 'The Seeding Twenties, Part 1: A Paling Darkness', *Punch*, 6 December 1961. The reference is to Franz Lehár's enormously popular 1905 operetta, *Die Lustige Witwe* (The Merry Widow).

[24] Gwyn Thomas, 'A Touch of the Boasts', *Punch*, 23 March 1966.

[25] Gwyn Thomas, 'Out of the Air – Llef', *The Listener*, 13 March 1975.

[26] Gwyn Thomas, 'That Night Still Shines', in Treorchy Male Choir, *Excelsior: The Voice of Treorchy Male Choir, Record for the Year 1954* (Treorchy, 1954), 7–8.

[27] *Artists in Wales*, 69.

[28] Gwyn Thomas, *A Hatful of Humours* (London, 1965), 9.

[29] Glamorgan Archives, County Entrance Scholarship Examination Results, 1909–1925, GD/E/23/1. The syllabus and examiners' reports are contained in GD/E/23/40.

[30] Owen Vernon Jones, *Porth County: The School and Its Boys* (Porth, 1991); Rhondda County Boys' School, *Jubilee Brochure, 1896–1946* (Tonypandy, 1946).

[31] *Y Brython*, 10 September 1914; William Davies and E. T. Griffiths, *The Tutorial Welsh Course* (Newport, 1914).

[32] *Aberystwyth Observer*, 26 July 1906; *Cambrian News*, 9 July 1909; *Y Cymro*, 23 January 1918.

[33] He in turn had replaced John Stradling Grant on his death. *Rhondda Leader*, 27 September 1913.

[34] Chris Williams, *Democratic Rhondda*, 157. Chalke won more than ten thousand votes and came second to the sitting Labour MP, David Watts Morgan. No Liberal (or Liberal Democrat) candidate has bettered this result (in Rhondda East, Rhondda West, or Rhondda) since then. In 1931, Chalke was the Liberal candidate for Swansea East, where he ran against the long-serving Labour MP, David Williams. Chalke eventually moved to Porthcawl where he was elected to the local urban district council. He served as chair between 1939 and 1941. *WM*, 8 July 1939.

[35] Gwyn Thomas, 'Foreword', in Stewart Williams, *Old Barry in Photographs* (Barry, 1977).

[36] Gwyn Thomas, 'The Improver', *Punch*, 9 October 1968.

[37] E. T. Griffiths and G. H. Rochat, *Higher Test Papers in French* (London, 1928–1929). Rochat went on to write a further textbook for the London publisher Macmillan a decade later. G. H. Rochat, *French Vocabulary and Syntax* (London, 1938). Both provide a strong indication of the material available to Gwyn as he was studying at Rhondda County School.

[38] Gwyn Thomas, 'On Leaving a Lover', *Punch*, 29 July 1953. It was reprinted in *Ring Delirium 123* (London, 1960).

[39] SEH Archive, Gwyn Thomas File; Testimonial from Georges Henry Rochat, 21 September 1931.

[40] D. Vaughan Johnston, 'Report on Porth County Boys' School, 31 October 1931', in Central Welsh Board, *Reports, Inspection and Examination of County Schools, 1931* (Oxford, 1931). Consulted at the Glamorgan Archives: GD/E/34/34.

[41] D. Vaughan Johnston, 'Report on Porth County Boys' School, 31 October 1929', in Central Welsh Board, *Reports, Inspection and Examination of County Schools, 1929* (Oxford, 1929). Consulted at the Glamorgan Archives: GD/E/34/32.

[42] Gwyn Thomas, 'The Call', *Punch*, 17 April 1968.

[43] Gwyn Thomas, 'The Seeding Twenties: It Figures', *Punch*, 20 December 1961.

[44] *WM*, 14 October 1933.

[45] *Artists in Wales*, 69. This fictional portrait of Gwyn's adolescence confused Michael Parnell who recorded that Gwyn 'went through a long period when academic success looked like the last thing on his mind.' *LFD*, 16–22. In letter sent home from Oxford in early May 1934, Gwyn had remarked that he 'bought Woodbines at the age of ten,' which is the likely origin of this part of the story. Letter from Gwyn Thomas to Hannah Thomas, 7 May 1934.

[46] Gwyn Thomas, 'Round the Forms (Lower), IIa', *Rhondda County School Magazine* (Porth, 1927), 21.

[47] Gwyn Thomas, 'An Hour in a Children's Library', *Rhondda County Magazine* (Porth, 1928), 21.

[48] 'The Literary and Debating Society', *Rhondda County Magazine* (Porth, 1930), 8.

[49] Jolson recorded the song for Columbia Records. It was number one in the leading record shops of London in the summer of 1920 and beyond. See, for instance, *Pall Mall Gazette*, 13 August 1920; *The Stage*, 1 June 1922. Gershwin's original score was also on sale in Britain at that time.

[50] *The Sphere*, 31 March 1928.

[51] NLW, GTP, J22/1: Letter from Gwyn Thomas to Walter Thomas, undated but summer 1931.

[52] Gwyn Thomas, 'First Exit', *Punch*, 5 June 1968.

[53] In fact, during the First World War, Emden had served on HMS Parker, a destroyer; his connection with submarines came during the Second World War when he was in command of the Oxford University Naval Division and accompanied a patrol in the Bay of Biscay.

[54] *AFSE*, 54.

CHAPTER TWO

St Edmund Hell, Oxford

The application form had thirteen questions. Surname: *Thomas*. Christian name in full: *Gwyn*. Age and date of birth: *18 years, 2 months; born July 6, 1913*. Nationality and place of birth: *Welsh; born at Porth, Glam*. Religious denomination: *Congregationalist*. Gwyn signed and dated it all on 19 September 1931 – a Saturday.[1] He was already in a state of despair. A few weeks earlier, Gwyn received the fateful news that two of the three scholarships, which he had been awarded on the basis of his exam results earlier in the summer, were to be withdrawn for financial reasons. Gone were the awards from Rhondda Urban District Council and Glamorgan County Council, together worth one hundred and forty pounds. All that was left was the state scholarship worth eighty pounds, which had to last him the year. It soon whittled away. Entry to the college had cost five pounds, matriculation to the university four pounds, and tuition fees were a minimum of eight pounds a term (three of those) with a supplement because of studying modern languages.[2] St Edmund Hall also charged its members two pounds in each of the spring and summer terms, as one contemporary recalled, to pay for steaks for the college rowing crew.[3] 'I was left,' Gwyn recalled three decades later, 'with the prospect of storming the land's oldest university on so short a shoestring my shoes even now keep falling off at the thought of it.' At the start of term, already desperate for money, Gwyn wrote to his brother Walt to tell him that 'I now want about £75 more in order to keep myself from falling into the merciless hands of Oxford's Official

74

Receiver and the subsequent incarceration in one of the city's prisons for recalcitrant debtors.' I suppose, he added,

> you think I am a fool to have started upon this brainless venture with such slender resources, but my Cynffig blood boils at the thought of capitulation, and I am prepared to go through with it and bag a few scholarships during the first year and obtain by this means some sense of comfort and security during the second year.[4]

Walt wrote back to offer a subvention from his salary. He had recently taken up a post teaching French at Neath Boys' Grammar School and was earning enough to ease, though by no means erase, Gwyn's financial troubles. 'I accept your offer,' Gwyn replied, 'on condition that you cease payments as soon as you find that you need the money for your own purposes.' Further relief came in the form of a Miners' Welfare National Scholarship worth ninety pounds, which Gwyn was awarded in the summer of 1932. He was the first person from the Rhondda to be awarded this scholarship to study at Oxford, and only the second from South Wales as whole.[5] It made possible the journey to Spain to study at the University of Madrid, an option otherwise out of reach, but provided little lasting material comfort in Oxford itself. In such conditions of poverty, Gwyn was never able to find happiness or contentment as a university student, even had he wished to do so. Whenever he was prompted by television interviewers or journalists to consider this period of his life, he often bristled and was never pragmatic about nor did he disguise those aspects of Oxford he thoroughly disliked.

As a young man, Gwyn simply avoided it all as best he could. 'I nearly got myself totally ostracised by my flat refusal to participate in any kind of sport,' he told his brother Walt. He was absent, too, from the traditional matriculation photograph of new college members (as freshers were known) taken before being inducted as members of the university. 'I keep my distance in silence and gloom,' he wrote home, 'when one of them utters a remark that falls outside the landed estate of conventional greeting or farewell, the next abandon all thought of nourishment or the future, and stand magnificently to attention, saluting the one who has gone.' Gwyn continued,

> There was a time when they tried to cajole me into singing their merry roundelay of balls. But I slung their balls around into a Celtic metre and threw them back with a force so cruel and certain that their understanding went mad, laughed shortly and hysterically for a moment, and retired to its source, unknown and unexplained. And now they leave me to me. I can stare at them in peace. When my hand moves ... to compare their idea of life and death with mine, my language becomes fouler than the ambition from which language was born.

There were, according to Gwyn, two factions amongst the undergraduate Aularians: 'those who revelled in the orthodox piety that gave the college its tone of chirpy altruism' and those who were 'political zealots.' By inclination Gwyn gravitated towards the latter but soon discovered they had the wrong sort of politics. 'In the valley a seam of socialist dogma took up nine-tenths of the mental space,' he wrote later, but in St Edmund Hall politics was High Tory. 'I was,' Gwyn added, 'impressed by its assurance, bewildered by its flavour.' It was a fractious time. Six weeks before term, the minority Labour government led by Ramsay MacDonald had collapsed over its continuing response to the global financial crisis caused by the Wall Street Crash of 1929. MacDonald remained as prime minister of a new National Government, which was in practice dominated by

Stanley Baldwin's Conservatives, and called a general election to gain legitimacy for his actions. Britain went to the polls at the end of October, not long after the start of Oxford's Michaelmas term. In much of England and Scotland, Labour was wiped out. There was not even a contest in Oxford: the sitting Conservative MP, Robert Bourne, was returned unopposed. At home in Rhondda East, the choice was between the Communist Party and the Labour Party. It was a world away.

Gwyn sought out like-minded students as best he could, typically outside of St Edmund Hall. He joined Oxford University Labour Club (OULC) as well as the 'Society for the furtherance of Oswald Mosley's New Party – not because I believe in the efficacy of Oswald's proposed measures,' he told the family in Porth, 'but because there are plenty of refreshments.' Once the free sandwiches and drinks were gone, Gwyn made his escape. The New Party's ethos in Oxford was more aristocratic and conservative than branches in working-class areas of the country, such as Bradford or Merthyr Tydfil, where members were drawn from the disgruntled ranks of the Communist Party (men such as Merthyr's Arthur Eyles, who later joined the British Union of Fascists), the ILP, or Labour.[6] In the aftermath of the election, British politics became ever more polarised. On the right, the New Party was dissolved and its more authoritarian figures, led by Mosley, formed the British Union of Fascists in the autumn of 1932. 'Its adherents, who are nearly all young men,' remarked the Labour-supporting *Daily Herald*, 'are busy being measured for black shirts.'[7] On the left, the Communist Party stepped up its attacks on the Labour Party which it regarded as weak and ineffective in the face of austerity and unemployment and the growing dangers of fascism and war.

Gwyn watched from the side lines as a small group of no more than a dozen students, including Frank Strauss Meyer

(1909–1972), a Jewish-American who later became a close associate of the right-wing commentator and journalist William F. Buckley (1925–2008), Dick Freeman (1910–1997)[8], John Windsor Farnsworth (1912–1987)[9] and Owen Papineau (1910–1970)[10], broke off from the OULC to establish a new, radical group in December 1931. It was called the October Club and aimed at studying 'communism in its world, social, economic and cultural aspects.'[11] The society built on an earlier study group and set about inculcating communist ideas and values amongst the student population of the city. At Balliol College, for instance, Frank Strauss Meyer convinced his fellow Junior Common Room members to subscribe to the *Daily Worker* in response to an apparently growing demand for 'revolutionary propaganda.'[12] In his letters home, Gwyn wrote about the October Club obliquely telling his family that the 'undergraduates of this university are agitating for free speech.' He was equally circumspect in later life. The only hint of the October Club to appear in Gwyn's published writings was in *A Welsh Eye* when he discussed the anti-Means Test protests in the Rhondda in 1935. 'One of the visiting contingents was of members of the October Club, a very militant outfit at the University of Oxford,' Gwyn explained. 'I had been a student there, on some of the most tenuous State-aid ever devised, until the previous year. The October boys called on me and requested that for Oxford's sake, I should march behind their banner.'[13] Gwyn refused on the grounds that he was marching with his family. The October Club contingent in the protest consisted of forty undergraduates who had travelled up from Oxford. Their presence was widely reported, even though they were a miniscule minority amongst the tens of thousands of locals who marched that day.[14]

Given his schoolboy radicalism, Gwyn was neither immune to the appeal of the October Club nor to the political and intellectual fervour it offered in the otherwise conservative atmosphere of the university and his own college, St Edmund Hall.[15] It is possible, therefore, that Gwyn, together with his friend John Wynne Roberts who was studying French and Italian as the Doncaster Scholar at Magdalen College, was one of at least three hundred undergraduates drawn into the October Club's activities by the end of 1932.[16] The pair certainly took an active interest in what was going on. In January 1933, the proctors (the university authorities) moved to prohibit the October Club: first by banning membership to individuals from outside the university; then by banning meetings of all political societies including the OULC; and finally by banning the October Club outright and preventing them from meeting in university buildings.[17] Gwyn set out his version of the story in a letter home, referencing the portrait of events in the family's newspaper, the Labour-supporting *Daily Herald*. He wrote,

The communists up here are thinking of moving to another planet. You may have culled the prominent facts from the 'Herald' but in case you haven't, here they are. The proctors who look to the disciplinary side of the joint seek to ensure the safety of the world and conservatism by expelling from the university all those weak-minded enough to wear a thoughtful look from time to time, meaning that strong antagonism has been jostled between the more free-thinking societies and the proctorial authorities ... Because of the absence of thought and freedom of thought up here are one and the same thing, depending for the distinction in terms upon the public school from which one crawls into this warren. Anyway, communism has now taken its place upon the field. (What a field, brothers and sister. What a field!) They formed a club and declared that they desired the abolition of all things except the right to blush at the mention of Russia. Up till this term, the proctors smiled with dignity upon them safe in the belief that a bunch of morons could accomplish nothing save hoarseness. But now, as I told you before, the delegates of our present govt. have demanded that all socialist or communist ideas be stamped out in Oxford. (It was generous of them to think that there were ideas in Oxford.) With the result that the proctors are now rushing about like elephants, stamping things out.

In the early days of the October Club's existence, when its status as a discussion group was more ambiguous, most participants were not actively involved in the Communist Party and the club attracted a range of left-wing speakers including the playwright George Bernard Shaw and the novelist H. G. Wells.[18] Such nuance belied the club's external reputation as the university's communist society. The red-baiting *Western Mail* was unequivocal insisting that 'it is a fact' that the October Club 'exists for the serious propagation of Communism.'[19] The *Merthyr Express*, which otherwise took little interest in the affairs of university undergraduates, pointed out to its readers that the ranks of the October Club were filled with '1500 a year incomed members.'[20] But the appeal was palpable. By the start of Gwyn's final year in Oxford, in the autumn of 1933, the October Club could boast the largest membership of any student organisation in the university. 'This theory,' the *Western Mail* warned its readers, referring to communism, 'has an increasing appeal to the young intellectuals, men of mental virility.'[21] Men including Gwyn. In a notebook compiled in the early 1940s, whilst he was teaching in Cardigan, he wrote that 'at the age of twenty, I became a Marxist. With this new perception, I foresaw that before I obtained the age of thirty, imperialism would be experiencing a series of crises sufficient to induce a war.'

It was not an inevitable progression. In his first year, Gwyn was a loyal member of the OULC and attended its meetings week after week. But, like many undergraduates, he became frustrated by Labour's lack of radicalism and the willingness of some in the OULC to continue to engage with those disgraced by their support for the National Government. 'I've already told you that I'm a member of the Oxford University Labour Club, I think,' he wrote in a letter home in November 1931. 'Malcolm MacDonald was there last night speaking on the Manchurian Question. There were a lot of Indians in the club, from Balliol. Red hot, flaming anarchists whose grammar gives all to the devil when they become excited and they are almost always in that unhappy state.'[22] Several of the Indian radicals Gwyn described would go on to be important figures in the October Club, including the philosopher Baba Pyare Lal Bedi who, with his partner Freda Marie Houlston, wrote a series of books on the Indian nationalist struggle from a communist perspective.[23] They were all there that night to listen to Malcolm MacDonald, then under-secretary of state in the Dominions department in Westminster. His father, Ramsay, of course, was the prime minister.

In his speech, the younger MacDonald warned of the probability of war between China and Japan over Manchuria should the League of Nations fail in its efforts to broker peace. 'This is going to be the real test,' MacDonald said, it 'has not been successful so far. If Japan goes out of the League, the League's prestige will suffer, and if the machinery of peaceful settlement breaks down there is going to be a very big war. The war would not stop in Manchuria.'[24] He faced a difficult crowd. But he was not alone. In June 1932, the left-leaning MP George Lansbury, who was a few months shy of his election as the leader of the Labour Party, was heckled by members of the October Club at a meeting of the OULC and asked what he had done personally to 'rouse the opposition against the means test.'[25] They were not convinced by Lansbury's reply. Then in November 1932, a few weeks after that year's national hunger march, a meeting of the October Club in support of the communist-leaning National Unemployed Workers' Movement was stormed by hostile undergraduates and a fight broke out. 'Many blows were exchanged,' it was reported, with conservatives singing 'God Save the King' and communists responding with 'The Internationale.'[26]

Students like Gwyn joined the October Club because it was the primary means of expressing a particular type of political view, usually an anti-fascist view, and was in the context of the rising tide of authoritarian and fascist regimes in Europe. That would have been Gwyn's purpose. Behind the scenes, the October Club formed part of a clandestine network of student societies established by the Communist Party, all linked together by its secretive Student Bureau. Its aim was to recruit undergraduates – and thus future civil servants, parliamentarians, academics, and journalists – into the party's ranks. A very small number of individuals were involved in the Student Bureau: Frank Strauss Meyer, Dick Freeman, and James Klugmann – the man at the heart of the Cambridge spy circle.[27] The Bureau's newspaper, the *Student Vanguard*, launched in the autumn of 1932, fitted this dual purpose of voice and recruitment and was ostensibly written by 'students who are convinced that conditions in every section of social existence are more and more forcing a radical alteration of society.' Its line was generally agreed with Communist Party officials in London, who regularly consulted with Comintern officials in Moscow. A national Federation of Student Societies (FSS) came into being in 1933 with the aim of overshadowing and then overtaking the Labour-aligned University Labour Federation (ULF).

Frank Strauss Meyer came to the attention of the authorities early in 1932, when the Chief Constable of Oxford City Police forwarded a copy of the October Club's term card to the intelligence services in London.[28] They in turn opened a file on the man. Much of what is now known about the October Club derives from this source, which was added to in the years which followed. At its heart is a confession made to the FBI and delivered to the British Embassy in Washington DC in February 1952, at the height of the post-war red scare in the United States. Meyer had already rejected communism by then and converted to Catholicism. He set down how the October Club came to be, who were its leading figures, and what its relationship with the Communist Party had been. 'I had been active in the Labour Club,' he explained, 'had organised a Marxist study group, and became impatient first with the Labour Party, then with the left wing of the Labour Party.' Meyer continued,

> We decided to organise the October Club quite on our own, with the idea of using it to attract those interested in communism and forming a guiding group inside it. At the beginning we had considerable contempt for the official Communist Party, and we had not decided whether to join it or whether to, rather romantically, organise a special group of our own in general sympathy with the Communist Party.

Keen to draw the October Club into the orbit of the Communist Party, as it was doing in Cambridge with that university's Socialist Club, officials in King Street (the CP's headquarters in London) appointed the economist and writer Emile Burns (1889–1972), then of the Labour Research Department, as go-between.[29] Further support and guidance came from William Gallacher, then the national head of the Young Communist League, and from 1935 member of parliament for West Fife, and from the Russian émigré D. S. Mirsky, who was known to the club as Prince Mirsky. He 'came down as a speaker,' Meyer recalled, 'and met with us afterwards.' Mirsky returned to the Soviet Union from exile in September 1932. To maintain the semblance of independence, and to protect the network being established, only the core of the October Club – its officers and 'most promising members' – were brought into the Communist Party, the rest were simply encouraged towards a Stalinist perspective on world politics. As Meyer noted, 'at the time I left England [in 1934] we had some 75 members of the Communist Party in Oxford.' Some were deployed as infiltrators of the OULC with a view to turning it over to communism. That takeover occurred just before the Second World War when the OULC was led by Communist Party members such as Denis Healey and Iris Murdoch.[30]

By then, the October Club had been long banned. The official edict was passed by the university authorities on 7 November 1933 after a series of high-profile protests. To celebrate May Day that year, members joined the Cambridge Socialist Society in London and marched through the streets wearing red shirts and ties, chanting 'We won't fight for King or Country.'[31] A few weeks later, members invaded a meeting of the Oxford University German Society which was being addressed by the London correspondent of the official Nazi newspaper *Völkischer Beobachter*.[32] Matters reached their climax in the autumn when the university proctors, those charged with maintaining discipline and order at Oxford, announced that undergraduates were prohibited from making statements in opposition to societies such as the Officer Training Corps. In protest, the October Club, the Labour Club, and the Peace Group, which came together as the Oxford University Anti-War Committee, organised a mass rally in favour of free speech. The rally itself was prohibited by the proctors and the clubs were forced to sanction members who had attended. The October Club committee refused, and the proctors reacted harshly, banning the club from all university buildings.[33] In the autumn of 1934, the club was revived albeit with meetings held at the independent Ruskin College which lay outside the proctors' jurisdiction. The new version of the club lasted a year before it merged with the OULC in December 1935.[34]

Gwyn's name appears in none of the surviving records and his letters home suggest engagement in the club's affairs on the fringes only. His role was always as the observer, never the actor. But he was by no means naïve as to what was going on and was politically aligned with the October Club, in principle, if not in practice. Mentioning the October Club and its activities to friends and family was Gwyn's way of signalling that these were his politics. He was an idealist and certain enough in his beliefs that this could be off-putting to those who failed to understand. But we should be careful in assuming that the 'kind of deadly seriousness and intensity' which Gwyn displayed at Oxford 'would hardly have endeared him to students of very different backgrounds and convictions.'[35] Such a conclusion misses the point of what was going on in St Edmund Hall and the wider university. In the college-focused passages of *A Few Selected Exits*, Gwyn's narrative is thoroughly distracting. His story seems to have no clear sense of itself, nor is it readily apparent what he is trying to describe. Except, that is, if one recognises that Gwyn is writing about the ease with which fascism can take hold in a conservative mind, and about the prevailing Teutophilia of Britain's ruling class (up to and including the Royal Family).[36] Many of the students at St Edmund Hall, Gwyn wrote,

> spent vacations in Germany, and they had come back full of praise for the plans and notions of the then emergent Hitler. The stables of pacifism and decadence, said these lads, were in for a scrubbing and you could see the bristles sticking out of

their every syllable. ... One of the pro-Nazis, an aquiline fellow who had made a regular breakfast of loathing on toast, told me that he had seen it announced somewhere that the Welsh stock had been heavily drenched by infusions of Jewish and Negro blood. I felt pleased, enlarged.

This might seem like typical Thomasian hyperbole to prove a point, but it was entirely rooted in truth. In February 1933, less than a fortnight after the Nazi takeover in Germany, the St Edmund Hall Debating Society considered the motion that 'This House Prefers Germans to Welshmen.'[37] It was a one-sided affair, easily won by the Teutophile conservatives who defeated a counter-motion that 'the Red Flag be sung at the conclusion of every meeting' proposed during the same debate session.[38] It was also a deliberate act of bullying and there is no reason to assume that Gwyn was anything other than the direct target. He had no choice but to defend himself. 'Oxford is an interesting place,' he explained in a letter to a relative in the United States, however 'it is the hive of unmitigated snobbery and painful politeness, where, as you may expect, a Rhondda lad seems a little out of his element. It grated on my nerves during the first term, but, by dint of incessant sarcasm and a constant display of a don't care a damn attitude, they're beginning to treat me with a little respect.'[39] Or rather, they began to leave Gwyn very much alone. Just as he wished.

Finding a hostile environment in college, aside from those occasions where he could join in with the small group of radicals discussing motions at the debating society such as 'this house has no faith in capitalism' or who proposed that Marlene Dietrich and Greta Garbo be elected 'to joint principalship' in place of the 'autocratic' Emden, Gwyn sought friendships in the wider university.[40] Some of them he met through the OULC and the October Club, others he knew because of mutual connections with the Rhondda. In fact, all of Gwyn's closest friends at Oxford either came from the Rhondda or Pontypridd – a clear indication of his yearning for South Wales. In a letter home, he described his relationship with one of his Rhondda friends:

> I met Sam near the portals of Balliol. He looked distant and unearthly, as if he were going over within himself all the age-old and never-to-be described thrills of the synagogue. ... He hadn't seen me for a long time. He asked me to come to his lodgings that night for supper. ... At half past seven I arrived trembling and eager ... The chips were all that Sam had claimed and were served in prodigious quantities. As Mrs Green, the landlady, laid them on the table, the four of us uncovered our heads, stood reverently to religious salute and sang in unison: 'Nearer my chip to thee.' We ate bread and butter and chips, drank tea and talked until our vocal chords were numbed.

Sam was Samuel Shriberg (1912–2006), a Jewish student and Cardiff graduate, who was studying classics at Balliol.[41] A year older than Gwyn, Shriberg was born and grew up in Tonypandy, where his father, Morris, was the rabbi at the local synagogue.[42] Gwyn and Sam Shriberg were close throughout their time at Oxford, and it was Sam who introduced another friend. As Gwyn explained to Nan, 'I met a genuine fellow last week. His name is Trevor Morgan. And where do you think he's from? Pontypridd.' Gwyn continued,

> He took a degree at Cardiff and is now at Balliol, relying, as far as I understand such a strange confession, upon his father's money until someone offers him a scholarship. Before Sam introduced me to him, he (Sam) warned me to avoid any of my callously poisonous cracks because Morgan is not accustomed

as yet to the torture of meeting anyone with an active mind up here. However, when I started, I found him responsive and now everything is on a footing of friendship. His Welsh accent, like mine, is perfect … Sam says he looks something like me. So set your imagination to work boys and girls.[43]

Trevor Morgan was the ideal replacement for Gwyn's best friend in his first year at Oxford, Wynne Roberts, a companion from Penygraig and Rhondda County School who graduated from Magdalen College in 1932. Shriberg, Morgan and Gwyn had a familiar routine: talking, singing, listening to music, and making plans for an intellectual revival in the Rhondda when they returned home.[44] It was all akin to the Sixth Form common-room chatter Gwyn had loved, and was the closest he could find to family life. The wireless sets owned by Roberts and Morgan were, he explained to Nan, '196 and its kitchen' and their gramophones '196 and its middle room.' This group of student dark philosophers was never quite enough to satisfy a young man yearning for home, however. 'There is clearer, more universal philosophy in 196 High Street,' Gwyn wrote, 'than in all the academies of Europe.' But what he took from his friendship with Trevor Morgan, Wynne Roberts, and Sam Shriberg was the comfort of knowing that even in Oxford there was someone who could sing along in tune.

*

Nestled in the east wing of the neo-classical Ashmolean Museum is the Taylor Institution – better known to students as the Taylorian, the home of modern languages at Oxford University. Gwyn was hardly an enthusiast, either of the building or the learning which took place inside. 'The lectures,' he wrote, 'were languid. The lecture rooms rustled with a whispered gentility that reminded one of the rubberoid surface of the Institute's floors, which muted shoes and brought one's sense of identity and direction dangerously low.' He eventually gave up attending lectures and instead took to reading in his lodgings. In effect, to hiding away. Gwyn's tutors were not those he described in *A Few Selected Exits* – they are fictional characters of his imagination. The 'small man with many malignant undertones,' although unnamed in Gwyn's memoir, was almost certainly Dámaso Alonso (1898–1990), a member of the avant-garde Generation of '27 alongside Federico García Lorca (1898–1936), who taught at Oxford between 1931 and 1933. Alonso was an expert on Spanish Baroque poetry, notably Luis de Góngora (1561–1627). Gwyn described his tutor as hating England. 'He was, he made it quite plain, dying of disgust and regarded me as having been paid to come along and finish him off.'

Alonso subsequently left Oxford to take up a chair at the University of Valencia before moving to the University of Madrid in 1939. As one of the most high-profile literary figures to make peace with the post-Civil War dictatorship in Spain, Alonso 'survived to become one of [Francisco] Franco's laureate bards,' as Gwyn put it. In fact, the poet was elected to the Royal Spanish Academy in 1945 becoming its director in 1962. Such an accommodation undoubtedly coloured Gwyn's portrait. His other tutors at Oxford were William James Entwistle (1895–1952), who was the King Alfonso XIII Professor of Spanish Literature at Exeter College, and Herbert James Hunt (1899–1973), the fellow in French at St Edmund Hall. Entwistle arrived at Oxford from Glasgow University in 1932, where he had been the pioneering professor of Spanish at that institution. He had previously taught at the University of Manchester. His research interests focused on medieval Spanish literature, including Hispanic retelling of the Arthurian legend and

European balladry; with other publications including a major study on the philological development of Spanish, Portuguese, Catalan, and Basque (1936) and Russian (1949). Hardly the writings of a tutor who 'detested the Middle Ages' and whose knowledge 'was only a short ballad ahead of mine,' but certainly someone who would instil in Gwyn a life-long enthusiasm for the literature of the Spanish Golden Age.[45]

Hunt, by contrast, was an expert in nineteenth-century French Romanticism, completing his study on socialism and romanticism in the French socialist press between 1830 and 1848, in 1935.[46] Later work included studies of the epic in nineteenth-century France and the writings of Honoré de Balzac. In his letters home, Gwyn described some of his tutors with a degree of affection, particularly Entwistle, telling Nan in the spring of 1934 that he was 'a great fellow, it's a pity he's a professor. He has a sense of humour something like ours.'[47] Another tutor, who taught Gwyn in his final weeks at Oxford, but cannot be easily identified, was reportedly 'a lonely gentleman, as lonely as I am.'[48] Nevertheless, Gwyn had little enthusiasm for someone he thought a 'venerably lousy tutor.'[49] He explained to Nan: 'the better you wrote for that man, the lower his estimation of you becomes.' None of the work Gwyn did at Oxford now survives. In fact, it does not seem to even have survived the day it was read out at a tutorial. At the end of one session with Hunt in the autumn of 1933, the essay which Gwyn had prepared 'was received and praised by the tutor, burned by myself on returning to my room.' He added, in a moment of confession: 'I despise the monuments of my own labour.'[50]

Notably, although he read French and Spanish at Oxford, none of Gwyn's studies in the former language made their way into any of his descriptions of university life, either in *A Few Selected Exits* or elsewhere. Nor do volumes of French literature, which Gwyn purchased in small numbers in this period, survive in his library to the same extent as those in Spanish. The exception is a volume of short stories by Guy de Maupassant (1850–1893) which Gwyn bought in a cheap Everyman's Library edition from 1934. Perhaps because of his dislike of his tutor, Herbert Hunt, or because he regarded French as his second subject, Gwyn's studies at Oxford were dominated by his Spanish interests, and his memory of the tutorials he took in Spanish and Catalan with Dámaso Alonso and William Entwistle remained vivid into middle age. It was to Spain, of course, and especially to Madrid, that Gwyn escaped in the spring and summer of 1933 – an essential part of his studies, so he said, otherwise he 'would not have stirred.' In truth, any escape from Oxford was welcome. Gwyn arrived in Spain in April after a calamitous journey through France. In later years, it regularly featured in his repertoire of talks and belly-aching anecdotes for television and radio.

Gwyn began the trip in London. Meeting his travelling companion, James Lawless, a fellow linguist at St Edmund Hall, at Victoria Station, where the bus from Oxford terminated, the two headed off to the cinema to pass the time before the midnight train to Paris.[51] They watched the Oscar-nominated Mervyn LeRoy drama *I am a Fugitive from a Chain Gang* (1932) starring Paul Muni and Glenda Farrell. Heavily censored in the UK, although not in Spain, the film was compelled to carry a disclaimer stating that the scenes depicted, featuring a brutal chain gang, could never happen in the British prison system.[52] Suitably entertained, the pair travelled on to Paris and from there, by train, to Bordeaux, where they caught the steamer to Spain. They arrived a few days later, thoroughly exhausted, at their lodgings: the Gran Pension Suiza on the Carrera de San Jeronimo, 'a mere shout away from the Puerta del Sol,' in the heart of Madrid.[53] The pension, Gwyn wrote in his memoir, was 'cheap, ornate, [and] full of Moorish doorways.' It was here that he first experienced the full blast of anti-Republican sentiment which was never far from the surface in certain quarters of interwar Spanish society.

> In the dining room our fellow guests were thickly bourgeois. Conversationally, lunchtime, dinnertime, the pattern did not vary by a comma. From the soup right through to the fruit they cursed the Republic roundly.[54]

Gwyn filled in the gaps during an interview with the makers of the documentary *The Colliers' Crusade*, about Wales and the Spanish Civil War, in 1979. The voice, initially, is that of a captain in the Spanish army:

> Of course, it will have to be destroyed. I said what do you mean, destroyed. Well, he said, this peasant government, this system of ideas will have to be destroyed. I said, you mean voted against. An obscenity, he said, voting, voting, voting. Destroyed. Cataclysmically destroyed. Well by what means? Are you going to agitate? Organise propaganda? See this (he grabs his lapel), see this insignia of the Spanish artillery. The guns that won South America will again regain Spain for the faith and traditional values.

The language was astounding but starkly honest in its ambition. Though he could hardly have known that in just three years Spain would be plunged into civil war, the discussion remained with Gwyn for the rest of his life. As he explained:

> This was it you see; this was it in a capsule. This marvellous idea, that if you have a hundred thousand people in a state organised in one small system of ideas – and ideas based on a technology, which is the technology of death – you were on to

a winner. And so it proved ... It was that man, sitting next to me on that table in Madrid who decided the issue. He knew precisely what he wanted, he knew precisely what he hated, and he won.

Precisely when that conversation took place is unknowable, it may even have been an amalgamation of the many political utterings which Gwyn heard in central Madrid. There is no doubt, however, that the raw politics of the Spanish Republic in the early 1930s shook him deeply.[55] After a month of studying in Madrid, he wrote to the Bursar at St Edmund Hall explaining how he was getting on. 'We are now entering our fourth week of study at Madrid University,' he explained, 'we have experienced little but discomfort since we arrived here and although this is being assuaged, at the moment, by the progress of our own work, it now shows every sign of degenerating into the gangrene of perplexity. We have had no one to initiate us into the Spaniard's art of living without being alive.' He added,

First there is the heat of the day, to which I object on parliamentary grounds. Then there is the cold of the night with which I deal similarly but with a more internally British countenance. Everyone sits about, looking sweaty and political, praising or cursing the Republic according to the position of the sun. This fever of political partialities sickens us. It breaks out here like whooping cough among the children of the North and causes the whole populace to scamper here and there in a dreadful effort to regain their breath. In addition, I am not at all pleased with the enthusiasm with which the Spanish nation takes to the delights of bomb-throwing. They almost make it a winter sport, specifying that government permission is necessary for its practice in summer. They have set up civil slaughter as a rival attraction to the public dispatch of bulls. The unemployed of Spain, preferring the free to the expensive, the indiscriminate to the discriminate, are flocking to the former. While the bulls remain scornful and rightly so, for the outlook of an infuriated bull, compared with the mentality of a Syndicalist in this particular setting, would be a criterion of gentility and tolerance.

Financial troubles dogged his entire time abroad and Gwyn was compelled to borrow money from James Lawless to survive day to day. He ate little and subsisted on coffee and cigarettes. He read voraciously, wandered the streets often in the direction of the Guadarrama mountains, and occasionally went to the cinema. He also travelled to the mining villages near Oviedo in the Asturias in north-western Spain, an experience which, more than any other in Spain, left Gwyn with the feeling that he was 'walking into villages in the Rhondda.' There was, he recalled years later, the same warmth, the same kindliness, and the 'same marvellous intensity' possessed by the people of South Wales. At the end of term, as Lawless headed south for Granada, Gwyn turned his attention northwards to the 'cold, enduring, studious place which my native surroundings ... afford.' The train journey back was arduous and slow, winding its way from Madrid through the Basque Country to the border town of Irun. France passed by 'like a breeze' and soon Gwyn was back in London. At Paddington, he washed off 'four or five pounds of dense, Peninsular dirt. I had been able to identify the various Spanish provinces in the layers of ochre waste' and made his way to the Rhondda.

The remainder of the summer vacation of 1933 was spent suffering from ill health, the result of an as-yet undiagnosed thyroid problem which had been aggravated by malnutrition in Spain and long-distance continental travel. Gwyn wrote to his tutor to explain that he would likely be late for the start of term. His third year at St Edmund Hall was to be spent in rooms at the college itself. That meant a new routine and innovations such as a servant (known in Oxford parlance as a scout) which flummoxed him almost immediately. He explained to Nan,

> I had an embarrassing fifteen minutes this morning. I slept until nine. Breakfast ends at quarter to nine. Even my half-comatose intelligence realised that I was about to miss my first official breakfast in college. I washed. Then with my curving features plastered all over with suds, I found that there was no towel in the room. I scrambled about having no concrete idea as to the manner of removing them. I fumbled about with my shirt for a moment but pushed away that possibility as dead from the start. Frantic, I wandered onto the narrow landing and nearly fell down the staircase … I weighed my chances of borrowing someone else's … I crawled into the bedroom of a neighbour and spent some delicious moments wiping myself in his towel. Then my scout, Joe, came in when I had dressed, looked at me intently and gasped with astonishment … he told me that I had not been expected until Saturday. So he hadn't brought me my hot water, hadn't called me and hadn't brought me a towel. Thus became my first day.

The next few weeks were little better. Partway through the term, he discovered that he had accidentally forgotten to pack any bedding, required once his scout had decided to put away the ones borrowed from the college. He wrote apologetically to his sister to ask that some be sent up, 'if I don't get them … the chances are that Wednesday night will be spent in a constant shiver under rigorous weather conditions.' In *Punch* in the 1960s Gwyn added to his assessment of his new lodgings. 'The bedroom had a window that would not close. I stared through it for hours. It overlooked a graveyard, immensely old and untended, which probably accepted its first customer when the college laid its first stone in the 14ᵗʰ century.'[56] His opposite neighbour on the landing was 'one of the most earnest and persuasive Oxford Groupers who ever aired a sin.'[57] Gwyn withdrew from meals in the college dining hall objecting both to the cost and to the alien experience of standing to attention as the fellows shuffled in and the Latin recitation of the college grace before any meal was served. He sought solace in a restaurant opposite: 'a melancholy place' where a 'miserable waitress ... serves the miserable Gwyn Thomas, from day to day, with miserable crumpets.'

Apart from James Lawless, with whom he met almost every day, Gwyn spoke to few people in the college itself. Those he did acknowledge, and who acknowledged him, were men who absented themselves from the institution's conservative Anglican functions. 'I nodded my head to them and cast off a mordant remark pertaining to the general hellishness of Sunday in an Anglican College,' he wrote, 'which they appreciated by loudly laughing.' On one occasion, his offer of cocoa was bewilderingly taken up by two students who were 'as unhappy here as I am.' Lacking cocoa, Gwyn offered tea instead. 'They opened up and told me about themselves.' One was Ralph Abercrombie (1914–1968) who had recently arrived from Leeds Grammar School. His father, the poet Lascelles Abercrombie (1881–1938), taught at the University of London having previously been Professor of English at Leeds University. A proficient piano player, the younger Abercrombie appealed to Gwyn's musical enthusiasms – 'he's going to give me a short recital next Saturday,' he explained to Nan – and gave Gwyn a copy of his father's poetry collection, *New English Poems* (1931). The other was David Floyd (1914–1997), a state scholar from Swindon, where his father was a GWR inspector, and an enthusiastic communist – for a period he served as secretary of the October Club and in the summer of 1933, as

Gwyn put it, he 'spent three days in the local jug' for his 'political frenzies.'[58]

Abercrombie and Floyd provided a welcome set of friends in a college where Gwyn had seldom made any. Now that he was in residence, he could less easily hide away in his lodgings outside the city centre – in any case, there were exams to think about. And politics. Early in 1934, Gwyn observed that year's national hunger march as the Lancashire contingent made its way through Oxford to London.[59] He may well have been one of the 'hundreds of students marching out to meet the Hunger Marchers' as they arrived in Oxford on 19 February.[60] Or as one Scottish newspaper put it, 'with banners aloft, and singing *The Internationale*, some two hundred Oxford undergraduates of the militant socialist persuasion left their colleges yesterday to greet a contingent of hunger-marchers on their way to London.'[61] When Gwyn came to write up the event for *Punch* in 1960, he said that he had simply watched from a side street and claimed instead that on the 25 February – the day each contingent from across Britain joined together for a rally in Hyde Park in central London – he had 'cadged a lift' to London from a lorry driver and met up with the Welsh contingent there. 'Hymn-singing started and Hyde Park Corner has never known such miraculous plangency.' When Gwyn got back to college, he found that no one had missed him.

In the summer of 1934, Gwyn sat his final honour school examinations. They were all taken, in one intense week, in the middle of term. He wrote home to explain what awaited him:

I sit some dozen papers, set me by a man who has probably forgotten the answers to whatever questions he may care to ask me. If that was all, Thomas would have little cause for protest. But after asking them, they take care to consult friends and books with an eye to discovering the answers. And then, when

97

I have offered up my small sacrifice in the Small Examination Schools (the sacrifice smaller than the Schools) with innocence in my heart, they pounce upon me with the information that I've got a wrong line on every subject that fell my way. I will have to express surprise at that revelation and suggest that I am not yet of an age to compete with their powers of mature judgement and discretion. That remark, without having any relevance to my status as a love of the Book will possibly make the difference between one degree class and another. So I may as well go and pay my compliments to them now and get a First without sitting the papers. That will save me thirty-three hours, thirty-three head-aches, thirty-three heartburns, and roughly one square foot from the seat of my subfusc trousers.

When the results were tallied, Gwyn had narrowly missed a first. He graduated in the upper second class. In the last few months of his degree, Gwyn had reluctantly pondered the next phase of his life. Speaking with tutors, he considered research; with friends, his attention turned to the more realistic possibility of teacher training. The Civil Service offered a third option although it was not one that he seriously entertained, in comparison with his friend James Lawless who set himself firmly on that path. There was little possibility of staying on at Oxford, however. His ill health and rebellious behaviour had established him, as Entwistle wrote in a private letter to the Principal of St Edmund Hall, as 'the most anxious problem in our department.' Entwistle continued:

Coming to Oxford has completely disorganized him mentally in a way that he would have been spared in a junior university. There he would have had prescribed work, terminal examinations, and a wigging when he did less than a conventional minimum; and perhaps such an arrangement, though not enfranchising the mind, would have held him to the rails. Coming here to an atmosphere of self-expression and discussion, he has, I think, lost his way; and his very considerable cleverness has been shown in erratic thought, while his inner nervousness seems to have given offence as if it were arrogance.

One knows he is clever and hard-working (perhaps too hard, for his health does not appear good), but one can prophesy little about his future, especially at so near a date as July. I should much doubt whether research is his calling and at any rate most doubtfully at Oxford, where he is still far from happy.

Between them Entwistle and the Principal considered Gwyn's options. The former added in his assessment that:

Mr Thomas is open to suggestions as to a more practical career and I have proposed he should seek to know more about various branches of the Civil Service. The Home-and-Indian is too heavily weighted in favour of Classics, History and Economics to be really within the reach of a Modern Language man, who is also a less finished product than those of other schools. But Inland Revenue, Factories, and perhaps Municipal Service might offer him a less brilliant but safer career, and there is always teaching. In research he may easily run up a blind alley which, with his antecedents, he cannot afford.

Of the options before him, teaching was the only one which held any real attraction for Gwyn, perhaps following the inspiration of his brothers Walt, who had settled comfortably into the profession in Neath; Eddie, who was by then training in London; or Emlyn, who had been a music teacher in the Rhondda. Gaining a teacher's certificate at least provided a further year of study, a further year of delaying unemployment, which was the intention. Gwyn discussed the matter with Sam

Shriberg, who was himself destined for teaching. Together they concocted a plan: gain a teacher's certificate at the university college in Cardiff, funded by means of a further grant from the Board of Education. There was but one snag, Gwyn thought: the queue of hopefuls already looking to teaching as a way out of the economic turmoil at home. With a first-class or upper second degree from Oxford, he reasoned, with Sam's assistance and reassurance, that it should be okay. All that remained was the application. Gwyn never applied. Whether the pressure of his finals or his increasing depression or his obvious bewilderment at academic bureaucracy got the better of him is not clear. Gwyn left for the Rhondda at the end of June 1934. He would not return to Oxford, or to St Edmund Hall, for more than twenty years.

---

[1] SEH Archive, Oxford, Gwyn Thomas Personal File: College Application, 19 September 1931.

[2] F. Homes Dudden, *Handbook to the University of Oxford* (Oxford, 1932), 428.

[3] Claude Hayes, 'The Awakening World', in *Hall: Memoirs of St Edmund Hall Graduates, 1920–1980* (London, 1989), 42. Hayes (1912–1996), an old boy of Ardingly College in Sussex, later studied at the Sorbonne and taught at New College, Oxford, for a period. He served as Principal Finance Officer for Harold Wilson's Ministry of Overseas Development between 1965 and 1968. Hayes recalled 'managing moderately ... on about £225 a year,' which places Gwyn's arrival with just eighty pounds to sustain him very much in context.

[4] NLW, GTP, J22/3: Letter from Gwyn Thomas to Walter Thomas, undated but October 1931.

[5] *Colliery Guardian*, 10 June 1932; *WM*, 3 June 1932; *DH*, 3 June 1932.

[6] Matthew Worley, *Oswald Mosley and the New Party* (London, 2010). The Oxford New Party branch was led by the journalist and England rugby captain Peter Howard. He later joined the Conservative Party. Anne Wolrige Gordon, *Peter Howard: Life & Letters* (London, 1974). Sellick Davies, who stood as the New Party's candidate in Merthyr in 1931, and was the party's national treasurer, had come from the Liberal Party. He stood as the Liberal candidate in Evesham in 1929. William Lowell, who stood in Pontypridd in 1931, was an estate agent from Fontygary, near Rhoose in the Vale of Glamorgan and more traditionally conservative – he had previously been chair of the Young Conservatives in Cardiff.

[7] *DH*, 23 September 1932.

[8] An undergraduate at Hertford College, a friend of the journalist and future

Labour MP John Strachey. In the summer of 1931 had volunteered to work on a Soviet collective farm 'coming back full of enthusiasm' for the communist system in Russia. Geoff Andrews, *The Shadow Man: At The Heart Of The Cambridge Spy Circle* (London, 2015), 37. Freeman was later a county court judge, the libel lawyer for *Reynold's News*, and a prominent member of the British Peace Committee. *The Times*, 14 June 1997.

[9] An undergraduate in Politics, Philosophy, and Economics (PPE) at Balliol, matriculated in 1930. Originally from Stoke on Trent. Regarded by members of the Oxford Union Society as 'a really embittered revolutionary ... [who] would class all the moderates within the present government as "bourgeois reactionaries."' Edward Pearce, *The Golden Talking-Shop* (Oxford, 2016), 368. On graduation worked for the National Savings Commission and later for the Ministry of National Insurance.

[10] An undergraduate at Hertford College. Previously active in the New Party and secretary of the Oxford University Labour Club before his defection to the October Club. Later appointed an economic advisor to the government of Trinidad. Died in Durban, South Africa.

[11] TNA, KV 2/3501: F. S. Meyer MI5 File. The turbulence of the October Club is discussed in Matthias Schüth, *Englands Politische Universitätsjugend, 1931–1940: Ein Beitrag zur Erforschung politischer Kollectivmentalitäten im Europa der dreißiger Jahre* (Münster, 2000) and Georgina Brewis, *A Social History of Student Volunteering: Britain and Beyond, 1880–1980* (London, 2014).

[12] Balliol College Archives, Junior Common Room Minute Book, 18 October 1931.

[13] *AWE*, 24. Paul Burrough (1916–2003), who matriculated in 1934 and later served as Bishop of Mashonaland in Central Africa, recalled that 'some of us used to go rather fruitlessly to show solidarity with the ninety per cent unemployed of South Wales.' Paul Burrough, 'The Mid Thirties', in *Hall: Memoirs of St Edmund Hall Graduates, 1920–1980*, 62.

[14] *Western Morning News*, 25 February 1935.

[15] As H. R. Orton recalled, the October Club was 'particularly active, always in the limelight, enjoying a wide range of interest, favourable or otherwise.' By contrast, Orton considered the Labour Club to be the most 'prominent and lively' of the political groupings. Orton, 'Equitation', 54.

[16] John Wynne Roberts (1911–1966). Born in Penygraig and educated at Rhondda County School. Switched to study English part way through his degree. Subsequently English master at Ebbw Vale Grammar School. An accomplished pianist and talented cricketer. In 1958, he served as local secretary of the National Eisteddfod organising committee. See also, Meic Stephens, *Cofnodion* (Llandysul, 2014), ch 4. Stephens taught French at Ebbw Vale in the early 1960s.

[17] *DH*, 4 May, 8 November 1933.

[18] *Western Daily Press*, 30 May 1932; *Yorkshire Evening Post*, 27 October 1932.

[19] *WM*, 8 April 1932.

[20] *Merthyr Express*, 11 May 1933.

[21] *WM*, 28 September 1933.

[22] NLW, GTP, J22/8. Letter from Gwyn Thomas to 196 High Street, Cymmer, 14 November 1931.

[23] *DH*, 3 November 1932; *Derby Daily Telegraph*, 7 March 1933; Andrew Whitehead, *The Lives of Freda: The Political, Spiritual and Personal Journeys of Freda Bedi* (London, 2019).

[24] *Sheffield Daily Telegraph*, 14 November 1931.

[25] *Dundee Courier*, 11 June 1932.

[26] *Western Daily Press*, 8 November 1932.

[27] Andrews, *Shadow Man*; Geoff Andrews, *Agent Moliere: The Life of John Cairncross, The Fifth Man of the Cambridge Spy Circle* (London, 2020). Klugmann's voluminous intelligence service files date from 1934 onwards. TNA, KV 2/788–791.

[28] Memorandum from the Chief Constable, Oxford, 16 January 1932. TNA, KV 2/3501.

[29] Burns had joined the Communist Party in 1920. He too fell under widespread surveillance. TNA, KV 2/1760–1763.

[30] This itself led to a split spearheaded by Roy Jenkins and Tony Crossland and the creation of the Oxford University Democratic Socialist Society. This history is related in Daryl Leeworthy, *Elaine Morgan* and John Campbell's biography *Roy Jenkins: A Well-Rounded Life* (London, 2014).

[31] *Western Daily Press*, 8 May 1933.

[32] *DH*, 18 May 1833.

[33] *DH*, 9 November, 18 November 1933.

[34] *Belfast Telegraph*, 5 December 1935, p. 8.

[35] *LFD*, 33.

[36] Much the same theme runs through Kazuo Ishiguro's Booker-prize winning novel, *The Remains of the Day* (London, 1989).

[37] SEH Archive, Soc 6A/7, St Edmund Hall Debating Society Minute Book 1927–1933, Entry for 13 February 1933.

[38] Similar debates during Gwyn's time at the college included 'that undergraduates out of work should be able to draw the dole' (23 November 1931 – lost); 'that the industrial civilisation of the modern world leads to unhappiness' (25 January 1932 – carried); 'that the presence of women in Oxford is deplorable' (29 February 1932 – carried); and 'this House prefers the South of England to the North' (21 November 1932 – carried).

[39] Gwyn Thomas letter to Peggy Counsell, February 1932.

[40] Debating Society Minute Book, entries for 23 January 1933 and 6 March 1933. The latter meeting also noted a 'telegram from Trotsky [offering] to stand as president [of the Junior Common Room].' This was allowed to lapse since the Russian revolutionary 'failed to appear.'

[41] *Jewish Chronicle*, 8 July 1932, 24 August 1934. Samuel Shriberg later adopted the Anglicised surname, Shirley, and taught Latin for a time at University College Cardiff before becoming a schoolteacher in Birmingham. He was best known for his well-regarded translations of the writings of seventeenth-century Jewish-Dutch philosopher, Baruch Spinoza (1632–1677).

[42] *Balliol College Register* (Oxford, 1933); the Shriberg family originated in the Lithuanian Pale and had originally settled in Lancashire on their arrival in Britain.

They lived at 7 Holborn Terrace, Tonypandy. *Jewish Chronicle*, 6 November 1936. Part of the Shriberg house in Holborn Terrace was used as the local synagogue between 1912 and 1926. Thereafter, the congregation met at 38 Eleanor Street. Cai Parry-Jones, *The Jews of Wales: A History* (Cardiff, 2017), 42. Morris Shriberg, Samuel's father, was naturalised as a British citizen in 1928. TNA, HO 144/9123; HO 334/108/16066.

[43] Letter from Gwyn Thomas to Hannah Thomas, 11 November 1933; Trevor Morris Morgan was born 14 March 1912. He took part in the Normandy landings in June 1944 and was later an education officer for Lancashire County Council. His father was Henry Ivor Morgan, the senior booking office clerk for the Great Western Railway in Cardiff and a private house builder. Trevor Morgan's younger brother was the artist Glyn Morgan.

[44] NLW, GTP, J22/4: Letter from Gwyn Thomas to Walter Thomas, undated but spring 1932.

[45] *AFSE*, 58.

[46] H. J. Hunt, *Le Socialisme et le Romantisme en France: Étude de la Presse Socialiste de 1830 à 1848* (Oxford, 1935). Gwyn's relative indifference to Hunt contrasts with the warmer recollections of fellow students of French at St Edmund Hall. 'He had,' remembered one, 'a pleasant, dry sense of humour and a down-to-earth view of his subject.' H. R. Orton, 'Equitation and other things', in *Hall: Memoirs of St Edmund Hall Graduates, 1920–1980* (Oxford, 1989), 53. Orton, a student of French and German, and old boy of Stockport Grammar School, matriculated alongside Gwyn in 1931.

[47] Gwyn Thomas to Hannah Thomas, 16 February 1934.

[48] Gwyn Thomas to Hannah Thomas, 23 April 1934.

[49] Gwyn Thomas to Hannah Thomas, 16 February 1934.

[50] Gwyn Thomas to Hannah Thomas, 11 November 1934.

[51] James Lawless (1913–2002) was born in the Attercliffe district of Sheffield. According to *AFSE* (p. 65), his 'father was a maimed veteran of the first world war and did something connected with the Haig Poppy Fund ... My friend was later to become an eminent civil servant and even then showed signs of economic mastery.'

[52] Clive Emsley, *The English and Violence since 1750* (London, 2007), 89; Jeffrey Richards, 'The British Board of Film Censors and the Content Control in the 1930s: Images of Britain', *Historical Journal of Film, Radio and Television* 1, no. 2 (1981), 95–116.

[53] Gwyn Thomas, 'I Dreamt I Dwealt', *Punch*, 16 May 1962.

[54] *AFSE*, 70.

[55] The context and consequences of this period are explored in Paul Preston, *A People Betrayed: A History of Corruption, Political Incompetence, and Social Division in Modern Spain* (London, 2020).

[56] Gwyn Thomas, 'We are not living, we're hiding', *Punch*, 19 December 1962.

[57] As above. The Oxford Group was founded in 1921 by the American priest Frank Buchman. Its four tenets (or absolutes) were 'absolute honesty, absolute purity, absolute unselfishness, and absolute love'. Tom Driberg, *The Mystery of Moral Re-Armament: A Study of Frank Buchman and his Movement* (London, 1964).

[58] A diplomat and Soviet agent during the Second World War, Floyd later became foreign correspondent of the *Daily Telegraph* and was involved in the Profumo Affair. He went up to St Edmund Hall in 1932. Floyd had in fact been arrested and charged alongside A. H. Hanson for an anti-war protest during a showing of 'Our Fighting Navy' at a Swindon cinema. *DH*, 19 September 1933. They served a few days at Gloucester Gaol. Floyd's scholarship was suspended and eventually cancelled because of his activities. *Wiltshire Times*, 7 October 1933, 6 October, 13 October 1934; *DH*, 29 September 1934. H. R. Orton, who was also a friend of Floyd's, recalled that Floyd 'was bailed out [of gaol] by a personal appearance of the Abe' – the nickname afforded to Principal Emden. Orton, 'Equitation', 54.

[59] In his portrait for *Punch*, and for obvious effect, Gwyn suggests that this was the Welsh contingent, however that part of the hunger march in fact went via Reading. Gwyn Thomas, 'We are not living, we're hiding', *Punch*, 19 December 1962.

[60] *West London Observer*, 23 February 1934.

[61] *Edinburgh Evening News*, 20 February 1934.

CHAPTER THREE
Acts of Social Idiocy

In the summer of 1934, Porth was a truly miserable place to be. Almost four thousand people signed on at the employment exchange every week, all looking for work which did not exist. More than half of them had been unemployed for over a year. It was the same up and down the valley: twenty-five per cent of Rhondda's entire male workforce were on the dole. 'For a number of years,' wrote the district's chief medical officer in his annual report for councillors, 'a large proportion of the community have been obliged to lead a life of subsistence.' Thousands had already left, never to return, finding jobs in the new factories in the Midlands, at Cowley outside Oxford, in London and the Home Counties. Years later, Gwyn would make light of all of this trauma in a series of jokes and observations and radio sketches. One such referred to the habit of Rhondda folk, as they were vacating their houses to go away, of placing placards in their windows explaining where they had gone. Another, published in the *Neath Guardian* in the summer of 1966, recalled 'a small band of us' who carried a coffin in 1935 'up to Llethr Ddu, the Black Meadow, our huge hillside cemetery [in Trealaw], bearing the legend NOT DEAD, BUT GONE TO SLOUGH.'[1]

Gwyn's own situation was a desperate one. As a university graduate with no history of work, he had accumulated no national insurance contributions and was ineligible to draw the dole.[2] What little money he had was left over from the scholarships held whilst at Oxford.[3] His visits to the employment exchange in search of work were no less in vain than the out-of-a-job miners, but he knew that this was where the radicals would gather, where they would gather on a street corner or stand on a wall to rail against injustice and the failures of capitalism, and so he went along anyway. On one visit, Gwyn met Will Paynter – by then a communist firebrand who had lost his job at Cymmer Colliery for his political activities. Gwyn fell under Paynter's spell and was soon drawn into the social world of Rhondda communism and the allied unemployed workers' movement (though he never joined the party itself). He got to know Lewis Jones, the most charismatic of the communists of the coalfield, who had already had some short stories published in the *Daily Worker*, and the communist families of the valley including the Sweets, the Mortons, and the Paddocks, who filled the party's local ranks.[4] Some of them, including Jesse Sweet and Will Paynter, had even been to Moscow to study at the International Lenin School.

These new friends fascinated and excited Gwyn. Nearly half a century later, in a radio documentary for the BBC, he extolled Lewis Jones's virtues and declared him to be the greatest Welshman. 'The man I select as having greatness must be measurable by the standards of my own experience,' Gwyn told listeners, 'he must have stood under the sky of the same events, must have walked the same sort of streets as [me]. I must know of first-hand the evils against which he fought, and which strove to bring him low. If he sang in sunlight, I knew and shared the songs he sang; if he whistled in the dark, and that was a large part of the music he made, I was there, whistling right alongside him.'[5] The rest of the portrait was full of anecdote and reminiscence taken directly from the mid-1930s, embellished by distance and purpose, certainly, but never entirely outside the boundaries of reality. 'The speeches he delivered in his favourite meeting place, Judge's Hall, Tonypandy,' Gwyn said, 'were always lessons,' adding that Lewis Jones 'had thoughts and images that could turn lights on for the most unprepared audience. He had quotations from every nation and class which he would lay down as text.' This was a man possessed 'of startling, unorthodox powers.'[6]

In the autumn of 1934, Gwyn was passed an advert from the Egyptian Ministry of Education inviting applications for teachers. It was a last-minute opportunity. The deadline was the following day. He wrote urgently to Principal Emden at St Edmund Hall asking for a testimonial. 'I have filled up all the necessary forms,' Gwyn explained, 'this having entailed nearly as many words as are to be found in the complete works of Balzac or any such prolific writer.' He needed the testimonial to prove his Oxford credentials because he remained in debt to the college and had been unable to purchase his official degree certificate – something he never possessed. 'If I obtain this post, I may be able to remedy these grievances,' he suggested optimistically.[7] The effort was wasted: there was no job for him in Egypt. Gwyn's mental and physical health declined steadily, with only assurances from the doctor that things would improve once he found 'some solid place on which to place the fragmentary elements of my life.' Only the poverty bit was certain. Although not yet ready to laugh, Gwyn began to see in the people around him what he later called the 'unique vein of humour' which he believed to be 'waiting to be opened up among the socially aware and conscious working people of our epoch.'

To pass the time Gwyn read voraciously, absorbing himself in the intellectual world of communism and the anti-fascist movement. By the spring of 1935, he was more active and committed a Marxist than ever but remained, curiously though temperamentally appropriate, aloof from the Communist Party itself. He read the *Daily Worker*, Marxian classics of economics and philosophy and politics, and left-leaning histories, all of which he borrowed from the library at Cymmer Workmen's Institute at the bottom of the High Street. In notebooks he made an intense series of reflections on current affairs and scribbled down the key points of communist doctrine.[8] One of the books he read, and then made several pages of notes in response, was William Z. Foster's *The Great Strike and its Lessons* (1920), about the wave of industrial unrest in the United States in 1919 which Foster had led. Another was Bertrand Russell's 1918 study of anarchism, socialism, and syndicalism, *Roads to Freedom*. Gwyn interspersed his engagement with Russell's ideas by reading Nikolai Popov's recently published *Outline History of the Communist Party of the Soviet Union* (1934) and W. W. Craik's *Short History of the British Working-Class Movement* (1919), which had originally been published as a textbook for the Plebs League.

These influences were at a remove from the 'cheap Tauchnitz editions of English and American novelists and poets,' which Gwyn later said he had read in Spain, alongside 'the whole of Shakespeare in the original, washed down by the translations of Menéndez y Pelayo' and 'the output of Cervantes, Bentio Galdos, Dickens, Dostoevsky, Tolstoy in interminable toto.'[9] This was, however, indicative of the literary training in which a young, well-educated communist might engage with a view to becoming an effective cadre or propagandist, and echoed the reading material prescribed to students at both the International Lenin School and its London equivalent, the Marx Memorial Library.[10] Gwyn's ready facility with Marxist texts set him apart from those who made up the membership of the Communist Party in South Wales. In the main, they were working-class men and women with only an elementary education behind them and so tended to prefer reading the *Daily Worker* or the *Communist Manifesto* or short (and distilled) pamphlets about discrete topics, rather than the more theoretical or weightier tomes produced either by the party press or imported (in English) from the Soviet Union. That situation was only marginally altered by the introduction of the Left Book Club in the summer of 1936. Indeed, the most successful volumes in that series, such as Hewlett Johnson's *The Socialist Sixth of the World* (1939), were those furthest away from a dialectical idiolect and so did not require a high degree of specialism or intellectual power or education and training to understand.

The most obvious expression of Gwyn's absorption into a quasi-communist worldview was made during the general election of 1935 – the first in which he could vote. Held on 14 November, it marked the continuation of the National Government headed by Ramsay MacDonald but also the steady recovery of the Labour Party. In Rhondda West, the sitting Labour MP Will John was unopposed, which meant that all eyes were on the contest in Rhondda East, where there was a straight fight between the incumbent Labour MP, W. H. Mainwaring, and Harry Pollitt, the General Secretary of the Communist Party. In the words of the virulently anti-communist chief constable, Lionel Lindsay, Pollitt ran an 'eye-catching campaign,' which saw the communist drive around the constituency in a car equipped with a loudspeaker.[11] A coupé was brought down from London by the wife of a London barrister, too, who put her own financial resources at Pollitt's disposal. Another London activist wrote to Pollitt offering him 'two new tins of paint and a can of petrol' for more orthodox aspects of a street-based campaign and to run the cars.[12] For all that absurdity, Gwyn knew instinctively where his loyalties lay. 'I wished to express,' he explained to Nan, 'the fact I was willing to put myself to some inconvenience that I might render incontestable my allegiance to the Red Banner of communism and the class war.' Nearly fourteen thousand others in the constituency expressed a similar view, but Mainwaring and Labour held the seat with a majority of over eight thousand.

Months of intense reading and the excitement of a general election could not assuage the restlessness Gwyn felt. Nor could he ignore his continued ill health. 'This pain in my neck began as the anniversary of my first day of idleness took place,' he complained to Nan. Illness had already cost him his one piece of good fortune. In the summer of 1935, after a year of unemployment, Gwyn tried with a degree of intensity to secure a teaching post and received positive testimonials to assist him in that quest from E. T. Griffiths, who was by then in post as headmaster at Barry County School for Boys. Griffiths was effusive in his praise for his former pupil.[13] In the autumn, Gwyn secured the offer of a job as the French master at Ystalyfera County School in the upper Swansea valley. But before Gwyn took up the post, he sought an answer to the medical problem which had hampered him for so long. It came in early December, following a visit to a specialist at Llwynypia Hospital. The doctor's findings, Gwyn told Nan, were as follows:

goitre there was and is. And from his remarks and my imaginings it has been by far the most important thing in my life. For the last year or so it has been excreting, giving off some kind of dangerous poison which accounts for my sleeplessness, my debilitated nerves, and the unusual pallor and sunkenness of my face and body.

He added,

The gland has also forced my windpipe into an extremely dangerous position. The specialist remarked that I was lucky to be able to swallow. (I've never given it much chance to close up on me, fair play.) They're admitting me into hospital as soon as possible between now and Xmas. The operation, he told me, will not be serious except in the respect that it will mean a serious improvement in my condition which, as you know, has been two miles below hell-level for the last few years.[14]

Admitted to hospital a few days after that letter was sent, Gwyn remained on the ward in Llwynypia for more than a month. He was so weak when he went in for his operation that surgery was initially delayed whilst he gained the strength to withstand the anaesthesia in the operating theatre. 'When I came back into the world,' Gwyn wrote subsequently, 'the years of frenzy were finished. My jungle juices had been thinned out. The pressures that had driven my mind in and out of storm clouds had eased. I had been brought back to something like normal, and it was a peculiar feeling: utter sobriety after a long, cheap jag.'[15] After an all-too-brief period of recuperation at home in Porth, Gwyn reported to Ystalyfera to begin teaching. After twenty long months out of work, he was keen to start. Perhaps too keen. By lunchtime on his first day, he 'was on the floor. At 12.45 I was on the bus home and never went back.'[16] With more patience, Gwyn might have regained enough strength to grow into the job of teaching French at Ystalyfera. Certainly, it would have changed the direction of his life entirely. No longer as dangerously ill as he had been – although he still had depression to overcome – Gwyn returned to the Rhondda once again to reconsider his future. He made up his mind to write, to respond artistically to the social and political conditions of his age.

*

He began by writing history. In the months before his operation, Gwyn had been engaged in background research for a book he was planning to write with his brother. Gwyn told Nan that

'Walt had an idea of writing a short book on the labour movement in South Wales in the nineteenth century, centring the action round the personalities of Dr Price, the Chartist and active revolutionary of Llantrisant, and Dic Penderyn, who was hanged in Cardiff jail.' But Walt had set aside the project for a time to focus on his teaching career at Neath and so Gwyn had offered to collaborate on a new variation of the premise: 'a book dealing with every aspect of life in the Rhondda Valley from unemployment to this swelling in my neck. He's doing it for fame. I'm doing it for fags. He's writing the facts. I'm writing the fiction.' In the end, the book never got going, although Gwyn's obvious interest in South Wales' industrial development, William Price, Chartist, and Dic Penderyn, never faded. Something of the idea appeared decades later in *A Welsh Eye*, when he told readers that 'My father claimed to have seen Price. He used to come over to the Rhondda from Llantrisant, in his fur hat and riding a horse.'

Living in the Rhondda once more in the spring of 1936, following the catastrophe at Ystalyfera, Gwyn lost interest in the collaborative project with Walt and focused on his own ideas. He began to compile a series of notes and sketches for a novel. It was to become *Sorrow For Thy Sons*. Thirty years later, with his dates only slightly askew, perhaps because he was thinking of the book's chronology rather than his own, Gwyn recalled the impulse which drove him to write fiction.

A long way back I wrote a novel called, just for the laughs, SORROW FOR THY SONS. The date was 1935, plum in the middle of what, for me, was a uniquely unpleasant decade. Through my book ran a stream of volcanic protest ... The work is painfully personal and raw. But the flesh of past experience, however ineptly embalmed, is always significant for the person whose flesh it was.[17]

Progress on the novel was interrupted by the outbreak of the Spanish Civil War in July 1936, which directed Gwyn's attention elsewhere, and by intermittent absorption into the tutorial ranks of the Workers' Educational Association. At the beginning of September, Gwyn delivered a 'full, clear and intelligent picture of the truth about Spain' to an audience at Porth Unemployed Club.[18] The lecture lasted more than an hour and drew heavily on the experience of studying in Madrid and wandering through Spain in the spring and summer of 1933. The ordinary people, he explained, lived in conditions which were 'tragic and revolting, an unpleasant mass of starvation and illiteracy, prayers, suicides and blind revolts.' Spain was riven with class conflict and the old landlords benefitted too easily from obsolete laws 'which can be compared with the mills of God for their efficiency in grinding together in a ghastly porridge the blood and bone of toil-broken, poverty-stricken, passive ignorant and superstitious land labourers.' The country's misfortune arose because 'there is no known technique of transforming a Spanish landlord into a socially useful member of the community [and] the peasants regard his complete removal as the first step towards the establishment of a happier and more productive life.' This, he concluded, was the agony of the Spanish people.

Gwyn's fierce critique of the nationalist rebels – whom he labelled 'a malevolent tumour that has eaten deeply and painfully into the health of Spain since 1920' – left his audience in little doubt as to the nature of the conflict which had broken out. They are, he continued,

dynamic parasites who borrow the political and social complexes of the seventeenth century and foist them on to the nation with the help of ammunition borrowed from the twentieth. They are tigers who kill by superior strength, under cover of night and instigate a reign of terror in the minds of timorous and superstitious villagers. Their political philosophy, on the one occasion when it rises above the dirty, indecent and sub-human pornography of an officers' mess, consists of detesting democracy, which, as the ordered will of the common people, would like to put salt on their be-medalled tails and see them do something useful for a living.

Gwyn's mind drew back to the conversations he had overheard in the cafés of central Madrid. The Catholic Church, which gave ample backing to the rebels, also came in for a scalding. It was, Gwyn said, a political instrument 'more intent on collecting rents than spreading light.' This was a tremendous window into Gwyn's oratorical power, and earned the praise of the session organiser, John Gwynne. 'The audience's enthusiastic attentiveness,' Gwynne remarked, 'was completely justified.' Despite the warmth of the late-summer sunshine, which might otherwise have tempted the audience outside, the lecture proved to be a stimulus to a series of further talks on 'subjects of national and educational interest' which, Gwyn said, were designed to 'liquidate some part of the political apathy and confusion that rest upon Porth.' Gwyn might have been a regular participant, but the vigour of his Spanish lecture masked increasing personal turmoil.

Within days Gwyn had fled the Rhondda seeking solace in Eddie's flat in London. His depression, exacerbated by more than two years of unemployment and physical emaciation, pushed him to the brink of despair and breakdown. 'The time had come for me to leave South Wales,' he explained to Nan, adding that there was 'nothing there except the possibility of a strike.' Home provided no comfort or respite. 'Economic conditions at 196 High Street are cruel,' he said, 'my presence there only added to the cruelty. By nature I am a kindly person.

That just sums up everything that is wrong with me. I cannot be comfortable while inflicting either pain or discomfort upon others.' He knew that piecemeal lecturing with the WEA or the Quaker educational settlement at Maes-yr-Haf, Trealaw, offered some means of bringing in money and that such work 'would have suited me.' However, 'anything I might have earned would have been used by those poisonous toads of the Means Test to reduce the benefit now received by Dad and Gwilym to nothing. As it is, when the Act begins to function in all its Christian glory next November, they will both be automatically cut from 17/- to 10/-. After cuts like that, you'll have to keep your head bowed all day to catch sight of them.'[19]

London was a mistake, of course. The metropolis did not suit Gwyn any more than Oxford had done and he remained with his brother no more than a month before moving on, in October, to Somerset, and to the maternal surety and comfort provided by Nan.[20] She had married her sweetheart, Bill Thomas, in the autumn of 1935 and the pair soon moved from the Rhondda when Bill got a job as a branch manager in a gentlemen's outfitters in Wells. They settled in Lewmond Avenue, half a mile from the city's medieval cathedral. 'You have an idea that I hate London,' Gwyn confessed to his sister, 'no more correct idea ever came into the human head. I do hate. It's an ugly, parasitic scab that ought to be trimmed, beautified, then buried. I have no patience with it. It is possible that I'll be very unhappy here. Don't be disturbed by that. I'm talented. That's why I'm out of a job.' The situation seemed almost as hopeless as the Rhondda. 'There's eight million other people here with me all trying to get a look at the sun,' he wrote from London, 'but, despite this volume of fierce competition, I am still as good as I used to be which is pretty bad with market values as they are.'[21]

Gwyn's letter, sent in a moment of depressive honesty and political ferocity, was laced with what he called his 'revolutionism.' When the Hunger March arrives, he told Nan, 'I hope they smash parliament to bits – I'll stand on Westminster Bridge as they do it, laughing – I've got a couple of laughs coming to me anyway.' The National Hunger March, made famous by the Jarrow contingent headed by Ellen Wilkinson, arrived in London at the end of October. With patience, Gwyn might have still been living there and been able to meet them on their way into the city centre, but he could not disabuse himself of the notion that the only place to be called home was somewhere in South Wales, if not the Rhondda, and had already fled the capital. South Wales, he told Nan, 'is a place of struggle, it is the richest field any author or politician could wish for, that's why I will always go back there.' And so, he did. After a few weeks of recuperation in Wells, he moved back in with Walt and Nest in Neath, remaining there until Christmas.[22] Only then, and with not inconsiderable reluctance, did he return to the Rhondda and to the miserable life at 196 High Street from which he had run away three months before.

It was in this period of to-ing and fro-ing between South Wales, London, and Wells, that Gwyn seriously focused on writing his novel, picking up where he had left off earlier in the year. He was given no little incentive by the appearance, in the October 1936 issue of *Left News*, of a notice advertising a competition being run by the publisher Victor Gollancz for the 'best genuinely proletarian novel by a British writer.' The prize was an advance of two hundred and fifty pounds on royalties, payable on publication. Completed novels were to reach the publisher's London office in Covent Garden by 1 August 1937.[23] As he confessed later, he wrote 'as fast as my sixpenny fountain pen could travel.' The source material for the novel was obvious and, as he noted in his autobiography many years later, 'I felt that as far as this problem was concerned I was the national dipstick.' In the confines of Neath, the novel Gwyn had started to write in earnest in Wells proceeded apace. He wrote to Nan to tell her of his latest endeavour. 'When a man is crazy enough to go in for creative work, work that devours more and more of his conscience and intelligence as he goes along, he ceases to be very much concerned by what he does or leaves undone,' he explained, adding that

> I refer, of course, to my not having written before. But the task of getting this novel of mine into some sort of final and satisfactory shape has turned out to be much more difficult than I had imagined when I left Wells. That, perhaps, is as it should be. To be satisfied, in my eyes, is to be accursed. The struggle for perfect self-expression is everlasting and drags me along with it as murderously and ruthlessly as a down-coming dram on an incline would drag a rider whose foot happened to slip.[24]

Gwyn's still depressive mind was increasingly guided by a singular desire for artistic self-expression, and he sought the means of fusing his politics with his honed ear for telling observation. 'I would be unhappy anywhere,' he told Nan, 'something must have gone wrong between me and the world right at the very beginning, far back in time. One day, weather permitting, I'll take myself, my books, and my pen, up to the stratosphere and try cultivating cheerfulness and adaptability there. If I'm not too disturbed by passing balloons, I should get on.'

By December, the novel was coming 'slowly to a close.' By Gwyn's calculation he had been writing for three months: 'not bad going.'[25] It was not to be completed for several months, however. 'I am,' he confessed to Nan in early June 1937, 'trying to finish a novel.'[26] It was still the same book. The text was diligently typed by Wynne Roberts, but since 'he can't understand my writing. I don't understand his typing. We'll

both have to be present when the thing is read by a publisher.'[27]
The result was a three-hundred-page typescript, which Gwyn
sent to the Gollancz office in London. He heard nothing more.
In October, after months of frustration, he lamented the novel's
apparent failure telling Nan that 'I was gambling on having
made some money by this time from that novel I wrote.' He
had, he insisted, submitted the novel on its own merit but
'apparently it has got caught up in a competition.'[28] The
Gollancz readers judged the novel as a powerful work of fiction,
but were unable to stomach 'its unrelieved "sordidness"' adding
to their lamentation that 'if there had been anything in it at all
which had been pleasant and beautiful it would have heightened
the effect of the rest.' If only it was more like the work of Rhys
Davies. 'It was said,' Gwyn later remarked, 'that the publisher's
readers ... wore asbestos breeches in self-defence when they
rested the manuscript on their knees.'

Into the narrative, Gwyn poured everything of significance
which had happened to him since the beginning of the 1930s:
unemployment, the Means Test protests, leaving the valley for
university, hearing Lewis Jones in full flight, even writing
articles for the local newspaper. However, as Dai Smith has
argued, their fictional presentation was 'neither naturalistic
documentary nor heroic epic.'[29] This verisimilitude differed
substantially from Gwyn's later work, which disguised the truth
rather than tell it directly. For the moment, though, he was
occupied with thoughts about the fluid, indiscernible
boundaries of fact and fiction.[30] *Sorrow For Thy Sons* captured,
in the raw, the contractions of a Rhondda gripped by economic
Depression but rich in social solidarity, and Gwyn's own sense
of dislocation being in the heart of both. The novel told the
story of an orphaned family of three brothers: Alf, the eldest,
whose work in a grocer's shop gave him a sense of importance
and the snobbery of upward mobility; Herbert, the tallest of the

three, an unemployed miner with a 'ready-made smile in constant wait around his mouth'; and Hugh, the youngest brother destined for a life away from the valley if only he can escape. Herbert was modelled on Gwyn's older brother, Gwilym, who had followed their father underground. Alf shared more than a few personality traits borrowed from Gwyn's eldest brother, John. Hugh's education and life experiences mirrored Gwyn's own.

In its final form the novel spanned the period from May 1930 until December 1935. The set pieces, such as the lingering effects of the 1926 lockout, the great demonstrations against the Means Test in the spring of 1935, and the everyday anxieties caused by life on the dole, were all real. As was Hugh's departure for university in the second act – a section of the novel set, in common with Gwyn's own experience, in 1931. Other elements offer disguised autobiography, too. The novel opens a month after the death of the brothers' beloved mother – a motif to which Gwyn regularly returned in his domestic writing, notably in *The Keep*. Likewise, the politically laced discussions which occur frequently throughout the narrative were unlikely to have been too far from those which occurred at 196 High Street. *Sorrow For Thy Sons* is the most classical of Gwyn's novels, framed by the social realism prevalent in nineteenth-century fiction. Gwyn had some recent local models on which to draw, too. There was *Times Like These* (1936) by the Blackwood writer Gwyn Jones or Jack Jones's *Rhondda Roundabout* (1935) and the book which Gwyn's mentor, Lewis Jones (who appears in Gwyn's own novel as 'Howells'), was writing: *Cwmardy*. It was published by Lawrence and Wishart in 1937.

Whereas Lewis Jones composed material in which the 'trumpet-notes of the revolution must sound' and wasted little time in getting to the point of dialecticism, Gwyn had a different audience in mind; one more general than that which read Britain's communist daily in the early 1930s, but no less radical. His was to be a literature of the popular front, bringing together the disparate parts of the labour movement to fight against their common enemies of unemployment, fascism, war, and the venal disinterest of the capitalist ruling class. But he struggled to cope with the unrelenting bleakness of the time, to say nothing of the darkness of his own experiences and did not yet possess an alternative to social realism to guide him in his writing. 'No writer could deal with it,' observed Dai Smith of the interwar conditions in South Wales, 'except through melodrama, through anger, through brute realism.' Gwyn took liberties, all the same, ignoring traditional scene setting and characterisation, and offering no apology for making the Rhondda and its people the narrative centre rather than a periphery of someone else's milieu. His readers were not to be treated as outsiders pulled into the world of Walter Greenwood's Hanky Park in Salford, the setting of *Love On The Dole*, or the Salinas Valley which dominated John Steinbeck's writing of the 1930s, but instead shown life as it truly was. In doing so, Gwyn created one of the great masterpieces of interwar working-class fiction.

*

Work on *Sorrow For Thy Sons* slowed the first months of 1937 because Gwyn was once more offered the opportunity to teach for the WEA. His classes in international relations were held at either end of the Windy Way in Trebanog and Porth, with those in the 'political history of South Wales' held in Ton Pentre and Cwmparc, near Treorchy.[31] 'The previous tutor was a moron, probably a fascist,' he explained to Nan after one session at Cwmparc, 'When I took over, the membership had dwindled to about five. My job now is to get the thing back on its feet. I'm a poor one to put anything back on its feet. Half the time I don't know whether I'm standing on my head or not. Still, I think the Cwmparc boys like me.'[32] Amongst the local tutors for the WEA in the Rhondda was Sidney Jones, who later taught with Gwyn in Barry. Jones's class in his native Ferndale, at the top end of the Rhondda Fach, covered social history from the fifteenth century onwards before turning his attention to international relations. Gwyn's brother Gwilym taught a music appreciation class.[33] Piecemeal community-based adult learning little eased Gwyn's financial troubles, for all that he was enthused by the experience of teaching and discussing contemporary and historical issues. 'Whenever I enter one of these unemployed clubs (the classes are held there),' he explained to Nan, 'I get seized by such a violent hatred of the capitalist system that condemns men to rot and waste away in such mean, disreputable shanties it takes my breath away for a while.'

For all that, Gwyn was no longer fully unemployed. In the 1937–38 session, he taught as many as eight classes across the Rhondda and secured a place on the approved tutor list for the YMCA Community College as well. This added to his income, allowing him to buy books again, something he had not done since leaving Oxford, but also to his physical burden and he soon looked for a way out. 'These classes,' he told Nan just before Christmas 1937, 'are at best a stop gap, but I can't forget these classes can serve as an inspiration to people fighting a pretty grim struggle with death.' Gwyn conceived of his teaching as a 'full-blown political campaign in favour of the bright dawn.' He had to be careful not to get caught by the inspectors or earn the scorn of his employers who insisted on being 'unsectarian' and 'non-party in politics.' Sidney Jones was temporarily dismissed from teaching in Ferndale, for instance, when he was found to be teaching 'subversive,' left-wing material. He had fallen foul of the unwritten rule that the more radical WEA tutors produced two syllabi – one to deliver and one to deliver to the inspectors. His reinstatement came only after the class went on strike.[34]

In the late 1930s, Gwyn's reading was dominated by books published Victor Gollancz and by Allen Lane's Penguin Books. Both played an important role in shaping mainstream left-wing and popular front thought through series such as the Left Book Club and Penguin Specials. With money in his pocket from teaching, Gwyn subscribed regularly to the Left Book Club between 1936 and 1946, supplementing his interests with copies of the inexpensive Penguin Specials. The latter habit he continued into the 1960s. Other material found its way to 196 High Street, too, including an edition of Marx and Engels's writings on literature and art, published by the French Communist Party – almost certainly purchased through the British Communist Party's publishing networks. Frustratingly, Gwyn's thoughts on the material he read and absorbed in this period of his life are largely lost save for fragments related in letters to his immediate family or recorded in his private journals, which are not themselves voluminous. He remained absorbed intellectually in the tenets of Marxism and the political enthusiasms of communism: the earliest Left Book Club volume which survives in Gwyn's library, Shirokov's *A Textbook of Marxist Philosophy*, published by Victor Gollancz in May 1937, is a clear indication of that. The volume's English language editor, John Lewis, explained that it was 'the best example of the philosophical teaching now being given in the Soviet Union' – that of the Leningrad Institute of Philosophy.[35]

The only other volumes from Gwyn's 1937 Left Book Club subscription to survive are Edgar Snow's *Red Star Over China* and Arthur Koestler's *Spanish Testament*. The former was published as the monthly choice for the Left Book Club in October 1937. Gwyn read it immediately and wrote to his sister to suggest that she read it too.[36] He was transfixed by Snow's portrait of the situation in China, of the contemporary battle between nationalism-fascism and communism, of the Long March and the rise of Mao Zedong. An American journalist, Edgar Snow was the first westerner to interview many of the leading figures in the Chinese Communist Party and his book became a bestseller in Britain and the United States. Whereas recent scholarship has clarified Snow's composition and his willingness to submit interview transcripts for editing and official approval, this process was hidden from readers in the 1930s who were encouraged to link events in China with those elsewhere, particularly Spain. Gwyn certainly did.[37] Agnes Smedley's equally sympathetic and pro-communist *China Fights Back*, published in December 1938, further shaped Gwyn's ideas about contemporary China and its communist party.

Spain, of course, Gwyn knew about, but Koestler's memoir of his own time in the country since the outbreak of the Civil War – as spy and as war correspondent – extended Gwyn's sense of what had happened to the country since he left in 1933. The basis of Koestler's work, as he described in *Spanish Testament*, was a trip taken to General Franco's headquarters in 1936 as a Comintern spy; Koestler had used manufactured credentials from the London *News Chronicle* as his cover. Able to observe the military and strategic support being provided to the Spanish Nationalists by Fascist Italy and Nazi Germany, Koestler gained the evidence which Moscow and the Spanish Republican government hoped, forlornly, would prompt the western allies (chiefly Britain and France) to intervene. Koestler's findings were first published in France as *L'Espagne Ensanglantée* – Bloodied Spain – before being expanded into *Spanish Testament*, which was published by Gollancz in English in December 1937.[38] Gwyn's response to Koestler's writing cannot now be known, but the survival in his library of *Spanish Testament* and not Orwell's *Homage to Catalonia* published in London by Martin Secker in April 1938, gives some indication as to Gwyn's thought process and his wider allegiances. He was not simply absorbing every possible leftist work on Spain but navigating a carefully curated literary and philosophical course.

In fact, Gwyn owned little of Orwell's work and the only survivor in his library is *Animal Farm*, although it is certainly possible that he read Orwell's other books in library editions. Gwyn continued to buy and to read Koestler, on the other hand, even after the latter's break with the Communist Party in 1938. In the 1950s, hinting at his own intellectual development, Gwyn purchased the first volume of Koestler's autobiography, *Arrow in the Blue* (1952), and *The God That Failed* (1950), the collection of essays by ex-communists such as Stephen Spender and André Gide compiled by Koestler and introduced by Richard Crossman.[39] In the 1960s, Gwyn turned to Koestler's 1939 novel *The Gladiators*, an allegorical study of the European left since the Bolshevik Revolution of 1917. There are notable absences, of course, not least *Scum of the Earth* (1941), *Darkness at Noon* (1942), and *Invisible Writing* (1954), Koestler's second volume of autobiography, but these appear so only because of Gwyn's other holdings. Orwell himself identified Koestler as a literary influence: the lineage between *Darkness at Noon* and *1984* is clear. So why Koestler and not Orwell (or both) in Gwyn's reading habits of the 1930s? The answer surely lies in Orwell's early rejection of Soviet communism at a time when Gwyn still had his own faith.

He could be especially hostile, at this time, to those who had no political fervour. This was notably true of Gwyn's older brother and sister-in-law, John and Gwen, who themselves ran out of patience. 'This house is as jittery as ever it was,' Gwyn told Nan in the spring of 1938, 'John is incredibly foolish and moody over this monstrous impostor of a wife of his as before. She has now added a few more complaints to her list. One culminating and fatal complaint would not come amiss. I don't like people who smarm me to my face and poisonously slander me behind my back. You'll probably be getting a letter from one of them soon, complaining of my "strange conduct."'[40] But Gwen and John were not alone. Unbeknown to Gwyn, Nan had written to Walt and Nest appealing for their support in reining in their increasingly turbulent brother. Walt readily agreed and told Nan that, 'the great work shall be commenced when I see the young reprobate tomorrow. I shall set about it quietly and subtly, with no heat, no acrimony, no noise. I shall appeal not to his head with political argument and philosophical claptrap, but to his heart and bowels because they are easily and profitably attacked.'

Walt's intervention, in the end, had little impact and so it was left to Nan to deliver the final, cutting reproach. Gwyn refused to speak to her for weeks afterwards. Towards the end of the summer term, 1938, he picked up his pen once more, pouring his irritation with life at 196 High Street onto the page. 'I've neglected you for quite a while. The reproach you administered me in your last letter was very well deserved but my skin has become so pleasantly thick to taunts of all kinds and my distaste for letter writing so pronounced that I have been able to go several weeks without using my pen.' It was the closest he came to apologising. 'There isn't much to say,' he continued,

I am quite happy. My relationships with the Cymmer people are not inspiringly friendly. John seems to spend most of his time in another world, and frankly I cannot stand his wife or any member of her benighted family. John attacks me bitterly because I say nothing to her. What in the sweet name of hell is there for me to say, I don't believe in fibs. I believe fortune tellers should be burned and I would advise a tearing out of the gall bladder as a fitting punishment for all spiritualists. So what have Gwen and I in common? She claims to have been like a mother to me. 'Nan never did anything for him. It's I who looked after him when he was homeless and sick.' That's the line they put over. That's the rubbish they pour into the ear of every goddam gossip in Cymmer and district until I am known to all and sundry as a kind of parasitic liver-fluke living on the proceeds of Gwen's sewing. Never a word about the money they got from Walt which will never be paid back. Never a word about the money (£44) which they got from me last year and the like sum they'll get from me this year. No, not a word. It's poor little Gwennie's sewing that keeps us all alive.

God blast her buttocks!!! She smarms up to me when I am there and does her feeble best to tear my name, your name, and the name of all our peculiar clan to tatters when I am not there. Our John's 'martyrdom' has given him many of the characteristics of a half-wit. Eddie noticed it when John went to London. I'll be going to London soon. To settle for good, I hope. As near to Eddie as possible. When I have a place of my own you will never lack for hospitality. We should be able to offer you a nice variety of concert and air raids. (Still, at the back of my mind, there is a small and pungent doubt as to whether I'll ever leave these walls. In the years immediately ahead there might be more security here than elsewhere. The times are fully of danger.)[41]

Sensing that he had better leave Cymmer as soon as possible, and unable to secure an immediate transition to London, which would have been a disaster, in any case, Gwyn applied for and won a post teaching at a government instructional centre in Norfolk. He arrived at Cranwich Heath at the end of June having had little respite since the end of his WEA duties. He quickly discovered that he had arrived in the most 'sceptically depressing place I shall ever know.'[42]

*

The Ministry of Labour Instructional Centres – established in the 1930s as one of the government's starkest responses to mass unemployment – were Britain's equivalent of the *Arbeitslager* found in Nazi Germany. At Cranwich Heath, the centre comprised fifteen wooden huts arranged around a central parade ground and a flagpole on which the Union Jack insistently fluttered. Everything was run along military lines.[43] The routine was 'horrible and revolting at first,' Gwyn told Nan, 'but becomes converted with a kind of charm that belongs to stability once the first bitter pang of it has passed off your tongue.'[44] The inmates – officially, trainees – were mostly from the North East of England. Gwyn thought them 'pleasant enough' albeit 'noisy as the devil.' I understand them, he told Nan, 'and I trust that they respect me.' Gwyn's political convictions were strengthened by what he saw in the camp, however he had no choice but to learn to be more cautious in openly expressing his feelings. 'Don't imagine that this experience is making me less of a communist,' he told Nan, '[I am] profoundly committed to revolutionary principles.' He added:

In any case, even had I been a member of the Primrose League before coming here, the sight of these morons, and consciousness of the fact that there is not one of them whose life is not in a hell of a mess could suffice to dye me as red as the poppies of the field.[45]

Gwyn wrote again a few weeks later, this time full of disgust and restlessly determined to leave at the first opportunity. 'If I don't find something more to my taste pretty soon,' he told Nan, 'I'll be heading for the bin.' But there was also a change in his attitude to the outside world and to the misfortune of others:

> Here you see the pitch black tragedy of unwanted men against the snow-white background of Norfolk desolation. You might think you see it in its entirety in the Rhondda. I thought so too. But you don't, not by a mile … These poor birds here are dumb shuttlecocks in a nasty, ugly game that passes their understanding.
>
> I see no need for these centres, yet they are being extended, improved and made to conform with regulations that become more severe from year to year. The official reason is that the men must be made to leave their hometowns for a substantial period and re-accustom themselves to the atmosphere of regular work. It does not need a very sensible wit to demolish those arguments. First, however loathsome and degenerating the slum life of some of the workless might be, it cannot be as demoralising as the life they lead when herded, forty at a time, into those wretched huts. Second, the work which is done at these centres is so trivial, stupid and laxly enforced as to make it valueless as an agent of reconditioning. The old gibe that slave camps were places where holes are dug merely to be filled in is not wide of the mark … The world is rotten. What are these centres but areas of pure, gangrenous infection? You cannot rid society of such things as that by moral persuasion. If there must be a purging, it is our duty to make it as brief and intelligently directed as possible.[46]

To make sense of his own experiences and to foster public anger enough to force the closure of the network of instructional centres, Gwyn resolved to write a novel. He sent a speculative letter to Victor Gollancz hoping to discuss the possibility of sending the manuscript for consideration when it was complete.

The novel was never finished but since his departure from the Rhondda, Gwyn had begun to recover from the mental ill health which had tormented him for years. 'Looking back, I seem to have been so terrible unhappy, so needless unhappy, for so many years,' he explained to Nan, 'In my lighter moments it makes me think that there must be [some] glorious and brilliant fulfilment awaiting me.' He added, 'this experience is slowly not surely making a valuable human being out of me ... that is, if I survive the experience without going nuts. My temperament is a dangerously wild one, I'm afraid. I have been ... acquiescent for the last few years but that was due entirely to immeasurably violent student and an exceptional load of physical sickness. As circumstances move me back to normal, I will tend, presumably, to become more violently critical and implacable.' Finally, with a clear head, and obvious respect for his sister's views, he apologised for his behaviour:

> You yourself have commented on the extreme contradictions of my personality. It takes an artist to be supremely contradictory. It takes an artist to observe the contradictions of others. Thank you.

Gwyn left Cranwich Heath in October 1938 and headed to London, where he lodged once more with his brother Eddie. He found a job as a trainee manager in the children's department at Selfridges. It lasted all of three weeks, 'shook me up so badly,' and little endeared him to the worlds of commerce and middle-class consumption. Besides, it interrupted the novel he had been writing on the camps. The three or four months spent in Norfolk had a tremendous effect nevertheless and they were never forgotten. In an interview with Denis Mitchell in 1975, Gwyn recalled the camps and what he saw. His anger had little dissipated in nearly forty years.

And then these camps that they started in this country, around about the 1937, 1938 period. And they were called, I believed, instructional camps for the unemployed because you had to have been unemployed for about eight years to qualify for a place at one of these camps. And I was sent there as a teacher and about the only thing on the curriculum was knotting – making knots. And I'd never made a knot in my life, I had no idea what to do. But they gave me a board full of all kinds of knots, you know, and the poor chaps in the camp, they were desperate men, they were very sad men. And I gave these lessons in knotting now; you know, how to attach a yacht to a mooring point. These chaps were on about four shillings a week in the camp. But it's a very funny thing because so many of these lads would come up to me and they'd say: what is the execution knot? Well, I didn't have much of an idea and I probably gave them some instruction in knotting for something totally different. But one of them at least acted on the shape and killed himself. These men were men of great strength, great dignity, who had had their backs broken by an act of social idiocy.

By New Year, 1939, Gwyn was back in the Rhondda, reading and writing, continuing his mental recovery, coming to terms with what he had witnessed. He had just finished Phyllis Bottome's 1937 novel *The Mortal Storm*, regarding it as 'very interesting.' Bottome 'writes with a good heart' he explained to Nan, who was by then heavily pregnant with her first child.[47] She named him David Gwyn. As for his own future, 'my general feeling is that I am nearer the mark as a writer than I have ever been in the past.' He added: 'my writing is more tolerant, my plots are more human, my outlook more sanguine.' Gwyn had all-but abandoned the long-form novel again, perhaps still annoyed at the failure of *Sorrow For Thy Sons*, and preferred instead to concentrate on 'shorter tales.'

As for work: 'influence is being used to get me a job in the advertising business,' he joked, 'it will be a sad step from writing epics for the world's workers to writing puns for Oxo.'[48] Reflecting on the Cranwich affair, he felt glad to have left noting that there was really 'only one way in which I will ever advance myself. That's on a soap box.'

Mindful of not remaining in the Rhondda too long, lest he fall back into old habits and the darkness which accompanied him there, Gwyn applied for, and won, one of two new posts being created by the Derbyshire Association of Social Centres – itself part of the National Council of Social Service (NCSS). He was to become warden of the Association's centres at Bolsover, Carr Vale, Clowne, and Shirebrook. The role primarily involved organising leisure activities and educational classes, and co-supervising a holiday for more than one hundred unemployed men from across Derbyshire at a hostel in Cheshire.[49] One of his first acts on arriving in the county was to deputise for the Association's secretary, Rowland Hill, who had fallen ill, at the annual weekend conference on The Clubs in Modern Social Life.[50] 'I had to give two speeches on "cultural developments,"' he told Nan, 'at the end of my second speech two ladies advanced excitedly to shake my hand, saying that they were enraptured. What is it that I have got that other people haven't got? God alone can tell.'[51] More than twenty social service centres were represented at the conference, held at Overton Hall Youth Hostel in Ashover, and it provided a golden opportunity to make his name in a new part of the country.[52]

In September, just as war broke out, Gwyn accepted the post of education officer with the NCSS in the towns and districts just north of Manchester: Bury, Prestwich, and Rochdale. The role was more formal than his previous work and involved a good deal of contact with the local councils – for a period Gwyn was also a contact officer for Civil Defence. He recalled his duties some years later:

> I myself once did, in those dim twilit days of the late Thirties, a semi-governmental job which required me to attend endless sub-committees of a whole group of municipal councils. It was a period of black and maddening tedium. It was a nightmare of triviality and bland unreason. And luck would always have me sitting next to the least civilised member of the council: some crafty, sub-literate scheme with eyes like clinker and apparently dead except when he gave me a fierce nudge and said it was bra-a-ass that made the mare go round or, his only other punch line, that life was the best university.

Alongside the council meetings were a seemingly un-ending series of talks delivered to unemployed clubs, Rotary clubs, branches of the Women's Co-operative Guild, and the likes; and if Gwyn was not delivering the talk, he was presiding over the session.[53] At the time, the NCSS were working to develop a network of Citizens' Advice Bureaux and it fell to Gwyn to convince residents in Rochdale and nearby Littleborough to establish local offices. The Rochdale Bureau opened in late 1939 with Littleborough following a few years later.[54] In many respects, Gwyn was an effective social servant. He was committed to ameliorating as best he could the conditions of the unemployed, and social service work suited his political instincts. But in the process of getting to know 'practically every distressed area in Britain,' he felt compelled to do something more. He explained to Nan in a letter written at Christmas, 1941, that

> I became so calloused by the spectacle of misery liberally administered and patiently, enduringly borne I became something

of a John the Baptist. I sensed that a terrible vengeance would come upon the agents and the victims of such inhumanity. But not even J the Bap could have foretold a vengeance quite as horrible as the one that the joint Imperialisms of Germany and Britain are now pouring nightly and daily from the skies of Europe. Men asked for this by their refusal to be decent. In odd corners, in the unemployed clubs of our great land, I preached the gospel of dignity and brotherliness. But the corners were too odd and too dark and my voice and all the voices like mine were as whispers compared with the roar of the tool-makers and the lie-makers who were forging the new instruments of force and injustice.[55]

Life in Prestwich had been made the more enjoyable by being able to live, for the first time since they had married in secret in January 1938, with Lyn. Born on 31 January 1911, Eiluned Thomas was a miner's daughter (her father worked at the Lewis Merthyr Colliery in Trehafod), and originally met Gwyn through his nemesis of a sister-in-law, Gwen. Lyn was close to Gwen's own sister, Dilys. By the time Lyn and Gwyn met, in around 1937, the former was working as a typist for the Unemployment Assistance Board and going out with Ivor Thomas, brother of future Labour MP for Cardiff Central (1945–1950) and Cardiff West (1950–1983), cabinet minister and Speaker of the House of Commons, George. Life at 9 Laburnum Grove, Prestwich, was not for Gwyn and Lyn alone, however: Lyn's mother, Gwen, now widowed, moved north with them, as did her younger brother, Richard. Tragedy soon struck. In the summer of 1940, Gwen Thomas, Lyn's mother, died suddenly. Not long afterwards, Walter senior, Gwyn's father, also passed. These losses were coupled with the traumatic sound of the air raid siren, a regular over Greater Manchester in the spring of 1940 as part of government preparedness tests.

Gwyn became so alarmed that 'despite all the efforts of my wife to calm me, I rushed on to the landing and went down the stairs with both my legs in one leg of my trousers. I hurt my skull and gashed my hand against the front door.'[56]

Gwyn resolved on moving once more and began applying for teaching jobs as far from air raid sirens as possible. One advert he saw was for a languages master at Cardigan County School. He wrote to the headmaster, Tom Evans, who travelled north to Liverpool to interview Gwyn.[57] Offered the job, Gwyn thought he had struck gold. He and Lyn prepared to leave Prestwich just as the first air raids occurred over Manchester that summer. For effect, Gwyn merged fact and fiction in his portrait of this period in *A Few Selected Exits*, remarking on the bombing of central Manchester and the substantial blaze which lit up the night sky. Those events, part of the Christmas Blitz, took place just before Christmas 1940, several months after Gwyn had moved, but the earlier, moderate raids which destroyed the Palace Theatre and other buildings were enough for him to yearn for 'a cloister, a school, something quiet and timeless.'[58] Given a 'nervous system that imperialism does not quite consider to be up to the high standard necessary for the dignified task of ensuing by violence that the sacred persons of Lords Derby and Nuffield shall not perish from the earth,' Gwyn was declared unfit for military service.[59] His war would be a civilian one.

*

Neither Cardigan County School nor Cardigan itself could sustain Gwyn for long, of course. He always knew that West Wales was a temporary measure, providing a degree of peace, quiet and safety from the bombing. The absence of air raid sirens calmed Gwyn's nerves and he was able to mourn the death of his father. He found the headmaster, Thomas Evans

(1896–1965), an interesting individual and someone with whom he could discuss current affairs despite sharp disagreements. Evans had completed a master's thesis in politics on the 'background to modern Welsh politics' and served as a member of the town council. 'When I met him,' Gwyn wrote years later, 'I found him to be the sort of man I had expected from his letter to me: very Welsh, very charming, charged with an almost overpowering vigour of mind, imagination and tongue; a man capable of living intensely on so many levels of life as to make the average schoolman seem a monkish drab.' Another of the teachers Gwyn got on well with was Leslie Wynne Evans (1911–1985), with whom he co-produced *The Mikado* as the school's Christmas show in December 1940.[60] But he was not fond of Cardigan itself, nor of the Cymric natives. This place, he told Nan,

> has but one virtue. It has the quantity of alcohol in it that will act as a preservative on bodies irrespective of whether or not they deserve to be preserved. Frankly, I am of the opinion that the air of Cardigan, which I assume possesses this rare property of bestowing immortality, is throwing its virtue about without due regard to the facts of the case. For Cardigan is a town which, in spite of a relatively small population, contains a greater number of people whose inner and outer characteristics demand that they should be knocked off than any other town. I know you are familiar through the medium of legend with the miserliness of these same Cardis, but legend can never give you the full repulsive quality of the hoarding activity that gives the older folk here such a passionate longing to keep looking at their odd scraps of property that they simply forget that nature ordinarily sets a term upon human life and they forget to die.[61]

He added,

The slightest trifle of domestic gossip zooms throughout the town like a flying fortress. So you can imagine that I, marooned upon this place which to me has in every respect the appearance of a desert island, feel a certain amount of uneasiness and disgust.

Bored with the company of miserly West Walians, Gwyn took to writing once more, this time with a renewed vigour and sense of creative purpose. In January 1941, he began the novella eventually published as *The Alone to the Alone*, a rich allegory of Europe in the 1930s full of the tensions between fascism and socialism, and the failures of liberal democracy.[62] What else could it be but that: 'I'm political to the roots of my hair,' Gwyn insisted, 'I look like a red.'[63] In other notebooks he set down his more private thoughts about contemporary life and became obsessed with the idea that the world had gone wrong with the outbreak of the Spanish Civil War. The international tragedy of Spain, as he now called it. He wrote:

The climax of her struggle occurred just when the major powers of Europe were moving up for their own clash. The Spanish war was a basic war waged round the eternal problems of human society. Spain [was] a pointer to the new Europe. The coalescence of international interests in a ruthless war of ideas ... Spain is one of the most sinister lynchpins of European fascism and post-war policy should be directed on that assumption. In exactly the same way as a victorious democratic outcome in Spain in 1939 would have brought unassessable benefit to Europe, so a victorious fascist regime contributes powerfully to the forces of oppression and backwardness throughout the continent.[64]

Despite the culture differences evident in West Wales, Gwyn relished being in the classroom. 'I began school teaching in

1940,' he wrote in 1965, 'and felt I had come home – it was my first bit of ringing happiness since early childhood.'[65] He yearned, though, for a return to Glamorgan and to his earth's warm centre. In February 1941, there was a chance to join Walt at Neath, but the interview coincided with the devastating blitz on Swansea, the sights and sounds of which terrified and horrified Gwyn. He returned to Cardigan resigned to the isolation necessary to remain safe. But as luck would have it Gwyn had struck up correspondence with his old headmaster, E. T. Griffiths. 'I've had some grand letters,' Gwyn told Nan, 'he's a nice fellow and he seems to have quite an opinion of me as a kind of boy sage. Don't blame him. He's pretty wise at that.' The original purpose Griffiths had had in writing to Gwyn had been to ask for the return of the money given to help at Oxford in 1931, but the departure of the Spanish master at Barry part way through the 1941–42 academic year left an opening. Gwyn was given the job. At the end of September 1942, having worked his notice in Cardigan, he and Lyn arrived in Barry.[66] The long years of trial and torment were finally over.

[1] Gwyn Thomas, 'Rhondda Retrospect', *Neath Guardian*, 1 July 1966.

[2] Will Paynter, *My Generation* (London, 1972), 49.

[3] *AFSE*, 99.

[4] Smith, *Lewis Jones*, 24. These included 'Young Dai', *Daily Worker*, 1 July 1932; 'Power of the Pit', *Daily Worker*, 23 August 1932; 'Boots, Shiny, Big and Heavy...', *Daily Worker*, 28 April 1933; 'The Pit Cage', *Daily Worker*, 21 June 1933.

[5] NLW, GTP, G234: Script for Wales and the Welsh: The Greatest Welshman, Episode Four, Lewis Jones, by Gwyn Thomas, 4 February 1977. A recording of the broadcast is held at the SWML: AUD/77.

[6] Dai Smith, *Lewis Jones* (Cardiff, 1982), 17.

[7] Letter from Gwyn Thomas to A. B. Emden, St Edmund Hall, 11 October 1934.

[8] The surviving notebook from this period of absorption dates the early summer of 1935.

[9] *AFSE*, 70–2.

[10] The Marx Memorial Library was founded in 1933 as the Communist Party of Great Britain's central training school.

[11] Letter from Lionel Lindsay, Chief Constable of Glamorgan, 2 November 1935. In KV2/1037.

[12] Letter from Iris Parsons to Harry Pollitt, 2 November 1935. In KV2/1037.

[13] Testimonial from E. T. Griffiths, 1 July 1935.

[14] Letter from Gwyn Thomas to Hannah Thomas, undated except 'two weeks until the feast of the nativity', c. 11 December 1935.

[15] *AFSE*, 115.

[16] *Punch*, 13 September 1967.

[17] Gwyn Thomas, 'Note on Sorrow For Thy Sons,' September 1966.

[18] *Glamorgan Free Press*, 5 September 1936.

[19] Letter from Gwyn Thomas to Hannah Thomas, 9 September 1936.

[20] Letter from Gwyn Thomas to Hannah Thomas, 17 January 1937.

[21] Letter from Gwyn Thomas to Hannah Thomas, 9 September 1936.

[22] Letter from Gwyn Thomas to Hannah Thomas, 17 November 1936.

[23] *Left Review*, (October 1936), 667.

[24] Letter from Gwyn Thomas to Hannah Thomas, 17 November 1936.

[25] Letter from Gwyn Thomas to Hannah Thomas, 13 December 1936.

[26] Letter from Gwyn Thomas to Hannah Thomas, undated but c. 5 June 1937.

[27] As above.

[28] Letter from Gwyn Thomas to Hannah Thomas, 26 October 1937.

[29] Dai Smith, 'Introduction', in Gwyn Thomas, *Sorrow For Thy Sons* (London, 1986).

[30] Dai Smith, 'The Early Gwyn Thomas', *The Transactions of the Honourable Society of Cymmrodorion* (1985), 71–89.

[31] South Wales District of the Workers' Educational Association, *Annual Report for 1936–37* (Cardiff, 1937), 56; South Wales District of the Workers' Educational Association, *Annual Report for 1937–38* (Cardiff, 1938), 40. The previous tutor in social and political history in that part of the Rhondda was Leonard Hugh Doncaster (1914–1994), a Quaker, then connected with the educational settlement at Maes-yr-Haf and later a lecturer at the Quaker education centre, Woodbrooke College, in Birmingham.

[32] Letter from Gwyn Thomas to Hannah Thomas, 7 February 1937.

[33] Letter from Gwyn Thomas to Hannah Thomas, 2 December 1937.

[34] My thanks to Ceinwen Statter (née Jones), Sidney Jones's niece, for relating this story to me.

[35] John Lewis, 'Preface', in M. Shirokov, *A Textbook of Marxist Philosophy* (London, 1937).

[36] Letter from Gwyn Thomas to Hannah Thomas, 28 October 1937.

[37] Letter from Gwyn Thomas to Hannah Thomas, undated but c. spring 1938.

[38] *Spanish Testament* combined *L'Espange Enslanglantée* with those elements which

Koestler later decoupled and which Gollancz published as *Dialogue with Death* in 1942. Having, by then, turned away from the Communist Party, Koestler refused the republication of *Spanish Testament*, allowing the propaganda sections of the book to fall by the wayside. Arthur Koestler, *The Invisible Writing* (London, 2005 edn.), 411.

[39] Coincidentally, Gwyn appeared at the Cheltenham Literature Festival in 1969 in a line-up which included Koestler, Michael Foot, and the poet Cecil Day-Lewis. *Birmingham Daily Post*, 17 October 1969.

[40] Letter from Gwyn Thomas to Hannah Thomas, undated but spring 1938.

[41] Letter from Gwyn Thomas to Hannah Thomas, undated but c. May/June 1938.

[42] *AFSE*, 103. Here Gwyn locates the camp in 'an area of reclaimed bogland in Staffordshire.' Parnell (*LFD*, 65–67) followed this misrepresentation and sought to reconcile the available evidence. The result was a manufacture of the truth, which I have corrected here.

[43] John Field, *Working Men's Bodies* (Manchester, 2013), 166.

[44] Letter from Gwyn Thomas to Hannah Thomas, 12 August 1938.

[45] Letter from Gwyn Thomas to Hannah Thomas, 12 August 1938.

[46] Letter from Gwyn Thomas to Hannah Thomas, 11 September 1938.

[47] David Gwyn Thomas was born on 22 February 1939.

[48] Letter from Gwyn Thomas to Hannah Thomas, 1 January 1939.

[49] *Derby Daily Telegraph*, 16 January, 26 May, 31 July 1939.

[50] *Derbyshire Times and Chesterfield Herald*, 27 January, 10 February 1939.

[51] Letter from Gwyn Thomas to Hannah Thomas, 14 February 1939. The topic was reported as cultural activities in the *Derby Daily Telegraph*, 20 January 1939.

[52] *Derby Daily Telegraph*, 6 February 1939.

[53] *Rochdale Observer*, 11 November, 9 December 1939, 18 January, 27 April 1940; *Bury Times*, 22 February 1940.

[54] *Rochdale Observer*, 13 December 1941.

[55] *LFD*, 74.

[56] *AFSE*, 104.

[57] NLW, GTP, B10, 'A speech given at Cardigan County School, 17 October 1963'.

[58] Graham Phythian, *Blitz Britain: Manchester and Salford* (Gloucester, 2015).

[59] Letter from Gwyn Thomas to Hannah Thomas, 6 December 1941.

[60] Leslie Wynne Evans later earned his doctorate for a study of education in Wales during the industrial revolution. It was published as *Education in Industrial Wales, 1700–1900* (Cardiff, 1971). He left teaching to take up a post at University College Cardiff, rising to become Reader in Education.

[61] Letter from Gwyn Thomas to Hannah Thomas, 6 December 1941.

[62] NLW, Welsh Arts Council Manuscripts, MS 20778B: Gwyn Thomas Notebook, January–June 1941. Containing four sketches for novels: *The Alone to the Alone, The Flute*, and two untitled works. For the spirit of *The Alone to the Alone* see GTP, M27: Interview with Dai Smith conducted by Michael Parnell, 27 February 1985.

[63] Letter from Gwyn Thomas to Hannah Thomas, 6 December 1941.

[64] NLW, GTP, N2: Cardigan County School Notebook, 1942, 11–12.

[65] *A Hatful of Humours*, 11.

[66] *The Barrian: Magazine of the Barry Boys' County School* 29 (June 1943), 5.

CHAPTER FOUR

Rhondda Runyon

Twenty miles south of Porth and ten miles south-west of Cardiff, the seaside-port of Barry had been the shock town of the Welsh industrial revolution. Until the opening of the docks in 1889, it was little more than an area of moorland, woodland, and a tiny fishing village nestled near St Nicholas Church. Apart from some fishermen's cottages and the church itself, the only other building which pre-dated the rapid construction of Barry in the last decade of the nineteenth century was the Ship Hotel. It overlooked the island, which was then linked to the mainland by a ford across the Cadoxton river. By the start of the twentieth century, Barry teemed with life. It was soon to be the largest coal exporting port in the world, overtaking Cardiff. On the streets, Arabic mixed with Spanish, French with Norwegian, and a variety of English and Welsh accents provided the local flavour. It was, Gwyn observed sardonically in 1958, a 'schizophrenic borough, torn between demands for a third tide daily to buck up business at the languishing dock and the brash revelries of Barry Island' and the sort of place where 'a strong strain of Somersetshire peasantry' rendered singing – Gwyn's code word for Rhondda-esque social democratic collectivism – 'about as unWelsh as can be.'[1]

151 Gladstone Road, the house into which Gwyn and Lyn settled in 1942, was a product of that rapid expansion of Barry in the 1890s and 1900s. It was the direct result of the council's desire to create a wide boulevard linking the eastern part of the town to the centre, a scheme on which it embarked

just before the turn of the century.[2] The house itself was a two-storey redbrick terrace with imposing bay windows on each floor: the clearest sign yet of Gwyn and Lyn's increased social mobility. They occupied lodgings on the upper level. It was an ideal location. Just along the road stood Gladstone Primary School, the small open space called Gladstone Gardens, and the town's memorial hall. Gwyn's daily 'commute' to work involved a walk along the steep rise of Buttrills Road to where Barry County School for Boys was located. It was a school with a reputation. E. T. Griffiths's predecessor as headmaster, Edgar Jones (1868–1953), considered the Thomas Arnold of Wales, had shaped the Boys' School into one of the foremost state schools in Wales. Although Gwyn later joked that 'the two years at Cardigan in a mixed grammar school are so sweet in recollection that my twenty years in the Barry Boys' Grammar School seem relatively penal in flavour,' there can be little doubt as to which of the two he always preferred to teach in: Barry.[3]

The marvellous welcome to Barry given by E. T. Griffiths and his wife, Jane, certainly made the difference to Gwyn. Regular Sunday lunches with E. T. and Jane (as Gwyn knew them) at their house on Colcot Road added to the charm and congenial atmosphere. After one encounter, a bemused Gwyn wrote to tell Nan that 'Griffiths thinks I have calmed down considerably, that my passionate temper has been blunted considerably by the tolerance that comes with age and experience.' It's not true, he insisted, adding that 'there has been no more calming down in me than you would find in a self-respecting volcano.' Instead, Gwyn concluded, 'I now adhere strictly to the New Commandment "thou must not address thy neighbour as a bloody nuisance unless thou art at least ten years away and speakest in an inaudible mumble."' This was, Gwyn remarked sardonically, 'quite a load of practical wisdom.' His political convictions had been shaken during the war, particularly after the entry of the Soviet Union in the summer of 1941. The old sureties were gone. 'All parties rally like joyful hounds around the heels of the Tory masters,' he complained to Nan, adding that even the communist leader Harry Pollitt 'sounds like a Union Jack.'

By 1943, Gwyn's admiration was reserved for the small number of individual politicians endeavouring to maintain the semblance of democratic debate in the face of the wartime coalition. Chief amongst them was Aneurin Bevan, the de facto leader of the parliamentary opposition and one of the prime movers behind the People's Vigilance Committee in 1940 and the People's Convention, held in London, in January 1941. 'The people,' he wrote, 'with pathetic blindness, kiss the pasteboard millennium of the Beveridge. The Fascist jackals of the Court and Carlton Club yelp with ecstasy at the sight of the workers destroying their own defences to forward the farce of National Unity. Miners worn down to skeleton thinness by years of unemployment and overwork are exhorted by communist leaders to do and say nothing that will cause the least offence to those paragons of human goodness, the coal owners. But behind the delusions and absurdities of this war, there are men who retain the sense to see that German Nazism and British Toryism are merely the two sides of one vile, horrible medal.'[4] Much of this was kept to the privacy of letters to Nan, although the essence of Gwyn's political surety and the great battle between good and evil, labour and capital, and democracy and fascism, soon found its way into his writing.

During the war years, whether in Cardigan or Barry, Gwyn composed dozens of short stories and two full-length linked novellas which he titled *The Alone to the Alone* and *The Dark Philosophers*. This was in addition to two completed but unpublished novels, *Sorrow For Thy Sons* (1936–7) and *O Lost!* (1938–9), the novel about the instructional centres which was cast aside, and several short stories and fragments written in the 1930s. Identifying the exact chronology of this body of work is tremendously difficult, the writer's secretive nature meant that he rarely discussed their composition in his letter, even those intended for Nan. The clearest evidence relates to *The Alone to the Alone*, which was written in the early part of the war and begun when Gwyn was still living in Cardigan. *The Dark Philosophers* followed thereafter, probably also in West Wales, although its original manuscript is seemingly lost. Both tales were then edited and shaped after Gwyn moved to Barry. A flavour of his style in this period can be found in the pages of *The Barrian*, the school magazine. The short stories published there, such as *Harvest*, which appeared in 1944, were the first to appear in print since Gwyn's Sixth Form efforts over a decade earlier. They serve as the clearest indication of his wartime creativity.

Harvest was based on a series of events in 1943. That summer, Gwyn's first in Barry, was partly spent in charge of a group of boys at a potato-picking residential camp at Penmark, five miles west of Barry. The camp itself was run by the Glamorgan Agricultural Committee. Officially, the experience provided 'three weeks of complete change of environment, devoted to work of national importance done under expert supervision with first-class food, proved an excellent tonic.'[5] Gwyn's take was rather different. In a letter to Nan to mark his thirtieth birthday, he noted that 'I am scheduled to promote the war by taking a band of the cannibals whom I teach in term time to harvest the crops for a month or so.'[6] He wrote up the experience as a short story under the imaginative pseudonym 'Gwynt,' the Welsh for wind.[7] The story began:

It is a large field, running down a hillside towards Culverhouse Cross. The sun is striking at us as if it had singled us out. The

144

field looks vast. Sheaves of barley are lying on the ground as far as the eye can see. The high hills around look cool. We envy them. A fair-haired foreman is talking to us.

'Those sheaves need bindin' an' stookin''

He leaves us. The terms mean little to us. Our ignorance of farm-labour is broad as the field, intense as the sun. We sit down to talk it over. We worry through to a solution. We find a fat ball of twine in the corner of the field. Moore is appointed number-one twine-cutter. He finds a shady place and cuts with a will and a knife. The strings pile up around him. We dig him out in time for dinner.

The literary voice is unmistakable, as is the humour and the gathering of voices to debate and discuss a problem. The tone is markedly lighter; a clear indication of the literary direction Gwyn *could* take. It was not yet certain that he would. He continued,

Someone sees a lake in mirage and the rest of us paddle in it. We feel we deserve well of the country. At five we pack in and wait for the truck. The silence is complete save for the moan of someone squeezing the hundredth thistle sting from his leg and the soft rasp of knife on cord as Moore cuts his millionth length of binder-twine.

'What's this barley stuff used for, mostly?' a dim voice asks, breaking the drowsy stupor of our group.

'Beer.'

We become Prohibitionists on the spot.

Throughout the 1950s and 1960s, Gwyn made frequent use of the school environments in Porth and Barry as source material, not least in his 1953 novel, *A Frost On My Frolic*. Anecdotes and wry observations also found their way into regular articles for *Punch* and the National Union of Teachers' magazine, *The Teacher*, wherein he satirised and lampooned his various colleagues or the technocratic changes he felt were ruining education and removing from children the opportunity to have a bit of light – the aesthetics of literary and artistic culture – shone into their lives. In a much calmer frame of mind than he had been in the claustrophobia and economic misery of 1930s Rhondda, Gwyn also drew from his experiences the comedic material he needed for his Meadow Prospect stories. 'Two things I miss,' he reflected after retirement, 'staff-room gossip, at which I was a dab-hand, and the laughter of boys when they and I, in our stammering communion around the totem poles of grammar, stumbled over the great jests of the universe.' This was all underlined in the depiction of his teaching career in *A Few Selected Exits*. 'There is little about himself in it,' Parnell lamented, 'and what there is, is presented comically and quasi-fictionally.'[8] That was the point.

In fact, chapter three of *A Few Selected Exits* was a recycling and weaving together of a series of *Punch* articles Gwyn had written a few years earlier, beginning with a series titled 'The Man With The Chalk' first published in the autumn of 1962.[9] As ever, much of his loathing was reserved for those whom he thought reactionary and whose intellect he rated lower than the average county councillor. To serve as foils, Gwyn 'invented' several teachers who symbolised the traits he disliked. When writing about his own sixth form days in Porth, he used the figure of 'Mr Rawlins,' a miserly but ambitious deputy headmaster.[10] His equivalent in Barry, and thus in *A Few Selected Exits*, was 'Mr Walford.' His debut appearance was in September 1962, in part two of 'The Man With The Chalk.'[11] Walford reappeared in April 1964 in a piece called 'Hitting The Track,' before returning once more in 'Fighting Fit' and 'Bowdler, What Are You Bowdling Now?'[12] For the memoir,

Gwyn reversed the last two articles, concluding the chapter with 'Fighting Fit' and two new paragraphs which he added as epilogue – the original article had ended 'anyway, I never went back and he never came back.'

Mr Walford was based almost entirely on an elderly colleague: David W. Walters, the school's chemistry master. Gwyn made the revelation in his foreword to *Old Barry in Photographs*, published in the 1970s. Walters had trained at the University College of South Wales and Monmouthshire at the turn of the century and, after a brief time teaching in Mold in North Wales, spent most of his career in Barry.[13] Relatively undistinguished as a pedagogue, he had been a prominent athlete before the First World War, with particular success as a hurdler and middle-distance runner. In 1906, he competed at the Intercalated Games in Athens and two years later was part of the British team at the 1908 London Olympics.[14] For several years he was the Welsh hurdle champion and a key influence in the Welsh Amateur Athletics Championships. Gwyn's fictional portrait hinted at these achievements. 'In his youth,' he wrote,

> Mr Walford had been a notable athlete. He was a hurdler and he put his phenomenal ability as a runner and a jumper down to nights of evasive action down west in flight from gamekeepers and landlords. He had been one of the British Olympic team that went to Athens in the early years of the century. That had been his only trip abroad. It had left no light or joy in his mind.

But Gwyn had little love of such things and his dislike, together with the need to maintain the fictional pretence, led to an exaggeration. Walters had, in fact, competed in Denmark and Sweden, and honeymooned in Switzerland, although he rarely left Wales after 1918.[15] By the time Gwyn knew him, Walters was old-fashioned, conservative, and narrowly focused in interests, hardly someone to whom Gwyn would warm. In *Punch* and later in Alan Plater's television adaptation of *A Few Selected Exits* in the 1990s, the fictional version of Mr Walford appeared to have a laughable enthusiasm for agricultural life and other rural habits. Such activities, in a town such as Barry, and certainly to an observer such as Gwyn, seemed oxymoronic.

> His main reading was an Agricultural Gazette, from which he would occasionally read some opaque message about the operation of the Seeds Act of 1919 or the vagaries of milk profits around Llandeilo. He also received free copies of the local paper, published in the township of his birth, which always contained in any given week so many incidents of sexual daring in places like cow-byres, we often asked whether this platoon of immoralists did not constitute a knock to the dairy trade in his natal zone.

Such passions were not only the result of a rural background but also an experiment in multilateral education carried out at Barry in the early part of the twentieth century – when Edgar Jones was headmaster. Jones was convinced that the 'orthodox type of Grammar School education, leading to Matriculation, was by no means suitable for a large proportion of our own pupils' and set about remodelling the school into four departments: general, technical, commercial, and agricultural.[16] David Walters, having retrained in agricultural science through courses at Aberystwyth, took charge of the new department, alongside his duties as science master.[17] By itself, this was not sufficient to justify scorn, but Walters's obvious disinterest in literature and the arts, and his West Walian provincialism, made anything more than a remote professional relationship unlikely. Gwyn experienced a similar difficulty with George Young Smith, a Barry native and old boy of the school, characterised as an 'apostle of cricket, High Toryism, and mathematics.' The two men accordingly 'argued passionately about social questions,' rarely seeing eye to eye.

Not all colleagues were kept at arm's length. Brynmor Ashton, who appeared in Gwyn's stories as Mr Selley, joined the school in 1950. 'Our classics man,' Gwyn wrote, 'held himself spellbound describing aloud, through a whole free period, the dark blue loveliness of the Aegean, the petrified world-mind of the Parthenon, the dusty pathos of eroded hills and frustrated heroes, who lived in poverty and desolation far below the last gleam of the Homeric sun.' Ashton edited the school magazine alongside Gwyn. They had inherited editorial responsibilities from the former English master, J. Howard Francis, upon his retirement in 1951. Francis was a 'connoisseur of contemporary writing and for long a dynamo of the Barry Arts Society,' exactly the sort of compatriot Gwyn favoured. But his strongest associations were with E. T. Griffiths, at least until the latter's retirement and departure for Australia in 1948; with Teifion Phillips, the gifted history master and later headmaster, who arrived in 1946; and with Sidney Jones, Gwyn's old WEA colleague from the Rhondda, who joined the school in 1942. Very short in height, with thick glasses, bald plate, sallow complexion, and a tiny, toothbrush moustache, Jones quickly became known as 'Tojo,' after the wartime Japanese prime minister. By all accounts he was hopeless at maintaining discipline in a classroom full of teenage boys but for Gwyn, he was a welcome reminder of home.

Teaching was never a vocational calling. It provided a stable income and not much more, and from the time of Leslie Mathews's arrival as headmaster in 1949, Gwyn was in constant search of a way out of the chalkface. He steadily became convinced that education was the basis of a 'schlemiel joke,' an archetype of Yiddish humour. The best response was to draw attention to the absurdity. In an interview with Michael Parkinson broadcast in 1971, Gwyn explained that

> you had this marvellous sense of a great jest that was going on all the time because there is something rather absurd, of course, about a domineering man with thirty captive children in a room, you know, teaching things which are going to be totally irrelevant to them for most of their lives. But, I must say, that I achieved a very good compromise most of the time: I mean, I didn't want to teach and they didn't want to be taught. That was the only way to make sense of it.

In an episode of the BBC series *One Pair of Eyes* broadcast in May 1968, Gwyn was pressed by the actor Robert Morley (1908–1992) to defend the teaching profession from the accusation was your schoolmaster really necessary? The episode was pitched in the *Radio Times* as revealing Morley's 'certain loathing of schoolmasters' and his belief that they were 'a corrupt body of creatures.' A graduate of Wellington College, which he often threatened to burn down in later life, Morley thought his acting career – which saw him win an Oscar in 1939 as the best supporting actor in *Marie Antoinette* – a form of 'revenge' on his former teachers. 'You're a second-class lot,' Morley began, 'purveying second-class information, why can't you come out of it? why can't you say we're going to teach children what they want to know? why can't you teach children cooking and sewing and useful things?' With a gurning grin on his face, which quickly became stern, his left hand resting beneath his suit jacket on his right shoulder, Gwyn turned to Morley and replied:

> The things at which they are going to be bored to death for the rest of their lives. This idea – set up a little factory in the school,

teach them to be handy with their hands – these poor schlemiels are going to leave school at fifteen or sixteen and do these ghastly, repetitive things until they die. There must be one period in their lives when somebody, even the shabby oafs that you are denouncing now, will open a few windows on the world.[18]

Perhaps because of his obvious understanding of the situation inside a classroom, Gwyn was warmly remembered by former pupils, who noted his ability to make them laugh – a precursor to, and a testing ground for, his television personality. Most are also honest in recalling that he showed relatively little interest in the day-to-day functions of either the classroom or the training of young minds. Gwyn's greatest and most successful efforts were reserved for extra-curricular activities where his ability to perform unencumbered was at its best, something classroom visitors also picked up on. Writing in 1950, one school inspector noted that,

The Master responsible for the teaching [of Spanish], who has had ten years' experience, eight of which have been spent at this school, is an Honours graduate in Spanish of the University of Oxford. He brings to his work enthusiasm and scholarship. He speaks the language fluently, having spent a term at the University of Madrid, and has made two further useful stays in Spain. Some very effective *lecture explique* in the foreign language was heard.[19]

Gwyn was a popular speaker at the literary and debating society. As one enthusiastic observer reported in *The Barrian*, 'Mr Thomas is a favourite and never fails to attract a large crowd.' Audiences of several hundred listened to Gwyn extemporise on topics as various as famous Welshmen, the growth of the entertainment industry, castles, youth movements, and Spain, of course.[20] As he had been in Cardigan, he was an important influence in the development of the drama society, and he worked alongside Sidney Jones to run the Barry branch of Urdd Gobaith Cymru, the Welsh-language youth association. Given his vocal antagonism towards the language throughout his adult life, Gwyn's support for the Urdd during his teaching career was notable, although it seems likely the chance to work alongside Sidney Jones was the chief motivation.

Gwyn's earliest lecture to a school society seems to have been about his visit to Spain as a student, which he described as an 'uneventful journey from South Wales to Madrid, via France.' He spoke about the meals he bought, about his travels around Spain, and about the University of Madrid 'which was a magnificent new building at the time of [his] visit. It had been built with money obtained from a State lottery but was unfortunately destroyed in the Civil War.' He concluded with remarks on bull fighting, pointing out that the sport was 'not as popular in Spain as we foreigners imagine.'[21] The exact contents of the talk have been lost, but the contours were sufficiently outlined in *The Barrian* in 1943 as to echo the Spanish passages present in *A Few Selected Exits*. They may even have been the first draft. Gwyn's next talk about his Spanish adventures followed a holiday he took with Lyn in San Sebastian in the summer of 1947. It was his first return to the country he regarded as his second home. The talk was published in full in *The Barrian* in 1948 and is repeated here.

The journey to the South was full of clatter. We saw the fantastic barricades of half-demolished ferro-concrete emplacements at Boulogne, decayed teeth in a madman's mouth. It is to be hoped that they will be removed and the roofs restored to Boulogne's poorer quarter before they unleash another and more efficient war; there is nothing like leaving the road to a fuller civilisation tidy behind one. On the way down to Paris we sat in a stifling compartment, windows open, with a furious side-wind laying every particle of grit from the engine upon us. Every garment we wore was discoloured and one hour more of it would have seen us certified as patent-fuel briquettes and dumped forthwith in the tender. Paris was a parched, tired, bad-tempered place. We had two meals featuring a brand of sausage based on the same principles as those buna-bonzo balls that held the record for the highest bounce in my generation. We left both helpings on the plate explaining that we were only going as far as Spain and asked them to allow us to have another chew at them on the way back. The waiter smiled because I did not have quite the right idioms to call all I meant without carrying gestures too far.

The approach to Spain must always be a major source of enchantment to all who have not been knocked flat and under the seat by the long journey down from Paris. Our train was packed tight and got so hot they did without coal for the last hundred miles. They showed us the water and it bubbled. There was a host of Boy Scouts, earnest and wholesome, diligently giving up their seats in every compartment except our own which was filled with some of the finest and dourest sitters I ever wish to see outside those Indian sects that are reputed to do it for a living. We tried every cunning device, even introducing ourselves as George Marshall and consort, and putting our hands significantly into our pockets from time to time, but the French had made their last concessions to the Anglo-Saxon powers, for that trip anyway. Still, to see the dark-green mountains rise out of Spain as one approaches Irun, especially after the endless tedium of the fir-country, the pit-prop acres of the Landes, casts an immediate spell. That excitement of the spirit survives even the shock of walking across the International Bridge and doing business with customs-officials dressed formally in white suits, smoking cigars

thick as a tree and staring at you with eyes so muddily dull with
knowledge and acceptance of chicanery among men that all
sense of innocence drops promptly away from you. We were
asked whether we had any contraband. We had some ideas
about freedom that would have wrung the Caudillo's withers
but, as we wanted to see what went on to the South of those
tall, castellated mountains, we said nothing.

We made our centre in San Sebastian. It seemed, in 1947, a
species of trough at which most of the folk in West Europe with
money to spare got their heads down and ate hard. Everyone in
Spain with anything to sell or steal had come there to get away
either from the broiling heat of the Meseta or the people they stole
from. The stretch of sand seemed hardly adequate to the throng
who queued up for the chance to leave their mark on it. Along the
Concha, the famous bay, there is a string of luxury hotels where
the prices are so high the cashiers have to do their work in an
oxygen tent. Everything in San Sebastian is so slick and new it
makes the warm sea look ridiculously old-fashioned. It is a
paradise for the children of the rich who teem on the tamarisk-
lined boulevards, escorted by nannies dressed in the authentic
fashion of 1900, vast, noisy women with tiny bonnets and
monstrous, propeller-shaped bows four feet broad bringing up in
the rear. It was instructive for one who has brooded much on the
austerities of the North to see all the pampered brats of Iberia
sucking away intermittently at small ice-cream cones at one and
eight a time. In the background, less favoured humans, not nearly
as addicted to sleeping as the sturdy British think they are, work
hard for wages which, with careful saving for a year or so, might
promote them a whole ice-cream wafer in lieu of social justice.

Flanking the town are the two mountains of Igueldo and Ulia,
miracles of cool graciousness. From Igueldo one sees eighty
miles down into the Basque country. At least, I was told that,
and when ten or more miles from home I always permit myself

the luxury of a nit-witted credulity. On the summit of Igueldo, reached by a funicular railway so jerky in its movements one's mind keeps hiccoughing with panic for a good hour after getting to the top, there is a small pleasure park in which thin donkeys do what they can under great loads of heavy children. There is a cageful of monkeys too, seeming in their assorted antics to be even more transparently frank under the strong Spanish sun than in the nonconformist dimnesses of Regent's Park. From the southern summit of the mountain, we see a white, beautifully eloquent hill-road whirling out of sight over the dark range towards Castille, the heart-land. At the spot from which we watch the road, there is a large bear in a small cage built into the solid rock. Its name is Ursula. A board above the cage tells us that it was captured as a cub and adopted as a mascot by a General Miranda who performed a triumphant march through the Asturias in 1938, picking up what besides bear cubs we are not told. Nor does Ursula care. It has long outgrown its cave, its belief in any dignity on earth. It is dirty, distracted. Occasionally it climbs up the little tree stump which has been stuck into its concrete floor to remind it of the roving freedom of which the thoughtful and triumphant Miranda deprived it. It gobbles up apples and nuts and looks as if it would much prefer to be nibbling a sample of fresh Spaniard from among those who are grouped around the cage's top, crying its name, lovely and sad to hear in Spanish, Oorsoola, Oorsoola. And she, looking at them with a dimming malignancy and slumping back into her prison of rock and concrete, glances at the wonderful road across the valley which plunges over the mountains to Castille. A thousand feet below, the sea washes in, gelatinously slow. To the right, where the bay sweeps around, there is a gaol, a very large gaol, guarded by soldiers who sit in the stale shadow of an unswept porch. They, like Ursula, are bored, but stupefied beyond even malignancy.

Opposite Igueldo, Monte Ulia, a hillside lined with shadowed paths that wind spirally to the summit. Half way up one comes across a secluded, inviting corner. This is the English cemetery, hedged around with evergreen bushes and primly kept. It is dedicated to our dead of the Spanish War of Independence. An impressive monument in granite shows grenadiers of 1812 manhandling a gun carriage. There are few things more joltingly poignant than the lines of toilsome agony on their faces. On the rock face, the words, in both tongues, 'England, Spain thanks you.' One looks down at the Atlantic and at the thin line of coast that curls up to Bordeaux; one thinks of Rupert Brooke who himself saw this soundless and dignified nook; one remembers the other lads who left Britain to hold Madrid against the Moors when they poured over the Guadarrama in 1937 and who, like Wellington's grenadiers of granite straining immemorially around their unmoving gun, will be forever in Spain. And for their gesture, no thanks have yet been given.

So much to tell, so painful to select the things for telling. Let us end with a Sunday afternoon in late August. The San Sebastian bull arena was crowded to a point where even the bulls felt stuffy. There is something about a bullfight, a hint of its having been one of man's first gestures of defiance at the outrageous antics of fear and death that have hustled him along, that hurts the clean, air-conditioned notions of the Northerner. We saw the ace-torero of Spain, the slender melancholic Manolete, idol of every bull-fighting crowd in the land until his fame and fortune curdled their affection and created in them a yelling wish to see his blood spilled. He moved around the bull's head with the languor of a snake. He seemed at moments to beard the bull's very horns and ride them with a brief indifference, as we would a bus. Off and on, he flipped a glance up at the crowd cold as the handle of a coffin, caustic as only a loveless wisdom and mastery can be. It seemed as if he were being struck for the first time by a clear wondering glimpse into the whole apparatus of sadistic horror of which for ten years, from the day he broke loose from a Cordoban slum to make music with his cape, he had been so ineffably graceful and nerveless an agent. A month after we saw him, fighting a Miura bull in Linares, he was killed. The crowds that had wished to see him fall ceased to yell and wept. He was buried with a lush extravagance and Ursula from her hole in the rock watched the white road, eloquent and swift, that sped across the mountain to Castille.[22]

The same trip was described with rather less enthusiasm by Lyn during interviews with Michael Parnell in the 1980s, when the latter was researching his biography of Gwyn. Lyn recalled being 'increasingly frightened' by the atmosphere and by the potential risks her husband took given the pro-Republican company he kept during their time in Spain. 'The thought of the proscribed books in their luggage,' wrote Parnell, 'terrified Lyn as they passed through Customs for the return journey and underwent the scrutiny of stern-faced and suspicious officials.'[23] As the historian Sasha Pack has observed, foreigners were often 'subject to what amounted to legalized extortion' by the border guards who required visitors to 'convert an extravagant amount of currency into Spanish pesetas at inflated exchange rates.'[24] No wonder Lyn, who had never before been abroad, and was much less politically engaged than her husband, was unsettled by the experience. For Gwyn, Spain experienced as a permanently employed schoolteacher in 1947 was considerably easier than as a penurious student in 1933; though he was far from naïve about the political circumstances of the Caudillo's regime. As he later put it, 'all around me were Spaniards and Spain and I had no real wish to know.'[25]

Alongside the sternness of officials, the watchful eye of the

Civil Guard, the stale but dangerous, right-wing atmosphere of Franco's dictatorship, and Gwyn's activities whilst on holiday namely visiting Republicans and seeking out anti-fascist publications and newspapers, which no doubt drew attention and certainly made Lyn nervous, was the reality of travelling to and from Spain so soon after the Second World War. It was by no means an easy or straightforward prospect. The border between France and Spain had been officially closed to traffic on 1 March 1946 in response to the execution of the communist Cristino García by Franco's regime and did not open again until February 1948. The only way through for visitors was to walk across the international bridge between Hendaye and Irun. Relations remained frosty. British tourists required a visa to enter and there was little desire on the part of the Labour government for improving relations between Britain and Spain, either.[26] Despite these constraints, and the complexity of their journey, Gwyn and Lyn were part of a growing wave of European tourists to post-war Spain and were (ironically) an early part of the rehabilitation process which slowly but steadily reintegrated the dictatorship into the international mainstream. In 1946, even with the border between France and Spain closed, eighty thousand people visited; by 1950, the figure had climbed to nearly three hundred thousand.[27]

Arriving home in early September 1947, Gwyn wrote to his brother-in-law, Bill, to let him know they were back and to complain of feeling 'dog tired' rather than refreshed. Getting home from Spain 'was a nightmare,' he added, 'two whole days without sleep improves nobody.'[28] With the new school year set to begin, Gwyn hardly relished the thought of returning to the classroom – he already had a profound sense of being trapped in an environment which was not entirely suited to his enthusiasms or intellect. He wanted, more than anything, to get on with writing. And so, he invented a character to contain the boredom he felt, imagining himself in the world of Ring Lardner, Raymond Chandler, Dashiell Hammett, and Damon Runyon. The latter, as Gwyn was to observe, had 'some of the most excitingly horrible material in modern life to turn into fiction, and by that oblique, sidling style of his managed to create the highest comedy.' For the moment, Gwyn had the classroom. There, his fast-paced American patter and his gangster-style slouch hat and trench coat, which made him look like a B-movie film star, earned the nickname Killer. 'I would have been more at home in New York or Chicago,' Gwyn might have thought privately to himself as he tried to teach verbal conjugations and would later say aloud for an HTV television crew, 'I would have been a more significant writer in many ways.'

*

Killer's American world soon found its way onto the page. The association was first made by the communist literary critic, Allen Hutt.[29] 'This may sound an odd, incongruous – a fantastic combination,' Hutt wrote, 'but the sardonic, dry, occasionally devastating manner of the celebrated Damon [Runyon] has been brilliantly transmuted into Welsh mining-valley terms by Gwyn Thomas.' Hutt had in mind the punchy, street-level episodic crime stories written by Runyon (and Ring Lardner, who adopted a similar style) and published in the 1930s. Gwyn heartily approved of the comparison. It came from 'the kind of world into which I was born in the valley,' he explained in an episode of the BBC's *Bookstand* in March 1962, 'at a time when militancy was everywhere, where the people were a ferment of discontent, where irony, contradiction, absurdity, were the common idiom of the day.' He continued:

when I decided to use this material in fiction, I was faced with a very, very great problem. I was living in a society so complacent that it would not readily accept the material that I was using. Quite apart from the fact that there was a kind of fad of disliking literature that came out of mining valleys because they are damnable and undesirable places, but the very idiom of these people the kind of apostolic, evangelical note that they struck was certainly out of tune with the prevailing English idiom of the time which was restrained, gentlemanly, indirect.

And the first novels that I wrote were so angry, so searing, so wild, that there was a legend that all publishers' readers in London who had to do with my books were equipped with firefighting equipment, asbestos underclothes and so on, which enabled them to read these books without undue discomfort. And this might have gone on, of course, for the remainder of my life – these wonderful things that I had discovered there in my background, these wonderful absurdities, these great nourishing absurdities that a writer should really dream of – ... had I not found the kind of idiom that I needed I might have gone through life silent.

But it was my encounter with Damon Runyon, an American writer not of the first class by any means, most emphatically of the second class, and I would say this is a specific for all writers: if they are to cherish a writer let him be of the second rate for it is a second-rate writer who yields his secrets most easily. Now Runyon was dealing with an environment quite as repellent, quite as incredible in its way as the one that I inherited in South Wales. His was the world of Broadway. His was the world of the kidnapper, the extortionist, the hipster, the thug. The men who were in and out of Sing Sing[30] and Dannemora[31], whom he got to know intimately well, of course, as a journalist. And it is this platoon of journalists, I think, these hard-bitten men whose souls were absolutely pockmarked with disillusion – the Lardners, the Benchleys[32], and the Runyons – who I think have contributed some of the most interesting literature of this century because they are dealing with an underworld. And it's an attempt to find an answer to the underworld that underlies most of the wisdom in writing.

With humour, slang, and colourfully named characters, Runyon's world of the New York hoodlum was easily translated into a Rhondda accent. 'Harry the Horse' from Broadway could easily have presented his ticket to 'Charlie Lush the Ush' at the Coliseum in Meadow Prospect without the slightest bit of confusion. 'Many of Runyon's stylistic tricks,' Gwyn recalled, 'the use of the present tense, the avoidance of "man" and "woman" in favour of sub-human terms like "guy" and "doll", are common in the everyday speech of hoodlums. More credit to Runyon for having made such good literary use of it. It is so right.'[33] More credit to Gwyn, too, although there was a cost: amongst literary critics, both contemporary and in more recent times, the lighter work of the 1950s and 1960s has tended to be regarded as both less impressive and less significant than the novels and short stories with which Gwyn announced his literary career in the second half of the 1940s. It was a distinction he himself acknowledged:

I suppose, if I were to appear as a ghost at some bar of literary history one hundred years from now in the company of Maxim Gorky on the one hand and Damon Runyon on the other representing the two extremes of serious and indifference, that I might indeed feel, that with the sort of material that I have had to deal with, that great, resounding, sulphurous novels of the Dickensian sort could have been written. Instead of which I have compromised with what possibly I, were I a severe critic, would denounce as the verbal equivalent of tiddly winks.

He defended the choice he had made pointing to the literary accessibility provided by his Rhondda Runyonism. Gwyn concluded, 'I go back to my first point: had I written these great, solemn, reverberating novels, it is likely that they would never have seen the light of day. At least I have crept into a little bit of light, with this strange trick of slyness learned from a master in his field whom I salute: Damon Runyon.'[34]

But how had Gwyn learned of the American? It seems very likely that he became aware of Runyon from radio adaptations, which were first broadcast on the BBC in 1939, or from the cinema, rather than printed collections of short stories.[35] The first book-length collection of Runyon's work to appear in Britain, *Guys and Dolls*, was released by the Norwich-based publisher Jarrolds in 1932. Although this introduced Runyon to the British market, the cost of the volume – seven shillings and sixpence – put it well out of the reach of working-class readers. In fact, when the London-based publisher Constable decided to release its own volumes a few years later, they were able to claim that the writer was unfairly neglected and unknown. More accessible were the short stories published in *Nash's Pall Mall Magazine* between April 1932 and June 1934, although this was not one of the periodicals Gwyn read.[36] By the time the BBC began broadcasting its adaptations, Constable had released three volumes of Runyon's work: *More Than Somewhat* in the summer of 1937, *Furthermore* in January 1938, and *Take It Easy* in October 1938.[37] These brought a relatively wide readership, amplified further by the release of a cheap edition of *More than Somewhat* in October 1939.[38]

Gwyn was securely employed at that time and could afford to buy books, especially in their more affordable form. It is therefore surely not a coincidence that when asked by *The Teacher* in the 1960s for a list of ten books for the budding humourist writer, Gwyn chose *More Than Somewhat*. It was, he wrote, the key to understanding Runyon – and surely the key to understanding the origins of Rhondda Runyonism. Gwyn was drawn to the story, he explained, because it was one in which 'one goon shoots another to get his place as a second tenor in the vocal quartet.' Gwyn's American enthusiasms were well-served in the late 1930s. The BBC broadcast several anthologies of humour and satire in that period, staging readings of the work of Will Rogers, George S. Kaufman, Clarence Day, and Dorothy Parker. A further flourish of interest followed in the spring of 1946 with 'Laugh That Off,' a Sunday lunchtime series on the Home Service which showcased, in addition to the writers featured in earlier programmes, the work of James Thurber, the poet Ogden Nash, and, of course, Damon Runyon. It all formed the creative context as Gwyn set about writing *The Alone to the Alone* and *The Dark Philosophers* and became ever more overt as his career developed. American critics immediately allied Gwyn's writing with Runyon and hinted at the probable influence. It was as if, wrote Lewis Gannett of the *New York Herald Tribune* reviewing *The Dark Philosophers* in May 1947, 'Thomas Hardy met Damon Runyon over a loving cup of small beer.'[39]

Gannett added that the novel was peppered with the 'doctrine of Karl Marx in the rarefied form once known as Christian Socialism.' Another observer thought Gwyn had fused Runyon with the seventeenth-century allegorist, John Bunyan. Reginald Moore, Gwyn's erstwhile literary patron, made the connection himself in his introduction to *Modern Reading 16* in the autumn of 1947. Moore noted that the Welshman had 'already been compared with Dickens, Anderson, Steinbeck, Runyon, Thurber and Dumas, and a *New York Herald Tribune* staff writer recently bemusedly speculated where this would end – whether the thing would become a national game. And this, mark you, before publication. Personally, were I Mr

Thomas, I should cable "Am willing to settle for Dickens and Thurber!" His publishers are free from blame: it is just something which has happened, and I am sorry about it because he will find himself forced to live up to a reputation forged by other people.'[40] The comparison was a flattering one: James Thurber (1894–1961), one of the leading humourists of the mid-twentieth century, a regular contributor to and cartoonist for the *New Yorker*, was best known for his short story *The Secret Life of Walter Mitty*, which was adapted for cinema in 1947 by Norman McLeod (1898–1964).

Throughout the short stories and novellas written in the early 1940s, Gwyn appropriated both the 'laconic style of the American detective hero,' as popularised by Raymond Chandler, Dashiell Hammett, and James M. Cain, and the Runyon-style buffoon. The result was a set of characters who spoke with an accent 'derived from the cinema and popular fiction.'[41] This suggests that the often-sharp distinction drawn between the supposedly 'darker' early Gwyn Thomas of the 1940s and the 'lighter' novelist of the 1950s has been overstated. For a long time, they existed side-by-side as Gwyn toyed with various creative means of translating the lived experience of the valleys into fiction, and in different forms. The lighter version won out in the 1950s, in large part because of commercial necessity. But in the 1940s, having failed to find any useful models in contemporary British literature, Gwyn had turned to, and adapted, American forms. In so doing, Meadow Prospect and the Kingdom of the Chip quickly replaced the political panorama and social melodrama of Lewis Jones's *Cwmardy* (1937) and *We Live* (1939), or Gwyn's own *Sorrow For Thy Sons*, without ever losing its authentic sense of place or capacity for critique.

By 1947, Gwyn had committed to writing a second novel for Nicholson and Watson, the British publishers of *The Alone to the*

Alone. The result showed the writer's continued experimentation in style and form, whilst satisfying his desire to expose the flaws of the post-war New Jerusalem. Set in a contemporary Rhondda, it was a comedy of manners rich in foresight about social democracy, the onset of affluence, and the compromises involved with living 'decently after reorganising within oneself the ambitions that spring from commercial and conservative values.'[42] The completed manuscript, titled *The Thinker and the Thrush*, although at one point known as *Another Night, Another Day*, was submitted in the autumn of 1947 with publication due by the end of 1948. The character at the heart of *The Thinker and the Thrush* was Stobo Wilkie, an ambitious assistant to an ageing greengrocer called Mr Ellicott. Although born into a society full of collective values, Stobo Wilkie wants to 'get on' and doesn't much care how. Except, of course, that to do so he must engage with a society and with systems of government which are themselves absurd. 'At bottom,' Parnell concluded, Stobo Wilkie is 'despite everything, optimistic, tough and resourceful, and we care about the dilemmas he is negotiating.'

But was the novel, as Parnell concluded, written 'at an important stage in [Gwyn's] realisation that his searing social anger was more effectively conveyed obliquely than through the direct attack he had tried using in his younger days?' It was certainly composed in a period of experimentation but had its roots in the Runyonesque style developed for *The Alone to the Alone* and *The Dark Philosophers*. Characters met in a Greek café, rather than an Italian one, but the effect was the same, and there was the ever-present pub and the cinemas, The Comfy and The Cosy. The latter eventually gets renamed The Taj. Set in Bandy Lane, rather than Meadow Prospect or the Windy Way, these subtle differences suggest a writer not yet settled on the precise form of his creation but nonetheless clear about his intended message. The published version of the novel, edited by Parnell to amplify its prototypical status, lost some of the rhetorical detail and Gwyn's political voice. Thus, said the editor, allowing a more 'sinewy and muscular text to emerge.' It is not at all clear that this was the original intention. Instead, the novel deserves to be understood as part of that wave of Gwyn's writing to emerge from the Second World War. Those were its roots, even as the author was in a period of transition.

No sooner than work on *The Thinker and the Thrush* was completed and submitted to Nicholson and Watson had Gwyn moved on to his next project. It was to be the most ambitious novel he ever attempted. Writing furiously and at high speed, he quickly filled numerous exercise books in longhand. 'Gwyn is working like a maniac,' Lyn confessed in a letter to Nan and Bill sent just before Easter 1948, adding that the book 'will be about six hundred pages when it is finished.' About three hundred pages had already been written and typed leaving Gwyn, in Lyn's words, 'very weary and tired.' In a separate letter to his sister, Gwyn said much the same. 'I've been working pretty constantly this holiday,' he wrote, 'and I shall probably feel like a miller's husk by the time I go back to school. Never mind, there is something about the sight of a class which makes me go slow as surely as the thought of a novel makes me go fast.'[43] The working title of the new novel was *My Root On Earth*. Assuming that his two-book contract with Nicholson and Watson had been met following the submission of *The Thinker and the Thrush*, Gwyn offered it to Michael Joseph Ltd.

My Root on Earth drew on Gwyn's substantial knowledge of the early industrial history of the coalfield and its semi-mythical figures such as William Price, Dic Penderyn, and Guto Nyth Bran. He was, in effect, picking up the threads of the collaborative project dreamed up with Walt a decade earlier and his old WEA teaching. To establish the novel's structure and environment, as well as how to approach the mythology, Gwyn penned a short story called *Thy Need*, which was published in the *Welsh Review* in the summer of 1948 – the first time any of his work had been taken on by the Welsh literary establishment. He explained to Nan, 'the Gito [sic] mentioned in the story as having inspired Uncle Onllwyn is that very character from Nyth Bran whose record of achievements was shown us proudly by the Jake [i.e. Gwyn's father] when he took us on our first walk up to Llanwonno and left us marvelling in the graveyard while he nipped around the corner for a pint.' Set in interwar Meadow Prospect, which had first been introduced to readers in *Where Did I Put My Pity?* in 1946, the story was a classic of Rhondda Runyonism. Three friends observing the world, an Italian refreshment vendor, and an upstart whose ambition and determination were absurdly at odds with the community around him.

'Mine is a selfish wish,' Uncle Onllwyn tells the three friends, 'I want tools, a smallholding and the feel of fertile earth for myself.' But as always in Gwyn's writing, the upstart begins to soften and falls back in line with communal habits and ambitions. Having won the race at the heart of the narrative through whatever means necessary, he hands over the prize money to his rival Cynlais Moore, who has many needs but spends some of his new wealth buying drinks for the friends like a ha'penny philanthropist. At the end, the group of friends make their way to the Library and Institute 'where, that evening, the librarian, Salathiel Cull, known as Cull the Lull, because he was a political quietist and a proponent of gradualist views, was going to give them a talk on why the world's greatest herds of driven folk should huddle into a compact and cosy mass and let evil bite them to the heart until its teeth were worn to the unhurting stump.' *Thy Need* had a long-lasting afterlife indicative of its enduring popularity: it was selected by Gwyn Jones, who had been the editor of *Welsh Review*, for inclusion in his *Welsh Short*

Stories collection published by Oxford University Press in 1956 and was one of three short stories by Gwyn Thomas to appear in the Library of Wales collections *Story I* and *Story II* in 2014 – the selection made in that instance by the editor, Dai Smith.[44]

As he was planning *My Root on Earth*, Gwyn realised that he needed to shift the setting and narrative away from either the end of industrialisation in the 1930s, or the compromises of the post-war New Jerusalem, which were the focal points of his other published work, to the beginning of South Wales a century earlier. He wanted to explore the origins of the social and cultural conflicts between labour and capital. Since Meadow Prospect in the 1830s had been no more than a few hillside farms, it too had to be set aside. Gwyn needed a new setting and turned to the only logical alternative: Merthyr Tydfil, which he translated into his literary universe as Moonlea. 'Towns like this here have grown up all in a space of about ten or fifteen years,' he had one of his characters explain, 'Streets, churches, chapels, courts, taverns, all around and serving the foundries. At first it was fine. It stayed fine for as long as Penbury and his friends were riding their particular tide and the world kept calling out for iron and more iron.' Gwyn had never written in this way before. Having escaped the over-familiarity of the Rhondda, he could set his creative talents to work telling South Wales' unique industrial history.

On the surface, the novel offered a straightforward historical drama with socialist realist inflections. Arrayed against the oppressed ironworkers were the up-and-coming ironmasters such as Richard Penbury (Gwyn's take on Richard Crawshay and his descendants) and the older, aristocratic landowners such as Lord Plimmon (or the real-life Lord Bute) – they too were threatened by the ironmasters but were no less reactionary and ruthless. Set in between the two sides was the artist, Alan Hugh Leigh, a travelling harpist, who could speak to both.

Music appealed to the wealthy in a way that, as Penbury's daughter, Helen, put it, the savagery of protest and appeals for better wages did not. 'I've been in a thousand little poverty-bitten places on the bare slopes of unkind hills,' Leigh explained, the voice as much Gwyn's own as a fictional creation, 'where men and women lead meagre bitter lives.' But hope had not been exhausted, for 'in Moonlea and places like it the people for the first time are not quite helpless. They are close together and in great numbers. Their collective hand is big enough to point at what is black and damnable in the present, at what is to be wished in the future.'

The first full draft of *My Root on Earth* was completed in the summer of 1948. Gwyn packaged the typescript and sent it off to Michael Joseph's offices in London. Then he wrote to Nan once more to complain of being 'mortally tired' and that 'trying to teach Spanish and packing the writing of a pretty big novel into the compass of a year have nearly landed me on my back.' And not just a novel. Alongside *Thy Need*, Gwyn had had four short stories and essays published on both sides of the Atlantic, a fifth, which was written in 1948, appeared in America early in 1949. Gwyn was overworking, perhaps fearful that if he took a break the opportunities would soon dry up. He was also fed up with life in Barry and the routine of the schoolmaster and so wrote for comfort and with the hope that writing would eventually offer a way out of the classroom. As he explained to his friend Glyn Jones, a fellow teacher and writer, 'I think I'd like to shift. I've been here for what strikes me as a tediously long time. I'm going up to Cumberland for the summer holiday and if the place suits me and I see a really fine opportunity I might try to sink a root there. I seem to have reached the tether's end here, to have signed a kind of sinister pact with the pupils to denounce Spanish with equal vehemence.' In a more reflective mood, Gwyn added that when the first abundant vigour is gone, teaching becomes incompatible with even the most tenuous intention of doing original literary work. Under the burden of this horrible and exhausting double-life one finds it less and less easy to keep away from the sharp-toothed mouth of one's own deadly mannerisms.[45]

There was to be no such luck. Just before setting off for the Lake District, Gwyn received a letter from Michael Joseph agreeing to publish *My Root on Earth* but only after the excision of almost two hundred pages of text, characters, incidents, and the replayed trial of Dic Penderyn. Fed up but pragmatic, Gwyn got on with the required changes, believing in the end that 'books come, books go.' He nevertheless felt, as he told Glyn Jones later, that the 'book has never possessed the balance that it struck me as having when the last page came out of the typewriter.'

With *My Root on Earth* complete, at least for the moment, Gwyn immediately turned his mind to ideas for his next novel. It was to be another historical epic which he had already titled *The Dark Neighbour*. Taking inspiration from his experiences in Spain and rich knowledge of Golden Age Spanish drama, he planned an allegory of interwar fascism and the extinguishing of the Spanish Republic and its democratic values – all set amongst the Spanish Moors of the fifteenth century. Although cautiously happy to publish the novel, Michael Joseph again pushed for extensive cuts to the original. Gwyn found the experience dispiriting. 'The novel which is now with the publishers is having a pretty bleak time,' he told Glyn Jones, 'and as far as I can see is not likely to emerge into the light of day. I am in no mood to go bargaining and cutting. They probably sense in me a potentially best-selling two-rapes-a-chapter man and if that's what they want, that's what they'll get, with the rate being jacked up to three in any novel appearing in time for the Christmas rush. My raw material in this line is inexhaustible.'[46] Gwyn withdrew *The Dark Neighbour* from Michael Joseph not long afterwards and set about finding a more sympathetic publisher.

Commensurate with the disarray at Michael Joseph, Gwyn learned that Nicholson and Watson were unable to publish *The Thinker and the Thrush* on schedule in 1948, preferring an early 1949 release instead. A clash with the release of *My Root on Earth* – by then known by its final title, *All Things Betray Thee* – was inevitable. Michael Joseph had already lined up adverts to appear in the press from January 1949 to build anticipation ahead of the novel's release in May. Just as Reginald Moore had warned in 1946, Gwyn's desire to get his work into print at any cost almost brought his still emerging writing career down on top of him. This time Gwyn made the right decision: *The Thinker and the Thrush*, the weaker of the two novels, was sacrificed and *All Things Betray Thee* was published to critical acclaim in the spring. The experience was scarring, however, and it was no surprise that Gwyn was 'in no mood to go bargaining.' But if he was to continue as a writer of fiction, and find a happier professional future than the current compromise afforded him, he needed the right outlet for his work. Ironically, given the fate of *Sorrow For Thy Sons* ten years earlier, this proved to be the left-leaning but increasingly anti-communist, Victor Gollancz whose publishing empire was now moving away from the popular front politics of the Left Book Club into contemporary fiction.

Gwyn's agent offered Gollancz sight of both *The Thinker and the Thrush* and *The Dark Neighbour* but the publisher rejected them instantly having been made aware that they had been handled by rivals. Instead, Gollancz proposed a refashioning of Gwyn's writing into something lighter and distinctive – social comedies better suited to the rising affluence of 1950s Britain. The first taste of this new Gwyn Thomas was a short story, 'Tomorrow I Shall Miss You Less,' which appeared in the National Coal Board magazine, *Coal*, in December 1950.[47] Its litany of characters included what were to be staples of the next decade of novels and short stories: Paolo Tasso the Italian café owner, Luther Cann the owner of the Coliseum cinema, Charlie Lush the Ush 'ticket-taker and thrower-out' at the Col, and Salathiel Cull, the librarian at the Library and Institute in Windy Way. But these were hardly new inventions. Most had appeared in short stories written since the early 1940s and some had already made it in print, and recently. They all reappeared in *The World Cannot Hear You*, Gwyn's first novel for Victor Gollancz, and the only one to be deliberately subtitled and designated 'a comedy,' which was published in June 1951. To the eternal regret of those who most admired the artistic achievement of *All Things Betray Thee*, Gwyn never returned to Moonlea.

*

The topsy-turvy relationships Gwyn developed with his publishers in the second half of the 1940s prompts the question of what might have happened had he been able to find greater consistency and development of his literary identity. What sort of career might he have had? Could he have escaped teaching much earlier, as he wished? A useful comparison can be made with the working-class County Durham writer and Gwyn's near contemporary, Sid Chaplin (1916–1986). The two appeared alongside each other in *Saturday Saga* released by Progress Publishing in 1946, although Chaplin had previously secured publication of short stories in magazines such as John Lehmann's *Penguin New Writing* and Woodrow Wyatt's *Short Story To-Day*. Chaplin's debut collection, *The Leaping Lad*,

which won the Atlantic Award for Literature, was issued by
Phoenix in 1946, and established his reputation as an
authentic, appealing voice, and gave him enough money to take
time out from working underground to write his first novel. *My
Fate Cries Out* appeared in 1949. It was followed in 1950 by
The Thin Seam. By then, Chaplin had begun working for the
National Coal Board as a publicity officer and wrote a monthly
column for *Coal*. This led to a long delay in writing novels, with
Chaplin's later works all appearing in the 1960s.[48] The second
wave led to Chaplin's association with the 'Angry Young Men'
of the late fifties and early sixties, writers such as Yorkshire's
Stan Barstow and David Storey, Nottingham's Alan Sillitoe, and
the South Walians Alun Richards and Ron Berry.

In America and Europe, readers and reviewers were unaware
of the inconsistencies which affected Gwyn's career in Britain.
Often, a single publisher was responsible for issuing Gwyn's
novels – Little, Brown and then Macmillan in the United States
or Feltrinelli in Italy – and so they were able to manufacture an
image somewhat at odds with Gwyn Thomas the comic writer,
which was the perception which came to prevail in Britain after
1950. In Europe, Gwyn was regarded chiefly as a socialist
realist; in America he was understood as a follower of the hard-
boiled tradition of Chandler, Hammett, and Runyon, funny at
times but laced with progressive ideals. This distinction was the
direct result of decisions about which novels were to be
published, when they were published, the formatting, and
whether they were to be made available in English or in
translation; and in Little, Brown's case, as Jack Aistrop explained
to Elizabeth Berridge, with an eye on shaping a prize asset:

> Gwyn Thomas is well fixed in the States. Little, Brown intend
> to spend a lot of money on him and say that they have a winner
> in him. Another Moore discovery well on the way to stardom.[49]

The Dark Philosophers, the first of Gwyn's writings to be published abroad, which appeared in the United Kingdom in the compendium *Triad One*, was thus issued in the United States, continental Europe, and the Soviet Union as a stand-alone novella.[50] Titles also changed, especially in America: *All Things Betray Thee* became *Leaves in the Wind*, *The Alone to the Alone* became *Venus and the Voters*, and *The Love Man* became *A Wolf at Dusk*. Gwyn's first short-story collection, with the central short story 'Oscar,' was not published at all outside of Britain.

The first European release of Gwyn's work was in Norway in the autumn of 1948, when the Oslo-based Tiden published Fredrik Wulfsberg's translation of *The Dark Philosophers*.[51] *Pastor Emmanuel og hans Kjærlighet* was sold as the work of one of the 'freshest and funniest' writers to have emerged recently from Britain, and it was warmly welcomed by Norwegian reviewers.[52] Per Gottschalk, a prominent music impresario and author, told readers of the intellectual weekly *Morgenbladet* that 'irony leaps from every page of the book,' although he warned that Gwyn's 'observations are sometimes overpowering.'[53] The communist journalist and critic, Johanna Bugge Olsen, thought the book a 'sparkling, talented and original work,' and praised the writer's freshness and clarity in depicting his people.[54] Similar views were expressed across the Norwegian spectrum, from social democratic newspapers to those more typically associated with liberal and conservative opinion. That of the Telemark *Arbeiderblad* was typical. 'Thomas,' the newspaper recorded, 'is practically unknown in this country, but in England he has already made a name for himself. *The Dark Philosophers* came out in 1946 and was his first book. ... [it is] full of such cracking humour that one is tempted to pick it up and start all over again.'[55]

Gwyn had a similar reception in Switzerland, where the

German language translation of *The Dark Philosophers* appeared in 1951.[56] As in Norway, Gwyn's work was picked up by a left-wing publisher. Büchergilde Gutenberg was founded in Frankfurt in 1924 as a co-operative – the company name translates as Book Guild – with the intention of publishing cheap editions of socially-committed novels and other progressive literature, and making them affordable for working-class people across the German-speaking world.[57] Gwyn was treated unquestionably as a socialist writer and the novel likewise. One reviewer, writing for the Social Democratic Party's *Rote Revue* thought Gwyn a poet and enthused that they could think of no other book which would be as successful in turning its readers into socialists.[58] As if to underscore this potential, parts of *The Dark Philosophers*, translated by Lina Fankhauser as *Die Liebe des Reverend Emmanuel*, were serialised in the press of the Swiss labour movement.[59] Most fittingly the book's cover, featuring one of the Belgian artist Frans Masereel's remarkable charcoal illustrations, declared that Gwyn's novel was a 'masterwork of world literature'; fittingly it was published that year in German alongside *The Stranger* by Albert Camus and *The Bridge of San Luis Rey* by Thornton Wilder.

The reception given to *The Dark Philosophers* in Norway and Switzerland presaged the Italian publication of *The Alone to the Alone* and Gwyn's final novel, *The Love Man*, by the communist publisher Feltrinelli towards the end of the 1950s.[60] By coincidence, 1957, the year Lucia Demby's translation of *The Alone to the Alone* – which in Italy took the American title, *Venus and the Voters* – appeared, was the same year in which Feltrinelli published Boris Pasternak's *Doctor Zhivago*, the manuscript having been smuggled out of the Soviet Union, and earned enduring fame. Gwyn's novel, although widely available in Italy, was overshadowed by the global storm which accompanied *Doctor Zhivago*, and to a lesser extent the Italian publication (also by Feltrinelli) of Doris Lessing's *A Proper Marriage*. For Gwyn, however, the concern was a more practical one: 'profits for the author,' he explained to Nan in 1954, referring to the process and experience of having his work translated abroad, 'are huge.'[61] But it was not cynicism which drove Gwyn, as much as he joked about money, so much as finding the right publishing house for his writing; hence the left-leaning connections of the Norwegian, Swiss, and Italian publishers with whom he worked. Profit was an added bonus.

The only other western European country where Gwyn's work appeared in the 1950s, albeit in English rather than in translation, was Sweden.[62] In 1956, one of Gwyn's short stories, *Little Fury*, which appeared in Britain in John Pudney's *Pick of Today's Short Stories 5* in 1954 (and again in *Gazooka* in 1957), was included in a collection intended for English-language and literature education in Swedish secondary schools.[63] Alongside *Little Fury* were stories by Roald Dahl, A. A. Milne, and V. S. Pritchett, amongst others. Although Swedish reviewers found Gwyn's work entertaining, and a useful insight into the nature of what they perceived to be Welsh humour, they admitted that up until that point Gwyn was almost entirely unknown in the country.[64] Previous encounters had been limited to occasional articles in the social democratic press, which were themselves syndicated from their British counterparts.[65] Unfortunately, a school textbook did little to encourage publication of Gwyn's other writing and the appearance of *Little Fury* proved to be an exception rather than a precursor to a wider phase of translation. Interested readers had to import copies from Britain, for instance, or rely on the Norwegian edition of *The Dark Philosophers*. The result was a limited appreciation.

Elsewhere in Europe, notably in France and on the Iberian

Peninsula, Gwyn was unknown. Only in Ireland was he actively banned. When the Irish Censorship of Publications Board made the decision to place *The World Cannot Hear You* on the register of prohibited publications, ostensibly for its politics and sense of humour, it marked the beginning of a period of more than five years in which every new novel was promptly censored.[66] Gwyn was by no means alone in falling victim to one of the most stringent regimes in the western world: Rhys Davies's novels and short stories including *The Red Hills* (1932), *Jubilee Blues* (1938), *Boy with a Trumpet* (1949), and *The Perishable Quality* (1957) were placed on the list of outlaws, as was Ron Berry's *Travelling Loaded* (1963). By the mid-1950s, the extent of Gwyn's writings still in circulation in Ireland amounted to *The Alone to the Alone*, *All Things Betray Thee*, and the two short stories in Gwyn Jones's Oxford University Press collection, *Welsh Short Stories*. Only with the passing of *Gazooka* by the Board in 1957 was the prohibition ended, although when *The Love Man* was allowed through in 1958, most Irish reviewers wondered what all the fuss was about. The *Irish Times* critic expressed confusion as to what the novelist was trying to say, adding that 'anyone's guess is as good as mine.'[67]

That comment would have raised eyebrows in communist Europe, where Gwyn was hailed as one of the pre-eminent socialist realist novelists of the west, especially from Britain. In the Soviet Union, unlike many of his erstwhile rivals and compatriots including Dylan Thomas, he was published numerous times: *The Dark Philosophers*, which was translated into Russian in 1958 for a series on the 'Modern Foreign Novel,' even went into a second edition in under a year.[68] Copies circulated, together with the Russian edition of *All Things Betray Thee*, published in 1959, amongst the Russian-speaking enclaves in the Baltic states of Estonia, Latvia, and Lithuania. It was followed by translations of short stories such as *Little Fury* in the 1970s. A Bulgarian edition of *All Things Betray Thee*, translated by Radost Pridham for Narodna Kultura, appeared in Sofia in 1961.[69] The foreword to the Russian edition was written by Alexander Anikst, a leading Soviet Shakespeare scholar, and illustrated Gwyn's reception in Moscow.

> The name of Gwyn Thomas is relatively new to the Soviet reader. Some time ago we had a translation of his novella *The Dark Philosophers*, but only now, with the arrival of *All Things Betray Thee*, will Russian readers get the opportunity to truly get to know this writer.
>
> A few words about the author. Gwyn Thomas was born in 1913. He lives and works in Wales. A schoolteacher by profession, Gwyn Thomas takes an active part in the social and political life of England and is a member of the Labour Party.
>
> In literature, Gwyn Thomas spoke for the first time after World War II. His main works are: *The Dark Philosophers* (1947), *All Things Betray Thee* (1949), *The World Cannot Hear You* (1951), *Now Lead Us Home* (1952), *A Frost On My Frolic* (1953).
>
> The stories and novels of Gwyn Thomas are dedicated to the life of Wales. For many of us, this geographical name means little. It is most often found in print due to the fact that the heir to the English throne has been called the Prince of Wales for many centuries. Even this brief title, however, is fraught with something that we don't usually think about.

So far, so good. But then the foreword took a turn into territory which showed a striking distance between Gwyn's views and the Soviet perception of what he was trying to say.

> The world economic crisis of capitalism in 1929–1933 had a grave impact on the position of the working people of Wales.

Many enterprises closed and unemployment reached enormous proportions. The protracted nature of the crisis forced a significant part of the population to emigrate. But the masses of Wales were by no means inclined to passively relate to the calamity that befell them. The crisis generated great discontent, and the people, not without reason, considered the lack of independence as one of the reasons for their difficult situation. A national liberation movement arose. It, of course, met with resistance from the British imperialist bourgeoisie. After the Second World War, the national liberation movement gained new incentives ... The work of Gwyn Thomas reflects the rise of the national liberation and social movements of the people of Wales after the Second World War. As far as we can judge, not a single writer of modern Wales has expressed with such clarity and artistic power the main social trends in the life of this people.

True, already at the beginning of World War II, a work appeared in the literature of Wales which attracted the attention of all reading Europe and America. We have in mind the novel by Richard Llewellyn, *How Green Was My Valley*. It depicts the life and struggle of ordinary workers in Wales, even class contradictions are reflected. But the author remained captive to petty-bourgeois philanthropism and reformist ideology. Reformist and philanthropic motifs are common to most of the works of Gwyn Thomas. But in the novel *All Things Betray Thee* he rose above this, creating a book truly revolutionary in its spirit and meaning ... It was Gwyn Thomas's historical novel which turned out to be the most modern.

The origins of this take evidently lie in the turn by some in the Welsh District of the CPGB towards ideas of, as they saw it, 'national liberation,' ideas which were then fed back to Moscow as *verité*. Those involved included district secretary Idris Cox, the dentist T. E. Nicholas, and the former Plaid Cymru member-turned-communist from Bangor, J. Roose Williams. The effort began in the 1930s with a series of pamphlets, accelerated in the 1940s particularly around the 1948 centenary of the *Communist Manifesto* (and its translation into Welsh), and culminated in communist support for the failed Parliament for Wales Campaign in the 1950s.[70] There were to be echoes of that support in subsequent decades, particularly during the 1979 devolution referendum. None of this had anything to do with Gwyn, of course, who agreed with Arthur Horner that it was all a distraction and alien to the British labour movement.

Nevertheless, with official endorsement Gwyn's writing was to be the subject of considerable study and discussion in the Soviet Union and mentioned frequently in literary circles and in essays and books on democratic and progressive western literature during the Thaw of the late 1950s and early 1960s.[71] It was a similar situation in Hungary, by then firmly under Soviet influence, where *The World Cannot Hear You* appeared in 1959.[72] According to outside observers writing for an American audience, the novel was not well received and Gwyn seemingly disappeared from public discussion.[73] However, Hungarian sources suggest that this was not true. In fact, the novel was widely and favourably reviewed, with short stories and essays published in Hungarian at around the same time, including 'A Spoonful of Grief to Taste' in 1958.[74] Even in countries where Gwyn's writing was not directly translated, such as in Czechoslovakia, he was known to newspaper readers and discussed in literary journals – all with official endorsement. As early as 1952, the Czech Communist Party's newspaper *Rudé Právo* identified Gwyn as being at the forefront of western progressivism.[75] A few years later, *Sv⬜tová Literatura* (World Literature) published an essay by the English Marxist critic, Arnold Kettle, in which he described Gwyn as having 'a beautiful, subtly lyrical sense of human nobility and a wonderful sense of humour.'[76]

Not every communist country took the same decision as to what to translate. A good example of the distinction can be found in the different treatments of *All Things Betray Thee* in East Germany and Poland. Given the choice of the American or British title, the East German censors recorded that 'there is unanimity that the novel should appear under the English original and not under the title of the American edition,' that is as *Leaves in the Wind*.[77] The opposite decision was taken in Poland.[78] The East German edition published by the Leipzig-based Paul List Verlag in appeared in English, the only example in eastern Europe, whereas the Polish edition was translated. Gwyn had relatively little to do with overseas markets once discussion about how to translate his work had been completed – at most he received royalties, if they could be removed from the country of origin, and they were generally paid in kind rather than in scarce western currency, and a boxful of copies none of which he could read. For the most part, he remained ignorant of the appreciation for his writing apparent in Eastern Europe, except that it is in Romania. For reasons that are no longer readily discernible, though illustrate the regard with which he was held in communist circles, Gwyn was approached in the early 1950s to undertake reviews of books from Romania for the *New Central European Observer*.

The magazine was a fortnightly based in London and run by the Communist Party with the purpose of reporting favourably on events and culture in Central and Eastern Europe – it was funded primarily by the Czechoslovakian government. Amongst the other regular contributors to the magazine were the historian Eric Hobsbawm, who much admired Gwyn's writing, and the composer Alan Bush, who had been a key force in the Workers' Music Association in the 1930s and a collaborator of

Lewis Jones.[79] Gwyn's first published review was of the English translation of Zaharia Stancu's autobiographical novel, *Barefoot*, which was published in Bucharest in 1948 but which appeared in Britain in 1951.[80] The themes of *Barefoot*, namely the long-lost world of the peasant village and the arrival of modernity, no doubt echoed those of *All Things Betray Thee* in the minds of the *NCEO*'s editors. A favourable review prompted various Romanian publishers to begin sending Gwyn copies of books, including the short stories of Geo Bogza, one of the most prominent writers in communist Romania, and a collection of folk art. They still survive in his library, since deposited at the South Wales Miners' Library, and are a curio of Gwyn's literary relationship with communist Europe. Perhaps out of recognition for this quirky bond, *All Things Betray Thee* appeared in Romania in the early 1960s.[81] In Eastern Europe, at least, Gwyn was recognised as the political writer and the revolutionary artist to which he had aspired as a young man.

Indeed, something of the pride Gwyn took in being published in the communist world can be discerned in the letters sent to Nan when he furnished her with a copy. He knew she could not read their contents. He sent them, he said, as 'examples of book production.' Adding that 'I think the jacket and the actual book cover of the Hungarian one are very striking.' The hardboard cover was primarily purple and blue with a small patch of bright yellow on the bottom right-hand corner featuring a sketch of a single man leading a horse. The jacket was starkly modern – even abstract – with blues, blacks, and yellows, painted as though to capture a dawn breaking through the slats of an old wooden shutter. The Russian edition of *The Dark Philosophers* was more direct, four men sat conspiratorially next to a gramophone. As for the Russian edition of *All Things Betray Thee*, Gwyn found that 'rather moving.' A motif of a shattered harp recalled a wreath seen at his older brother, John's, funeral in 1949 – just before the original publication of the novel in Britain. He told Nan, 'that novel was one I would have liked John to read, he and I talked so often of the Dic Penderyn story on which it is based ... And now the image [of the harp] turns up again on the cover of a book from several thousands of miles away.'[82]

*

Gwyn always believed that he had 'not had much success, you know, in the recognisable sense of selling millions of copies ... I've always had a very, very limited readership. I once defined my readership as being large enough to be accommodated in a reasonably sized catacomb or vestry.' He did not fully appreciate that at the height of the Cold War no other Welsh writer was as widely available to international audiences; indeed, few British novelists were quite as able to speak to audiences on both sides of the divide. In 1950s Britain, too, Gwyn was used as a measure of the success of other writers, particularly those starting out in their own glittering careers. The classicist Peter Green, writing for the *Daily Telegraph*, recorded that future Nobel laureate V. S. Naipaul was 'a kind of West Indian Gwyn Thomas – pungent, charitable, Rabelaisian, who deals in the small change of human experience as though it were minted gold.'[83] When Menna Gallie's first novel, *Strike for a Kingdom* was published by Victor Gollancz in 1959, one reviewer argued that she had adopted 'a kind of Gwyn Thomas approach.'[84] Another suggested that the novel's protagonist, D. J. Griffiths, 'stands out as a real character among the Welsh types that Gwyn and Dylan have familiarised us with.' Even when the comparison with Gwyn's writing rankled, as it did for Kingsley Amis, there was an acceptance that when publishers thought of Wales, they thought of Meadow Prospect.[85]

It was in Australia that the three publishing identities – American, British, and European – which had emerged in the 1940s came together. Gwyn was embraced effusively, even despite a censorship regime which rivalled Ireland's for its viciousness.[86] Writing in the *Sydney Morning Herald*, Keith Newman remarked in 1951 that such a welcome 'is partly a reflection of the dislocation of our times. It is always pleasant to meet good writing, and when it is shot through with golden seams of laughter, then we have every excuse for becoming lyrical amid our mid-century gloom.' He added that 'Mr Thomas has emerged from the same drear valleys as Mr Aneurin Bevan and the two Welshmen appear politically akin (or at least they both sometimes throw stones at the same targets). But, where the politician roars into the fray, searing his foes with the flame-thrower of invective, the writer comes armed with a smiling irony, which deepens pleasantly often into the belly-laughs of sheer good fun.'[87] Responding to *A Frost On My Frolic* for the *Sydney Morning Herald* two years later, L. V. Kepert added that 'stuck out on his own among the current of modern novels, owning no real model either English or Welsh, ancient or modern, Gwyn Thomas makes a beautiful haven for the reader in search of freshness.'[88]

As always, Gwyn received his most enthusiastic and enduring support from the left-wing press. 'Gwyn Thomas lovers are akin to Marx Brothers adherents,' observed the Sydney *Tribune* in December 1957, 'you either love him, or you don't, with no in-betweens. Me, I am a Thomas fan with many a sore rib gained after a session with his "voters" and "thinkers", his earthy characters whose people depressed Welsh villages.' The reviewer concluded, 'as well as being a superb humourist, Thomas is a social writer with a penetrating insight into his fellows. His characters are inevitably poor, desperately so, but they are never caricatures never dehumanised. Come to think of it, Steinbeck could profitably learn some lessons from Thomas.'[89] *Tribune* was the successor to Sydney's earlier communist newspaper, the *Worker's Weekly*, published in the city from 1923 until 1939, and provided the official journalistic voice of the Communist Party of Australia. In its advertising columns, Gwyn's work was promoted alongside that of Mulk Raj Anand, Upton Sinclair, Leo Tolstoy, and the American Howard Fast, as exactly the kind of literature for progressive Australians to read – all available at the Pioneer Bookshop in downtown Sydney.

In the 1960s, the bookshop became known as the New World. It continued to stock Gwyn's work. One of the editions available was the East German version of *All Things Betray Thee*.[90] On the face of it, a rather unusual presence. But the imprint, Panther Books, was intended by its East German creators to be a 'propaganda project on an international scale.'[91] Run by Gertrude Gelbin and her husband Stefan Heym, the imprint served as a way of channelling financial support to writers suffering in the United States because of the Red Scare. Heym recalled later that 'Gertrude pointed out the dire straits in which men like Howard Fast, Alvah Bessie, etc. found themselves. A writer must be published to be able to function and live ... and we might succeed in bringing progressive literature precisely where it was banned, the USA.'[92] That is almost certainly why Gwyn agreed to the East German publication in the first place. He was, after all, no stranger to the ban which had been imposed on Fast, Bessie, and others, and his own work was to fall victim to the McCarthyite reaction of the 1950s. He was no stranger, either, to the personal privations experienced by these men because for several years they were his correspondents, his reviewers, his supporters, and, above all, his friends.

[1] Gwyn Thomas, 'Bread and Cymric Circuses', *Punch*, 16 July 1958.

[2] *Barry Dock News*, 14 October 1898.

[3] In an article for *Punch*, published in 1967, Gwyn described Barry as 'a colder, coarser ambience than the one before.' Gwyn Thomas, 'Walking Away from the Impotent Halls', *Punch*, 13 September 1967.

[4] Letter from Gwyn Thomas to Hannah Thomas, undated but c. autumn 1943.

[5] J. H. Francis, 'Editorial', in *The Barrian* 34 (1944), 7.

[6] Letter from Gwyn Thomas to Hannah Thomas, 7 July 1943.

[7] Gwyn Thomas (Gwynt), 'Harvest', *The Barrian* 34 (1944), 17–19.

[8] *LFD*, 81.

[9] The seven-part series ran in *Punch* between 29 August and 10 October 1962.

[10] Gwyn Thomas, 'The Man With The Chalk, Part One: A Season for Wizards', *Punch*, 29 August 1962. Rawlins appeared across a number of *Punch* stories following his debut in 'That Vanished Canaan', *Punch*, 23 September 1953, namely: 'Of All The Saints', *Punch*, 13 October 1954; 'Lo, Hear The Jumping Gene', *Punch*, 29 December 1954; 'New Every Morning', *Punch*, 4 January 1956; and 'A Pace Or Two Apart', *Punch*, 7 May 1958.

[11] Gwyn Thomas, 'The Man With The Chalk, Part Two: The Cool Eye', *Punch*, 5 September 1962.

[12] Gwyn Thomas, 'Hitting The Track', *Punch*, 8 April 1964; 'Fighting Fit', *Punch*, 13 May 1964; 'Bowdler, What Are You Bowdling Now?', *Punch*, 27 May 1964.

[13] *Chester Courant*, 25 September 1901.

[14] *Evening Express*, 16 March 1906; Theodore Andrea Cook, *The Fourth Olympiad: Being the Official Report of the Olympic Games of 1908* (London, 1908), 61.

[15] *Barry Herald*, 17 September 1909; *Carmarthen Journal*, 12 September 1913.

[16] Barry County Schools, *Jubilee 1896–1946* (Cardiff, 1946).

[17] *Barry Dock News*, 14 July 1916.

[18] Gwyn Thomas in discussion with Robert Morley, *One Pair of Eyes: Was Your Schoolmaster Really Necessary?* (BBC TV, 4 May 1968).

[19] TNA, ED 109/9725: *Report by H. M. Inspectors on Barry County School (Boys), Glamorgan, 14–16 February* 1950 (London, 1950), 9–10. The inspector's report also noted some of the literature Gwyn used in his teaching, namely Pedro Alarcon (1833–1891) who was most famous for his 1874 novel *El sombrero de tres picos / The Three Cornered Hat*; Emilia Bazán (1851–1921) whose work was particularly noted for its feminism and links with the realist literature of Émile Zola (1840–1902); and Vicente Ibáñez (1867–1928), whose work, appropriately for Gwyn, was widely adapted for American cinema in the 1910s and 1920s.

[20] Also noted by the school inspector who thought such talks 'broaden the course and consequently increase its value materially from the cultural point of view'.

[21] *The Barrian* no. 29 (1943), 17–18.

[22] Gwyn's notes for the speech can be found at NLW, GTP, E92.

[23] *LFD*, 94.

[24] As above, 43–44.

[25] *AFSE*, 71. Compare with Barbara Prys-Williams's rather curious – and incorrect – reading of this passage as being indicative of a 'phobic reaction to being vulnerably away from his home-base' (p. 105). It was Franco's Spain that he had no wish to know, rather than Spain in general.

[26] *LFD*, p. 47.

[27] Sasha D. Pack, *Tourism and Dictatorship: Europe's Peaceful Invasion of Franco's Spain* (London, 2006), 39.

[28] Letter from Gwyn Thomas to Bill Thomas, 9 September 1947.

[29] Cambridge University Library, G. Allen Hutt Papers, MS Add.9814/E/57, Letters from Gwyn Thomas to Allen Hutt, 1947; *Daily Worker*, 10 July 1947.

[30] A maximum-security prison in New York State. Most famous as the site of execution of Julius and Ethel Rosenberg in 1953.

[31] A maximum-security prison in New York State, officially known as the Clinton Correctional Facility.

[32] That is, the American humourist and writer Robert Benchley (1889–1945), who was most famous for his contributions to the *New Yorker*.

[33] *A Hatful of Humours*, 82.

[34] Gwyn Thomas, 'The Influence of Damon Runyon', *BBC Television* 7 March 1962.

[35] The BBC began broadcasting Runyon stories that July starting with 'Bloodhounds of Broadway'. *RT* 30 June 1939. 'Butch Minds the Baby' followed on 26 September. *The Listener*, 21 September 1939.

[36] Damon Runyon, 'A Story Goes With It', *Nash's Pall Mall Magazine* (April 1932), 56–112; 'That Ever Loving Wife of Hymie's', *Nash's Pall Mall Magazine* (October 1932), 48–108; 'Earthquake', *Nash's Pall Mall Magazine* (April 1933), 16–74; 'Twilight of the Gangster', *Nash's Pall Mall Magazine* (June 1933), 44–47; 'Ransom', *Nash's Pall Mall Magazine* (June 1934), 18–121. The magazine was owned and controlled by the American tycoon William Randolph Hearst, for whom Runyon worked. See also the letter from E. C. Bentley (1875–1956) in *The Spectator*, 15 October 1932.

[37] *TLS*, 3 July 1937, 22 January, 29 January 1938.

[38] *TLS*, 21 October 1939.

[39] *New York Herald Tribune*, 6 May 1947.

[40] Reginald Moore, *Modern Reading 16* (London, 1947), 42.

[41] Victor Golightly, 'Gwyn Thomas's American "Oscar"', *New Welsh Review* 22 (1993), 26–31, p. 30; Dai Smith, 'Breaking Silence: Gwyn Thomas and the Pre-History of Welsh Working-Class Fiction' in Clive Emsley and James Walvin (eds.), *Artisans, Peasants and Proletarians, 1760–1860: Essays Presented to Gwyn A. Williams* (London, 1985), 104–23.

[42] Michael Parnell, 'Introduction', in Gwyn Thomas, *The Thinker and Thrush* (London, 1988), 6.

[43] Letter from Gwyn Thomas to Nan Thomas, undated but early April 1948.

[44] The others being *Gazooka* and *A Spoonful of Grief to Taste*. The character of

Salathiel Cull had a similar longevity, cropping up in *The World Cannot Hear You* in 1951, *The Stranger At My Side* in 1954, and in several other short stories. 'As it was in the Beginning', *Coal* 2, no. 10 (February 1949); 'Tomorrow I Shall Miss You Less', *Coal* 4, no 8 (December 1950); and 'The Short Spell', *Punch*, 17 July 1963.

[45] NLW, Glyn Jones Papers, A12/18.

[46] NLW, Glyn Jones Papers, A12/18.

[47] Gwyn Thomas, 'Tomorrow I Shall Miss You Less', *Coal* 4, no. 8 (December 1950), 30–31.

[48] *The Big Room* (1960), *The Day of the Sardine* (1961), *The Watchers and the Watched* (1962), and *Sam in the Morning* (1965).

[49] BL RMP: Letter from Jack Aistrop to Lisa Berridge, undated but 1947.

[50] Gwyn Thomas, *The Dark Philosophers* (Boston, 1947). It was published in the United States on 4 May 1947.

[51] Gwyn Thomas, *Pastor Emmanuel og hans Kjærlighet* (Oslo, 1948). Tiden was then owned by the governing Labour Party; *Tidens Nyheter* 14 (October 1948).

[52] *Arbeiderbladet*, 22 December 1948.

[53] Per Gottschalk, 'Ironisk Proletar', *Morgenbladet* (Oslo), 30 December 1948. My translation of the Norwegian original.

[54] *Beyers Bokservice*, 1948. Copy contained in the Tiden Archive Collection at the Norwegian Labour Movement Archives and Library, Oslo: AAB/ARK-2120/D/L0112: Gwyn Thomas, *Pastor Emmanuel Og Hans Kjærlighet* (1948).

[55] *Telemark Arbeiderblad*, 29 January 1949. My translation from the Norwegian original.

[56] Gwyn Thomas, *Die Liebe des Reverend Emmanuel* (Zurich, 1951). Production details are held at the Swiss Social Archives in Zurich: Büchergilde Gutenberg, Ar 201.10.8.

[57] The German headquarters switched to Berlin in 1928, with separate but linked branches founded in Vienna, Prague, and Zurich by 1931. The Swiss branch became independent in 1933 in response to the Nazi rise to power in Germany and rose to become the most important of the four with more than one hundred and ten thousand members by the end of the Second World War.

[58] *Rote Revue: Sozialistische Monatsschrift* 30, no. 6 (June 1951), 275.

[59] *Industrie Arbeiter* (Zurich), 12 July 1951; *Der VHTL*, 20 July 1951. The latter was the organ of the Swiss lorry drivers' union.

[60] Gwyn Thomas (transl. Lucia Drudi Demby), *Venere E Gli Elettori* (Milan, 1957); *L'Uomo Dell'Amore* (transl. Bruno Tasso) (Milan, 1960). The former was the twelfth title to be released in Feltrinelli's 'Narrativa' series, launched in 1955; the latter appeared as the three hundred and twenty-fourth title in the company's 'Universale Economica' series.

[61] Letter from Gwyn Thomas to Hannah Thomas, 9 August 1954. Parnell suggests (*LFD*, p. 226) that *The World Cannot Hear You* and *All Things Betray Thee* were released by Einaudi and Feltrinelli in 1954 and 1955, respectively; this is inaccurate.

[62] Although in areas of Belgium, Denmark, France, and the Netherlands, where listeners could pick up the BBC on the radio, it was possible to listen to Gwyn's

words, even if they could not be bought in a bookshop. For instance: *Nationaltidende* (Copenhagen), 9 August 1953.

[63] Johannes Hedberg (ed), *Six Stories by Six Modern Writers* (Stockholm, 1956), 49–56. Others in the volume included A. A. Milne, Roald Dahl and V. S. Pritchett.

[64] Olof Sager, 'Review of Six Stories by Six Modern Writers', *Moderna Språk* 51 (1957), 165.

[65] *Arbetartidningen*, 18 November 1953.

[66] *Irish Times*, 20 July 1953, 30 April 1956, 5 May 1956.

[67] *Irish Times*, 26 July 1958.

[68] Other books in the series included John Steinbeck's 1947 novella, *The Pearl*.

[69] The translation was largely based on the Russian language edition, but Pridham also sought Gwyn's advice and guidance. NLW, GTP, J2: 'Letter from Radost Pridham to Gwyn Thomas, 1 October 1961'.

[70] Douglas Jones, *The Communist Party of Great Britain and the National Question in Wales, 1920–1991* (Cardiff, 2017); Daryl Leeworthy, 'A Miner Cause? The Persistence of Left-Nationalism in Post-War Wales', in Evan Smith and Matthew Worley (eds), *Waiting for the Revolution: The British Far Left from 1956* (Manchester, 2018).

[71] The wider phenomenon is discussed in Eleonory Gilburd, *To See Paris And Die: The Soviet Lives of Western Culture* (Harvard, 2018).

[72] Gwyn Thomas (transl. Tamas Kaposi), *Ősi Vágyak Komédiája* (Budapest, 1959).

[73] Eniko Molnar, 'Notes on English Literature in Hungary Today', *Books Abroad* 36, no. 4 (1962), 383.

[74] Gwyn Thomas (transl. Péter Balabán), 'Bánatkósoló' in *Mai Angol Elbeszélők* (Budapest, 1958), 333–344.

[75] *Rudé Právo*, 23 March 1952.

[76] Arnold Kettle, 'Pohled na současnou britskou literaturu / A Look at Contemporary British Literature', *Světová literatura / World Literature* (1958), 125.

[77] Federal Archives of Germany, Berlin, German Democratic Republic Collection, Records of the Ministry for Culture, Author Files, 1953–1965, BArch DR 1/5089 ff.213–215: Gwyn Thomas, *All Things Betray Thee*, Paul List Verlag, 16 June 1955.

[78] Gwyn Thomas, (transl. Tadeusz Jan Dehnel), *Liście Na Wietrze* (Warsaw, 1955). The novel was similarly referred to as *Leaves in the Wind* in Czechoslovakia. *Rudé Právo*, 23 March 1952.

[79] TNA, KV 2/3515, Personal File of Alan Dudley Bush. Of particular interest here is an intercepted letter (f. 7a) from Bush to Lewis Jones sent in June 1938. For an assessment of Bush's career see: Joanna Bullivant, *Alan Bush, Modern Music and the Cold War: The Cultural Left in Britain and the Communist Bloc* (Cambridge, 2017).

[80] Zaharia Stancu, *Barefoot* (London, 1951). The edition featured an introduction from the Anglo-Australian writer and literary critic, Jack Lindsay. Gwyn Thomas, 'Review of Zaharia Stancu, *Barefoot*', *The New Central European Observer* (1951),

416.

[81] Gwyn Thomas (transl. Ticu Arhip), *Totul Ti-E Potrivnic* (Bucharest, 1961).

[82] Letter from Gwyn Thomas to Hannah Thomas, undated but 1959.

[83] V. S. Naipaul, *Letters Between a Father and Son* (London, 2009), 447. The review was in response to Naipaul's debut novel, *The Mystic Masseur* which was published in 1957. *Daily Telegraph*, 14 June 1957.

[84] *Belfast Telegraph*, 16 March 1959.

[85] Kingsley Amis, 'Letter to Philip Larkin, 25 June 1956', in Zachary Leader (ed.), *The Letters of Kingsley Amis* (London, 2000), 471–2. Amis's second novel, *That Uncertain Feeling*, set in Wales, had been published by Victor Gollancz the previous year.

[86] Nicole Moore, *The Censor's Library* (St Lucia, Queensland, 2012).

[87] Keith Newman, 'A Fine Novel from Wales', *Sydney Morning Herald*, 17 November 1951.

[88] L. V. Kepert, 'A Comic Novel of Brilliance', *Sydney Morning Herald*, 7 November 1953.

[89] *Tribune* (Sydney), 18 December 1957.

[90] *Tribune*, 28 January 1959.

[91] Letter from Getrude Gelbin to Erich Wendt, August 1961; cited in Nicole Moore and Christina Spittel 'South by East: World Literature's Cold War Compass', in Nicole Moore and Christina Spittel (eds), *Australian Literature in the German Democratic Republic: Reading Through the Iron Curtain* (London, 2016), 16.

[92] Stefan Heym, *Nachrüf* (1988) quoted as above, 16.

CHAPTER FIVE
Gusto of Genius

The letter arrived in Barry from New York in October 1950. It was a piece of fan mail sent by the Brooklyn-based poet and playwright, Norman Rosten (1913–1995). Gwyn wrote back immediately to thank Rosten for his letter and explain that 'it was a kind and delightful gesture, the sort of pleasant surprise which more than makes up for the almost sombre lack of success, in strictly commercial terms, which the books had when they came out. Fortunately for me, the background and experiences which gave me the material to produce the books gave me also the patient understanding to accept as a sufficient and fine reward the occasional appreciation of isolated and shrewd connoisseurs of the human scene like yourself.'[1] Rosten had read the American editions of *The Dark Philosophers* and *The Alone to the Alone* (published in the United States as *Venus and the Voters*) which had been published a few years earlier. He mused in his letter about the possibility of turning one of them into a play for the New York stage, perhaps even Broadway itself. Gwyn was tickled: 'as far as the London theatre is concerned,' he explained to the American, a close friend of Norman Mailer, Arthur Miller, whom he had met whilst studying at the University of Michigan in the mid-1930s, and the ill-fated Marilyn Monroe, 'just the faintest whiff of this type of material would have managers and actors howling for the police.'

The thrill of receiving such correspondence was palpable. Gwyn admitted to Rosten that his offer 'to try an adaptation makes me feel very happy.' It was the start of an encouraging friendship, which lasted through several years of correspondence and mutual aid at a time when the United States was entering Red Scare paranoia. With his reply to Rosten, Gwyn enclosed a copy of *Where Did I Put My Pity?* which had not been published in the United States, as a thank you gift. With his next letter, Rosten sent copies of his own early work, all of them books of poetry: *Return Again, Traveller* (1940), *The Fourth Decade* (1943), and *The Big Road* (1946). None of them could be easily acquired in post-war Britain, where Rosten was largely unknown. Gwyn devoured Rosten's writing and was soon penning his own fan letters to send back across the Atlantic. 'Why in god's name isn't your work better known over here,' Gwyn said, 'what kind of pin-headed morlocks are these publishers of ours? Here we are, the intelligent of this land, crying to heaven for a poetry that will catch all the pity and passion of our own sense of this epoch, and yet knowledge of your work which catches every footstep, every heart cry of our bloody journey, every wound of loss and grief, is denied us save by chance.'

Taking it upon himself to become a one-man propaganda machine for Rosten, Gwyn used what opportunities arose to deliver public talks about 'a poet whose strength of voice, depth of pity, proclamation of a healed and united mankind would shake [audiences] out of their seats.' In a letter sent in mid-December 1950, Gwyn explained that,

> On Tuesday night – I was due to lecture to the British Poetry Society at Cardiff. I had not given a subject. The title space had been left blank, a privilege afforded to the more garrulous swamis in this belt. The arrival of your volumes transformed me into an evangel, sent me to the meeting with a sense of mission. I would announce and illustrate [your] work ... Most

of the audience were miners down from the valleys of Rhondda, Garw and Aberdare, men whose essence could have gone to dyeing your verse the brilliant colour it is. Every wind of a torment from hell and British Toryism had moulded the shape of their faces and hearts. Your words moved into them like food or love, with passion, without a moment's doubt or pause. You might have been born for the sake of speaking to just that group at just that moment.[2]

Sensing a meeting of minds, Rosten then sent a copy of Thomas McGrath's 1947 collection *To Walk a Crooked Mile*, which had not yet been published in Britain. McGrath (1916–1990) was not an entirely unfamiliar choice: his work had previously appeared in the American communist literary journal *Masses and Mainstream*, to which Gwyn subscribed. 'Now I can settle down and get a fuller view of his landscape,' Gwyn explained to Rosten, by way of thanking him for the present, 'there can be few things to equal in richness the experience of having before one enough material on which to form a judgement and an enthusiasm about a poet of one's own time and kind.' Gwyn added, 'when I evangelise here about the work of men like yourself and McGrath, spokesmen of as broad and passionate a humanity, as we can find in the whole range of modern letters, my listeners are astounded that people like yourselves can have been produced from the same matrix as Trumans and MacArthurs.'

Norman Rosten was by no means a random correspondent. Born into a Jewish family in New York City, he studied at Brooklyn College (graduating 1935), New York University (1936), and then the University of Michigan (1937–38), where he was a classmate of Arthur Miller. Together with Miller, and whilst working for the Federal Theatre Project in New York at the end of the 1930s, Rosten wrote the plays *Listen My*

Children (1939) and *You're Next* (1939). At this time, he was a regular contributor (as poet and reviewer) to *New Masses*, the American popular front literature and culture magazine – the equivalent of the *Left Review* in Britain – penning poems about the death of Lorca, on the one hand, and the electoral defeat of Winston Churchill, on the other.[3] At the time Gwyn and Rosten were in direct contact, in the early 1950s, the latter was sharing an apartment in Brooklyn with Norman Mailer and mentoring the younger man in the art of writing. The two also shared a publisher, Rinehart and Company. Mailer's first novel, *The Naked and the Dead*, had been published two years earlier, in 1948; his second, *Barbary Shore*, appeared in 1951. Speaking to Dai Smith at the Hay Festival in 2000, Mailer recalled this period of his life and, albeit more vaguely, Rosten's enthusiasm for Gwyn.

Thomas McGrath had a similar set of associations, particularly in his role as film critic for *New Masses* in 1946. After studying at the University of North Dakota, Louisiana State University, and at Oxford on a Rhodes Scholarship, McGrath settled in Los Angeles where he taught and wrote. He was one of the editorial team involved in planning the *California Quarterly* at the start of the 1950s. The *CQ* was envisaged as the successor journal to *The Clipper*, the West Coast literary journal of the communist-aligned League of American Writers, which had been edited by the novelist Sanora Babb. Babb used both *The Clipper* and the *California Quarterly* to provide opportunities for emerging and established progressive writers and poets on both sides of the Atlantic. Amongst the names appearing in issue one of *California Quarterly*, which appeared in the autumn of 1951, were the American science fiction writer Jay Williams, with whom Gwyn also struck up a lasting friendship, the historian E. P. Thompson, and Gwyn himself. Future editions featured Ray Bradbury, Nelson Algren, Ralph

Ellison, and the Chicagoan radio presenter and historian Studs Terkel, as well as Mailer, Miller, and Rosten. This was the literary circle in which Gwyn now moved much to his obvious delight.

The story published in that first issue of *California Quarterly*, 'Where My Dark Lover Lies,' did not appear in Britain until it was included in *Gazooka* in 1957.[4] According to Michael Parnell, it was one of Gwyn's favourites – 'the one about the rain-beset funeral at which the mourners forgetfully [leave] the coffin in a pub.'[5] It was a classic of Rhondda Runyonism written when Gwyn was at the height of his powers and an ideal introduction to his work for the West Coast's literary left. If they needed it. Gwyn's biographical snippet in the magazine noted that he was 'the distinguished Welsh novelist of *Leaves in the Wind*, *Venus and the Voters*, and *The Dark Philosophers*.'[6] Already his work had appeared and been reviewed in *Masses and Mainstream*, the New York counterpart to the *California Quarterly*, which launched in March 1948, and he was known to readers of the *Daily Worker* on the east coast and the *Daily People's World* on the west. In fact, *Venus and the Voters* had been reviewed in the first issue of *Masses and Mainstream* by the Russian-born Jewish New Yorker Ben Field, the nom de plume of Moses Bragin/Brahinsky (1901–1986). A graduate of City College of New York and Columbia University, Bragin's own writing career, which included short stories and reviews in *New Masses*, *Partisan Review* and the *California Quarterly*, has long been forgotten.[7]

In his review of *Venus and the Voters*, Bragin correctly linked the novella with *The Dark Philosophers* noting that 'the philosophers ... resume their places on the brick wall in the yard and continue their wry commentary on the world.' Clearly impressed by what he had read, Bragin concluded that '*Venus and the Voters* has sharper character delineation, broader and more spontaneous humour, and a richer plot than *The Dark Philosophers*. The earlier book should also be read because it has an abundance of Gwyn Thomas's gifts and starts us with the history of its fantastic, yet down-to-earth philosophers.'[8] The following year Bragin reviewed *Leaves in the Wind (All Things Betray Thee)* for *Masses and Mainstream*. This time he was less enthusiastic thinking that this 'historical novel of revolt' had stretched Gwyn's literary powers too far. In *Venus and the Voters* and *The Dark Philosophers*, he wrote, 'it was enough for them to begin and end on a wall or in a confectionary shop; this was their action in the main and was enough. But *Leaves in the Wind* is an historical novel of revolt. Action is demanded by its theme and plotting on the part of the novelist so that the plotting of the enraged workers has more head and body too.' Gwyn, the reviewer concluded, was not 'the master of plot, action and character to the degree that he is of commentary and dialogue.'[9] For all that, Bragin nevertheless felt that Gwyn appeared

to be one of the few contemporary English novelists who have something to say. He comes to grips with the central problems facing his people. A master of incisive plangent prose, wise and tender, and full of an earthy humor, he shows that he is definitely on a hard, bold road, which should put his gifts to their fullest use and help him solve every one of his problems as an artist.

Gwyn owed this close relationship with the post-war American literary left, and particularly to *Masses and Mainstream*, to the novelist, playwright and screenwriter, Howard Fast (1914–2003), who was one of the magazine's contributing editors. Fast had reviewed *The Dark Philosophers* for the New York *Daily Worker* in late December 1947, observing that it was not only a work of genius but 'a masterpiece, a warm, beautiful, splendid book that sets a new standard in proletarian literature.'[10] The review was then republished in the Los Angeles *Daily People's World*. When, a short while later, Gwyn read what Fast had written, he responded immediately telling the American in a letter that 'your word of praise makes up for a lot of setbacks. From the critics of this green and Social-Democratic land I get a fairly thin time. The Tories say nothing until they can serve me with a police-notice. The "Third Force" boys who are going all the way to hell with Bevin and read only when they get the stars out of their eyes regard as quaintly vulgar anyone who goes raking up the facts of social and industrial decay in the basic "black areas" that made up the life-view of those who now make up the vanguard of the British Labour movement.'[11]

It was a fortuitous engagement. At the time, Fast was widely connected to the literary milieu of the American left and able to open doors for Gwyn which might otherwise have remained closed. The pair struck up a regular correspondence, lasting over a decade, sharing ideas and political anxieties. The impact on Gwyn's American fortunes was almost immediate. Fast arranged for *The Dark Philosophers* to be reprinted by the Liberty Book Club, an American equivalent of the Left Book Club, in the summer of 1948, and provided space in *Masses and Mainstream* for Gwyn's short stories.[12] It seems likely that Howard Fast learned about Gwyn from Angus Cameron, the left-leaning editor-in-chief at Little, Brown in Boston. Little, Brown published both Fast and Gwyn. Cameron himself was the key to bringing *The Dark Philosophers*, *The Alone to the Alone*, and *All Things Betray Thee* to the American market and evidently targeted those journals and reviewers – in addition to standard literary ventures such as the *New York Times* and the *New Yorker* – which he knew to be sympathetic to Gwyn's politics and artistic ambitions. They were Cameron's ambitions, also, and had already got him in trouble in 1947 when he refused to publish George Orwell's *Animal Farm*.

Cameron's decision was by no means controversial – the novella was rejected by four mainstream publishers in Britain alone – but prompted the Harvard academic (and later court historian to the Kennedy administration) Arthur M. Schlesinger Jr. (1917–2007), himself a Little, Brown author, to begin a red-baiting tirade against what he saw as Stalinist interference. In his version of events, published in his memoir, *A Life in the 20th Century*, Schlesinger recalled that he had 'urged the editors to publish this wonderful satiric tale about the Soviet Union. As I talked on, I felt a chill arising, especially from an editor I had not previously met named Angus Cameron.'[13] Schlesinger made enquiries – during the war he had worked for the Office of Strategic Services, a precursor to the Central Intelligence Agency – and learned that Cameron had a history of fellow travelling activities. This led Schlesinger to write to the head of Little, Brown, Alfred McIntyre, to explain that he had no desire to be published by a company in which one of the leading members was 'taking an active part in opposing the democratic effort to check the spread of Soviet totalitarianism.' Schlesinger then moved over to the Boston-based publisher Houghton Mifflin, where he remained until his death.

It was not long before this spat was picked up and amplified by various conservative and liberal, but firmly anti-communist, organisations including the American Legion. Within a few years, red baiting was to bring about Cameron's downfall at Little, Brown and a sudden halt to Gwyn's publishing career in the United States. At the centre of the storm was Howard Fast's 1951 novel, *Spartacus*, which formed the basis of Stanley Kubrick's 1960 film starring Kirk Douglas and Laurence Olivier. Fast had written the novel, at speed, in the aftermath of a prison term served in the summer of 1950 for contempt of Congress. Having refused to co-operate with the House Un-American Activities Committee (HUAC), he saw his incarceration as that of a political prisoner. Fast used this self-description regularly in his letters to Gwyn. The Welshman readily accepted what Fast was telling him, as he sought to understand what was going on in the United States during the Eisenhower administration and in the era of HUAC. At Mill Point in West Virginia, Fast grew interested in the historical figure of Spartacus. His initial thoughts had been sparked by reading about Rosa Luxemburg in the prison library and wondering why her group had been called the Spartacus League. In and out of prison, Fast devoured as much as he could on ancient Rome, even taking a crash course on Latin. Armed with the information, he began writing.

Fast's *Spartacus* depicted the class struggle, albeit as Duncan White has observed with 'lashings of sex and violence.' Rome is decadent and cruel, as imperial Washington was perceived to be, and the ruling classes overfed and oversexed. White continues, 'in the first fifty pages alone, we get a member of the Roman nobility trying to seduce a houseguest ... the nobleman's wife trying to seduce her nephew, and that nephew having a gay romp with a distinguished general.' The general being Spartacus's eventual nemesis, Crassus.[14] It cannot have escaped Fast's attention, either, that Arthur Koestler, by the 1950s a vehement anti-Stalinist, had also written about the Spartacus rebellion in his 1939 novel *Gladiators*. In Koestler's telling, the slave revolt was not about class conflict per se, but rather about a revolutionary mass that cannot be controlled, and the compromises made by the European left since the advent of the Soviet Union. Fast's novel was completed in the spring of 1951, and he duly sent the five hundred and fifty page manuscript to Angus Cameron at Little, Brown, convinced that the new work was a hit in waiting. With sales of his previous novels running into the millions, Fast was a well-known and commercially saleable name, but the political situation in America was changing rapidly and, following his showdown with HUAC, Fast was increasingly toxic for mainstream publishers.

Even at Little, Brown, several directors were nervous about their association with Fast. Nevertheless, Cameron stuck by his friend, pushing the board at Little, Brown to publish what he thought was an 'entertaining and meaningful novel.' In a letter to Fast, enclosing the reader's report, Cameron added that 'it is a novel we can publish with pride.' Unfortunately for both men, events were to conspire against them. Louis Budenz, the former editor of the *Daily Worker*, who turned coat after the Second World War and became a professional witness for Congress in its conduct of the Red Scare, testified to the Senate Internal Security Subcommittee chaired by Senator Pat McCarren that Angus Cameron, amongst others, was a member of the Communist Party. Nine days later, Cameron's letter to Fast, together with the reader's report, both of which had been intercepted by the FBI, was published in *Counterattack*, the weekly anti-communist bulletin published by the New York-based American Business Consultants, Inc. It had been founded in 1947 by three former FBI agents for exactly this purpose. *Counterattack* devoted an entire issue in the summer of 1951 to denouncing not only Angus Cameron but also more than thirty 'fellow travellers' whom he had published. Little, Brown was smeared as a communist-front organisation.

'How long,' the bulletin demanded, 'will [they] be able to continue publishing the works of so many communists and front supporters without incurring bad publicity and suffering financially.' Cameron called a meeting of the Board to clear his name and defend the position they had previously taken to publish works regardless of their political implications, but he found himself stuck in Maine due to bad weather. In his absence, the Board voted through a motion to ask Cameron to seek permission for his external political activities. On hearing the news, Cameron resigned telling his former colleagues that the request was unbecoming of a publisher. *Spartacus* was quickly excised from the Little, Brown list. Both Cameron and Fast were soon blacklisted. *Spartacus* was rejected by every major publisher in the United States and in the end Fast resorted to self-publication with financial support (that is, a commitment to buy a copy) from his friends, including Gwyn. Angus Cameron set up on his own as an independent publisher based in New York City, eventually joining forces with the similarly blacklisted journalist Albert E. Kahn. Their most famous production was Harvey Matusow's *False Witness*, published in March 1955, a sensational repudiation of the McCarthy witch hunt and the part the author had previously played as a paid informer for the FBI.[15] Other books included Ring Lardner Jr's *The Ecstasy of Owen Muir* (1954), Herbert Aptheker's *History and Reality* (1955), and Abraham Polonsky's blacklist novel *A Season of Fear* (1956).

Gwyn was supportive: copies of several Cameron and Kahn books survive in his library. He had been more fortunate, for a short while, at least, than either Fast or Cameron. Little, Brown did not withdraw from its commitment, which in any case had surprised Gwyn, to publish *The World Cannot Hear You* in March 1952.[16] As early as 1950, Gwyn had been convinced that he would not be published in the United States 'for a long while.'[17] In the event he was off in his calculations, but only by about eighteen months. To repair the damage apparently done by the *Counterattack* accusations and to move on from Angus Cameron's period as editor-in-chief, Little, Brown sent their subscribers a pamphlet insisting that 'the apparently deliberate attempt of that account [in *Counterattack*] is to show that Little, Brown has recently become a Communist-front publishing house. Those who know us well understand that such a charge is absurd.' They went on to explain that the objectionable authors totalled no more than four per cent of the in-print Little, Brown list. Authors identified as 'problematic' included Ernest Simmons, Lillian Hellman (partner of Dashiell Hammett), Albert Deutsch, and James S. Martin. But, remarked Clem Hodges in *Masses and Mainstream* in an article defending Angus Cameron published in November 1951, 'Little, Brown failed to specify in the brochure other authors and their work who could conceivably be included in the same listing: Albert Maltz and Howard Fast and Gwyn Thomas and Richard O. Boyer and Stefan Heym and Abraham Polonsky and a number of others.'[18] The article reappeared in 1955, when it was used as evidence in Senate hearings on the Matusow scandal.[19]

With Angus Cameron gone from Little, Brown, and *The Dark Philosophers* also referenced in the Congressional proceedings because it had been reprinted by the Liberty Book Club in the late 1940s, Gwyn was regarded as a problematic author and the Boston publisher refused to release another of his Gollancz novels or any of the short-story collections. It was a serious and highly politicised situation. Not until 1968, when it agreed to publish *A Few Selected Exits*, did Little, Brown rescind this 'ban.' The American edition of *A Welsh Eye* was released by the small, but well-regarded Vermont publisher, Stephen Greene in 1965.[20] As for Gwyn's fiction: the only other novel published in America in the 1950s was his Don Juan tale *The Love Man*, retitled by Macmillan as *A Wolf at Dusk*. It appeared to warm reviews in 1959.[21] In effect, Gwyn had been blacklisted along with many of the writers and poets with whom he had been published since 1947. It was not the case, as Parnell erroneously suggested, that Little, Brown had 'lost interest.'[22]

Gwyn's work was steadily forgotten by all except a few of the older radicals and those writers with whom he maintained an active correspondence. That neglect made it possible in the late 1960s, in a different era from the Red Scare of the 1950s, to 'restart' his American career with the help of his friends and supporters.

One of the few in the United States outside of Gwyn's immediate circle of friends to engage with his work on an intellectual basis was Irving Grablowsky, a master's student in Lionel Trilling's Department of English and Comparative Literature at Columbia University. In 1963, Grablowsky defended his dissertation called 'Gwyn Thomas and the Welsh Renaissance' in which he argued for the need to place Gwyn's writing at the centre of the post-war Welsh literary revival.[23] Grablowsky was not all that far outside Gwyn's American circle. Born in 1917, he was a working-class, Jewish New Yorker. He had seen active service during the Second World War and afterwards earned his degree at the renowned New School for Social Research. Whilst there, Grablowsky got a few of his short stories into print – chiefly in collections edited by faculty members such as Don M. Wolfe and Frederic Morton.[24] The stories reflected Grablowsky's wider interests in proletarian literature, Marxist literary aesthetics, and communism – he was a member of the Communist Party – and provided both an indication of Gwyn's appeal and the origins of Grablowsky's interest in his work.

Another who took an active interest in the early 1960s was the Jewish New Yorker, Lewis J. Amster (1910–1991). A novelist, playwright, and erstwhile Hollywood screenwriter, with credits such as 1942's *Tough As They Come* and 1943's *Mug Town*, Amster had been active in the literary left since the 1930s writing for *New Masses* and the *Daily Worker*.[25] For a period in the Depression, he claimed he had even been a professional boxer to make ends meet. His wife (from 1961), the Cuban-American Emma López-Nussa Carrion Amster, better known by her stage name Melitta del Villar, a former medical student, was a leading figure in the Medical Aid to Cuba Committee (formed March 1962, dissolved January 1963) and the Fair Play for Cuba Committee. Therein she worked closely with the journalist William Worthy (1921–2014), made famous by his un-passported trips to Cuba in 1961; Bayard Rustin (1912–1987), the African American labour leader who was a key behind-the-scenes influence in the Civil Rights Movement; David Dellinger (1915–2004), who was one of the Chicago Seven put on trial in 1969 following the riots at the 1968 Democratic National Convention; and Freda Kirchwey (1893–1976) the veteran former editor of the progressive magazine *The Nation*.

Lewis Amster first wrote to Gwyn in the summer of 1962 proposing, as Norman Rosten had once done, an adaptation of *Venus and the Voters* for the New York stage.[26] The pair maintained an intermittent correspondence about the idea until May 1964.[27] Although it does not seem that the project ever came to fruition, Amster was sufficiently proud of the idea as to include it as part of a biographical paragraph accompanying his story 'Center of Gravity' in William Saroyan's *Best Modern Short Stories*.[28] Echoing Nelson Algren's *Never Come Morning* (1942), Amster's story of 'under the bridge' life told through the lens of a Jewish narrator, was first published in the *Saturday Evening Post* in 1965. The last of this generation of erstwhile supporters was Barbara Giles (1906–1986), another of the *New Masses* circle and the author of the 1947 novel *The Gentle Bush*, who reviewed *Wolf at Dusk* for *Mainstream*, as *Masses and Mainstream* was now known, in August 1959. But it was a different time, the aftermath of the Soviet invasion of Hungary in 1956 and Nikita Khrushchev's 'secret speech' had forced many communists to reconsider their worldview, and Giles (who remained in the American Communist Party) was not entirely sure that Gwyn had achieved his aims. 'We would hardly expect a Don Juan as the author presents him to become a revolutionist,' she wrote,

> we might, however, expect a Gwyn Thomas to interest himself more in the characters that we merely hear about, who may end as corpses displayed in the village square for the edification of other 'grumblers,' but who take that risk for the sake of life. As it is, the resemblance to twentieth-century Spain, even under Franco, is incomplete, and the story seems over-old, sad and rather oppressive, burdened by the monotony of its elegant verbalisms as well as by the unbroken round of bestiality and death.[29]

In the second half of the 1960s, with the Vietnam War raging and the counter-cultural forces on the left growing rapidly, Gwyn's fortunes in the United States were temporarily revived. In this case by two Chicagoans – Nelson Algren (1909–1981) and Studs Terkel (1912–2008) – and a New Yorker, Maxwell Geismar (1909–1979). One pre-eminent Hollywood star who also read Gwyn's work was the actor Roddy McDowall (1928–1998). His library, now held at Boston University, contains a copy of the American edition of *A Welsh Eye*. As a child, McDowall had played Huw Morgan in the Hollywood adaptation of *How Green Was My Valley* and had starred alongside Richard Burton and Elizabeth Taylor, both of whom knew Gwyn, as Octavian in *Cleopatra* in 1963. It is possible that Burton made the introduction. Nelson Algren had positively reviewed *Venus and the Voters* for the Chicago *Sun* newspaper in January 1948, writing that:

A story like this will startle; it ought to shock. Its antic tone is a way, perhaps the best way, of expressing the author's protest against everything that blocks the road to decent, intelligent, hopeful living. It is certainly the way to express his people – Celtic, lyric, humorous, and immemorially sad.[30]

Terkel himself had known about Gwyn for almost as long, before he used his eponymous radio show broadcast on WFMT in Chicago to discuss Gwyn's work, comment on and read out extracts from *A Welsh Eye* and the novels and short stories in December 1965.[31] He returned to Gwyn's work in the 1970s.[32] Both Terkel and Algren had been staple fixtures of the Chicago left in the 1930s and 1940s, and both were members of the Communist Party – although Terkel's membership was kept secret to prevent him from losing his valuable radio job.[33] Algren's politics, on the other hand, cost him his career: as biographer Colin Asher relates, the attack on former communists-turned-informants in his 1949 novel *The Man with the Golden Arm* prompted the FBI to take revenge.[34] Behind-the-scenes manipulation and blacklisting ensured Algren blamed himself for what seemed, to him, to be personal failure and for the paranoia and depression which followed. The writer 'decided his books were not being published because no one wanted to read them.'[35]

Neither Algren nor Terkel, despite the latter's determination to provide airtime in Chicago, were powerful enough to encourage a publisher to take on the task of reissuing Gwyn's writing for a new generation, but the critic, editor and academic, Maxwell Geismar, was. Geismar wrote to Gwyn in February 1967 to discuss the idea of republishing *Leaves in the Wind*. Gwyn was flattered, excited, and clearly buoyed by the idea of his best work becoming available once more in the United States.[36] In the context of the civil rights movement, the anti-war protests, and the apparent resurgence and renewal of the American left, it was encouraging that he was thought of as relevant once again. The new edition, with an introduction by Geismar, was to be published in January 1968 by the New York-based Monthly Review Press, one of the principal outlets for emergent New Left opinion in the United States (although its roots were firmly in the Old Left). Geismar's introduction appeared separately in the *Monthly Review*, a linked but independently-operated Marxist journal, in October 1967.[37] As Dai Smith has noted, Geismar 'comprehended the pared-down bleakness of [Gwyn's] imagery' and regarded the novel 'as fiction, as art, as a beautiful story ... a remarkable achievement.'[38] In the opening gambit of his introduction, Geismar insisted that Gwyn's 'more recent novels should be picked up by American publishers'; adverts for the edition also reminded readers of, or introduced them to, *The Dark Philosophers*.

Geismar's faith in Gwyn was soon rewarded when *Leaves in the Wind* went to a reprint in March 1968. The New Haven *Register* declared, in a widely circulated review, that 'seldom has more beautiful writing gone into a work which depicts so horrifying a struggle.' With the arrival of the American edition of *A Few Selected Exits* from Little, Brown in November that year, not only was Gwyn's reputation steadily being restored he now had a new generation of potential readers with which to engage. Temporarily at least. The arrival of Richard Nixon as president in 1969 and the steady rise of the 'New Right' in the 1970s, with Ronald Reagan as its leading figure, brought an end to the optimism of the 1960s and the liberalisation of American society under Presidents Kennedy and Johnson. As at the height of the Red Scare of the 1950s, when Nixon had been Vice President, Gwyn found his work once more out of favour. He was not published again in the United States in his lifetime – neither the *Lust Lobby* (1971) nor *The Sky of Our Lives*

(1972), which enjoyed a good reception in Britain, found their way to America except as imports, nor did any of his plays, not even the prize-winning *The Keep*.

The journalist Edwin Milton Yoder Jr., writing in the *Chicago Tribune* early in 1969, summed up the change of mood in his review of *A Few Selected Exits*. He remarked that the book was 'a kind of autobiographical snapshot album, [which] recalls like an old melody the Welsh paradox. Reading it, I felt the same stuffy failure to dig this race of artists; and Welsh humor remains as elusive to me as their passion for the game of Shove Ha'penny.' Yoder had almost understood, even as he complained that Gwyn's jokes were 'more American frontier' than they were '*Punch*-like.'[39] It was left instead to Richard Burton's mentor Philip Burton (1904–1995), by then director of the American Music and Dramatic Academy in New York City, writing in *Saturday Review*, to explain Gwyn's intentions and context to an audience no longer quite attuned to either. 'Gwyn Thomas,' Burton wrote, 'transmutes the commonplace into the delightfully grotesque by means of his keen perception, his twinkling compassion, his cartoon comedy, and his deft way with words.'[40] He was not entirely successful. By the end of 1969, in the absence of reviews for *A Welsh Eye* and relatively little attention afforded in the mainstream press either to the republication of *Leaves in the Wind* or to *A Few Selected Exits*, the American dream was finally over.

*

Gwyn was never entirely a victim of circumstances beyond his control. He recognised the stakes involved in the Cold War and made decisions about his friends and his publishers accordingly. Like his namesake, Dylan, Gwyn fought in the literary and cultural conflicts of the 1940s, 1950s, and 1960s, adding his

name in support of a range of initiatives. There was the World
Peace Council, which he supported alongside the composers
Aaron Copland and Dmitri Shostakovich and the writer Norman
Mailer. There was the campaign against German rearmament,
the international petition to prevent the execution of Ethel and
Julius Rosenberg in 1953, and the campaign to free the
Hollywood Ten – writers, actors and directors, including Dalton
Trumbo, Edward Dmytryk, Ring Lardner Jr., and the former
International Brigader Alvah Bessie, who were imprisoned in
1950 for contempt of Congress.[41] The same charge sent
Howard Fast to prison and its threat forced others, notably the
actor Edward G. Robinson, to renounce and repudiate
organisations and friends with whom they had previously
associated. Robinson, a liberal Democrat and New Dealer,
famously wrote an article for the right-wing *American Legion
Magazine* in 1952, in which he explained, with reference to his
testimony before the House Un-American Activities Committee,
'how the Reds made a sucker out of me.'[42]

By then, of course, Gwyn was fully engaged in his
correspondence with Norman Rosten and Howard Fast, and the
three men often set down their concerns about the political
atmosphere in the United States. Fast made Gwyn aware of the
torment of the Red Scare as the HUAC net closed in on him.
For his part, Gwyn set out his antipathy to the British
government's prosecution of colonial conflicts in Asia and Africa
as the empire began to unravel. Each fed the other's anxieties.
In one of his earliest letters to Fast, written in March 1948,
Gwyn complained that several Labour MPs he had previously
respected seemed to have mislaid their socialist principles since
coming to power. Amongst the names on Gwyn's list was that
of the Minister of Health, Aneurin Bevan.[43] It was a curious
moment, in retrospect, for Gwyn to launch into his critique,
even in private. Bevan was in the process of steering through

the creation of the National Health Service, which began operating in July 1948. James Griffiths, the former president of the South Wales Miners' Federation and since 1936 the Labour MP for Llanelli, was busy delivering the social security infrastructure and national insurance reforms necessary for the welfare state.

Outside cabinet, Ness Edwards, the Caerphilly MP, who had written early histories of radicalism and trades union struggle in the South Wales Coalfield in the interwar years, was a junior minister at the Ministry of Labour and National Service and was appointed to the privy council in 1948. Hillary Marquand, the Cardiff East MP, who had written insightful studies of unemployment in the coalfield in the 1930s, and whom Gwyn knew through the Fabian Society in Cardiff, was the Paymaster General and took up his role as Minister of Pensions in the summer of 1948. Welsh Labour members of parliament, in other words, had never had such influence on the direction of government, and yet in his correspondence with Fast, Gwyn spoke only to the flaws rather than to the possibilities of power. From Fast's point of view, Gwyn's gripes at Labour's foreign policy was an invitation to begin writing in much clearer detail about his own fears. Fast felt that post-war American society was losing its grip on the ideals of liberty as the republic slipped towards authoritarianism, or worse. 'We have already begun our own brand of fascism,' Fast told Gwyn, '[although] cloaked in The Star Spangled Banner [it] is as frightening as [any] Adolf Hitler ever cooked up.'[44]

Fast looked around at the landscape of anti-communist organisations, whether new ones such as the FBI-supported American Business Consultants Inc., or long-standing ones such as the American Legion and (in Hollywood) the Motion Picture Alliance for the Preservation of American Ideals. The latter, headed by actor John Wayne between 1949 and 1953, had widespread and powerful support within the Motion Picture industry from studio executives like Walt Disney to directors like John Ford and Clarence Brown, to actors such as Clark Gable, Gary Cooper, Ginger Rogers, and Ronald Reagan. Fast explained to Gwyn in a letter sent in April 1948 that 'storm troopers' were being organised across the country. 'Is it known in Britain today,' he added, 'there is a condition of cold and cruel terror in America that competent observers say matches what went on in Germany and Italy before the war?'[45] Gwyn could say only that it was not. His letters matched Fast's tone, especially after the outbreak of the Malayan Emergency in June 1948. 'This is nightmare stuff,' Gwyn wrote, 'this sending of our premier musclemen, the Guards divisions, to fight colonial wars that are even more brazenly disgusting than those we fought in Africa and the Far East a century ago.' He added, 'colonial crimes of the Malaya type ... proceed smoothly to their hideous climax with our "militant and fiercely anti-middle class" Mr Shinwell shedding tears of affection over the military gorillas as they set off for Singapore from Southampton.'

Gwyn's dislike of Manny Shinwell, the Secretary of State for War, was palpable. As a former member of the Independent Labour Party and an avid supporter of the Spanish Republic during the Civil War, Shinwell was a left-leaning member of the cabinet. He was one of those whom Gwyn had once admired but whom he felt had turned coat in the face of the new, nuanced realities of the post-war world. Stafford Cripps, the Chancellor of the Exchequer, who had been at the forefront of the campaign for a united front across the Left in the 1930s, a campaign Gwyn had supported, was another. Gwyn dismissed him as a 'perfidious eunuch.' Behind the scenes, ironically, the Truman administration were concerned that Cripps was guided by 'personal sympathy for the Soviets.'[46] Gwyn's greatest scorn was reserved for Ernest Bevin, the Foreign Secretary, 'whose conduct in this Berlin affair has made us ... utterly sick.' The reference was to the Berlin airlift, which began at the end of June 1948 and was intended to supply food and other goods to the people of West Berlin to prevent the entire city falling into the hands of the Soviet Union. Gwyn's dislike of Bevin was so thorough that even in his letters to Norman Rosten, who was more measured than Fast, he could not resist denouncing a man he regarded as a 'myopic Neanderthal lout of a latter-day imperialist.'

Like his American friends Gwyn initially struggled to adapt to the circumstances of the Cold War and spoke at times in a rhetoric and with an imagery which had not moved on from the fixed, pre-war binary of fascism versus anti-fascism. He was dismayed at what he regarded as the failed promise of the Labour Party in office and lashed out at those on the left who did not stand up for what he thought was morally right, especially in the field of foreign affairs. Britain's Atlanticism, the creation of the North Atlantic Treaty Organisation (NATO), and the steady reintegration of West Germany into the western alliance, all left a sour taste. It was the mirror for Howard Fast's similar attack on the political situation in the United States. There, at least, the two men agreed, there was a third way: the nascent left-wing presidential campaign of Henry Wallace. Vice President during Franklin Roosevelt's third term (1941–1945), Wallace was removed from the ticket during the 1944 presidential election by conservative elements within the Democratic Party. Keenly aware that Roosevelt was ailing and was almost certain to die in office, they were aghast at the idea of Wallace, who was thought pro-Soviet, succeeding to the presidency. Harry Truman, a moderate, hawkish senator from Missouri, was selected as the vice-presidential nominee instead. Truman became president less than four months after Roosevelt's fourth inauguration.

In 1948, Truman was up for election to his own full term. By then Wallace had become a stern critic of the administration and was nominated by the Progressive Party as a third candidate. With its platform of desegregation, a national health insurance programme, the introduction of a welfare state, and nationalisation of the energy sector, the Progressive Party was a clear retort both to the Democratic and Republican establishment and was intended as a platform for extending New Deal legislation. The Progressive Party was widely supported by communists, anti-war campaigners, members of the American Labor Party such as New York congressman Vito Marcantonio, and a variety of left-wing writers and intellectuals including Howard Fast, Studs Terkel, Aaron Copland, Arthur Miller, Albert E. Kahn, and Norman Mailer. Angus Cameron, Gwyn's American editor, was himself chairman of the Progressive Party in Massachusetts and treasurer of the Wallace for President National Committee.[47] We have, Fast told Gwyn in August 1948, 'great hopes in the growing third party movement.'[48] A reaction from Truman's supporters within the Democratic Party was guaranteed. 'It would surprise not one of us,' Fast explained to Gwyn, 'if the government, in its bestial and reactionary desperation, attempted to destroy this movement with physical force.' He added, 'these baboons seem ready to stop at nothing. Hitler may have thought that he had a propaganda machine, but it was a tiny tin trumpet compared to the blast the American press, with its ten thousand controlled newspapers, is letting loose today.'

To the right of the Progressive Party was the liberal-orientated Americans for Democratic Action (ADA) whose luminaries included Eleanor Roosevelt, future vice president Hubert Humphrey, and Arthur M. Schlesinger Jr, as well as most other prominent New Dealers. The ADA framed the Progressive Party and its Democratic counterpart, the Progressive Citizens of

America, as, at best, dupes of the Communist Party and the Soviet Union, and supported the government in its swoops on those who were active communists.[49] In July 1948, twelve members of the National Board of the American Communist Party were arrested and charged under the 1940 Smith Act with conspiracy to teach and advocate the overthrow of the US government by force and violence. Fast denounced the arrests, telling Gwyn that those sent to prison had been 'framed' and expressing concern about his own fate.[50] 'I am,' he explained to Gwyn, 'waiting on a day-to-day basis' to be thrown in jail.[51] A few months later, around the time of the presidential election, Fast added to his despairing portrait. 'For the first time in American history you have a group of people who have been indicted, tried, condemned, sentenced – and yet remain at liberty.' He continued,

> The probable reason for this lies in the enticing contradictions of the whole case. Eleven men and women, on the one hand, are sentenced to prison without having committed any crime under the written or unwritten laws of the land. On the other hand, to make the real cream of the jest, the chairman of this obscene unamerican committee which originally framed us, Mr Parnell Thomas, representative from New Jersey, has just been indicted himself on the charge of defrauding his employees.[52]

Gwyn followed Fast's descriptions avidly and seems to have generally believed in their veracity. They chimed with the material he was reading in *Masses and Mainstream*, the British *Daily Worker*, and other left-wing magazines. Britain, too, he said, perhaps as spiriting comfort for Fast, had its own third party.[53] There is some confusion as to what exactly he was referring. In his article discussing the correspondence between Gwyn and Howard Fast, the literary critic Victor Golightly speculated that the former 'presumably meant the "third way" then forming in the Labour Party around [Aneurin] Bevan.'[54] That is, the Tribune group which at the time included Bevan, Harold Wilson, Michael Foot, Richard Crossman, Ian Mikardo, and Barbara Castle. Their pamphlet, *Keep Left*, published in 1947, had advocated a European third force between American and Soviet foreign policy. But Gwyn was not yet in the frame of mind to begin his transition towards Bevanism, and his criticisms of Bevan and other left-wing Labour MPs earlier in 1948 suggests that the Tribune group was not (yet) what he meant by a third party. Instead, this was most likely a reference to Gwyn's still instinctive allegiance to the Communist Party of Great Britain, which was then at the height of its influence. He had in mind, surely, Harry Pollitt's near victory in the Rhondda East constituency in 1945 (when he came within a thousand votes of toppling Labour's sitting MP, W. H. Mainwaring), Arthur Horner's position as general secretary of the National Union of Mineworkers (NUM), and talk of Will Paynter as the successor to Alf Davies as president of the South Wales Area of the NUM.

Indeed, Gwyn was forthcoming with his American friends in his critique of the Labour government, usually from a position resonant with that of the Communist Party. Writing in September 1948, he told Fast that 'many members of the working class are beginning to believe that in foreign affairs the victory of Labour in '45 is likely to turn out one of the bitterest tragedies of our epoch. It left the ruling class still with enough strength of will and reserves of wealth to play a sharply reactionary role in world affairs and found the Labour Party bossed by such elements as Attlee and Bevin whose anti-proletarian bias is still disguised well enough not merely to fool the workers, but to draw them into the active prosecution of imperialist folly.'[55] He added, 'It makes me mad with rage when I think of the wonderful things to which we could be dedicated if fascism and its American inspiration were truly dead.' But as always, Gwyn remained silent on the domestic policies which were beginning to reshape post-war Britain. That was to prove his route towards Bevanism in the early 1950s. In fact, as he was writing *All Things Betray Thee* in the autumn of 1948, Gwyn was starting to change his mind about politics. 'We need to reinvigorate the wonderful creative legends of the people that first made socialism,' Gwyn told Fast, 'the legends of irreducible valour, humanity and friendliness ... our struggle gains wings and a splendid face as artists sing out the hymns of the common folk in the torment of their growth.'[56]

It was as if Gwyn's mind was focused on the role of the artist – in his case, the writer – in a changing world. He read Fast's new novel, *My Glorious Brothers*, a depiction of the Maccabean uprising against the Greek-Seleucid Empire in the second century BC and an allegory for the current conflict in Palestine and the emerging state of Israel. Gwyn recognised in Fast's work the possibility of historical drama as a means of conveying present-day politics: exactly his purpose in writing *All Things Betray Thee* and the unpublished *The Dark Neighbour*. 'It's a grand and lovely book,' Gwyn told Fast in November 1948,

> The theme, and the way of its telling will have a deep interest for the people of these mining valleys ... The Scriptures have been grafted into the marrow of their revolutionary tradition as intimately as the words of Marx, Keir Hardie and Lewis Jones. (This last you may not have heard of. I'll tell you about him one day. An authentic Maccabee of the fight against finance capitalism, a miner of genius who turned out to be one of the great proletarian teachers and died woefully young.) One of my friends told me he was reminded of Lewis when reading your sentence: 'And then I went back to weep with my brothers; and above the sound of the rain I could hear the people weeping.'

Those words could mount on every wind that blows out of the Rhondda.[57]

When Fast came to read *Leaves in the Wind*, as *All Things Betray Thee* was known in the United States, just six months later, he was no less fulsome in his praise, and felt sure that Gwyn had answered his own questions about artistic and revolutionary purpose. 'I have just finished a most incredible experience,' Fast wrote,

> the reading of your book, LEAVES IN THE WIND … I don't know what would be wholly adequate to say about this book [it is] a new level in the truest kind of socialist realism and humanism … you deal for the first time in our writing with the beginnings of a conscious struggle for the elimination of exploitation by the working peoples. This is real meaty stuff for any book. You go into fields that were never plowed before, and you turn over a lot of new soil. But, transcending that fact, here in this book you have put in the mouths of your characters, in a singing beautiful Celtic cadence, not what they probably said but what they would have said if they had been able to voice their dreams, their passions, and even the force of our splendid historical destiny.

He concluded,

> the beautiful thing for me is the fact that you bring to these men who made such a splendid struggle on behalf of freedom an understanding which both history and Marxism gives us. Out of this understanding, you made of their lives a poem to hope and to beauty.[58]

Such was Fast's level of enthusiasm for *Leaves in the Wind*, he devoted an entire chapter to the novel in his work of literary criticism *Literature and Reality*, which appeared in the United States in 1950. Gwyn was presented as a writer 'armed with great talent and a lyric intensity of language' and possessed of an 'inner truth [like] a ringing and lovely song,' who had written 'one of the best achievements in socialist realism that we know in Western literature.'[59] Fast's discussion, the first major piece of literary criticism to deal with Gwyn's writing at length, had much in common with the thoughts of Jack Lindsay, the Anglo-Australian novelist, translator, and communist, who included Gwyn in his *After the Thirties: The Novel in Britain and its Future*, published in 1956. For Lindsay, as for Fast, 'Thomas in all his writings has a warm and poetic feeling ... but here [in *All Things Betray Thee*] he writes with a consuming and sweeping passion.'[60] There was one distinction, writing in the aftermath of Stalin's death in 1953, Lindsay avoided any mention of 'socialist realism,' the official Soviet definition of high art and the sanctioned aim of communist and communist-aligned writers the world over. Lindsay was himself moving away from older left-wing orthodoxies – Fast would do the same in the wake of events in Hungary and the Soviet Union in 1956.

For Gwyn, corresponding early in 1950, recognition of the political underpinnings of his writing was enough to prompt an over-enthusiastic, almost childlike reply. 'I cannot describe to you the delight, the sensible unconceited delight, with which I read the pages you devoted to myself,' he told Fast having read *Literature and Reality* shortly after its publication in January 1950, 'you have made plain my innermost aims and convictions about how our class, its life and viewpoint, should be expressed in literature, better than I, with my perverse shyness, could ever have dreamed of doing.' There is a sense in Gwyn's letters to Fast, supplemented by correspondence published in *Masses and Mainstream*, of his getting involved in the political situation in the United States and bringing its terms to bear on life in South Wales, not always with a clear eye for relevance or nuance. In a letter published in *Masses and Mainstream* in March 1949, Gwyn explained that he had recently been lecturing to audiences in South Wales about contemporary American literature which 'becomes a topic of greater and greater interest to the militants over here.'[61] To aid his preparation, he confessed to having plagiarised an article from the February edition by the magazine's editor-in-chief, the literary critic and Walt Whitman specialist Samuel Sillen (1911–1973), called 'Writers and the American Century.'

Gwyn further claimed to have led a 'workers' verse-speaking group' in reading and performing the poetry of the Chilean poet-diplomat and communist senator Pablo Neruda, who had recently gone into hiding. 'We got hold of enough copies of the October [1948] issue,' in which part of Neruda's *Canto General* had appeared in translation, Gwyn said, 'to arrange a recital ... it was wonderfully moving.'[62] It was not enough to create art, even as a revolutionary artist, Gwyn thought, he also had to ferment working-class awareness and understanding to democratise access. As he explained to Nan, 'there is a strong preaching impulse in every Celt which must find vent in some way or another.'[63] The publication of Dudley Fitts's *Anthology of Latin American Poetry* in the early summer of 1948, which included excerpts from Neruda's work suggests that Gwyn was not engaging entirely in make-believe, though the exact nature of the 'workers' verse-speaking group' cannot be established at this distance. As the *Manchester Evening News* noted in response to Fitts's collection, 'one or two of these writers, like the Chilean Pablo Neruda, are already known in England, Neruda's poems are romantic, highly coloured, and extravagant, what most of us think of as typically South American.'[64]

By the autumn of 1949, Howard Fast's position in New York had become precarious. A matter of days before judgement was passed in the first wave of Smith Act trials, Fast wrote full of despair and paranoia. 'There are spies, informers, and various kinds of touts at every street corner,' he explained to Gwyn, 'Berlin at its worst was not quite as bad.' The American government 'had gone truly berserk.'[65] Gwyn was sympathetic, but at a remove there was little he felt he could do, save provide moral support and join in with protests as they arose. It is clear from Gwyn's correspondence that he had absorbed much of Fast's point of view, repeating it where it suited the moment. 'When artists in their thousands can be bludgeoned into flight and shameful silence by the repressive phobias of sick-minded fanatics and rogues,' Gwyn wrote forcefully in a letter to Fast sent in April 1950, 'the community deals itself a mortal wound.'[66] He said much the same to Nan six months later. 'The tide of panic against writers of the Left,' he said, '[is] getting almost as bad here as in the States.'[67] The conservative reaction to the post-war world, in Gwyn's view, seemed to be circling in Britain: at the general election in February 1950, Labour's parliamentary majority was reduced to five although the party had secured more than one and a quarter million additional votes compared with 1945. In Rhondda East, always the bellwether for Gwyn, Harry Pollitt's vote collapsed to fewer than five thousand from the nearly sixteen thousand won in 1945. Labour's W. H. Mainwaring added ten thousand to his tally.

Gwyn had worked hard to secure the redrawn Barry constituency for Labour in 1950, in the face of a concerted opposition advance. He liked and admired the party's victorious candidate, Dorothy Rees, a fellow teacher and a long-serving member of the town and county councils – she would later serve as only the second woman chair of Glamorgan County Council in 1964. Gwyn told Glyn Jones that 'I did some meetings ... and I went at it with the tempestuous hwyl of Lear in the storm.

My heart was in it. Behind every word was the remembered torment of the wasted, stupid years and not a Tory in the Barry land dared a second reprimand. Every anti-Labour vote in the national result was a hot coke on my body and I still feel as scarred and charred as an ancient chimney.'[68] It was a temporary reconciliation with the Labour Party. In June 1950, the Korean War broke out and Gwyn's antipathy to Attlee's foreign policy was reawakened. 'It would be wrong to say that there has been a quick or considerable revulsion of opinion in this country against the danger of a world war brought on by the war in Korea,' Gwyn explained to Howard Fast, 'we are cursed by the fact that the sending of troops to discipline [other countries] has always been epidemic in British history.'

Gwyn also felt the jingoistic British media had been complicit in creating a society lacking in compassion or critical awareness. He told Fast, 'The butchering of whole nations in the Far East which are trying to usher in a new epoch in human organization will mean very little to people put fast asleep by a Press which has presented the war as just another police operation against a covey of insubordinate riff-raff ... the masses are in a really catholic stupor and count the beads of their anti-communist ritual by the minute.'[69] Gwyn said much the same thing to Norman Rosten a few months later. 'The sort of government which we have,' he wrote, still attacking the Attlee's Labour administration, 'a sly, dangerous travesty of a real producers' democracy, reveals the state in the clearest light as an insolent thief which strips you of your substance any way you turn.' A week before Gwyn wrote to Rosten, Aneurin Bevan had been removed from his post as Minister of Health and reshuffled to the less senior Ministry of Labour and National Service, in large part because of Bevan's increasingly fractious relationship with his moderate colleagues. Gwyn's change of attitude was immediate. He told Rosten,

The rich do as well as ever. (A week in the London West End or in the snug bar parlours of our pursey little market towns where the gentleman farmers dream of the blackest counter revolution and threaten to shear Aneurin Bevan over their hot toddy, will convince one of that.) The poor are robbed with traditional ferocity with one difference: the escape routes of protest and rage which lay wide open in the days before our apostles of egalitarian democracy came to power are now closed and inside the working class movement itself I should say that at this moment, but not for much longer, the professional party bosses and coalition fanciers like [Herbert] Morrison could get a clear majority for out and out aggression alongside MacArthur and a revived Germany.[70]

A few weeks later, in early March 1951, Bevan was passed over as Foreign Secretary following Ernest Bevin's effective retirement due to ill health – Bevin died on 14 April. Bevin's successor was the 'coalition fancier,' Herbert Morrison. On 23 April 1951, Aneurin Bevan formally resigned from the cabinet citing, in his resignation speech to the House of Commons, the introduction of prescription charges and the military spending which had made them necessary. 'It is now perfectly clear,' Bevan stated, 'to any one who examines the matter objectively that the lurchings of the American economy, the extravagant and unpredictable behaviour of the production machine, the failure on the part of the American Government to inject the arms programme into the economy slowly enough, have already caused a vast inflation of prices all over the world, have disturbed the economy of the western world to such an extent that if it goes on more damage will be done by this unrestrained behaviour than by the behaviour of the nation the arms are intended to restrain.'

Even as Gwyn was moving away from communism and

towards Bevanism, he remained attached to his American friends, whose descriptions of what was going on were ever more alarming. Released from prison and in the middle of writing his new novel *Spartacus*, Fast did not hold back when, in September 1950, he told Gwyn that 'we now live in a fascist country, the madmen scream that those who talk of peace should be rewarded with the death sentence.' A couple of months later Fast went even further: 'America is now an enormous concentration camp.'[71] Gwyn's reply focused on what artists could and should do in such a situation: speak up. He told Fast that,

> We have retreated enough while the proponents of illiteracy and greed have cemented their black marriage in our midst. We are all threatened. But we are men as well as writers, and if this persecution of the free mind continues, we fail as both. The writers and thinkers are the people's tongue. Let that tongue be ripped out and the people can be assured that the process of amputation will not stop there. The legs and arms of all their fundamental freedoms will follow and the damp helpless trunk of a community enslaved will be used as it was by Hitler in 1939, to fuel whatever fire is needed to warm and solace the terrible, freezing minds of those who cannot visualise or accept life without a proper measure of hate and butchery, whose own private unease prompts them to regard the torment and disunity of man on earth as ends good in themselves.[72]

In his own way, Gwyn did just that – speak out – but always on terms he felt able to control. In May 1950, for example, during the build-up of tensions which led to the outbreak of the Korean War, and despite the physically exhausting impact of this kind of political activity, he addressed peace rallies around South Wales, passionately invoking the need for more mature solutions to the world's problems. 'The cause is good,' he told Nan, hoping to convince her his actions were worthwhile.[73]

The tone of Gwyn's correspondence, particularly with Howard Fast, led earlier biographers to dismiss the views of both men as 'naïve.'[74] But this is to misjudge both the atmosphere of the period – especially in the United States, where the Red Scare really did produce a high degree of paranoia – and the nature of Gwyn's political convictions. His communism, which lingered into the early 1950s, was instinctive, rooted in his anger at what had happened economically and socially during the 1930s, and reflected to a large degree the clarity of anti-fascist, anti-nationalist, and anti-imperialist purpose provided by the Communist Party in the interwar years. His use of terms like 'revolutionary artist' were as stereotypical as they were refulgent, and in retrospect hollow-sounding. If Gwyn was more a romantic than an ideologue, he nevertheless read voraciously, seeking out books, pamphlets, newspapers, and magazines, from both sides of the Atlantic, all with a view to developing and rationalising his position on the left. Gwyn was a subscriber as well as contributor to *Masses and Mainstream* and its predecessors *Mainstream* and *New Masses*, telling a very sceptical Glyn Jones, who was himself on the left but aloof from the Labour Party and no friend of the Communist Party, that these were 'about the most elaborate of the Left Wing quarterlies.'[75]

Books from Gwyn's library which survive from this period and suggest something of his intellectual habits include Emery Reves' essay in favour of a federal world government, *The Anatomy of Peace*; V. A. Firsoff's essay on a federal European Union, *The Unity of Europe*; John Hersey's essay on Hiroshima; and studies on the Red Scare in America published by his friend and editor Angus Cameron. He was also interested in the anti-Soviet writing of Arthur Koestler. For a while, Gwyn remained an avid reader of the *Daily Worker* and the other British left-wing magazines such as the *Communist Review*, *Labour Monthly*, and *World News and Views*, although that diminished after his political shift in the 1950s. But this was a cerebral absorption in the left, rather than card-carrying political activism, as was always the case with Gwyn. He preferred to set out his politics in the republic of letters, and through artistic endeavour, hence his attachment to the idea of the revolutionary artist, rather than by amassing a string of memberships to the Communist Party, to Labour, to the Campaign for Nuclear Disarmament, and the wider peace movement. Which is not to suggest that he did not take the language of protest and anti-capitalism seriously, simply that he was not a great 'joiner.' As he mused with Norman Rosten in January 1951,

> I suppose the road gets as rough under foot with you over there as it does here. The present dilemma (to keep the commentary quite polite) must be even more appalling to you than us. You at least might be allowed the illusion that you could have progressed as a nation without any of the bloody tomfoolery of imperialism and aggression. We have grown used to the notion that at any time we might be called upon to be butchered in the cause of a tradition of snobbery and grab which at least a third of us detest. Our numbers grow. We are accustomed to the rhythm whereby the ruling group harvested our field of strength and hope roughly once a generation but when they start sounding the bugles with the flesh scarcely off the bones of the last offerings, even the most inert begin to feel that governments must be taught to mend their ways.[76]

The best indication of Gwyn's engagement with politics as a 'letter activist' was his work with and on behalf of the African American civil rights movement. Gwyn took an especial interest and followed the fortunes of the Civil Rights Congress, which was formed with support from Paul Robeson, W. E. B. du Bois, and the folk singer Pete Seeger, from its foundation in 1946. Gwyn was held in high esteem by his American counterparts because of the support he showed. In 1953, when Robeson was invited to be guest of honour at that year's South Wales Miners' Eisteddfod in Porthcawl but was unable to travel to Britain because his passport had been confiscated, Gwyn was asked to stand in and read out a message of solidarity.[77] The link had been made by Howard Fast. Three years before, around Christmas 1950, Gwyn received a parcel from Fast containing a recording of the Peekskill concert given by Robeson in the summer of 1949. Featuring the voices of Fast, Robeson, and Seeger, amongst others, the record was propaganda aimed at drawing attention to the anti-black rioting and racist abuse which marred the concert. Few who were present were necessarily surprised at what had happened.

The community of Peekskill, nestled on the banks on the river Hudson some fifty miles north of downtown New York, had an active branch of the Ku Klux Klan and holding a fundraising concert there for the Civil Rights Congress headlined by Paul Robeson was a deliberately provocative act on the part of the left-wing organisers. The racist abuse captured on the primitive wire recorder – 'get back to Russia, ya niggers,' 'you white niggers,' 'Jews, Jews, Jews' – was (and remains) shocking.[78] Gwyn was disturbed when he listened to the recording for the first time. He wrote to Fast early in January 1951 to thank him for that 'wonderful record you sent us by Paul Robeson, yourself and other comrades' adding that 'the earth's political crust [is] cracking wider every minute' but that 'not one person in a hundred here is aware of the ghastly foredoomed farce in which we are being involved by the world's white overseers.'[79] Recognising Gwyn's appreciation and understanding, Fast engaged him, via a telegram signed by Paul Robeson, in the international protest effort seeking a stay of execution in the case of Willie McGee.[80] A young African American, McGee had been found guilty of rape by an all-white jury in Mississippi in 1945. Famously, it took just two and a half minutes to reach a verdict. Gwyn agreed immediately. His name was added to a list of global cultural dignitaries including Albert Einstein, Jean Cocteau, Albert Camus, Dmitri Shostakovich, Sergei Prokofiev, William Faulkner, and Norman Mailer.

In addition to adding his own name to the protest, Gwyn wrote to several political figures in Britain to secure their support for the cause. 'Won the sympathetic assistance of a few,' he told Fast, but the 'indifference and timidity of some of the others to whom compliance with the American-British war set-up overrides every other loyalty' was damning in Gwyn's eyes. One of those he had in mind was the Barry MP Dorothy Rees, who refused to get involved in what she regarded as the internal affairs of another country. Gwyn's efforts, as well as those of the Civil Rights Congress and the wider international community, were in vain: Willie McGee was executed by the state of Mississippi's travelling electric chair on 8 May 1951. 'We were,' Gwyn confessed to Fast a few weeks later, 'terribly upset.'[81] Fast was himself heavily involved in the struggle against legal lynchings in the late 1940s and early 1950s. In his telegram asking for support with the McGee case, Fast also referenced the Martinsville Seven, a group of young African American men from Virginia convicted of rape in 1949 – the longest trial lasted under two hours. Despite appeals and the support of the Civil Rights Congress and the National Association for the Advancement of Colored People (the NAACP), the seven men were executed in February 1951. The Martinsville case, together with that of Willie McGee, was clear evidence of the racism embedded in southern law: in Virginia, for example, white men convicted of rape were not subject to the death penalty, it was reserved only for men of colour.

Cities with large African American populations outside of the South were no haven, either. There has been 'a new wave of this particular bestiality,' Fast explained to Gwyn in the summer of 1951, 'two nights ago, a Negro father was shot down by a policeman across the river in Brooklyn. A week before that, a Negro auto worker in Detroit was sentenced to death because he shot a cop, defending his home against a group of these hoodlums who had broken in, in an attempt to lynch his son.'[82] Gwyn could do little but support his friend from the side lines, of course, occasionally joining in activities by adding his name to protest letters or writing for pamphlets circulated by Fast, such as *Steve Nelson – A Tribute* (1952). It was dedicated to the political commissar of the Abraham Lincoln Brigade in Spain who had been convicted of attempting to overthrow the federal government and imprisoned in 1950. This brought Gwyn's name into circulation alongside Alvah Bessie, Albert Maltz and John Howard Lawson of the blacklisted Hollywood Ten, and the Australian communist writer and critic Frank Hardy.[83] Such company placed Gwyn squarely in the sights of the American authorities, confirming their growing suspicions.

On 20 June, scores of FBI agents swooped on the homes of leading communists in New York City charging them with conspiracy under the Smith Act. A fortnight later, Fast's friend, the crime writer and author of *The Maltese Falcon* (1930), Dashiell Hammett, appeared before federal prosecutors seeking a group of communist fugitives. Hammett refused to co-operate, citing the fifth amendment, and was sent to prison for six months for contempt. Three days after Hammett's court appearance, Fast wrote to Gwyn with information about Hammett, some of the incriminating evidence which Hammett and Fast wished to hide, and a letter which set out Fast's fear that his life was in danger and that he too might well be re-incarcerated.[84] The documents Fast sent have never come to light but by accepting them Gwyn directly involved himself in the court proceedings against Hammett. In his reply, Gwyn sent a copy of a recently published *Tribune* pamphlet, which he thought indicative of a way out of the malaise – the surest sign Gwyn gave to Fast of his shifting politics. The pamphlet, *One Way Only*, had been written by Aneurin Bevan, Harold Wilson, and John Freeman, who had each recently resigned from the government – Bevan and Wilson from the cabinet.[85]

Knowing the recipient, Gwyn was modest with his praise, but praise it was. 'It will probably strike you as sloppy and fatuous,' Gwyn told Fast, 'but it becomes slightly more admirable when viewed against the incredible background of cowardice and crypto-Tory crookedness now established in the Labour Party.'[86] Given his commitments to the peace movement and outspoken criticism of government support for West German rearmament and the Korean War, Gwyn found the politics of *One Way Only* to be encouraging. Bevan's introduction, which set out clear opposition to increased spending on arms, was the closest any major politician had come to Gwyn's point of view since the war. In Bevan's words: 'we fear the consequences if too much of our wealth and energies is canalized into the creation of a great war machine ... it is our view that the vast war machines to which the Western world is fast committing itself will obstruct and not open the paths to peace.'[87] Free of his cabinet responsibilities, and collective responsibility for the government's actions, Bevan re-emerged in the early 1950s as a cogent, alternative left-wing voice able to present an independent, democratic socialist perspective on foreign and domestic policy. Precisely the sort of political figure Gwyn admired and willingly followed.

From the start of 1951 onwards, Gwyn allowed his

communist instincts to wither as his Bevanism developed apace. The catalyst, he explained to Norman Rosten, was the western alliance's reconciliation with West Germany, which Bevan opposed even when the Labour Party's leadership did not. 'There is no town of any size which did not extend its cemeteries after the fall of German bombs,' Gwyn wrote, 'and this is a fact which might penetrate the fog bank of patriotic stupor in the mind of some of our most cretinous Tories and cause them to denounce the wicked futilities of policies that make us walk in such mortal and shrinking circles.'[88] In 1954, Bevan and a group of left-wing MPs including Harold Wilson and Barbara Castle penned a robust response to Labour's policy statement, *In Defence of Europe*, which pushed for rearming West Germany and the country's rehabilitation – in effect accepting the division between East and West.[89] Bevan refused and argued instead that Germany could be reunited if the Western powers were willing to discuss the matter with the Soviet Union. To arm West Germany was antagonistic and counterproductive, and potentially dangerous to all sides. 'The twelve divisions [of the new West German army] will be Nazi-led and Nazi-trained,' Bevan warned.[90]

A few months later, Bevan added to his points in a speech in the House of Commons. 'Does anybody think that the people of this country will feel safer against the prospect of war if German armies with Nazi officers have atom bombs?' It was a position which Gwyn shared, together with the leadership of the South Wales Area of the NUM, much of the Welsh Parliamentary Labour Party, as well as the Welsh Regional Council of Labour, and the Communist Party. In 1962, Leo Abse, who had been elected to parliament as MP for Pontypool in 1958, pointed out that whereas 'the Labour Party and the Trades Union Congress, at their annual conferences, have made it unequivocally clear that they regard the coming of the

Panzers, under officers who supported the unspeakable horrors of the Nazi regime, as an insult to the memory of millions who died to preserve liberty and democracy from the German menace.' Gwyn spoke in similar terms, both against West German troops taking part in military exercises at the Castlemartin base in Pembrokeshire and in support of the protest organised in Swansea by the All-Wales Campaign Committee Against German Troops. 'The lives of our children and the independence of Britain as a nation,' he said, in 1961, 'are being threatened.'[91]

*

The comedy novels Gwyn wrote in the 1950s were conceived at a time when his politics were changing, and this gave them some of their different flavour. He remained sceptical of Labour's Atlanticist foreign policy but found himself drawn to Aneurin Bevan, who emerged after his resignation from the cabinet as the left's leader-in-waiting. Gwyn's intellectual alignment with communism faded in the light of Bevan's leadership, although when Gwyn signed with Gollancz in the autumn of 1950, he was surprised that the publisher even took *The World Cannot Hear You*. Gollancz, Gwyn explained to Nan, had spent much of the previous decade 'trying to bury his pro-communist past by bringing out a spate of anti-communist stuff.' What he understood by then, however, was that to remain in print he would have to be pragmatic. 'If one writes frankly and honestly these days,' he confessed to Nan, 'one is lucky to be printed at all.'[92] Working with Gollancz, Gwyn perfected the technique he referred to later as 'sidling malicious obliquity,' switching the overt politics of *The Alone to the Alone* and *The Dark Philosophers* for a lighter, riotously comic voice. He had not surrendered the political ethos of his creative project, so much as learned better to smooth the surfaces and to employ 'overtones of literary cunning.'[93] Indeed, there were his politics on the dust jacket of the American edition of *The World Cannot Hear You*:

> What I write is tied umbilically to the astonishing Rhondda Valley where I was born and brought up. It is a great sprawling mining community between high, close hills. In the course of my childhood and youth this rapidly assembled and matured community of 200,000 people was shrunken and twisted under the impact of long strikes and a bitter depression. The people, largely of Celtic stock, already plagued by a vague 'mystique' of racial defeat and a passionately lyrico-religious temperament, found their life-view darkening as their economic and spiritual underpins were sent spinning ... I was ... never free from the fierce conviction that the essence of their strange wild humor could and should be communicated, making audible every tone of their bawled comment on a pitiless and crumbling environment. Into that humor went a comradeship in multiple discomfort and mutilated longings, the pervasive memory of a half-buried, brooding, bardic culture, tales of immemorial grief set to the sweep of harps and to frame man at his daftest, nature, in the shape of hills of a mould superbly smooth, and insistent rain mist edging down towards the valley bed.[94]

Knowing something of his disappointment with the non-appearance of *The Dark Neighbour* and *The Thinker and the Thrush*, as well as the significant cuts made to *All Things Betray Thee*, Howard Fast urged Gwyn to think carefully about his approach to writing. 'You are going to fall short of the job you set out to do,' the American explained, 'until you can conceive the story emerging head and shoulders over the verbal contest of ideas. There is your greatest weakness – the one which, I think, needs to be overcome for you to step onto a new level of work creativity. The essence of the ideas we stand for is contained in the struggle of men, and the literary reflection must carry the story and the excitement of that struggle ... You must fight with yourself to tell stories as well as to project ideas ... I think it is important for you to think about this because I know of no one in Great Britain who carries the same potential as you do for beautiful and splendid writing.'[95] Neither the prospect of better plotting nor literary trickery filled Gwyn with enthusiasm. Adopting a lachrymal tone, he complained to Nan that there seemed to be 'so little of what one wants to say that one can say [and] so little of what is really important in a man's heart that can really be said.'[96]

Gwyn was more successful in this new comedic technique than he realised. His radicalism seeped through in a cast of characters featuring corrupt or corruptible local politicians, wheeler dealers, and the voters facing the challenge of holding onto their convictions in an age of affluent plenty. Behind the scenes, the tension between the commercial saleability of comedy and the philosophical desire, which had propelled Gwyn to pick up his pen in the first place, remained. Gwyn reflected on the conflict in a letter to the Welsh-born Canadian novelist Robertson Davies. An admiring critic of Gwyn's work, Davies had written an encouraging review of *The Dark Philosophers* for the Ontario newspaper, the *Peterborough Examiner*.[97] However, the two men did not correspond with each other until the 1950s, by which time Davies was writing for the Canadian magazine *Saturday Night*. In 1953, Davies reviewed *A Frost On My Frolic* together with Dylan Thomas's *The Doctor and the Devils* and James M. Cain's *Galatea*; and in 1956 set Gwyn's *A Point Of Order* alongside Kingsley Amis's *That Uncertain Feeling*.[98] Davies was clearly no great fan of Amis: 'he is a writer of great resource and ingenuity, and he can be very funny indeed. But he makes me shudder.'[99] He had much greater affection for Gwyn, thinking him 'a much finer writer' whose prose 'rises to a splendidly poetic level.'

After reading Davies's reviews, Gwyn sent signed copies of his books full of notes and 'regrets that his sort of Welshman ever go further west than Swansea.'[100] He also took the opportunity to set down his views about contemporary literature, Kingsley Amis, and his own creative ambitions. The letter, written in July 1956, merits being transcribed in full.

Dear Robertson Davies,

First, a sprinkle of penitential ash upon myself and an explanation of my silence. A few months ago my general health started to curl up in a corner. Specifically my nerves and eyes seemed to lose touch with one another and only now are they being coaxed back into an uneasy alliance.

Your novel [*Leaven of Malice*] was one of the very few bits of delight I found during the period of rest. It was a joy and I loved it. At least half a dozen of the things have moved into my private funnybone anthology, notably the scene in which the Oedipus Complex suggestion is put to Vambrace. I would give much to have your clarity of eye and openness of ear.

Thanks for the very nice review of Point of Order. Structurally, as you suggest, the book is maimed. When I wrote it I was suffering from a most troublesome sort of inner split. My spirit was as weary as an old tramp, beaten up by an awful 'tedium novellae.' I resolved that sticking a book up annually for its need of contumely and slender gain was for suckers. Short pieces were to be the thing. But novel writing is not a vocation, not a choice. It is a disease of the marrow and that Councillor Eryl Prym was writing his own agendas in no time at all. You probably spotted the exact page where I forgot about Punch and returned to the game for which I was born and at which I will die.

We were deeply interested by the review on the Kingsley Amis novel [*That Uncertain Feeling*] you had alongside mine. What you said was exactly what we think. It is one of the saddest phenomena in post-war Britain that this chilly, deliberate guttersnipery of thought and expression should have reached the status of a cult, a school. Not a Sunday passes but that a new masterpiece is unveiled in The Observer written by some bellyaching little squirt of fifteen who was poisoning his parents and raping all his sisters while writing his last chapter with a blunt knife on the bare back of a masochistic uncle. I have a feeling that this exposure of shoddy and witless gaucherie undertaken by Amis and his friends has been given the cachet of a revelation at the instance of the Carlton Club. Those dim and tottering dodos need some assurance that their special type of breeding has an irreplaceable charm. It must be shown that the Welfare State has spawned a horde of whining underlings. If we cannot restore the confidence of our social elect with the sight of ragged bodies we'll do the best we can with ragged minds. Did you see what that canting mummy Maugham had to say about this?[101]

Gwyn's low opinion of Amis was the result not only of reading his work but also a face-to-face meeting several months before the letter to Robertson Davies was written. On 1 December 1955, Gwyn took part in an Oxford Union debate alongside Amis – the first time Gwyn had been back to Oxford since he left St Edmund Hall two decades earlier. The debate had been organised by the out-going Union president, Desmond Watkins, an undergraduate from Newport then reading law at Keble College, and was broadcast on BBC radio.[102] Its theme was inspired by Emlyn Williams's interwar play, *The Corn is Green*. The two writers, Amis and Thomas, were not overly disposed to each other: in the official photograph of the event, Gwyn sat uncomfortably two seats along from Michael Heseltine; Amis, whose enthusiasm for the setting and the occasion was obvious, sat next to Watkins. The debate itself was notable for the comments Gwyn made, live on air, about the 'imbecility' of Welsh nationalism and in its review, the *Western Mail* characterised an encounter between Amis, 'the Teddy Boy of literature' and Gwyn, 'the clown who could easily give a sensitive reading of Hamlet.'[103]

Gwyn's contempt for his British contemporaries, which he confessed in his letters to his American and Canadian friends, was mirrored in his enthusiasm for writers from the other side of the Atlantic. Nor were they always correspondents at a remove, as Fast and Rosten had been – although Fast did eventually meet Gwyn on a visit to Britain in 1969.[104] Americans such as Jay Williams and Ezra Jack Keats wrote to and visited Gwyn in Barry, the latter (who was also an illustrator) struck up a particularly close relationship with Lyn. Williams first got in touch with Gwyn in the 1940s and the pair exchanged letters for most of the next two decades; the dozen copies of Williams's novels which survive as part of Gwyn's library are a further testament to that friendship, as is a significant amount of correspondence to and from Gwyn and Lyn held at Boston University in the United States. Gwyn probably encountered Jay Williams in the pages of *The New Masses*, to which the latter contributed both articles and short stories in the 1940s.[105] Williams had first written to tell Gwyn that he was 'knocked over' by *The Dark Philosophers* and looked forward to visiting that summer.[106] As a result of several visits to Barry, Jay Williams produced a pen portrait of Gwyn in his 1956 travelogue, *A Change of Climate*. A variation of the chapter was also published as an interview with the *Barry Herald*.[107]

'Gwyn,' Williams observed affectionately, 'is large and fat and hearty, he is a lover of good food and good drink, and since giving up cigarettes ... he has made up for them in the quantity of beer he can consume. He wears thick-rimmed glasses and from behind them his massive face glowers.'[108] Williams's account is of particular interest because this was the first occasion, in print, that Gwyn had allowed any sort of acknowledgement of his unpublished Spanish novel, *The Dark Neighbour*. Williams wrote,

> Only once, I think, did he forsake the locale of the Rhondda in a book. That was when he did a very long historical novel about the Moors in Spain; he wrote me with characteristic violence and gusto:
>
> 'The Moors buried around Cordoba will spin a little in their graves to find a boy brought up among the Congregationalists so warmly cordial to their viewpoint. It's good gutsy stuff, with four more deaths than John Hersey got into his book *Hiroshima* and two blank pages to be drawn on by people who cannot read. I've even included a rape in case the Guild of English-Speaking Writers should make this a condition of membership.'
>
> Unfortunately, nobody liked that book, and the editor he and I shared at the publishing house said that he got so deeply into the thinking and feeling of the epoch he was writing about that he left the reader outside. Gwyn said to me later, 'That crack gave me a beautiful picture of the reader groping with a lantern around the Alcazar, tapping on the walls in search of a way in, and shouting to me inside doing research on nautch girls, "Come on, Thomas! Stop your blo-o-ody messing about, boy, and open up!"' He set the work aside and counted its time more or less lost.[109]

A Change of Climate was illustrated, in the American edition, by Williams' friend Ezra Jack Keats, the Brooklyn-born Jewish artist credited with introducing multiculturalism into mainstream children's literature in the United States.[110] Williams made the formal introductions with Lyn and Gwyn, and Keats visited the pair during a research trip in the summer of 1954. At the time, Keats was engaged in illustrating Phyllis Whitney's 1955 novel, *Mystery on the Isle of Skye*.[111] It was the start of a friendship which lasted until Gwyn's death.

Although of a different character to the correspondence-friendship shared with Howard Fast and Norman Rosten, which offered ample opportunity to engage in mutual anxieties, Gwyn's relationships with Robertson Davies, Jay Williams, and Ezra Jack Keats, were important to him precisely because they provided a North American literary circle, and one which was not overtly political. It was America, as much as Spain or South Wales, which held Gwyn's imagination – pondering, as he often did, the historically retrograde step taken by his grandfather to return from the New World to the Old. To say nothing of the cloak of Welshness adopted by Gwyn's American-born father, Walter. Gwyn's American friends – Fast, Rosten, Keats, and Williams – all shared another characteristic particularly prized by the Welshman: New York City. They were a link back to the city of Damon Runyon and of Gwyn's cinematic imagination. But if Gwyn was to truly emulate his literary inspiration, the novel was the wrong approach: Runyon had been, first and foremost, a journalist and short-story writer. Fortunately, Gwyn's success as a novelist in the 1950s brought invitations to write different pieces for newspapers and magazines. The shorter form suited Gwyn's lighter, comedic style and, when slotted in amongst other commitments and the day-to-day job of teaching, was much less onerous a task than novel writing.

Ideally there would have been a British equivalent of the *New Yorker* to which Gwyn could have contributed. The kind of work which yielded an income, as regular and as steady as possible, and allowed him to say the things he wished to say, to write in his own way, but which did not demand high levels of concentration or the deliberate work of creating plot and character. Instead, as Gwyn observed sardonically in a letter to the BBC producer Peter Duval Smith, with whom he had worked on an adaptation of Vive L'Oompa in the summer of 1955, he got himself 'landed with a weekly column for the Welsh *Empire News*. [How] in God's name can a civilised man find anything to say at intervals of seven days to the readers of a Sunday paper? And this stuff has to tie in with Welsh affairs. There isn't a Welsh affair in sight that isn't black and blue with polemical flogging. Last week I gestured like Moses over the library rate in Treorchy and the murder rate in Carmarthen. Never mind. I'm just over the page from Diana Dors. So if you hear a swift tearing sound you'll know what's going on or coming off.'[112]

---

[1] Letter from Gwyn Thomas to Norman Rosten, 30 October 1950, in Smith, *Wales: A Question for History*, 181.

[2] Letter from Gwyn Thomas to Norman Rosten, 12 December 1950. The date referred to would seem to be Tuesday 5 December 1950.

[3] Norman Rosten, 'Lorca', *New Masses*, 14 April 1942; 'Ode to the Departure of Winston Churchill', *New Masses*, 26 March 1946.

[4] Gwyn Thomas, 'Where My Dark Lover Lies', *California Quarterly* 1, no. 1 (Autumn 1951), 34–40.

[5] *LFD*, 153.

[6] *California Quarterly* 1, no. 1 (Autumn 1951), 2.

[7] Although it was warmly supported by American leftist writers such as Erskine Caldwell (1903–1987) and Jack Conroy (1899–1990). The fullest discussion of Moses Bragin's life and career can be found in Betty Ann Burch, *The Assimilation Experience of Five American White Ethnic Novelists of the Twentieth Century* (London, [1990] 2018), ch. 5.

[8] Ben Field, 'Welsh Comedy', *Masses and Mainstream* 1, no. 1 (March 1948), 80–82.

[9] Ben Field, 'Leaves in the Wind by Gwyn Thomas', *Masses and Mainstream* 2, no. 9 (September 1949), 82–84.

[10] Howard Fast, 'A Work of Genius', *Daily Worker* (New York), 28 December 1947.

[11] GT letter to HF, 3 February 1948. NLW, GTP, J35/1.

[12] An indicative advert, together with Fast's endorsement, can be found in the *Chicago Star*, 19 June 1948.

[13] Arthur M. Schlesinger Jr., *A Life in the 20th Century: Innocent Beginnings, 1917–1950* (Boston, 2000), 401–2.

[14] Duncan White, *Cold Warriors: Writers Who Waged the Literary Cold War* (London, 2019).

[15] Kahn later wrote his own book about Matusow, with a foreword by Angus Cameron, titled, *The Matusow Affair: Memoir of a National Scandal* (New York, 1987).

[16] It received a scattering of reviews, notably in the *Saturday Review*. Walter Havighurst, 'Humor But No Green Valleys' *Saturday Review*, 29 March 1952. Havighurst (1901–1994) was professor of English at Miami University in Ohio. In his view, Gwyn's novel was 'unique' in character because of the 'presence of tenderness in the midst of daftness and derision'.

[17] Letter from Gwyn Thomas to Hannah Thomas, 25 October 1950.

[18] Clem Hodges, 'Burning Books, Burning Authors – Crisis in Publishing', *Masses and Mainstream* (November 1951).

[19] Senate Judiciary Committee, *Strategy and Tactics of World Communism: The Significance of the Matusow Case* (Washington DC, 1955), 701.

[20] NLW, GTP, J67 – Letter from Stephen Greene Press regarding the publication of *A Welsh Eye*, 4 October 1965.

[21] 'When Don Juan Hit The Sunset Trail', *Washington Evening Star*, 8 February 1959.

[22] *LFD*, 132.

[23] Irving Grablowsky, 'Gwyn Thomas and the Welsh Renaissance' (Unpublished MA Dissertation: Columbia University, 1963). A copy is held in the Rare Book Library at Columbia. The Barry student was Dai Smith.

[24] Irving Grablowsky, 'Tiger, Tiger', in Don M. Wolfe (ed), *New Voices: American Writing Today* (New York: Perma Books, 1953), 142–147; Irving Grablowsky, 'Pierhead Jump', in J. Ernest Wright and Frederic Morton (eds), *American Vanguard* (New York, 1956), 171–179. Others at the New School in this period included William Styron and Mario Puzo. Maxwell Geismar noted later that 'the New School has become the richest center of new fiction among all our colleges and universities'. Cited in Peter M. Rutkoff and William B. Scott, *New School: A History of The New School for Social Researcher* (New York, 1986), 229.

[25] Lewis Amster 'Four Year Perspective', *The Screen Writer* 1, no. 9 (February 1946). One of his regular collaborators in the 1930s and 1940s was Albert Bein (1902–1990), a Russian-Jewish immigrant, former hobo, and Guggenheim Fellow.

[26] NLW, GTP, J31/1, Letter from Lewis Amster to Gwyn Thomas, 25 June 1962.

[27] NLW, GTP, J31/1, J31/2, Letters from Lewis Amster to Gwyn Thomas, 1962–8 May 1964.

[28] William Saroyan (ed), *Best Modern Short Stories* (New York, 1965), 486. Saroyan was himself no stranger to the literary left and had been part of Sanora Babb's circle in California in the 1930s.

[29] Barbara Giles, 'Don Juan in Purgatory', *Mainstream* 12, no. 8 (August 1959).

30 *Chicago Sun Book Day*, 7 January 1948.

31 Chicago History Museum, Studs Terkel Radio Archive, T2030 SRO: Terkel reads extracts from *A Welsh Eye*, 1 December 1965.

32 Chicago History Museum, Studs Terkel Radio Archive, T3299.01 SRO: Terkel reads 'The Teacher' by Gwyn Thomas, 10 November 1977.

33 Federal Bureau of Investigation, Archives: Louis Terkel File. Available online: https://vault.fbi.gov/louis-terkel [Accessed: 27 July 2019] For Terkel's party membership, see page four.

34 Colin Asher, *Never A Lovely So Real: The Life and Work of Nelson Algren* (New York, 2019).

35 Asher, *Algren*, xv.

36 NLW, GTP, J68/1–3, Letters from Maxwell Geismar to Gwyn Thomas, with replies, 12 February–24 March 1967.

37 Maxwell Geismar, 'Leaves in the Wind: An Introduction', *Monthly Review* 19, no. 5 (October 1967), 56–64.

38 Smith, *Aneurin Bevan*, 14.

39 Edwin M. Yoder Jr., 'The Welsh Paradox', *Chicago Tribune*, 6 March 1969.

40 Philip Burton, 'Ever Green Was His Valley', *Saturday Review*, 26 April 1969.

41 Dmytryk later wrote a memoir of his imprisonment and involvement in the Hollywood Ten, *Odd Man Out* (Carbondale, Illinois, 1996). Trumbo set out his perspective in a volume of his correspondence, *Additional Dialogue: Letters of Dalton Trumbo, 1942–1962* (New York, 1970), and in a more contemporary pamphlet published by the California Emergency Defense Committee to raise funds to defend those blacklisted. Gwyn purchased a copy, which survives in his library. Dalton Trumbo, *The Devil in the Book* (Los Angeles, 1956).

42 Edward G. Robinson, 'How The Reds Made A Sucker Out Of Me', *American Legion Magazine* 53, no. 4 (October 1952).

43 University of Pennsylvania, Howard Fast Papers: Letter to Howard Fast from Gwyn Thomas, 8 March 1948.

44 Letter to Gwyn Thomas from Howard Fast, 19 March 1948.

45 Letter to Gwyn Thomas from Howard Fast, 25 April 1948.

46 National Archives and Records Administration, RG 341, Box 747, Report by US Ambassador to London, 11 July 1947. Cited in Ken Young, 'Cold War Insecurities and the Case of John Strachey', *Intelligence and National Security* 29, no. 6 (2014), 905. Shinwell was thought equally suspect by the Americans.

47 Schlesinger, *A Life*, 456; Columbia University Special Collections, 'Reminiscences of Donald Angus Cameron, interviewed by Louis Sheaffer, 1977'.

48 Letter from Howard Fast to Gwyn Thomas, 1 August 1948.

49 Those involved in the PCA included Dalton Trumbo, Dashiell Hammett, Lillian Hellman, Edward G. Robinson, James Cagney, Frank Sinatra, Gregory Peck, Olivia de Havilland, Bette Davis, Paul Robeson, and Norman Mailer.

50 Letter from Howard Fast to Gwyn Thomas, 13 August 1948.

51 Letter from Howard Fast to Gwyn Thomas, 1 August 1948.

52 Letter from Howard Fast to Gwyn Thomas, c. November 1948. J. Parnell

Thomas (1895–1970) was the Republican Representative for New Jersey's 7th District, serving from 1937 until January 1950. Thomas was chair of HUAC from 1947–1948, during which the Hollywood Ten were first called to testify. He was indicted for tax evasion and fraud in early November 1948. *New York Times*, 9 November 1948.

[53] Letter from Gwyn Thomas to Howard Fast, c. August 1948.

[54] Golightly, 'We who speak', 75.

[55] Letter from Gwyn Thomas to Howard Fast, 24 September 1948.

[56] Letter from Gwyn Thomas to Howard Fast, 6 November 1948.

[57] Letter from Gwyn Thomas to Howard Fast, 6 November 1948.

[58] Letter from Howard Fast to Gwyn Thomas, 16 July 1949.

[59] Howard Fast, *Literature and Reality* (New York, 1950), 67.

[60] Jack Lindsay, *After the Thirties: The Novel in Britain and its Future* (London, 1956), 118.

[61] Gwyn Thomas, 'Neruda in Wales', *Masses and Mainstream* (March 1949), 96.

[62] As above. The full epic was published in Spanish in Mexico in 1950, with an English edition published by *Masses and Mainstream* in the same year. The translation in 1948 was by 'Waldeen', a professional dancer who befriended Neruda on his arrival into exile from Chile. John Felstiner, *Translating Neruda: The Way to Macchu Picchu* (Stanford, 1980), 19.

[63] Letter from Gwyn Thomas to Hannah Thomas, undated but September 1946.

[64] *Manchester Evening News*, 12 May 1948.

[65] Letter from Howard Fast to Gwyn Thomas, 12 October 1949.

[66] Letter from Gwyn Thomas to Howard Fast, 17 April 1950.

[67] Letter from Gwyn Thomas to Hannah Thomas, 25 October 1950.

[68] NLW, GTP, J39/6: Letter from Gwyn Thomas to Glyn Jones, February 1950.

[69] Letter from Gwyn Thomas to Howard Fast, 16 September 1950.

[70] Letter from Gwyn Thomas to Norman Rosten, 25 January 1951.

[71] Letter from Howard Fast to Gwyn Thomas, 10 September 1950; Letter from Howard Fast to Gwyn Thomas, 7 November 1950.

[72] Letter from Gwyn Thomas to Howard Fast, 17 April 1950.

[73] Letter from Gwyn Thomas to Hannah Thomas, 23 May 1950.

[74] *LFD*, 123–124.

[75] NLW, GTP, J39/1: Letter from Gwyn Thomas to Glyn Jones, 5 June 1948.

[76] Letter from Gwyn Thomas to Norman Rosten, 25 January 1951.

[77] *Daily Worker* (New York), 2 November 1953.

[78] Howard Fast, Pete Seeger, Paul Robeson, the Weavers, *The Peekskill Story* (New York, 1949); Howard Fast, *Peekskill: USA* (New York, 1954).

[79] Letter from Gwyn Thomas to Howard Fast, 2 January 1951.

[80] Telegram from Howard Fast and Paul Robeson to Gwyn Thomas, May 1951.

[81] Letter from Gwyn Thomas to Howard Fast, 26 May 1951.

[82] Letter from Howard Fast to Gwyn Thomas, 4 June 1951.

[83] Howard Fast et al, *Steve Nelson – A Tribute* (New York, 1952). A copy of the pamphlet is held as part of the Civil Rights Congress papers at the Schomburg Center of the New York Public Library.

[84] Letter from Howard Fast to Gwyn Thomas, 12 July 1951.

[85] Aneurin Bevan, Harold Wilson, John Freeman, *One Way Only* (London, 1951). The pamphlet was published in early July 1951. A follow up, *Going Our Way* (London, 1951) appeared a few weeks later.

[86] Letter from Gwyn Thomas to Howard Fast, 21 July 1951.

[87] Aneurin Bevan, 'Introduction', *One Way Only*. Cited in Foot, *Aneurin Bevan*, volume 2.

[88] Letter from Gwyn Thomas to Norman Rosten, 25 January 1951.

[89] Labour Party, *In Defence of Europe* (London, 1954).

[90] Aneurin Bevan, Barbara Castle, Tom Driberg, Ian Mikardo & Harold Wilson, *It Need Not Happen* (London, 1954), 13.

[91] *Daily Worker*, July 1961. NLW, GTP, K30. Gwyn's message was also publicised in East Germany. See, for instance, *Neues Deutschland*, 14 July 1961.

[92] Letter from Gwyn Thomas to Hannah Thomas, 25 October 1950.

[93] *Artists in Wales*, 71.

[94] Gwyn Thomas, *The World Cannot Hear You* (Boston, 1952). The politics were picked up by Robert Friedman in his review of the novel for the New York *Daily Worker*. The review was published in the edition of 16 May 1952.

[95] Letter from Howard Fast to Gwyn Thomas, 1950.

[96] Letter from Gwyn Thomas to Hannah Thomas, 29 November 1949.

[97] Robertson Davies, 'Weekly Book Review', *Peterborough Express*, 18 February 1948.

[98] Robertson Davies, 'Two Thomases and a Cain', *Saturday Night* 69, no. 2 (17 October 1953).

[99] Robertson Davies, 'A Matter of Morality', *Saturday Night* 71, no. 9 (7 July 1956).

[100] Queens University, Kingston, Ontario, Robertson Davies Collection, WMR/R1/S2: *A Point of Order* by Gwyn Thomas.

[101] Robertson Davies Collection, WS/R5/S4: *A Few Selected Exits* by Gwyn Thomas, with enclosed letter from Gwyn Thomas to Robertson Davies, 20 July 1956. Gwyn is referring here to W. Somerset Maugham's angry disdain for *Lucky Jim* and Jim Dixon, the hero, especially, expressed in a column in the *Sunday Times* at Christmas 1955. Dixon was a 'white collar proletariat [who] do not go to the university to acquire culture, but to get a job, and when they have got one, scamp it … They are mean, malicious, envious … Charity, kindliness, generosity are qualities which they hold in contempt. They are scum.'

[102] *WM*, 12 December 1955; *Liverpool Echo*, 10 December 1955.

[103] *WM*, 19 December 1955, 22 December 1955.

[104] Howard Fast, 'In Search of the Welsh', *Esquire*, 1 December 1969.

[105] Jay Williams, 'The End of the War', *The New Masses*, 23 April 1946; 'What Do Kids Read?', 10 June 1947.

[106] *LFD*, 113; Howard Gottlieb Archival Center, Boston University, Jay Williams Papers, Boxes 30–31: Letter from Gwyn Thomas, 1949, Letter from Lyn Thomas, 10 October 1949.

[107] *Barry Herald*, 6 September 1956.

[108] Jay Williams, *A Change of Climate: A More Or Less Aimless And Amiable Account* (London, 1956), 14–15.

[109] Williams, *Change*, 16–17. The editor was Angus Cameron. 'Nautch girls' is a reference to a form of dancing and dancers originating in India.

[110] Keats had been born Jacob Ezra Katz, but formally changed his name in 1947 – the anglicised form allowing him to evade what he perceived to be increasing anti-Semitism in post-war America.

[111] Keats, too, maintained correspondence with Gwyn and Lyn, albeit on a rather more modest basis. The letters are held at the University of Southern Mississippi. Ezra Jack Keats Papers, DG0001/U/1022-1026: Letters from Gwyn and Lyn Thomas to Ezra Jack Keats, 1955–1981. See also NLW, GTP, J40: Letter from Ezra Jack Keats to Gwyn Thomas, 20 August 1975.

[112] NLW, GTP, J53: Letter from Gwyn Thomas to Peter Duval Smith, 12 September 1955. The column was called 'Man to Man'. *WM*, 10 September 1955.

CHAPTER SIX

Clout that Dreamer

The *Empire News*, launched with pomp and ceremony on 3 October 1954, was Wales' first Sunday newspaper.[1] By the end of the decade 'no other paper printed outside London [had] a circulation to compare.'[2] Its appeal was based on an accessible tabloid style, rich in gossip and heavily illustrated, with celebrity columnists drawn from the worlds of entertainment, literature, politics, and the arts. The singer and actor Harry Secombe. The novelist Jack Jones. Miners' leaders Arthur Horner and Will Paynter. Politicians George Thomas and Jim Griffiths. And, of course, the leading sports stars of their day, including boxers Dai Dower and Jack Petersen. This was a Welsh newspaper, so went the advertising each Saturday in the *Western Mail*, written in Wales, printed in Wales, full of Welsh features, with 'more Welsh news, more Welsh pictures, gossip, Welsh sport,' and all for a Welsh audience. Gwyn joined the newspaper early in 1955, delivering his unique take on the changing nature of life of the Valleys.[3] He was already a known quantity to the editors and, more especially, to the paper's northern proprietors having written previously for the long-running Manchester-based original (known from 1955 as the *Empire News and Sunday Chronicle,* and which merged with the *News of the World* in 1960).[4]

Gwyn used his regular columns in the Welsh *Empire News* to write, perceptively, about the growing affluence of the post-war Valleys, and the implications of their regained prosperity for realising long-held social and cultural ambitions. In the spring of 1958, for example, he wrote a four-part series about the Rhondda, examining the transformation of the district since the dark, deforming days of the interwar Depression. 'Once the miner's wife scraped and saved for a day trip to Barry Island,' he remarked, indicatively, 'now she spends a fortnight at Bournemouth – even Biarritz. Once it was make-do meals, makeshift homes and make-mend clothes; now it's television and washing machines.'[5] The portrait Gwyn painted of rapid social and economic change was more overt in his journalism than in his novels, an appeal to readers armed with mug of tea and a round of toast on a lazy Sunday morning to think about what their lives had become since the war and to be more adventurous lest the good times come to a sudden end – again. It was not all that long ago, Gwyn reminded his readers, that 'life was raw; conditions of work hard, even brutal. And often, as a kind of wild hanging of rage and resentment against the light in many lives, there was a deal of violence.'[6]

As well as his clear-sighted understanding of post-war affluence, Gwyn also revealed a mind sensitive to the experiences and rights of women. In one entry in the *Empire News* in 1958, he observed that the Rhondda had once been 'a man's world and there were too many men who lacked the discipline to see that a woman's rights ranked equally with their own.' He made similar points on television, too, albeit a decade later. As he observed when visiting a new comprehensive school in Fairwater for TWW, 'it wouldn't be a bad idea for this work with ovens, rollers and fillers, were shared by the boys, it would enable the two sexes to share responsibility for the world's stock of indigestion, and it would spare women the shame of feeling that their first function is to keep men glutted and dozy.' Gwyn appealed to men to realise the truth of the modern world. 'Last week,' he continued, this time in the *Empire News*,

I was sitting in a club at Tonypandy talking with a group of miners long retired from the pits. The club was a survival of the period when such bodies as the Maes-yr-Haf settlement at Trealaw held the smelling salts to the townships that were almost on their feet. We talked of their womenfolk, of how, by contrast, they saw the young women of today. There were, of course, the usual complaints of married couples neglecting the minds and bodies of their children to hang on to all the privileges that could be bought only with a large joint income. … But the men I met were agreed that there had been elements of serfdom and intolerable misery in the lives of the women of their generation. And unanimously they praised providence, full employment, electrical wizardry and a more joyous social philosophy for having helped in the great liberation. How nice for a change to hear the typical valley wise crack of 1958: 'I'd have a twenty-four inch TV screen but I've only got a twenty-three inch front room.'

Viewing Welsh history through the eyes of women, Gwyn added subsequently, 'gives a measure of the forward steps that have been made.' Titled 'Seven Women of Rhondda,' the article identified a series of archetypes and historical staging posts: the Tonypandy mother who had come down to Porthcawl for the Miners' Eisteddfod and the housewife standing with her husband outside Notre Dame in Paris. 'He's been here on his own twice, with the rugby,' she said, 'But now he's here with me and the cricket.' There was the widow of the First World War who had starved during the interwar years but took full part in the action against the means test all the same; and there was Gwyn's childhood memory of one of the old women of Porth who had worked underground before that was banned. There was the woman he met at Trecco Bay who loved staying in the caravan because 'I've always wanted to cook and watch the sea at the same time.' And there were the two young women on their way down to Cardiff for a night out. 'The music of all freedom was in their eyes and I gladly suppose a fair provision of blessed cash in their glossy handbags.'[7]

The *Empire News* columns were inevitably promoted, in tabloid fashion, as 'forthright' and 'outspoken,' or as hard-hitting gazes at the valleys, their people, their possibilities, and their problems. Gwyn certainly lived up to the advertising bluster and to the necessary performance. But he also recognised a golden opportunity to write the first draft of jokes and the quick-witted observations which found their way into novels and short stories, and in later years into contributions made on radio and television. A good example of this process of invention lies in a discussion of Trecco Bay and its modern caravan park on the South Wales coast near Porthcawl. The first version of the joke was published in *Empire News*, a more refined version appeared in the script for a TWW programme on the Vale of Glamorgan a few years later. 'A tricky business all these caravans,' Gwyn wrote in 1958,

Did you hear about that chap from Maesteg? Down here with his family. Very poor head for direction in sand. Caravan right in the middle of the camp. Came back from Porthcawl one night. Few pints and a sing-song. On his own, of course, because of the kids. No moon. Very dark. Dunes very treacherous. Got lost. Couldn't find the alley his caravan was in. Almost crying now. Went creeping up to caravans in the dark calling very softly at the door his wife's name. 'Meg, Meg,' very softly like that. Before the night was out he found twenty women called Meg, got himself in four fights, [and] was given a ticket by the police for not having his feelings under proper control.

The 1962 television version showed the joke's development:

'there is the story of the miner returning from a jovial evening in Porthcawl. He had forgotten the exact site of his caravan and was not sufficiently in touch with the gypsies to make a good guess. He wandered up and down the endless avenues of caravans, tapping on windows and doors, calling out the name of his wife – Megan, Megan – he didn't find his wife, but he found five women called Megan and got a week's gaol for hindering sleep and undermining confidence.'

A similar process lay behind a joke discussed by Raymond Williams in a seminar paper on the Welsh Industrial Novel given before a university audience in Aberystwyth in September 1977. 'When Gwyn Thomas says of an unemployed miner that he has thought more deeply about rent than anybody since Ricardo, he is not just making the kind of easy joke which becomes characterised as quirky Welsh humour. The more you think about this, it's one of the bitterest things ever said because it reveals that sudden alteration of dimension between formal thought and the experience of suffering, which is concealed inside the joke.' Williams's reference, and the commentary provided, drew on Glyn Jones's discussion of the same bit of humour in *The Dragon Has Two Tongues* in 1968. Gwyn's joke was first made in print in *The Stranger At My Side* in 1954. It reappeared in a variation in the *Western Mail* in the 1970s, that time with the narrative distance removed and Gwyn himself inserted into the telling. 'As a precocious boy in a community where plentiful disease gave the only hint of family planning,' he wrote, 'I proceeded almost without pause from comics to the works of that sourest of economists, [Thomas] Malthus.'

Gwyn was an enthusiastic contributor to various Welsh newspapers throughout his professional career and readily accepted commissions when they were offered. He wrote intermittently for the *Western Mail* and the *South Wales Echo* from the mid-1950s onwards, and with notable frequency in the 1970s.[8] But he avoided, almost entirely, the Welsh literary magazines. He never wrote for Keidrych Rhys's London-based *Wales*, for instance, although it drew regular contributions from friends such as Alun Richards, Glyn Jones, and the poet Huw Menai, and published some of his aphorisms in its pages. Similarly, only one of Gwyn's short stories was ever published in Raymond Garlick's *Anglo-Welsh Review*. Set in Belmont, 'I Think, Therefore I Am Thinking,' appeared in 1959. Had he wished to do so, there is no doubt that Gwyn could have written frequently for such ventures and been as active a literary critic as his contemporaries. He chose otherwise, preferring instead to write for national journals and magazines such as *Coal*, the *Listener*, the *New Statesman*, the *Spectator*, and the *Times Educational Supplement*. Gwyn seems to have reasoned against speaking 'in-group,' to borrow a phrase from historian Eric Hobsbawm, to a Welsh audience about Welsh matters, and through magazines aimed at the small, and often disinterested, jealous and snobbish, Welsh middle class. Instead, he found editors in London willing to offer him money and space to write about his Wales. It was a gamble, but one which paid off: thanks, in large part, to Mr Punch.

*

On New Year's Day 1953, Malcolm Muggeridge (1903–1990), the deputy editor of the *Daily Telegraph*, succeeded the cartoonist Kenneth Bird (1887–1965) as editor of *Punch*. Muggeridge immediately set about transforming the ailing, century-old magazine into the British equivalent of the *New Yorker*. During a visit to the United States a few months after his appointment, Muggeridge explained in an interview with the American magazine that it was his intention to 'bring in some new writers ... and make [*Punch*] more topical.'[9] As his biographer has noted Muggeridge thought 'the business of a humorous or satirical magazine must be to ridicule the age in which we live, and particularly those set in authority over us.'[10] One of the writers approached was Gwyn, who had first come to the notice of the magazine in 1951 when Richard Mallett reviewed *The World Cannot Hear You*. The novel, Mallett suggested, and Gwyn's writing especially, was as brilliant as that of the contemporary Irish satirist and novelist, Flann O'Brien.[11] Muggeridge's offer was serendipitous. *Punch* had more than one hundred thousand subscribers and was an influential voice in the English literary world bringing together a range of writers from Kingsley Amis to John Betjeman, Keith Waterhouse, and Alan Coren. It was easily to prove Gwyn's largest audience outside of his television and radio work and an important gateway into the top tier of contemporary writing.[12]

'I have reservations,' Gwyn told Nan at the outset, 'because I have a feeling that the average reader of *Punch* would in no way consider me funny; or, at least, about as funny as I would consider him.'[13] These were soon cast aside and Gwyn set about writing to the best of his ability, gaining the support not only of Muggeridge but also the latter's successor as editor, Bernard Hollowood. Gwyn wrote for *Punch* for more than fifteen years. His first article, 'On Leaving A Lover,' appeared on 29 July 1953; his last, 'The Pausing Places,' on 23 October 1968. He appeared in the magazine with remarkable frequency and, in all, contributed well over one hundred pieces – far more than either Kingsley Amis or John Betjeman in the same period – and many of them were reprinted in other contexts.[14] At least four of Gwyn's books had their origins either in part or completely in this work: *Ring Delirium 123* (1960), *A Welsh Eye* (1964), the memoir *A Few Selected Exits* (1968), and *The Lust Lobby*

(1971).[15] Michael Parnell's posthumously published collection *Meadow Prospect Revisited* (1992) was also based largely on Gwyn's contributions to *Punch*. The relationship came to an end abruptly on the appointment of William Davis as editor early in 1969. Davis, the creator of the BBC's *Money Programme* in 1966, strongly disliked Gwyn's brand of humour and cut him loose.

Alongside *Punch*, Gwyn also joined the stable of writers including Sid Chaplin, Gerald and Lawrence Durrell, and J. B. Priestley, who were employed by the satirical magazine, *Lilliput*. At the time, it was edited by Jack Hargreaves (1911–1994), who also served as editor of *Picture Post*. He moved to ITV in 1959, presenting *Gone Fishing*, the magazine programme *Out of Town*, and creating the popular children's television programme *How* alongside presenter Fred Dinenage. Lyn thought the offer from Hargreaves was a signal, as she explained in a letter to Nan, that Gwyn was 'very near the top now, and although he may never make much money out of his books, he has made a very considerable reputation.' She added, 'although he is already committed to too much work, he has written some very witty stuff for Punch ... He has also been asked to write for Lilliput which has amused us very much, but the publicity value of these periodicals is terrific. They are worth cultivating.'[16] Lyn's amusement almost certainly arose from *Lilliput's* reputation for publishing 'tasteful' black and white nude portraits of women; but it was an important outlet. Gwyn's short story, *A Team of Shadows*, appeared in the magazine in November 1953.[17] Given an over-committed schedule, Gwyn did not write again for *Lilliput* until February 1959, when he contributed candid observations about the Brains Trust.[18]

If *Lilliput* raised a chuckle, Lyn's reaction to some of the other magazines to which Gwyn contributed must have been quite different. In the 1960s, Gwyn was commissioned to write for several of the emerging glamour magazines of the period. Top of the list was the short-lived *King*, which was initially underwritten by the strip-club owner Paul Raymond but later found support from celebrities including Peter Sellers, Bob Monkhouse, and David Frost. *King* sought Gwyn's services as an interviewer. In January 1966, for instance, a few months before the General Election, he was tasked with quizzing the Liberal MP Jeremy Thorpe about the party's prospects.[19] A few months later, Gwyn was back talking about 'a certain winner' in the magazine's regular 'Hard Word' feature.[20] Gwyn also had a brief engagement with *Town*, which originally launched as *Man About Town* in 1952, but was renamed in 1960 (initially as *About Town*) after it was purchased by Michael Heseltine and his Cornmarket group. Gwyn's short story, 'Trigger,' was published alongside work by John Updike, Graham Greene, and Ted Hughes.[21] Given recent biographical interest in Gwyn's sexuality and sexual behaviour, not least the author's frequent and enthusiastic expiation in his private notebooks 'on the zealous masturbation of his adolescence,' the fact he wrote for men's magazines in the 1950s and 1960s can easily be misinterpreted.[22]

The reality is that these were commonplace commissions and indicative more of the possibilities which writing for major national magazines had brought to the fore, rather than any overwhelming desire on the part of a middle-aged man to have soft pornography lying around the house for his wife to find: in fact, as well as many of his contemporary male writers both of Gwyn's editors at *Punch*, Malcolm Muggeridge and Bernard Hollowood, wrote themselves for *King* and *Town*. They most likely made the introductions. Men's magazines were part of an eclectic approach to publishing, a habit which became more pronounced after Gwyn left teaching at the start of the 1960s, when he was less interested in writing long-form fiction and when he needed to bring in a relatively stable freelance income with more than a decade before he could draw his pension. Gwyn does not seem to have been especially deliberate in his choice of magazines. Thus, he placed articles in periodicals as various as *Argosy*, *Holiday*, *Ingot*, *Magpie*, *The Montrealer*, *The Reporter*, *Twentieth Century*, and in both the American and British editions of *Vogue*.[23] The result was his work was set alongside that of other high-profile celebrities and the leading authors of the day: they became aware of him. American and Canadian magazines paid better than their British counterparts, too, which explains at least some of Gwyn's transatlantic appearances, although he was also courted by editors.[24]

One such approach was made by Harry Sions, a former correspondent for *Yank* magazine, a weekly published by the US Army during the Second World War, who first noticed Gwyn following publication of *The Love Man* in the United States in 1959. At the time, Sions was editorial director of *Holiday*, a glossy travel magazine packed with a starry array of household names including Joan Didion, Ernest Hemingway, Jack Kerouac, William Faulkner, and John Steinbeck. *Holiday*, it was said, did for travel what *Vogue* did for fashion, selling the idea of travel 'as enrichment, a literal path to spiritual betterment.'[25] Sions tasked Gwyn with writing about Wales and gave the essay, as he put it, 'place of honor' in the September 1960 issue for being written 'with humor and affection.'[26] Gwyn's essay was published as 'Journey Through Wales' and began in his typically ironic style. 'I don't belittle those wonderful piles of rock and earth,' he wrote, 'the queen mountains of the globe, the Everests and Kilimanjaros, that sit quietly just under the sun and stare down at you with those great icy eyes.'[27] Sions got from Gwyn exactly what he wanted: a retort to an earlier piece on Wales penned by Richard Llewellyn.

Llewellyn had originally written a fantasia full of pseudo-medieval romance and Celtic mysticism but the editors were after something more in tune with the idea of the valleys presented in *How Green Was My Valley* (1939) and, more especially, John Ford's Oscar-winning film adaptation.[28] The Americans quickly realised that the submission was a fake and tried to choreograph something better. 'It would be extremely interesting to American readers,' wrote one of the magazine's editors, 'if you tell more about the miners of today, their working conditions and way of life ... for Wales means coal and coal miners and their hardships to most American readers.'[29] Llewellyn lacked the requisite knowledge of Wales to do so, of course, whereas Gwyn's authenticity was guaranteed. So from 1960 to the spring of 1965, Gwyn was invited back to *Holiday* several times, producing articles on topics as various as Martin Luther, Cotswold Pubs, King Arthur, and Spanish literature.[30] But for a contractual dispute, which resulted in the departure of Sions and other long-standing editors in December 1964, Gwyn might have written much more for *Holiday* and found a happy platform in America for his work.[31] As it was, Sion's resignation meant that the commissions from the magazine quickly dried up. Fortunately for Gwyn, Sions soon found a new role as a senior editor at Little, Brown in Boston and he was able to use his influence to commission the American edition of *A Few Selected Exits*.

The experience with *Holiday* was common. Gwyn lost out as editors moved on. Gerald Taaffe, the Chicago-born editor of *The Montrealer*, Canada's equivalent of the *New Yorker*, who had been in post since May 1960, left the magazine at the end of 1965 to develop a freelance writing career in Ontario. During his tenure, Taaffe viewed Gwyn as one of the big-name contributors who would occasionally write for the magazine, together with the leading Canadian novelist Hugh MacLennan and the English writer Alan Sillitoe. Gwyn's first short story for

The Montrealer, 'Jennie Bell,' appeared a few months after Taaffe's arrival with at least one other, 'Violence and the Big Male Voice,' appearing in the magazine before his departure.[32] Taaffe had joined *The Montrealer* when the previous editor, David Hackett, a close friend of Robert F. Kennedy, left to join John F. Kennedy's presidential campaign.[33] The last of the three major North American magazines which picked up Gwyn's writing in the 1960s, albeit only once, was Max Ascoli's influential mouthpiece for American liberal internationalism, *The Reporter*. 'A Harvest Frenzy,' an unusually pastoral short story set on a farm in the 'borough' of Meadow Prospect, appeared there in late April 1966.[34]

By the end of the 1960s, Gwyn's links with the lucrative but fickle magazine market in London and New York began to diminish: his long-running relationship with *Punch* ended in 1969, a regular column in the National Union of Teachers magazine, *The Teacher*, which began in 1963, stopped at much the same time. A selection of his articles for the latter formed the basis of *A Hatful of Humours* published in 1965. By the 1970s, articles by Gwyn published in national magazines and newspapers were few and far between: some appeared in London *Vogue*, in the *New Statesman*, the *Daily Telegraph* magazine, and a series in the *Guardian* in the very hot summer of 1976. There was one avenue which remained open, and which allowed Gwyn to turn what might have been a difficult situation into a new opportunity: the *Western Mail*. Invited to become the paper's television critic, with regular book reviewing as an aside, Gwyn relished the assignment. His lengthy stint, characterised by an idiosyncratic and sometimes caustic approach, began in the autumn of 1970. He joined a relatively small band of household names from the well-established Maurice Wiggin at the *Sunday Times* to younger men such as Clive James, who joined the *Observer* in 1972.

*

Gwyn had been in front of the television cameras for almost twenty years when he became a critic for the *Western Mail*, which gave him an unusual depth of experience. Most of his colleagues lacked similar expertise. Television criticism only became a distinct journalistic specialism in the 1970s, with older writers having begun their professional lives as theatre or literary critics. And they frequently complained of the apparent loss of stature. T. C. Worsley, the critic at the *Financial Times*, wrote tellingly of an 'illness [which] plunged me overnight from the theatre ... (of which I had some twenty years' experience) into the television world (of which I had precisely none).'[35] Maurice Wiggin, too, confessed to being 'far more a reporter, an observer, a narrator, than an analytical critic' and that until he became a television reviewer had seen nothing 'but the boxing.'[36] Gwyn had no such qualms and revealed a catholic taste; his articles for the carefully wove social commentary and personal habits into his reflections on broadcasting. A typical column is this one from the summer of 1975, which began:

August 23.
A Sunday night series which has done much to deepen the solemnity of the Sabbath and send us into Monday uncheered is 'Against the Crowd' from ATV. The idea has been to study the plight of various categories of misfit, rebel, failure and outcast. It has been, in short, an album of our sorest and most publicised wounds.

Gwyn then considered the series as a whole (or as much of it as he had seen, at least): Fay Weldon's *Poor Baby*, which dealt with learning disabilities in childhood; Nigel Kneale's *Murrain*, with its examination of witchcraft and superstition; Howard

Schuman's study of contemporary racism and identity; and Kingsley Amis's *We Are All Guilty*. Of the latter, Gwyn wrote, 'Last Sunday, *Against the Crowd* was *We Are All Guilty* by Kingsley Amis. The title is a sour smile at the over-compassionate who, in the Amis view, are being taken for a disastrous ride by a growing horde of delinquents and parasites. The theme is one of the most frequently scratched areas of our social skin. Mr Amis is one of our wittiest novelists. [However] the play put one in mind of Hamlet trying to find a credible role in a Z Cars charge room.' What was missing, Gwyn thought, was humour: as though somehow the earnestness with which the series had been written betrayed a lack of understanding:

> One does not look for laughs in a leper-island, which is what the theatre of pity tends to be. But, all the same, from proceedings so consistently glum a curious comicality with a cosmic taste seeps through. Rebels and reformers seeking temples to outrage or hearts to change are clowns like the rest of us.

At times, Gwyn could hardly contain his deep disgust and anger at what had happened to the world in his lifetime. Thames Television's *The Final Solution*, broadcast in two parts in August 1975, prompted one such expression of horror. 'The viewing world should have felt scalded,' Gwyn wrote. Adding that,

> As I looked at it, I tried to keep my raging disgust in some kind of civilised control. Surely of all the events of this century which might have inflicted some kind of irreversible brain damage on our species this must be the most devastating. ... By a striking coincidence BBC 2 showed some days before *The Final Solution* two of the most memorable classics of German silent cinema, *The Cabinet of Dr Caligari* and *Metropolis* made twelve and five

years respectively before the coming to power of the Third Reich. Hitler and his demented master folk were foretold in both works. We saw the same irresistible rhythm of nightmare, the same bewitched automation, the same apocalyptic sense of humanity blowing its brains out that went to make Auschwitz.[37]

Although frequently funny, the column was laced with an underlying seriousness even when discussing programming such as *Doctor Who* or the Gerry Anderson live-action series *Space 1999*.[38] As Gwyn put it, 'with the progressive withdrawal of buses I hope one day to board the last Dalek to Pontyclun.' Gwyn's commentary on literature, theatre, and the arts, showed him to be an insightful observer: challenging where he felt trends or practitioners had erred, encouraging where they had shed genuine light on the human condition. 'Graham Greene,' Gwyn wrote typically early in 1976, 'has never been one to encourage humanity to have a good opinion of itself.' A few weeks earlier, just before Christmas 1975, he mused on the shift from the big to the small screen. 'The replacement of the cinema by tv as the main story-telling medium,' he wrote, 'has altered the whole landscape of fiction. During the cinema's boom-time it was ruled by men who rose from the lowest levels of personal culture to dictate the patterns of the world's sensibilities.' They were, he added, 'a gaggle of latter-day Romanovs – autocrats devoid equally of taste and truth who seized the world's most powerful medium' and turned it into a megaphone and a mirror for their own private lives and sensibilities. Television 'has made sociologists of us all.'

Few critics were able to pontificate so convincingly, in the space of a few paragraphs, on the failures of programmes such as *The Old Grey Whistle Test*, 'the worst idea ever conceived for tv,' the sadness of the life of Judy Garland, and the brilliance of *Dad's Army*. 'I will have a look,' Gwyn wrote in his

Christmas roundup for 1975, at the *Wizard of Oz* 'because when I first saw it I felt that a girl who so trenchantly proclaimed a belief in magic could find little in her own life.' As for *Dad's Army*: 'tribute must be paid to the best idea ever spawned by that perverse monster, situation comedy, and to the most splendid team of comic actors ever assembled in the canon of television.' Of course, given the column appeared in the *Western Mail*, there was an inevitable concern with forms of Welshness, as Gwyn's observations on his friend Windsor Davies's 1976 appearance on *This Is Your Life* (then presented by Eamon Andrews) demonstrated.[39] He wrote:

Then came Windsor Davies, a man who looks, sounds and is a Celt of courage and integrity. The comrades from the colliery in Nantymoel bore witness to Windsor's labours as a junior electrician. We heard of his long and often painful journey out of teaching into acting, a shining exception to the rule that keeps Welsh classrooms uniquely well-stocked with frustrated actors. Witty growlers and grimacers of high talent whose audiences have fallen quite still behind deposits of council chalk.

Watching him beam with pleasure as the past gave up its ancient traces in his honour, it struck me that the comedy-trick which gave him his first authentic home as the sergeant major in 'It Ain't 'Alf 'Ot Mum' reflects one of the most interesting details of life in the South Wales Valleys. That was the almost absurdly emphatic relish taken in the speaking of English by those whose Welsh had just departed. English consonants had never known such a heyday, stammers of delight trembling on the Silurian tongue as each new hard sound came up.

Gwyn's Saturday television review appeared for most of the 1970s and was his primary journalistic outlet in the final decade of his life. As Jeffrey Robinson and Brian McCann observe in the introduction to their collection of Gwyn's columns, *High on Hope*, published in 1985, Gwyn's reviews were 'ostensibly a criticism of the week's television [but] served mainly as a launching pad from which Gwyn was able to take off on many and varied tangents.' Thus, he was able to move thematically from the funeral of Charles de Gaulle in November 1970 to humorous discussions of Kermit the Frog and Yogi Bear, to the timeless observation that 'the last World War will be fought between the literate and thoughtful and the vandalistic mob. The cause of the war might well be a decision to repeat *Match of the Day* on all channels right through the week.'

Gwyn's book reviews for the *Western Mail*, which date from the start of the 1960s onwards, were similarly wide-ranging. He tackled Len Deighton's 1970 novel, *Bomber*; Walter Langer's 1972 psychoanalytical study *The Mind of Adolf Hitler*; Paul Johnson's historical study of the English, *Off-Shore Islanders* (1972); Trevor Fishlock's *Wales and the Welsh* (1972) and its sequel *Talking of Wales* (1976); Peter Tinniswood's comedic novels, *Mog* (1970) and *I Don't Know You Cared*, which first published in 1973 and adapted for BBC television towards the end of the decade; and Emyr Humphreys' 1974 novel, *Flesh and Blood*, the first part of the seven volume Land of the Living sequence. More esoteric reviews included treatments of Ken Baynes's *Sex*, part of the Welsh Arts Council's art and society series, and Kenneth Young's *Chapel*, both in the autumn of 1972. The most significant reviews were of Hugh Thomas's landmark and prize-winning history *The Spanish Civil War* in 1961; Raymond Williams's novel *Second Generation* in November 1964[40]; Rhys Davies's 1969 autobiography, *Print of a Hare's Foot*, through which Gwyn introduced the concept of the Welsh European, a decade before it was then used as a self-descriptor by Raymond Williams[41]; and of David Illingworth's

1975 play *Aneurin Bevan: Struggles Against the Iron Heel* published by the Welsh Drama Company.[42]

In his reviews, Gwyn began the process of stripping away some of the verbal masks which had disguised the political honesty of his novels and short stories of earlier decades. 'It is so sad,' he wrote, 'that so much South Welsh talent should have to grow from such a pungent compost of early mutilations.' He added, in a different column, that 'literature is basically the great freemasonry of loneliness. Writers wait for you. When a book is written the writer calls out in an empty street. For many years to come odd people come and answer the call. This silent intercourse is incomparably the most precious element in human existence.' But autobiography was not inserted without regard for purpose. Gwyn was an observer, placing himself into the story only when it was necessary. Otherwise, he used analytical asides and pen portraits of indicative figures – Aneurin Bevan, Roy Jenkins, and Charlie Chaplin among them – to make his case. Take Gwyn's twin observations about the economic turbulence of the 1970s, on the one hand, and Bevan's apparent turn away from the Labour Left in the final months of his life. Gwyn wrote,

what his [Bevan's] immutably radical friends would have called his mellowing duplicity, was simply an accident of late dusk. The fatigue of office and the onset of disease which made him a little more averse to solitude and struggle.

Compared with him, Lloyd George used the escape apparatus early on. He found himself a war he could applaud in company with the dukes he had earlier wished to dynamite. Bevan had no such luck. The things he had identified as social blights as he walked the mining valley streets and made his first calculations, looked no less vile to him even after he had taken many hints of luxury and indulgence aboard his life, and lived in a house that had nothing of the Tredegar stamp.

In a very real sense, Bevan's rise out of the valley to economic security was Gwyn's own post-war trajectory.[43] A detached bungalow in the tiny village of Peterston-super-Ely in the Vale of Glamorgan, trips abroad to Moscow, Berlin and New York, and a feted literary career, was a world away from the radical upstart living in an overcrowded terrace in the Rhondda who wanted to destroy every capitalist he saw and imagined himself a revolutionary artist. But neither man let go of their political core. In fact, Gwyn's antipathy to rising unemployment, industrial turbulence, and especially to Welsh nationalism, was based on what he saw as the echoes of the 1930s and the need to invoke a vigorous political response. What was nationalism, he thought, even its Welsh variant, but fascism by another name; an undermining of the universalism to which the revolutionary movements had aspired earlier in the century.[44] 'We have altered the tone,' Gwyn lamented, 'little more.' As for deindustrialisation, he wrote in a column for *The Times* in 1970 that 'Cardiff has a wry look, twisted painfully away from one source of gain and poised tentatively in the direction of another.' The impending demise of coal was really what lay beneath the sudden fascination in Welsh nationhood and capitalism, adding that the industry's decline 'has left as many vacuums in the mind of this region as its roistering phase made cavities in its earth. But this will swiftly pass. The shock of loss and change even on this scale becomes more and more treatable. We hope and stay wary.'[45]

Gwyn began writing columns of this kind in the 1960s when the success of *The Keep* brought a wave of invitations from the editors of the major London dailies. Counter-intuitively, perhaps, most of the offers came from right-wing or Conservative-supporting newspapers. In November 1961, it was announced that Gwyn had joined the *Daily Mail* as a columnist. His first piece, 'The Man Who Made Critics Laugh,' began in typical style: 'I am a social virgin,' he wrote, 'My ideal is a life so bare of artificial encumbrances that I could keep padding unscathed through blackness and H-bombs.' Gwyn gave a nod to his literary influences, too. 'My favourite corner in literature,' he wrote, 'is the group of sardonic Radicals who did their best humorous writing in the [thirties] in America – Dorothy Parker, Don Marquis, [James] Thurber, and the rest.'[46] Between November 1961 and October 1962, Gwyn produced six columns for the paper addressing youth offending, the campaign for nuclear disarmament, personal self-belief, the process and experience of deindustrialisation, the visit of Soviet tourists to Britain, and the rise of bingo in the South Wales Valleys.[47] And that was that. Gwyn's writing did not seek to fit in with the rest of the newspaper's style (to say nothing of its politics) and the arrangement did not last.

Writing for the *Daily Mail* was little more than a financial quickie and Gwyn hardly produced his finest work. Across Fleet Street, editors seemed to pick up on a lack of enthusiasm for this kind of journalism and the calls stopped, although invitations from provincial titles in England, such as the *Reading Evening Post*, continued to trickle in.[48] The best of the six pieces for the *Daily Mail* was the last, which served as a prototype for subsequent discussions about the decline of literacy and political debate in the valleys and the rise of commercial distractions. 'The impact of this plague on some of our small industrial villages is sad,' he wrote of bingo, 'the welfare halls with their cinemas were the eyes and the conscience of such places, and the one spot where the young could know the excitement of a big, shared pleasure.' Gwyn returned to the dilemma once again in *A Welsh Eye* in 1964 and in 'Plaster Saints in the Valleys,' an essay contributed to *Twentieth Century*'s provincial culture series in the winter of 1965–66. The articles Gwyn wrote for the *Daily Express*, which were published in 1962 and 1963, were of a similar character to those for the *Daily Mail* and tackled a range of issues relating to childhood such as one's first crush and the question of changing the age of criminal responsibility in England and Wales from being a mere eight years old.[49]

*

If Gwyn ever measured his success in terms of opportunities to write, and to make his voice heard, and he almost certainly did think in those terms, then by the 1970s he was conscious that his journalistic career was in decline. The last regular outlet, aside from his *Western Mail* television review column, was in the press allied to the BBC and ITV. He wrote regularly for the *Radio Times* and *The Listener* as well as for *Television Weekly* and the *TV Times*. Most of the articles were written to accompany a broadcast rather than being any kind of opportunity to debate or to argue a point. Nevertheless, they formed an important component of Gwyn's corpus of writing, and one which has tended to be overlooked or has been misrepresented.[50] At a time when overt advertising was not permissible on the BBC and trailing of programmes was much more limited, the articles acted as precisely that kind of promotional activity. But there was more to it than that. Gwyn's sequence of articles for *The Listener* came in the second half of the 1970s and linked together his television play on George Bernard Shaw and J. M. Barrie, his recollection of travelling (by bus) to Oxford for the first time as a young man, ideas about the meaning of spring festivals, and Spain.[51] They were reflections on a lived life and the idiosyncratic process of writing, more than they were pieces submitted in response to a commission or the transaction of a writer in financial need.

Take the article on spring festivals written for *The Listener*,

265

which in its autobiographical elements recalled *A Few Selected Exits*, albeit with the details altered to suit a new purpose. 'Once I had a period of insomnia that kept me up reading in the kitchen from midnight until dawn,' Gwyn wrote, 'fifty pages an hour, one cigarette every three hours, a short chat with the friendlier roaches when I got dazed by the traffic of ideas.' Then, at half past seven in the morning, Gwyn switched on the gramophone. 'I never had anything thrown at me. My melody at sunrise was always the adagio of Mozart's Clarinet Concerto. Then, one April morning, one of my brothers, drunk on the earth's swiftly rising sap, smashed the disc to bits. I have never really trusted the spring from that day to this.' In *A Few Selected Exits*, the music was by Rachmaninov instead – the adagio of his second piano concerto. 'My brothers would come down the stairs in varying states of grunting rage, wishing to hang Rachmaninov and flog me.' The truth of Gwyn's single-mindedness was contained in both anecdotes, whether the music blaring from the gramophone of a morning was by Mozart or Rachmaninov.

It was all a strange echo, at least for Gwyn. Forty years earlier, as an otherwise unemployed graduate, he had served his apprenticeship as a writer and as a journalist with the *Rhondda Leader*. As 'Our Porth Correspondent,' he wrote reviews of drama and cinema, covered sports competitions and elections, and penned obituaries of residents. As with the *Daily Mail* and *Daily Express*, Gwyn's politics differed significantly from those of the *Rhondda Leader*. The experience was to serve as the basis of Hugh Evans's short-lived and ill-fated turn as a journalist on the *Clarioneer* in *Sorrow For Thy Sons* – the newspaper's name intended to evoke a link with the Labour Party and was a stand in for the *Rhondda Leader*. The conversation Gwyn wrote between Hugh and Mr Anderson, the editor of the *Clarioneer*, was a telling one. 'Working for the press, Mr Evans, is a great responsibility and a great opportunity,' the scene began, 'you are never to be forgetful of that. A great opportunity. Were you conscious of that when you applied for the position of local correspondent of our paper?' Hugh Evans replied, bluntly,

> I was conscious of the fact it might provide me with pocket money. That's all. I'm fully qualified to teach, Mr Anderson. I don't see that you are doing me any great favour by giving me this job. In different circumstances I might be earning a good wage. But I'm not. So the less we talk about responsibilities and opportunities the better.[52]

All the way along, Gwyn used commissions for broadcast and for print, as well as his fictional creations, to shape and reshape the way in which he told his own story – the synergy between *Punch* and *A Few Selected Exits* is not a surprise when it is recognised. Observations which appeared novel at the end of his life had often appeared in print decades earlier: sometimes the words changed, the anecdote or joke told in a slightly different way, but almost always with the understanding that the audience was new and so was the performance. Seemingly ephemeral activity, such as the 'Gwyn Thomas Looks Again' column for *Television Weekly* in the 1960s, which was written in the knowledge that those words would largely disappear once that week's schedules had been and gone, could come back as an anecdote given in a radio broadcast more than ten years later and seem fresh and original. A story about travelling to Cardigan in a van in 1940, given to John Ormond in 1981, appeared first in a column in *Television Weekly* published nearly twenty years earlier in 1962. 'I was taken to Cardigan,' he wrote on a lorry belonging to a friend of mine. He was a man who never took his eyes off the road or his tongue off the topic he happened to be pursuing. The door on my side of the lorry had a defective lock. As we neared Carmarthen my friend was throwing the light on the situation in France, at that moment unusually murky. He swung the lorry around Carmarthen bridge, the door sprang open and I went rolling like a hoop towards the Towy. My friend was on the farther side of Carmarthen and still explaining France before he noticed that I had left the cab.[53]

The column was originally published to accompany the series of short films broadcast on TWW on *Wales And The West* which Gwyn co-wrote and in which he co-starred with the poet John Betjeman, one of his fellow *Punch* writers. They were an added reflection on the weekly visit. When writing about Pontypridd, Gwyn could point out the 'kaleidoscope of Mid Glamorgan ... [the] land of tough men, lovely women, tall mountains, deep seams, and a record collection of perpendicular streets.' And note, also, that 'South Wales has few places that can be singled out and lingered over. We have not had the good fortune to have towns of deep and striking beauty like Bath or Sidmouth. Even John Betjeman, with his masterly eye for spotting odd bits of neglected loveliness, would find it hard to view an average mining village with anything but a puzzled frown. We may not have deliberately gone after beauty with a hatchet, but in the majority of our townships beauty has managed to get itself scalped.'

Gwyn would drop in the phrases which worked so marvellously on television in later years, such as the encapsulation of his father, Walter, as 'an underground ostler with no love of coal and no luck with horses ... a catalogue of hoof-prints and a founder member of the Great Depression.' On television it featured in the opening narration of *One Pair of Eyes* broadcast in 1969 but was first run out in an autobiographical column published in *Television Weekly* in August 1962. In this way, writing for publication and writing for broadcast were rooted in the same source of self-image and black comedy. Gwyn may well have felt greater affinity for written word, observing that writing 'is utterly private and involves an enormous amount of sitting down,' but there is little doubt that broadcasting brought him the greater audience and the best chance to embody his character. He could observe sardonically that 'I have brought high principles to the novelist's craft. I eliminated adventure, romance and profit,' but the same could never be said about his broadcasting work. Television and radio were, except for *The Keep* on the London stage, to bring the greatest successes of Gwyn's career. For the generation which grew up after the publication of *The Love Man* in 1958, the last novel published in his lifetime, television was the primary basis of their familiarity with Gwyn's gifts with the English language. The result was a change in character from writer to broadcaster, from the Rhondda Runyon to the Great Communicator.

[1] *WM*, 1 October 1954.

[2] *WM*, 18 May 1959.

[3] *WM*, 10 February 1955. The article was published in the *Empire News* (Cardiff) on 13 February 1955. It was followed, from 20 February 1955, by a series of focused case studies about 'what is right and what is wrong' in the Valleys, including on the Rhymney and Sirhowy Valleys (*Empire News*, 13 March 1955) and Merthyr Tydfil, Brynmawr and Abertillery (*Empire News*, 20 March 1955). The series was curtailed, somewhat, by the outbreak of the national newspaper strike in late March 1955 and did not resume until late April. *WM*, 22 April 1955.

[4] Gwyn Thomas, 'My Heart Sang on a Hilltop', *Empire News* (Manchester), 13 March 1953; a further article was published in the newspaper on 24 March 1953.

[5] Gwyn Thomas, 'The Rhondda Rich', *Empire News* (Cardiff) 13 April 1958. Hereafter all references to the newspaper are to the Welsh edition.

[6] Gwyn Thomas, 'The Rhondda Rich', *Empire News*, 20 April 1958; the series continued in the editions of 27 April and 4 May.

[7] Gwyn Thomas, 'The Seven Women of Rhondda', *Empire News*, 11 May 1958.

[8] Amongst the earliest commissioned pieces were published in the *WM*, 23 April 1955, 19 December 1955.

[9] *The New Yorker*, 23 May 1953.

[10] Ian Hunter, *Malcolm Muggeridge: A Life* (Vancouver, 2003), 185–186.

[11] Richard Mallett, 'The Happy Breed of Voters', *Punch* 22 August 1951. O'Brien – the pen name of Brian Nolan – joined the *Irish Times* in 1940 and wrote his Cruiskeen Lawn column until his death early in 1966. He wrote two landmark novels in English, *At Swim Two Birds* (1939) and *The Third Policeman* (1967), and the Irish language classic *An Béal Bocht* (1941).

[12] Confirmed in 1958 when Gwyn was invited to lecture at the Cheltenham Literature Festival for the first time. His theme: 'contemporary humour'. *Tewkesbury Register*, 26 September 1958.

[13] Letter from Gwyn Thomas to Hannah Thomas, 25 May 1953.

[14] The high watermark of Gwyn's career at *Punch* was between 1960 and 1965 when he wrote fifty-six articles, the equivalent of half of the entire corpus he submitted from 1953 to 1968.

[15] Those parts of *A Few Selected Exits* which reused material from *Punch* include the entirety of chapter three and three of the six sections of chapter five.

[16] Letter from Lyn Thomas to Hannah Thomas, 12 July 1953.

[17] Gwyn Thomas, 'A Team of Shadows', *Lilliput* 33, no. 6 (November/December 1953), 12–15.

[18] Gwyn Thomas, 'How It Feels To Be A Subordinate Crumb On Television', *Lilliput* 44, no. 2 (February 1959), 24–27. *Lilliput* merged with the pin-up magazine *Men Only* eighteen months later. The article would be recycled for use in *A Few Selected Exits* (as the opening section of chapter five).

[19] Gwyn Thomas, 'Jeremy Thorpe in Interview with Gwyn Thomas', *King*, January 1966.

[20] Gwyn Thomas, 'Hard Word: Gwyn Thomas on a Certain Winner', *King* April 1966.

[21] Gwyn Thomas, 'Trigger', *Town*, 3 October 1962; NLW, GTP, C86.

[22] Prys-Williams, *Autobiography*, 107.

[23] Gwyn Thomas, 'The Little Baron', *Vogue* (London edition), April 1958; 'Welsh Hi-Fi', *Vogue* (New York edition), October 1959; 'My Day', *Vogue* (London edition), February 1972.

[24] Leader, *Amis*, 401.

[25] Michael Callahan, 'A *Holiday* for the Jet Set', *Vanity Fair*, 11 April 2013.

[26] Harry Sions, 'Editorial', *Holiday* August 1960, 3.

[27] Gwyn Thomas, 'Journey Through Wales', *Holiday* September 1960, 34–44, 132–135. The article mirrored other travel pieces such as 'One Welshman's Wales', written for *Travel and Camera* 32, no. 6 (June 1969).

[28] Richard Llewellyn, 'Wales', *Holiday* May 1951, 87–89.

[29] Harry Ransom Center, University of Texas, Richard Llewellyn Papers, Box 11, Folder 12: 'Letter from Richard L. Field to Richard Llewellyn, 1 July 1949'.

[30] Gwyn Thomas, 'Martin Luther: The New Piety', *Holiday*, January 1964; 'Quest for King Arthur', *Holiday*, August 1964; 'Tranquillity and Warm Beer: The Cotswold Inns', *Holiday*, September 1964; 'A Joyful Noise', *Holiday*, December 1964; 'The Passionate Authors', *Holiday*, April 1965.

[31] *New York Times*, 12 March 1964, 20 March 1964, 4 December 1964.

[32] Gwyn Thomas, 'Jennie Bell', *The Montrealer*, August 1960; 'Violence and the Big Male Voice', *The Montrealer* May 1960.

[33] Robert Thacker, *Alice Munro: Writing Her Lives* (Toronto, 2011), 162–165.

[34] Gwyn Thomas, 'A Harvest Frenzy', *The Reporter*, 21 April 1966.

[35] T. C. Worsley, *Television: The Ephemeral Art* (London, 1970), 11–12.

[36] Wiggin, *Memoirs of a Maverick*, 200–201, 207–208.

[37] Robert Wiene's *The Cabinet of Dr Caligari* was released in 1920; Fritz Lang's *Metropolis* appeared in 1927.

[38] Something of the humour evident in the columns can be found in Jeffrey Robinson and Brian Hope (eds.), *Gwyn Thomas: High on Hope* (Cowbridge, 1985).

[39] The episode aired on 7 January 1976.

[40] Gwyn Thomas, 'Review of Raymond Williams, *Second Generation*', *WM*, 8 November 1964.

[41] Gwyn Thomas, 'Review of Rhys Davies, *Print of a Hare's Foot*', *WM*, 3 June 1969; Raymond Williams, 'The Welsh Trilogy; *The Volunteers*' in Raymond Williams, *Politics and Letters* (London, 1979), 296.

[42] NLW, GTP, E29, p. 20.

[43] As it was, if on a more modest scale, the post-war trajectory of the coalfield itself – the point Gwyn had raised in his *Empire News* columns, particularly the *Rhondda Rich* series in 1958.

[44] And in this sense, Gwyn echoed the anti-nationalist position taken by Eric Hobsbawm throughout his work. For instance, and most obviously, in his *Nations and Nationalism since 1780: Programme, Myth, Reality* (Cambridge, 1990). See also, Eric Hobsbawm, *On Nationalism* (London, 2021). Gwyn's own engagement with Hobsbawm – as evidenced by surviving copies of the historian's writing – included *The Age of Revolutions* (1964); *Bandits* (1969); and *Captain Swing* (written with George Rudé, 1969).

[45] Gwyn Thomas, 'Changing Face of Cardiff', *The Times*, 2 April 1970.

[46] *DM*, 24 November 1961.

[47] Gwyn Thomas, 'Speaking as one who has a shady past', *DM*, 29 November 1961; 'My testament for the marchers', *DM*, 8 December 1961; 'Why you should NEVER give up the ghost', *DM*, 27 January 1962; 'How sweet is the valley', *DM*, 30 June 1962; 'What the Russians missed by not coming to Wales', *DM*, 4 September 1962; 'When it stops the Welsh Singing ... UNO Should look into Bingo', *DM*, 20 October 1962.

[48] *Reading Evening Post*, 18 October 1965.

[49] Gwyn Thomas, 'My First Love', *Daily Express*, 23 April 1962. The age of responsibility was raised in Scotland to twelve in 2019.

[50] Parnell thought that this work was the result of responding to anybody 'who thought of asking for a contribution', which was not an accurate appraisal.

[51] Gwyn Thomas, 'Mr Barrie and Mr Shaw', *The Listener*, 14 August 1975; 'Thomas, G.', *The Listener*, 2 October 1975; 'April's Eternal Fools', *The Listener*, 30 March 1978; 'Some Spanish Echoes and Shadows', *The Listener*, 21 December 1978.

[52] Gwyn Thomas, *Sorrow For Thy Sons*, 199.

[53] Gwyn Thomas, 'Gwyn Thomas Looks Again...', *TW*, 14 September 1962.

CHAPTER SEVEN

The Great Communicator

In the spring of 1948, the BBC's Light Programme broadcast a review of *The Alone to the Alone* as part of an episode of *New Books and Old Books*.[1] It was the first time that the BBC had noticed Gwyn's writing – there was no discussion of *The Dark Philosophers* in 1947, for instance – and marked the beginning of a decades-long relationship with Britain's national broadcasters. A year later, following the publication of *All Things Betray Thee* in the summer of 1949, it was the turn of the Welsh Home Service's *Arts Magazine*, itself launched only a few months earlier, to discuss Gwyn's latest work.[2] He listened intently, and then promptly wrote to the programme's producer, Elwyn Evans (1912–2004), to thank him 'for making room … for such an excellent notice of my book' and to add his especial thanks 'on the fine work you are doing. The Arts Magazine programme in particular is splendid and wins you the warmest esteem of the whole thinking part of Wales. It will provide for our intellectual and artistic efforts a fine spine of awareness and encouragement for lack of which they have tended to droop in the past.'[3] Evans replied a few days later, enclosing a copy of the script.

The following week, Gwyn received another letter from Evans, this time with a tantalising offer. 'Glyn Jones has been asked to enlist your aid in a new radio series for the Welsh Home Service,' Evans explained, 'I think the idea will appeal to you.'[4] Gwyn agreed, telling Evans that 'I had had a chat with Glyn Jones and the idea certainly does appeal to me. I will be delighted to do anything I can to help you and him make it a success.'[5] Gwyn let on to Nan about the venture, by then titled 'How I Write,' a few months later.[6] 'It seems that I am now regarded as one of Wales' five premier writers,' he said,

> It should be a very interesting series, especially the part dealing with the role played by a writer's early past in the way he writes and the purpose he has in writing. I wish I could illustrate what I will have to say with sound-records of the life we lived at Cymmer, the great lovable tumult of it all, the song, the laughter, the argument, and, above all, the genius and affection you gave to create the road along which we all came. There is so little of what one really wants to say that one can say, so little of what is really important in a man's heart that can really be said.

As was then common, the programme was carefully scripted albeit with the text drawing on a series of discussions between the presenter, Glyn Jones, and Gwyn prior to recording.[7] 'I enjoy writing very much,' Gwyn explained, 'in fact, I seem to get completely absorbed in the enthusiasm of the chase after words and ideas. No part of me moves except my hand.' In his letter to Nan, Gwyn predicted that the programme would explore the autobiographical roots of his creative imagination and the richness of Rhondda society in the early years of the century. He was right. Glyn Jones prompted the observation that, 'The people among whom I grew up spoke with a boisterous artistry. On certain levels of deprivation, life and speech cease to be cautious and hedged-in; humour then can express itself without inhibitions. Life in the valleys when I was a boy was a precarious and disquieting thing which encouraged an amazing vitality on people's tongues. We talked endlessly. That was one way of keeping up our spirits in a university that did not seem very encouraging. A cracked world and a love of poets gave us all the spiritual incentive and mechanical facility we needed. If we lacked sixpence for the pictures we could always float on a sea of metaphor in a session of high Socratic debate under a lamp-post in Porth Square or outside the Tonypandy Empire. Our imaginations had a ferocious quality. They roamed through our cosmos like hungry wolves, free to feed on whatever they fancied, finding nothing to make them fall back into a reverent hush.'

That was Gwyn's explanation for the darker elements of the stories including *The Dark Philosophers*, but then the writer turned to the idea of humour. 'People tell me there are comedic undertones in even my most sombre imagery,' he said, 'I can easily believe it. Humour is a sense of the incongruous or absurd, an aggravated sense of the contrast between man's divine promise and his shambling, shabby reality. There was enough incongruity between the way my people lived in the Rhondda of my early manhood, and the way in which they would have wanted to live, to have nourished at least ten thousand humourists of the first rank. But, of course, about the humour produced from such a situation there will be hints of the most extreme savagery; and the artist into whose spirit it may have entered too deeply will find his main task to be the rendering of his anger bearable to himself and acceptable to others.' Gwyn was then pressed by Glyn Jones to talk about the American nature of the Meadow Prospect idiom and the charge, made by reviewers and literary critics alike, that they all seemed to speak in the same way. Gwyn pondered for a moment. Accepting the premise, he pointed out that he did not see it as a problem.

'Literary convention insists that poverty of pocket must be matched with poverty of speech,' Gwyn remarked, adding that it 'has never made the slightest sense to me. Some of the most magnificent speech I've ever heard has come from the plainest and commonest people.' Insisting on the authenticity of his creations, Gwyn concluded that 'I like to imagine I am writing for one of those groups I loved as a boy, a circle of fruity, excitable characters sitting around me on the hillside at dusk, moved to a particular tolerance, perhaps, by a session of good harmonious singing or a cash windfall which enabled us to buy a bagful of well-salted chips apiece. ... Those Rhondda days are, for me, forever bathed in a brilliant light; the tumult of political enthusiasms, the white-hot oratory of the people's paladins; the festivals of folk-singing and hymn-singing in the vast chapels, moving groups on the hillsides at night ... the fermenting disquiet of the valley streets, ringing with every note of pain and laughter contrived since man's beginning.' These were the words spoken at the outset of a broadcasting career which lasted until Gwyn's death in 1981 and were as clear a roadmap to the central themes and ideas of his work as he would ever provide in public.

For various reasons, Gwyn did not appear on the radio again until 1952. Behind the scenes, Glyn Jones and Elwyn Evans had been trying to find a use for Gwyn's talents. Jones made the approach early in 1951. At first, with writing for *The World Cannot Hear You* getting under way, and conscious of needing to prove himself with a new publisher, Gwyn offered a rebuff explaining that 'I am afraid I have been somewhat vitiated by too much novel-writing in a vein where I have been able to say practically everything I wanted. After years of being able, in utter indifference to the scruples of publishers' readers, some of whom must sidle up to the ammonia-flask as soon as a new MS of mine steams up, to work off as much Radical wise-cracking and buttonless lubricity as I fancied, it would be hard to submit to the urgent discipline of word and impulses necessary to the broadcaster ... [But] there must be some themes to which even a loose-lipped Dionysian like myself might bring a fresh and useful nib.' With support and encouragement, particularly from Glyn Jones, Gwyn relented and agreed to provide a specimen piece of reminiscence about his childhood in the Rhondda picking up on the themes he had discussed in the earlier 'How I Write' episode on the *Arts Magazine*.

Conscious that he had no time to be writing anything new, Gwyn turned, for the first time but not the last, to a previous work and began the process of adaptation. Published three years earlier in *Coal*, the National Coal Board's literary-minded magazine, the short story 'Then Came We, Singing,' had been praised as 'refreshingly original' on initial publication, with one reviewer noting that Gwyn was 'incapable of writing a dull or unamusing sentence.'[8] It had music, the gathering of a group of voters in the terraces, ready-made dialogue, and humour, everything necessary to bring Rhondda Runyonism off the page and onto the airwaves. It was easily turned into a radio script and duly sent to the BBC offices in Cardiff. When he read it, Elwyn Evans was no less enthusiastic than the short-story reviewers had been but suggested just a few minor changes. One of which, as Gwyn told Nan, was to the title.[9] In place of the singing was a reference to the instruments played by the marching jazz bands of 1926: 'Gazooka.' The script was formally commissioned for a fee of sixty guineas just before Christmas 1951 and was broadcast on the Welsh Home Service on 11 January 1952.[10] Gwyn's life, and his career as a writer, was never the same ever again.

Welsh listeners generally enjoyed 'Gazooka,' as did most reviewers, although the *Western Mail* opined that the writing was not quite up to Gwyn's usual standards.[11] Nevertheless, the broadcast was successful enough that offers of more radio work were forthcoming, as Elwyn Evans had anticipated. A sequel to 'Gazooka,' called 'The Orpheans,' for which Gwyn earned fifty guineas, was broadcast in Wales on 2 September. This time the *Western Mail*'s reviewer commented that it was the one 'programme which pierced the gloom last week.'[12] Gwyn set about writing a third feature. News soon spread through the BBC about Cardiff's latest talent. Towards the end of 1952, Gwyn received the news that 'Gazooka' would be re-broadcast on the national Third Programme in early January 1953.[13] He also received a letter from Denis Mitchell (1911–1990), since 1950 a features producer for the Northern Region based in Manchester. Earlier in the year, Mitchell had produced 'Lorry Harbour' featuring the folk singer and left-wing activist, Ewan MacColl (1915–1989), and the voices and experiences of life on the trunk roads and in the transport cafés of the north of England. The following year, Mitchell would be responsible for the series *Ballads and Blues*, an exploration of American folk music and jazz, featuring MacColl, Alan Lomax, and Humphrey Lyttleton.

Mitchell's offer to Gwyn was the chance to write a script for the Northern Region. To sweeten the deal, Mitchell offered an increased fee of fifty-four guineas. The intervention rankled the Welsh Region who were now told by the central copyright unit in London that they would have to pay more to secure Gwyn's services in future. The surviving memorandum, held at the BBC's Written Archives Centre in Caversham, near Reading, has marginalia capturing the annoyance felt in Cardiff. 'Blast the "North" for interfering,' one producer wrote, 'So-and-sos! Why should we negotiate at an increased rate with him? He hasn't, as far as I know, questioned our offers to him.'[14] Mitchell's actions served to embarrass the Welsh Region, who had undervalued Gwyn's talents. The script Gwyn sent to Mitchell was titled 'Forenoon.' It was set in a secondary school not entirely unlike Barry Boys and followed the exploits of a Walter

Mitty-esque schoolteacher, Mr Walford, the first version of the character who would later appear in *Punch* and in *A Few Selected Exits*, as he tussled with his students. Gwyn had recently been reading James Thurber's short stories. He received a rapturous reception from reviewers across the north of England. The *Yorkshire Evening Post* declared the programme a 'gem of a broadcast' and that Gwyn was a 'radio writer to take notice of.'[15]

With the Welsh success of 'Gazooka' and 'The Orpheans' and the Northern success of 'Forenoon' behind him, as well as the astonishing success of 'Gazooka' at the national level – it was played three times in January 1953, including two repeats[16] – Gwyn became much more ambitious. 'I have mentioned to my Head of Programmes,' wrote Elwyn Evans in a letter sent to Gwyn in January 1953, 'that you would like to write three sixty-minute feature programmes for broadcasting in the Welsh Home Service this year, each programme to be about a different facet of South Wales life in the Twenties and Thirties. He is attracted by the idea and would like to commission you to carry it out.'[17] 'Gazooka' compounded the awkward position the BBC's Cardiff office found itself in, with a flurry of correspondence sent from London essentially accusing the Welsh Region of neglecting its star. 'You will have heard how appreciative our critics team was of Gazooka,' observed the London office in a memorandum to Cardiff sent on 6 February 1953, following broadcast of *The Critics* on 1 February, 'as a result, I think it possible that the programme may have still another broadcast.'[18] As it did on 9 October. The London office then asked the question which served to embarrass their colleagues in Cardiff still further: 'Also, I have been reading one of his novels, which impresses and amuses me a good deal. Have you used him as a talker or a short-story writer?'[19]

The Cardiff office replied a few days later, clearly irritated by the interference from Manchester and now, more problematically, London, and determined to assert their authority over Gwyn's development as a broadcaster. 'Thank you for your note of February 6th. The current interest in our author is not only widespread throughout the BBC but it has become an embarrassment to us. We have commissioned him to undertake another two or three features which will quite probably find a home in Third Programme as well as in Welsh Home Service.'[20] There was to be no such luck for the Cardiff producers who had been caught out. From London came a further note, this time copied to P. H. Newby, novelist and senior producer for the Third Programme, who had previously reviewed *All Things Betray Thee* for *The Listener*, pushing for action to be taken to secure Gwyn's services – and quickly.[21] They wrote,

> I am sorry to add to your embarrassments about him, but I am convinced from reading one of his books that he has a verbal ingenuity and humour which might provide admirable short story material if he can broadcast; and if he has sufficient leisure, I feel I ought to experiment with him in this form. I am prepared to back him – provided he is a capable broadcaster – for a good placing in basic Home Service. If you feel you are already so over-burdened, I will suggest that we should invite him to London at the Corporation's expense to discuss the matter and give us some opportunity of trying him in a studio with some of his own material.[22]

London successfully pulled rank and Gwyn was summoned to Broadcasting House for an audition. The result was that in 1954 he was included in a series for the national Home Service called 'Imaginary Journeys,' alongside writers such as Colin MacInnes and Laurie Lee.[23] Gwyn's script, 'Further on for

Paradise: A Journey in Innocence and Irony' was broadcast on 13 June 1954 and focused on the experiences of a whimsical bard seeking a haven of sensual warmth in eighteenth-century Glamorgan.[24]

Already Gwyn had completed a further feature for the Northern Region. 'The Deep Sweet Roots,' documented a visit to Pontefract and explored the manufacture of liquorice. Two of the three features commissioned for the Welsh Region by Elwyn Evans in January 1953 had been completed as well: 'Festival' and 'Our Outings.'[25] The first of the Welsh programmes, broadcast on 9 April, drew on similar themes to 'Gazooka' and 'The Orpheans' and suffered by comparison with those earlier scripts. The *Western Mail* reviewer thought that it was less successful; as they put it 'it did not grip me as Gazooka did.'[26] 'Our Outings,' which was broadcast in late October, was more appealing to listeners and took as its theme the various Sunday School trips to the coast – notably Porthcawl and Barry Island – then typical of valley life.[27] Not everything penned in 1953 made it to broadcast, although many of the scripts and treatments Gwyn wrote still survive. A third feature for the Welsh Region, titled 'The Rich Hills,' was apparently not produced; likewise, a more ambitious project for the Northern Region, based on a one-off documentary called 'Ballads and Blues' which was broadcast in March 1953, sadly fell by the wayside.[28] In a letter to Nan sent in April 1953, Gwyn explained that Denis Mitchell was

> eager about some scheme for throwing together a show using some very fine folk song material which he has collected from the States and here. He's had people like Josh White and so on singing the old railroad songs and stuff like that. He thinks that I may be able to weave for him the sort of comment and continuity that would make the whole thing come to dramatic

life. He wants me to come up to Manchester on Wednesday, so that, I'm afraid, is that. He's so keen on the project that he thinks that with proper handling it might even qualify for consideration as a candidate for the Italia prize which, as you probably know, is the European prize for the best radio writing and production. (Incidentally, I hear whispers that Gazooka is already on the cards for submission by the BBC in this competition.)[29]

Mitchell's intent was to turn the one-off 'Ballads and Blues,' as well as a trio of programmes he had been involved in a few years earlier – namely Josh White's *Glory Road* (1951–52) on the Light Programme; Alan Lomax's *Adventure in Folk Song* (1951) on the Home Service; and Lomax's sequel, *The Art of the Negro* (1951–52), which went out on the Third Programme – into a full series.[30] Although Gwyn's involvement foundered, the series nevertheless went to air in June 1953.

A similar offer for a similar programme, this time for the BBC's North American Service, came from Charles Parker – at the time, a radio talks producer and later a research fellow based at the South Wales Miners' Library. 'I have to plan one or two trips from Cardiff up the Rhondda and down the Afan Valley,' Gwyn explained to Nan about Parker's proposed venture. 'It struck me that there might be some good radiogenic stuff on the old Rhondda–Swansea Bay line. He's coming down next week-end to discuss some further ideas.'[31] The project was postponed when Parker was sent by the BBC on a fact-finding tour of American and Canadian radio stations that summer. On his return, Parker was promoted to the role of Senior Features Editor in the Midlands Region and ideas discussed with Gwyn for the North American Service went no further.[32] Despite his excitement, Gwyn was pragmatic in his response to the flurry of requests, including those which eventually came to naught, despite the time and effort he invested. Indeed, by the end of the year, he was able to report to Nan that he was doing 'lots of radio work.'[33] Encouraged by London executives, the Welsh Region commissioned two short stories to be read on air: the original version of 'Then Came We, Singing' and 'Teilo Topliss.'[34]

Gwyn was more modest in his judgement of what was going on than Lyn, who beamed with delight at her husband's broadcasting career. She told her brother-in-law, Bill, that 'the Welsh BBC have been marvellous to Gwyn. They have commissioned him to write a series of scripts for them. It is a tremendous turnup for Gwyn. At last the world is beginning to pay homage to the most brilliant and wittiest writer of the twentieth century. Gwyn will wear the mantle of Shaw and Shakespeare if he lives long enough. I do hope that this will be granted to me, that Gwyn's health will be such that he will live for a hundred years.'[35] But she was worried, too, especially about cumulative impact of teaching, writing, broadcasting, and public appearances, telling her in-laws that Gwyn's health was 'more important to me than the writing of books.'[36] It was not the last time that Lyn expressed some concern about Gwyn's level of exhaustion and her own isolation in the house. 'Gwyn is so wrapped up in his books,' she told Nan just before Christmas 1952, 'that he is not in this world half the time. I've grown used to talking to myself these days.'[37] And so she involved herself in the writing process, correcting manuscripts and proofs and replying to the fan mail which began to arrive after the national broadcast of 'Gązooka' in January 1953.

'I spent all yesterday and this evening replying to these very charming letters,' Lyn told Nan, 'Gwyn dictated the letters to me before going out and I worked like a slave to get them typed and completed by today. I find it a refreshing change from housework and it pleases me to think that I can help Gwyn in this way.' But, she confessed, 'I wish I could do so much more to help him. He works so very hard but I have discovered that he really likes working on his writing and is not happy to sit down and relax for long.'[38] Lyn struck up a friendship with some of Gwyn's American friends herself, notably Ezra Jack Keats and Jay Williams, and became almost as active a correspondent with them as her husband. Keats reciprocated the friendship by giving Lyn a watercolour he had painted. It was to find a place at 8 Lidmore Road, the new bungalow to which Gwyn and Lyn moved in October 1953, using the proceeds of the broadcasting work to fund the purchase. The house gave Lyn a project and eased some of the isolation and loneliness she had previously felt in Porthkerry Road.[39] There was also the sense that Lyn was overawed by the world into which she was being thrust by her husband's literary and media success.

In a letter to Nan sent in July 1951, Lyn enthused about a trip to a party held at Victor Gollancz's residence: '[We] had a most interesting time. Met all the critics and famous writers who were very enthusiastic about Gwyn's books, and as far as we were concerned the affair was most successful. Daphne du Maurier was there looking very beautiful in a wonderful gown that must have cost plenty. The Lord Chancellor and Viscountess Jowitt, Prince and Princess Frederick of Prussia, the Askwiths and also the Asquiths were there, and the most brilliant gathering of famous literary figures in the world. It was some "do", believe me. We received an invitation from some "nobs" at the party to spend a week-end at their country home, and we go to Suffolk on the 2nd August.' Following his radio success, Gwyn broke into television in the summer of 1954. It is 'a little job,' Lyn explained to Nan, 'but one never knows what it might lead to.'[40] Gwyn, too, was jovial about the prospect. 'On the 24th July I'm on television,' he told Nan, 'I'm doing the commentary on some kind of carnival shindig,' he wrote, 'There's a parade of gazooka bands and they should be good for a few smiles.'[41]

Gwyn's excitement about television never faded. *Gazooka Parade* (broadcast on 24 July 1954) was one of the programmes about which he wrote in *A Few Selected Exits* observing, with no sense of accuracy, that 'there was that day of autumn monsoon in Porthcawl, a seaside fun centre in South Wales. I was to put in some of the words at the televising of a carnival jazz-band competition.'[42] Drawing on his experiences in the classroom, where he used fast-paced and witty language to hold the attention of his otherwise reluctant charges, Gwyn proved himself adept at handling the curious paraphernalia of television broadcasting and was a natural in front of the camera. The following year, he was sought by the Cardiff-born producer Donald Baverstock as a regular guest for the daily television magazine show, *Highlight*. The programme launched on 22 September 1955 as a direct challenge by the BBC to its new independent rival, ITV, which likewise began broadcasting that day.[43] Gwyn sent his segments 'down the line' from the studios in Cardiff, with the main elements of *Highlight* produced from Lime Grove in London. But with ongoing commitments to teaching and to writing novels, Gwyn's broadcasting activities were otherwise restricted to radio. At least for the time being.

Called on to participate on-air as a contributor and behind the scenes as a scriptwriter, Gwyn found himself shuttling from Barry to a variety of studio and outside broadcast locations with increasing regularity, and he mixed with many of the celebrities of his day. In November 1954, for example, he travelled to Swansea to take part in *Young People's Question Time* for the Light Programme and featured alongside the captain of Glamorgan County Cricket Club, Wilfred Wooller, and the politician Megan Lloyd George. A second appearance on

Question Time in December 1955, this time from Ebbw Vale, saw him join broadcasters Wynford Vaughan Thomas and G. V. 'Geevers' Wynne-Jones.[44] These were the radio precursors to more famous appearances on the *Brains Trust* on BBC TV, the first of which was broadcast on 15 January 1956. Gwyn starred alongside the scientist Jacob Bronowski, the Liberal aristocrat Violet Bonham-Carter, and the historian and biographer Alan Bullock. This was the second of the television programmes Gwyn discussed in *A Few Selected Exits*. 'My most thorough exposure to the cameras,' he wrote,

> came when I sat in as one of the sages on the BBC Brains Trust. Its personnel is made up in the main of aristocrats, polymaths, tycoons and arch-administrators. No one has more emphatically been none of these things than I … Punditry in any shape or place is a base act. The ability to pontificate in public on a wide range of unlike subjects should involve a man in a kind of breathalyser test in reverse. If he has done it without being loaded above a certain alcoholic level he should be put down on grounds of brazen arrogance. That I should ever have got mixed up in it was quite against the run of my nature.[45]

In the immediate aftermath of those early appearances in January and February 1956, however, Gwyn was much more enthusiastic. He told his sister, Nan, that:

> This Brains Trust thing is fantastic. Once you've been on it it's got such a huge viewing public even dogs that watch TV stare at you. The team meets at Scott's restaurant in Piccadilly, one of the really fancy eating spots in London. The panellers are given so much to eat and drink it's a wonder they are not carried into the studio on litters. At the end of the meal, which is served in a private room, when the brandy is served with the

coffee (Bring your forks. There will be butter beans. Remember that? I told Lady Violet that in the middle of my oysters and she's still trying to figure what I found funny in the remark.) a trolley loaded with about a thousand cigars is wheeled in. Bronowski, whom most people around here seem to call Bronski, always picks the very biggest, a giant of a thing as long as his own torso. I take one too, same length, not to smoke, just to beat Lady Violet over the head during her longer and sillier memoirs. She's got an endless gusher of stories of the days when her father was Prime Minister. That last Sunday I got in a sly word through the palisade of country house chatter. I told her our father had been called the Jake. She was very impressed. She thought it was some kind of Arab title, a sort of Welsh Sheik.[46]

By the summer, he had appeared three more times – in April, June, and August.

Those early encounters with Bronowski lingered in Gwyn's mind. In *A Few Selected Exits* he presented a rich portrait of the polymath, who had once lectured in mathematics at the University of Hull and from 1950 until 1963 was, in effect, the chief scientist for the National Coal Board in his capacity as the director of the NCB's Central Research Establishment. Five years after Gwyn's memoir was published, Bronowski presented his television masterpiece, *Ascent of Man*, featuring the quite remarkable single-take sequence to camera filmed in Auschwitz-Birkenau. Bronowski, Gwyn wrote, 'is one of the marvels of the contemporary mind ... without strain he could give you the weight of the moon and the proportion of turpentine poured by your father into his second tin of paint for his second try at interior decoration. He is almost total intelligence. He came to Britain from Poland at the age of nine, a refugee from pogroms and speaking only Polish. He read his way through the large library of the bright and literate London slum where he settled.' Such was Gwyn's admiration that he paid to Bronowski the ultimate Thomasian tribute, 'he is the classic product of twentieth-century Europe and it is logical that, at a certain point of ripeness, he should move to America.'

In his public and private portraits of Bronowski, Gwyn never discussed how much of the man's biography he knew – the commitment to the Left Book Club in the 1930s, for instance, or his involvement in the People's Theatre Guild of the 1940s. Bronowski wrote poems such as 'how I hate war,' which was read out at one meeting of the Guild in Hull in 1941. The result of Bronowski's publicly identifiable leftist activity was the start of a long period of surveillance by the intelligence services and the compilation of a substantial personal file – most of it consisting of letters from informers and police follow-ups.[47] The file cost him senior posts in British academia, although not in the United States, and prevented his involvement in atomic energy research in the late 1940s. Gwyn was certainly familiar with Bronowski's famous broadcast on the BBC which detailed what the scientist had seen in Hiroshima and Nagasaki in 1945. The interview, which took place in July 1946 in response to American nuclear testing at Bikini Atoll in the Pacific, launched Bronowski's broadcasting career – he joined the radio version of the *Brains Trust* in November 1946 – and his role as a 'humanist intellectual for an atomic age.'[48]

Joining Bronowski on the *Brains Trust* in the mid-1950s was the culmination of Gwyn's early growth as a contributor and broadcaster, a figure upon whom BBC producers, whether in London or in the regions, could rely. At the same time, having belatedly realised the extent of Gwyn's talents as a broadcaster, the Welsh Home Service gave him a prominent and permanent role in their new English-language literary magazine show, *Present Indicative*. The title was a nod to Noel Coward's 1937 autobiography.[49] Aired monthly between November 1955 and March 1956, *Present Indicative* was designed as a showcase for new writing and provided critical discussion and an opportunity for the panellist to read excerpts on air – akin to the *Arts Magazine* which had been the springboard for Gwyn in the 1940s. He was involved in a similar venture for the national Light Programme, too, stepping in as a contributor to the arts magazine show *Review* in November 1955. Amongst the works discussed on that occasion were Burt Lancaster's directorial debut, *The Kentuckian*, and the French-language film *Loves of Lisbon* starring Trevor Howard and Daniel Gélin. Gwyn ended 1955 as the Cardiff presenter of the BBC's New Year's Eve extravaganza, joining colleagues from across Britain to 'look to the future that awaits.'[50] His own anticipation was palpable.

*

With broadcasting added to Gwyn's writing commitments, the tension between all of the elements of his life was becoming overwhelming, and it was obvious that teaching was getting in the way. As Lyn told Nan, Gwyn had to 'turn down so many offers because of the job he has to do.'[51] Gwyn had mentally switched off from the chalkface years before remaining at Barry Boys because it provided financial surety. Vocationally, he was a writer, although even that identity seemed to be under threat now that the studios and their executives and producers were regularly calling him. 'All this radio stuff is interesting,' he told Nan in March 1956, 'but I bitterly miss the days when there were no calls on my time and I could dawdle for twelve months on and over one particular book. Now it seems an age since I did any really serious work on a book.'[52] He added, 'writing has become such a devilish chore for me I have to drag myself to do any bit of it that isn't wrung out of me by the approach of a deadline.' In the end, Lyn intervened. In November 1956, Gwyn travelled to Eton College for a young people's forum on books. Because of teaching commitments, he had to travel back and forth in the same evening. Furious when she saw Gwyn, Lyn wrote to tell Nan that, 'I have made up my mind that he will not do it again.'[53]

Gwyn did not appear again on the *Brains Trust* until September 1957. Lyn got her way. In fact, her husband's absence caused confusion behind the scenes when he was booked for the programme that autumn. Kenneth Adam, controller of programmes for BBC TV, remarked in a memorandum that 'I thought Thomas a good newcomer.'[54] It was Gwyn's seventh turn on a *Brains Trust* panel. Adam's intervention resulted in further invitations early in 1958 and again a year later. In the spring of 1959, the offers stopped. 'I haven't been on that BBC Brains Trust for quite a time,' Gwyn explained to Nan that summer, 'and it won't bother me if I never appear again.' He was clearly fed up. 'That sort of thing gets very boring,' he wrote, 'and they are such a stuffy, self-important lot. It was a good experience and I wouldn't have wished to be without it. But I am temperamentally incapable of being fully at ease with such people. I expressed these feelings in an article I did for Lilliput magazine and after that I suppose I had my chips.'[55]

It was not quite the end. Gwyn was invited back one final time in August 1960, appearing alongside the Vice Chancellor of Reading University, Sir John Wolfenden, and the conductor Colin Davis (1927–2013), who had recently made his debut at the BBC Proms. For all his private disquiet, Gwyn recognised that broadcasting offered a route out of the classroom, if only he could find the right opportunity. One such was *Tonight*, the BBC's expanded daily magazine show for television produced by Donald Baverstock and Alasdair Milne, the future Director

General, and memorably starring the journalist and documentary maker Alan Whicker. *Tonight* had replaced *Highlight* in February 1957 and, in the words of historian Asa Briggs, 'deliberately blurred traditional distinctions ... [breaking] sharply with old BBC traditions of "correctness" and "dignity."'[56] It was ideally suited to Gwyn's public temperament, as he told fellow Rhondda novelist Ron Berry in 1961. *Tonight*, with its 'zany-spotting gambits' was capable of digging deep into 'the soil of idiosyncracy.'[57] Just as Baverstock had tapped Gwyn to appear on *Highlight*, so he offered a regular slot on *Tonight*. Gwyn leapt at the opportunity, telling Nan in late July 1958:

> Another thing that takes me up to London is an invitation from a very dynamic character called Donald Baverstock. Donald is the producer of a programme on TV called 'Tonight,' one of the best things in all that deplorable meadow of muck. He wants me to take a look at some lengths of film, miscellaneous things like 'Seventy-Five Double Decker Buses leave Treherbert for the sea' or 'Do Sheiks Smell Worse Than Oil?' and then do spoken commentaries on them ... We planned to do a TV piece about Guto Nyth Bran.[58]

The relationship with Baverstock, buoyed with several hilarious turns with Alan Whicker including the infamous interview about the great chip famine in the Rhondda in the early 1960s, was potentially lucrative. The programme brought welcome reviews by the major television critics such as Maurice Wiggin of the *Sunday Times* who observed of Gwyn's contributions that they were 'disenchanted but enchanting ... *pronunciamentos* ... [by] that most gifted and singular broadcaster.'[59] Behind the scenes Baverstock had even offered Gwyn the golden ticket. Gwyn told Nan, 'I was up in London at half-term doing some bits of work on the *Tonight* programme. The producer, Donald Baverstock, wanted me to come up and join them permanently. I was, as I say, tempted. But one becomes very much of a rock as time goes by, hard to change and hard to shift. I may regret not having decided to make tracks, I don't know. All I do know is that whatever dignity or delight I might once have found in teaching is no longer there.' The offer of permanent work must have been extremely difficult for Gwyn to turn down, although it did not impact his relationship with the programme too greatly and he continued to appear until his defection to independent television in 1962.

Having refused Baverstock, Gwyn tried to carry on as normal. He took part in magazine shows, he read his short stories, he penned features, and he provided testimony for documentary makers. He came up with marvellously inventive descriptions of various parts of South Wales – Barry Island, for instance, was dubbed 'the kingdom of the chip.'[60] And he began to take his part, finally, in the literary culture of Wales having earned, in the eyes of the *Western Mail*, the title of Wales' 'best-known novelist.' Early in 1959, he interviewed Alexander Cordell for the Welsh Home Service about the latter's new novel set in South Wales in the turbulent 1830s, *Rape of the Fair Country*.[61] Published by Victor Gollancz in January 1959, and subsequently by Doubleday in the United States, Cordell's novel had been distributed to reviewers with encomia from Aneurin Bevan, Emlyn Williams, the novelist Jack Jones, and Gwyn.[62] In his tribute, Gwyn observed that:

> It's a real shaker, a most remarkable bit of compassionate evocation. Knowing the places, the people, the sounds, it struck deep into me. For all the terror of which it tells there is a sheen of laughing goodness over it; a quick lyrical humour silvers even the savagery of it. Time and again I caught the authentic

astonishing smile of all the sardonic poetry that has ever moved in bitter mystery among the mutilated delvers and smelters who have lived out their odd lives in the tough, scuffed gulches of Siluria. The untidy anguish that nourishes the dreams of our nameless ones can rarely have received so vivid a tribute. A lovely book. I wish it very, very well.

Reviewing Cordell's novel brought back memories of writing *All Things Betray Thee* – it was the closest contemporary work of fiction to Gwyn's own masterpiece. Following on from his discussion of Cordell, Gwyn joined Gwyn Jones, Glyn Jones, Emyr Humphreys, and others, on the Third Programme to debate the concept of Anglo-Welsh literature. As the *Radio Times* observed, 'Welsh writers fall into two categories: those who write in Welsh and those who write in English. Is there a more fundamental difference between them?'[63] In the aftermath of the programme, the Abertillery MP, Labour's Llywelyn Williams, hit out at those 'playwrights and novelists who caricature public life in Wales,' telling local government representatives in Cardiff that 'something I deprecate very much is the childish way in which people such as county councillors are caricatured and parodied.'[64] Williams continued, 'some Welsh plays give a silly portrayal of a county councillor as though he were a moron doing nothing but meeting canvassers. It is a completely untrue picture.' The complaint was surely levelled at Gwyn, who readily held up the mirror to local government failure and to the petty-mindedness of some councillors and other public officials, although it had little impact on the wave of satires being produced. Glyn Jones's *The Learning Lark*, with corruption in education at its heart, appeared the following year.

Those early months of 1959 were symptomatic of a reflective turn; approaching fifty, an age Gwyn never expected to see, and increasingly conscious that his American Wales was disappearing, he began to reflect on history and the formative interwar years. One product was *Dusk and the Dialectic* broadcast on the Third Programme in the summer and repeated on the Home Service in January 1960 – the text itself was published in *A Welsh Eye* in 1964. 'There was a time when the Birchtown Institute was a very considerable place,' Gwyn told listeners, 'the walls were distempered to match the prevailing shades of philosophic determinism. Acid overtones of radical dissent had eaten into the dark didactic murals.'[65] But no longer. The growing influence of the drinking club, 'that genial but witless trough,' was symptomatic of serious social change. A few months before, in February 1959, Gwyn had taken part in Constantine FitzGibbon's provocative radio documentary, *The Hungry Years*, about life at the height of the Depression of the 1930s.[66] On its broadcast, the programme caused a storm with members of the ruling Conservatives charging the BBC with 'bias,' although the corporation had provided a copy of the script to Conservative Central Office prior to broadcast.[67] Gwyn, of course, thought the programme an effective one, and accurate, too, and wrote to FitzGibbon to say so.[68]

Completing the year was a re-broadcast, during the Christmas holidays, of *The Long Run*, Gwyn's dramatization of the life of Guto Nyth Bran on the Welsh Home Service. It had previously gone out on the national Home Service in July 1958, written to coincide with the Empire and Commonwealth Games held that summer in Cardiff. 'Top-class Gwyn Thomas writing,' observed the *Western Mail* fulsomely.[69] In an interview with another local newspaper, the *South Wales Gazette*, which was published in Abertillery, Gwyn explained the origins of the tale lay in the mythology of Guto Nyth Bran passed down to him by his father. 'Since then,' he said, 'I have had the wish to set Guto in the living social context of eighteenth-century Rhondda. I have called in imagination to give a warm rot for the final flowering of the story. Hence *The Long Run*, half fiction, half truth, all affection.'[70] As well, two scripts for the Welsh Home Service written for the series *Help Yourself* broadcast in February and March. The first of them, 'How To Become A Committee Man,' retitled 'How To Become a Welsh Committee Man,' was published as chapter five of *A Welsh Eye*, 'Self-Improvement.' It was the sort of satirical script guaranteed to give certain members of parliament a twitching eye.

*

By 1960, Gwyn had been working with the BBC consistently for a decade and had established himself as the go-to Welsh voice across the network, at home and abroad. In September that year, for instance, he was booked by the *Today* programme to provide an insight into the Ebbw Vale constituency. This was ahead of the selection of the Labour candidate for the autumn by-election called following Aneurin Bevan's death that July. It was to prove the first in a sequence of appearances on the *Today* programme discussing matters as various as 'bogus graduates,' the 'shift system,' 'Father's Day,' and 'gambling.' But it was also the beginning of increased tension between Gwyn and the BBC: partly because of a willingness on Gwyn's part to press for what he thought adequate compensation for his time. Convinced that broadcasting offered the means of retiring from the classroom, he asked for more money. Time and again in 1961 and 1962, letters and telephone calls were exchanged between Gwyn, Lyn, and the BBC, all on matters of contract and financial settlement. To little avail. The alternative was to defect to ITV. Yet Gwyn had shown little desire to do so since the launch of independent television in 1955 and had been only occasionally interviewed by the Welsh independent television network, TWW. He was, by instinct, 'Auntie's man.'

In the early 1960s, that affinity began to change. In January 1961, he appeared on TWW's *Two's Company*, providing what one critic thought a discussion 'radiating wit, good humour and epigram.' The programme clearly had an impact on producers; a few weeks later, the industry newspaper, *The Stage*, reported that TWW had commissioned six half-hour plays from writers including Kingsley Amis and Gwyn.[71] The plays failed to appear, but the advertisement was the first signal that Gwyn might well switch his allegiances given the right incentive, or, at the very least, follow the Pontypridd-born novelist and playwright Alun Richards in submitting work to both networks. An even larger indication of Gwyn's wavering loyalty to the BBC was the multi-part TWW series *Wales and the West*, which Gwyn presented along with John Betjeman. 'The contrast between them,' recorded *Television Weekly* in an introductory portrait of the two men ahead of broadcast in the summer of 1962, 'couldn't be more complete.' Even their approach to filming the respective segments was different – 'whereas Betjeman likes to accompany the director and suggest what should and should not be filmed, Thomas, like Betjeman, having accompanied the unit on reconnaissance, gives his impression to the director leaving the unit itself to put his thoughts on film.'[72]

In their individual ways, and certainly from different cultural perspectives, Betjeman and Gwyn provided a poetic, but no less astringent, critique of contemporary Britain. For Gwyn, especially, *Wales and the West* provided an opportunity to pierce contemporary ideas about the post-war New Jerusalem and to set down his views about social, cultural and political change. The first programme took Betjeman to Sidmouth and Gwyn to the Rhondda, 'home territory' as he still referred to it. Gwyn's portrait was sympathetic and characteristically focused on the achievement and potential of the people despite their absurd situation. 'Before one,' Gwyn began 'the earth splits in three.

Here, over the last hundred years, we have seen one of the world's greatest explosions: of music, work and thought. Every note of laughter and tears has been struck between these hills. Every variation on the theme of farce, courage and nobility ... the astonishing pageant of comedy and calamity which made up the life of the valley in those days.' He refused to paint a false picture of the Rhondda as it had become. He was neither romantic nor nostalgic. His realism was symptomatic of a long period of reflection. 'Coal has lost its dominance,' he explained to viewers,

> Once the mining activity was so passionate a man on his way out of the house would pause and wonder whether he would sink a pint or a pit shaft. So much digging even the moles carried union cards in self-defence. Now there are men who can only try in their memories to make sense out of forty, fifty years of tearing out the geological substrata of the Rhondda to provide a score of peerages for the stockbrokers of Cardiff and quite a few tidy funerals in the gulch itself.

The second episode saw Gwyn focus his attention on the Vale of Glamorgan concluding his segment in the caravan park at Trecco Bay, near Porthcawl. It was, he said, 'one of the great escape valves of Glamorgan ... grown out of the new world of plenty and leisure.' He added to his portrait in a column for *Television Weekly*:

> Any excuse to meander around the Vale of Glamorgan is a good one. The best excuse of all is to do so with fresh eyes for the purpose of presenting it to television viewers. The place has always been one of enchantment to me. As children we stood on the Trebanog ridge and surveyed the great expanse of coloured fields and tranquil villages merging into the sea. It was

all so different from the narrow, enclosed life we knew in the valleys. Later on, when our limbs could stand it, we ventured forth on walking tours down to the coast. The expedition would usually be disastrous. The family would pack enough food for us to justify them in the hope that they had seen the back of us for a week. We would take the road bent almost double beneath the fodder and a type of tent that went out of date in the Boer War. By the time we reached Pendoylan we had contracted every type of blister known and a few that were original.'[73]

From the Vale of Glamorgan, Gwyn next travelled to Pontypridd, Maesteg, and Merthyr Tydfil, before turning to Dylan Thomas's Laugharne, Tenby, and finally Aneurin Bevan's Ebbw Vale. *Wales and the West* was popular with viewers. One wrote to *Television Weekly* praising the 'wonderful descriptions of two different parts of the country' and hoped that 'the programme will continue.'[74] Another wrote to congratulate Gwyn, regarding him as 'nothing short of superb as narrator. His deep, rich Welsh voice and his own inimitable wit made the listening even more enjoyable than the viewing, an occurrence which is rare these days. I think it is a great pity that this programme was confined to Wales and the West. In my opinion it would have given people in other parts of the British Isles a chance to see the Rhondda as it really is and not a conglomeration of slag heaps and collieries, which I find is the popular conception.'[75]

Not everyone was happy with the series, or with Gwyn's perspective. The former vicar of St Catherine's Church in Pontypridd, George Shilton Evans (1886–1976), who had willingly supported the evangelical American preacher Billy Graham when he came to the town in 1946, wrote grumpily from his retirement home in Weston-Super-Mare that the visit to Pontypridd 'was a surprise and a disappointment. Shots were

given of the busy market and of the crowds in Taff Street,
including close-ups of people, in cafés, devouring fish and chips,
to the entire exclusion of the lovely park. Surely, a bird's eye
view of the town, with its beautiful church and spire, would
have given viewers, not acquainted with the district, some idea
of the layout. A crowded street, or a crowded café, cannot be
said to introduce one into the actual life of a town.'[76] Another
Pontypriddian thought the programme degrading and wrote to
complain. 'In common with other Pontypriddians to whom I
have spoken,' he explained, 'I would like to express my distaste
at Mr Gwyn Thomas' portrayal of the town of Pontypridd.' The
correspondent continued:

> Mr Thomas' view of Pontypridd [was] as a town of fish and
> chips, Be-bop and vagabonds. These aspects are common to
> nearly every town the size of Pontypridd throughout the United
> Kingdom, some better, some worse. But what town the size of
> Pontypridd can offer such beauty and tradition? I would like to
> remind Mr Thomas that Pontypridd is the home of the Welsh
> National Anthem and possesses one of the most beautiful parks
> in the country. If this view of Pontypridd was intended to be
> satirical then it was satire at its lowest and most degrading.[77]

Complaints came from the Rhondda, too: 'I am afraid Mr Gwyn
Thomas has been away from the Rhondda for so long he has
forgotten his way. It may have opened his eyes had he got out
of the van instead of speeding through the main roads of the
valleys ... The camera may have got shots of the improvements
in the valleys instead of broken-down pits and slag heaps. Mr
Thomas doesn't seem to dig us anymore.'[78] Those ideas of
change were picked up in the BBC Wales documentary, *The Long
Street*, fronted by Vincent Kane, in 1965 – although Gwyn was
absent due to his contract with TWW. Instead, the voice

observing what was going on in the Rhondda of the mid-1960s was that of novelist Ron Berry, who told programme makers that 'the history of the Rhondda itself is fading away, you know, which isn't to say that these things when they occurred weren't vital – because the Rhondda obviously gave a social impetus and gave social values to industry throughout the whole world.'

The weekly letters in response to *Wales and the West* generated their own autonomous debate in the pages of *Television Weekly* and in mid-October 1962, one correspondent writing from the new housing estate at Glyncoch, near Pontypridd, noted that 'every true artist has his critics, but it appears that the disgruntled viewers were more concerned about what other viewers would think of Pontypridd. A town does not make people; people make the town. The "famished ones" obviously devoured their fish and chips with great relish, and they appeared to be happily contented. Gwyn Thomas has an uncanny way of seeing not just the faces of people but also glimpses their minds and notes their characteristics – the hallmarks of a highly intellectual man and a true creative artist. I have nothing but praise for the series and Gwyn Thomas who, unlike John Betjeman, is not addicted to inanimate architecture.'[79] *Wales and the West* returned for a second series in November 1963. It took viewers to a new school in the western suburbs of Cardiff, to Butetown, to the Vale of Neath, and to Llanthony in Monmouthshire. Apart from the episode on Butetown, which captured the early stages of redevelopment in the docklands of Cardiff, the second series of *Wales and the West* was less memorable than the first, and certainly less personal. Taken together the ten programmes which made up the series established a broadcasting model and a narrative style, which Gwyn was to replicate in subsequent years for each of the networks he worked for: the BBC, TWW and HTV.

The success of *Wales and the West* prompted TWW to offer

Gwyn a lucrative, but exclusive, television contract in the summer of 1962.[80] Having retired from teaching earlier in the year, his novel writing days seemingly behind him, and now entirely reliant on freelance income from writing and broadcasting, he happily signed. His work for the BBC was thus consigned to radio for the time being. But nor did it dry up: in August 1963, producer Brian Evans (1919—2007) approached Gwyn with an offer to join the first broadcasts of *Good Morning Wales* which was due to launch that autumn with Vincent Kane as anchorman.[81] The last television programme Gwyn wrote for BBC TV, *The Slip*, was broadcast on 14 October 1962, just before his exclusive contract with TWW took full effect. At the heart of the story was the looming environmental disaster which threatened the communities of the coalfield: sliding coal tips. Actor Glyn Owen took on the role of Selwyn Dell, an enterprising (if short-sighted) local councillor who rushed around trying to solve the problem of the 'moving mountain' by proposing to build a containing wall.[82] As was typical of Gwyn's approach to writing for the BBC in the 1950s, he used comedy to convey his otherwise serious theme. Some reviewers thought this approach 'very disappointing'; others felt that they 'had to force the titters a little' although the overall impact of the piece was 'by no means a failure.'[83] Gwyn explained his intentions in the *Radio Times*,

The central character in *The Slip* is a figure that has fascinated me for a long time, the local councillor who represents a ward afflicted by a host of physical difficulties – chronic subsidence, irreparable slum-properties, an antediluvian abattoir, a glue-factory. He can plough this sterile furrow for the rest of his days and he will get no reward save a full set of corns and an astonishing amount of ill-will.

South Wales is full of townships so pitted with the errors of the past they are guaranteed to send the average councillor climbing up the mayor's chain. They are places from which most of the original mistakes of the Industrial Revolution set out. And to the councillor's door comes the procession of supplicants demanding a quick solution to problems that have been unsolved since time got itself buttressed by rates. People living in houses from which the sub-soil has quickly been withdrawn and in which a part of the roof will collapse at any twitch of the plumbing. Mothers with predatory broods complaining that the apples from the last orchard looted by her son upset him. Shy lovers demanding a recipe for a more brazen approach to affection. Hysterical calls from teachers whose nerves have been unravelled by thirty attempts to get a headship.

I have been amazed by the lack of information about local government. Once in a short spell as a quiz-master I asked the contestants the details of the controversial knock-down in the Dempsey-Tunney fight. They gave the answers instantly as if they had just been on the phone to Dempsey. Then I asked how the aldermanic bench was filled. The answers I got were 'slowly' and 'from right to left.' People who can tell you to the inch the length of the Lone Ranger's gun-barrel will not know the basic qualification to become a town clerk, unless the town in question happens to be Tombstone.

The basic problem which drives Councillor Selwyn Dell off the hinge in *The Slip* is a moving mountain, a landslip which threatens to engulf not merely a whole terrace of houses but Dell's majority at the next election as well. The causes of this nuisance are varied. Excessive rain, a honeycomb of old mine-workings, an utterly perverse geology. All could help to send a hill splurging downward. But there will always be some who will put it down to the ineptitude or neglect of the local councillor. Some, indeed, who will claim they saw the councillor himself giving the landslide a quiet shove.

The Slip is a comedy, and ridicule is not intended. I have wished merely to point out that there are areas of our country less stable than others, and that we should look with greater sympathy on those elected representatives whose lives are a maze of other people's concerns.[84]

Given the Aberfan disaster just four years later, about which Gwyn would so memorably broadcast, the play seemed retrospectively prescient.[85] It was part of a growing body of work from coalfield authors addressing the industrial landscape and the scarred environment, and which is now recognised as environmental writing.[86] Elaine Morgan's *Black Furrow*, which focused on opencast mining in the Cynon Valley and was the earliest of this new genre to make it to air, was broadcast in March 1958. She took up the theme of deindustrialisation once more in her autobiographical serial *A Matter of Degree* in 1960.[87] Ron Berry, the only major Welsh writer of this period to have worked underground, likewise explored 'ecocentric' themes.[88] Gwyn had, in fact, got there ahead of both Berry and Morgan. Although penned in 1962 as a teleplay, *The Slip* had its origins in the 1956 novel *Point of Order*, which famously ended with a deadly landslide. The tips, Gwyn said memorably in *Wales and the West* in the summer of 1962, were 'rather like the pyramids of Egypt but we could not persuade our pharaohs to be built into them.'

Gwyn's next teleplay, *The Dig*, was written whilst under contract for TWW and as a result aired on independent television in the autumn of 1963 in the series *Thirty Minute Theatre*. Set in a pub in South Wales, the play brought viewers into the world of Meadow Prospect and its darkly comedic voters in the terraces with Welsh actors Windsor Davies, Glyn Owen, and Philip Madoc in the leading roles. At the heart of the affair was Milo Morgan, played by Owen, a 'pub philosopher' with devious designs, and the script brimmed with gossip from the regulars.[89] A few weeks later, Gwyn returned to Meadow Prospect in a Christmas special for the arts programme *Tempo*, for whom he had been commissioned to write a seasonal short story. Introduced by presenter Leonard Maguire, Gwyn's reading of 'A Meadow Prospect Christmas' formed a double-bill alongside a dramatization of Anton Chekhov's 'The Dream.'[90] Maurice Wiggin, writing in the *Sunday Times*, declared Gwyn 'one of television's treasures' whose story was told 'inimitably.'[91] Writer Angus Wilson, on the other hand, thought Gwyn's narration 'rather wooden' and the effect of the solo recital left viewers 'cold and dazed.'[92] In the absence of any surviving recordings, we shall now never know which of the critics was right.

Behind the scenes, even without teaching to weigh him down, Gwyn's fatigue had not disappeared, and he ended 1963 completely worn out. 'I'm just managing to ride a thumping attack of exhaustion,' he told Nan before Christmas.[93] Some of his other work at that time, including an interview for TWW's *Here Today* programme, was thought to be 'not up to his usual standard.'[94] It was hardly surprising: for in 1963 alone Gwyn had been filming for TWW in Cannes, the two Germanies, and in the United States. He had been to London several times, finished recording the peripatetic *Wales and the West*, provided commentary for coverage of the Llangollen International Eisteddfod and the National Eisteddfod in Llandudno, and maintained his intensive recording schedule for BBC radio. The eisteddfods were particularly testing given Gwyn's antipathy towards them. 'There is so much that is deliberately quaint,' he told Nan of the Llangollen event, 'one has the feeling at times of being in some kind of lunatic nursery.'[95] Conditions were poor: Gwyn was recording from a tent late at night with the cool air blowing through. He wrote to Nan, 'Twice I left the tent shuddering and explaining that I was Captain Oates wishful to give Captain Scott a better chance.'

In truth, Gwyn was not angry at the weather nor even the eisteddfod (though it was not his favourite sort of gathering) so much as upset at not being able to visit his old school friend Wynne Roberts in hospital, where he was receiving treatment for a deadly brain tumour. A few years earlier, having observed Roberts's hair loss Gwyn had put it down to the absurdity of a world that was unfair. 'Look at Wynne Roberts,' he explained to Nan, 'the integrity of a rock and even less hair, poor schmoll.' But as the underlying cause became clear, Gwyn's concern and worry grew. He explained to Nan, 'the things one does when time, weariness and greed have rotted the hinges of one's first loves, enthusiasms and goodness. I fool and flunkey around on television, and my old fellow dreamer, Wynne Roberts, enters into the last muttering finale of his life commuting between Ebbw Vale and some brain-and-nerve clinic in Oxfordshire.' Gwyn was visibly hurt when Roberts died three years later, in August 1967. Two years later, it was Gwyn's turn to receive the diagnosis of ill health. In a letter to Ron Berry sent in August 1969, he explained that he had had 'a rough sort of year,' adding that

> after ignoring ten years of good advice I've had some kind of diabetic collapse with a sugar imbalance that would have startled even the West Indies. I seem for months now to have been sitting, chastened and ashen, in an awesome crater of silence. Compared with this the detached and sullen course I pursued before appears a golden time of gibbering geniality. I will wait for the evil to ease, lessen and go. Patience, guile and a few strokes of conciliatory magic are the words I stitch on my banners.[96]

Gwyn's diabetes had gone unmanaged for years and the chronic symptoms of exhaustion and fatigue, exacerbated by overwork, had taken their toll. As early as 1963, his fiftieth year, he was prepared to give it all up. 'I've grown to loathe writing in any shape and form,' he told Nan, '[so] that if a tidy sum of money were dropped in my lap I'd bury my biros in the back patch and lapse into the silence of stones.' On the surface he remained pragmatic, aware that 'television today is the god which a man can only ignore on pain of perishing.' But the long and often fruitless discussions involved in bringing ideas to the screen were disheartening, especially when they involved travelling to London, 'a place I find more and more pestilent' and the luxuries of TWW's expense accounts. His socialist morals kicking in, Gwyn complained to Nan of 'eating meals which had they not been eaten at someone else's bank account would break the bank in two: contributing in the meantime to conversations that have no end and to schemes that never seem to see the light. For which I'm grateful. If these teeming dreams ever reached the flesh and blood stage, I'd have to go into the studio and work. And that I don't like.'[97]

Gwyn disguised all of this in *A Few Selected Exits*, holding onto comedy and delighting in 'seeing Gregory Peck in the flesh' and talking to Richard Burton's brother, Graham Jenkins, about ambitious plans to develop Aberavon beach into a quasi-Mediterranean playground. 'Say what you like,' Gwyn quoted Jenkins as saying of Cannes, 'it's not a patch on Aberavon. Not a patch.' Gwyn was there in 1963 to record his latest documentary, 'Hot Spot,' with TWW. It was shown at the International Film Festival the following year and won the Television Viewers' Award at the Golden Prague Television Festival in 1965.[98] Gwyn wrote sardonically, 'the film was shown to minute audiences and improved the world not at all. It won a subordinate prize at the Prague Film Festival. Its vague humanitarianism might have made some appeal to the people of those parts.'[99] In actual fact, it was welcomed as an 'indictment against the threat of nuclear war and against hunger and misery in many parts of the world.'[100] For all the enjoyment Gwyn might have had on his travels, privately he was morose. 'These trips abroad,' he told Nan, 'were much too fast, too intense. Funny, the amount of time I've spent fiddling about with other people's languages and I still hate other people's countries. The sight of a frontier guard brings me out in hate-bumps.'[101]

*

The mid-1960s marked the highpoint of Gwyn's television career and the most expansive phase of his entire life. In all, he visited France, East Germany, West Germany, Italy, the Soviet Union, Spain, and the United States. Each documentary was accompanied by a blurb in *Television Weekly* with occasional reflective articles there and in *Punch* added into the mix; that describing the trip to New York City was typical. Viewers were offered 'a non-stop tour of what the Welsh playwright calls "this incredible and fantastic city" ... [he] gives his pungent impressions of a city which offers "chromium ulcers" to its hurrying workers.' He took in Fifth Avenue and Grand Central Station, 'the deceptive peace of Central Park,' and the United Nations headquarters. From the waterfront of lower Manhattan Gwyn made his way to Harlem and to the Bowery before moving on to the White Horse Tavern in Greenwich Village, once frequented by Dylan Thomas and a host of American writers and musicians including Jack Kerouac, James Baldwin, Norman Mailer and Bob Dylan. Gwyn's tour of the city ended at Broadway where 'a million lights [beckoned] a star's welcome.'[102]

He was in his element telling viewers that 'on this incredible island of Manhattan ... America has its mirror and heart,' although privately he hated the heat of the summer and the less than efficient arrangements made by TWW. Satisfying his own passions, Gwyn made a pilgrimage to Lindy's on Broadway, the café-restaurant Damon Runyon had immortalised in his writing as Mindy's, and wrote home to Lyn to tell her that this was 'the only time I've ever faced a pancake that was bigger than the table.' Producer Wyn Roberts, later a minister at the Welsh Office during the Thatcher government and member of parliament for Conwy, recalled that 'I took Gwyn on his first visit to New York. He knew all the mobsters' haunts in the 1920s from reading Damon Runyon and we filmed a good many of them.' [103] In *Punch* a few years later, Gwyn reflected on that trip to America and on his own 'tenuous' American identity, the gift of his father and the 'fugitive, eastward-homing ghost' of his grandfather. 'On my first visit to the States,' he added, 'there was no surge of spiritual overtones, no sense of returning to a birthright narrowly missed and poignantly regretted. The whole experience, despite its underlying clamour, was full of abrupt, unsettling silences.' [104]

Gwyn was in America in the late summer of 1963, a matter of weeks before President Kennedy was assassinated as his motorcade passed through Dealey Plaza in Dallas, Texas. The country was still dealing with the after-effects of the Cuban Missile Crisis and involvement in the escalating conflict in Vietnam. Gwyn's ideas of what America was like had been shaped in large part by cinema, reading the stories of Damon Runyon and others, and, more recently, by the letters sent back and forth from leftist activists and writers in the 1940s and 1950s. That explains Wyn Roberts's recollections about Gwyn knowing all there was to know about Lindy's restaurant. Gwyn's commentary on the documentary was telling of his discombobulation. 'This is like living bang in the middle of a nervous condition,' he said in voice-over, 'here is the great external image of schizophrenia, the split mind, in which one half of the mind, one half of the body, is not too sure and not too happy about what the other half is up to.' Confronted by the realities of contemporary America during that frenetic tour in the last days of the Kennedy administration, his imagined America, along with his vanishing American Wales, shrivelled as he beat a welcome retreat homewards.

His portrait of the Soviet Union, titled *The Growing People*, was striking. It provided an encounter with the realities of the social, cultural, and political system to which he had been sympathetic for so long. 'For me,' he wrote in *Punch*, 'the name and fact of Russia have been loud on the wind. In my valley the militants peered into every corner, looking for powers to subvert, pieties to trash, blacklegs to harass, bailiffs to outrage, orthodoxy to knock, and usually finding them. Occasionally these subversive lads would be collared and whipped off to gaol. We took an operatic joy in their martyrdom.'[105] In the documentary, Gwyn stressed the humanity of ordinary men and women. He stood apart from the Cold Warriors, whose politics he did not share, and set out to provide 'an assessment of the fact that human beings struggle and try to survive. The more fully they survive, the more passionately they feel that they need a common ground of understanding with nations like ourselves.' He looked at the young people of the Soviet Union, the generation growing up after the Second World War and the tensions of the 1950s and insisted that 'There is a place for a new and sweeter manifesto – that all men have a common interest in preserving the innocence and delight of children as a change from projecting their own prides, spites and delusions.' Gwyn continued:

The brightness of the faces of the young children ... full of enquiry. Their expressions reminded me of my youth in the Rhondda Valley. In the Soviet Union I felt I was looking at part of my own childhood – a picture of a people struggling for a new identity. Don't think the streets of Moscow are rubbish dumps of failure. They tingle with great vitality ... In Moscow people wanted to know so many things. There is a real blaze of interest in the West. I liked the taxi drivers, so relaxed and friendly. I didn't like so much the ritual for form-filling. As for Moscow night life, outside the big hotels where you needed a wad as broad as the Volga, it struck us as terribly dull.[106]

Less dull was the experience of a night of singing with a group of Russians at their hotel who could otherwise speak no English. Gwyn recalled, 'the great thing was that it took so little to establish human affection between us – as we sang we found a marvellous bridge of understanding. The barriers were broken down.' In this way, Moscow was 'a city like any other.' Gwyn noted the 'multitudes of people [going] about their immemorial business of working, walking, talking, standing. ... Always, always we must think of the man, the woman, making their way from bed to work, work to pleasure, beginning to end. Empires may topple, dictators may wither or vanish, the human reality remains.'[107]

Wyn Roberts recalled the trip to Moscow in his 2006 memoir, *Right from the Start*. Characteristically, Roberts reflected, it was a bureaucratic experience, chaotic, yet warm and enjoyable, with the team benefitting from Gwyn's established renown as a progressive Western author and from the material support of their handlers from the state broadcaster. The TWW team stayed at the Hotel Ukraina, one of the grander skyscraper-hotels built in Moscow after the Second World War, and at the time the tallest hotel in the world. Opened in 1957, four years after

Stalin's death, but ten years after building work began, the Hotel Ukraina exemplified Soviet – indeed, Stalinist – modernity. The visit was managed by a Moscow handler called Vitaly Seferiants, a native of Vladivostok, who turned out to be supportive rather than obstructive. Roberts remembered that Seferiants 'had a very distinctive badge on his lapel that commanded a great deal of respect from all and sundry. He got the policeman to hold up the traffic outside the Bolshoi so that our cameraman could get his desired shots. He took us to the furthest point of the German advance on Moscow, to the onion-domed precincts of the Kremlin, and to film the crocodiles of children visiting Red Square. At the end of the day, he took our film for processing and a security check.'

Gwyn's own view of his only visit to the Soviet Union was never entirely committed to paper. Writing to Nan just after Christmas 1965, by then back in Britain, he let on only that the trip had been a 'brief but delirious episode. Once the first pall of suspicion had cleared, they could not have been kinder.'[108] His conclusion in *Punch* was similarly guarded. 'I clapped eyes on the Kremlin,' he wrote, 'by this time the name and fact of Russia had become less emotive, sang more quietly on the wind. The old hot ardours had cooled and greyed into clinker. The world had been savaged, concussed and had become quieter. The warriors of the Marxist word had slipped into apathy or the earth. Their voices were not heard save in some bit of sardonic late-night musing.' What Gwyn could not have known, of course, was that deep in the official archives in Moscow, he had a file all of his own – it had been compiled by the International Department of the Communist Party of the Soviet Union and contained background material such as biography and, in Gwyn's case, information relating to publications in the USSR and involvement in the Soviet-led peace initiatives of the 1950s.[109]

Germany was Gwyn's first real encounter with a divided Europe, and the experience was not at all enjoyable. 'The greatest and least unpredictable nation in the world,' Gwyn told readers of *Television Weekly*, 'in turn, profoundly creative and utterly destructive. It has produced some of the world's wisest and gentlest men – and some of the world's wildest and damnedest fools.' The TWW crew travelled from the Berlin Wall, which Gwyn thought one of the 'most depressing and sinister [sights] on this earth,' to Wittenberg where Martin Luther had launched the Protestant revolution centuries earlier.[110] Berlin stayed with him most. It was, he wrote, 'a community with a thread of barbed wire running through its soul.' The experience was made worse by the attempts to cross the border into East Germany. Gwyn's fame in the German Democratic Republic opened doors which would otherwise have remained shut. 'Four times our unit presented itself at the frontier at Lunenberg,' he wrote. 'Each time poker-faced guards turned us back on the grounds that our documents were not in order. For four days we filled in forms. In despair, I thought of trying a fictious name. But it was my own name that finally got us in. By a stroke of luck an East Berlin official had read some of my books. Even more fortunate, he liked them! He heard of our dilemma and arranged our entry.'[111]

As with the Soviet Union, Gwyn found the atmosphere in East Berlin became much more comfortable after the initial suspicion faded away – his was not to be a critical or antagonistic voice. Indeed, his sympathetic and humanistic portraits of Eastern Europe won him plaudits and awards. *The Growing People*, broadcast in the autumn of 1966, two years after *Gwyn Thomas in Germany*, won several commendations at the annual *Western Mail* and *South Wales Echo* ceremony in February 1967 including best television production, best television documentary, and, for Gwyn, best television performer in English.[112] The fourth documentary in the sequence took the team to Venice and was the most straightforward of the assignments. *The Drowning City* was broadcast in March 1965 and posed Gwyn in a gondola as he toured the famous canals and gave his impressions of 'a city which is slowly sinking.'[113] In the absence of political tension and with little cultural or linguistic interest in Italy, Gwyn's trip to Venice produced the least memorable of his TWW documentaries. Writing in *Television Weekly*, Gwyn described the trip as 'a very moving experience' and suggested that 'everyone should see Venice. It has the face of a lovely woman whose beauty is fading, slowly and sadly.'[114]

Gwyn's final overseas documentary for TWW took him back to Spain. It was the worst experience of all. He had none of the fame there which he enjoyed in the Soviet Union and East Germany, and the regime, in Gwyn's mind, really was the enemy. In the view of Wyn Roberts, *The Darker Neighbour*, filmed in April 1966, was 'a lovely film history.' Its title was a near-direct borrowing from Gwyn's unpublished novel of Moorish Spain written in the 1940s, and the attendant imagery borrowed from those older ideas, too. As Gwyn explained in *Punch*, 'we had planned a journey to Spain. Its point was to make a film that would show glimpses of Holy Week and of the cities the Moors had left behind in the slow anguish of their departure.'[115] The crew stayed at the Hotel Fenix, one of Madrid's luxury hotels, where the Beatles had been in residence a year earlier. The journey to Spain was a nightmare: the director, Colin Voisey, went down with food poisoning and almost missed the flight, and the camera equipment was impounded at the border. 'The usual old racket,' Gwyn told Lyn, recalling the problems they had experienced twenty years earlier.

As the impasse at the border continued, Gwyn retreated to a corner of the Hotel Fenix and read as much as possible, writing letters home to Lyn to tell her as much as he dared commit to paper. 'When I get back,' he told her, 'I will have things to tell you about the efficiency of TWW that will blacken the walls of our lovely home.' His prediction that the issues with the cameras was simply a matter of the officials wanting their bribe proved correct and as soon as money changed hands the equipment was released, and the crew could begin filming. They travelled across Spain, from Madrid to Cuenca, Granada to Cadiz, Seville to Segovia. It was at Cuenca that they captured one of the most striking images in *The Darker Neighbour*: the stations of the cross. Gwyn's rich commentary added to the visual and aural spectacle. 'Easter dominates the year,' he said in voice-over, 'the facts of this nation's faith are projected with a ruthless passion. To impersonate the Christ bearing his cross to death is an honour fervently sought. The hooded penitents, the rhythmic movement of the men carrying the massive stations of the cross through the narrow streets, the incessant drumming convey the impression of a mysterious and invincible devotion. Jesus on this day literally walks back into life.'

The Darker Neighbour was the last time Gwyn travelled abroad for television work, the result partly of his own declining health, changing demands on his services, and because of the much poorer working relationship he had with HTV, which controversially took over the rights to the Welsh third channel in 1968. There was one other documentary which fitted into this sequence of reflections and explorations, however, and which was produced by Gwyn for TWW in the middle of the 1960s: *Return to the Rhondda*. Broadcast on 22 September 1965, it brought together several of the valley's most famous sons – Donald Houston, Tommy Farr, Stanley Baker, and Gwyn – to talk about growing up and the Rhondda's impact on their lives.[116] Baker confessed that the valley was 'my idea of hell' and was shown walking through the remains of the colliery in

Ferndale where his father had lost his leg working underground. In those ruins, Baker pondered the choice of escaping the pit by boxing or acting. Gwyn, who frequently pondered the same act of flight, emphasised the dark, sardonic humour of valley people as they confronted the absurdity of their situation.

Well, we've heard something about the tears of the valley but the laughter of the valley I think is much more interesting because it's very understandable against the background of the fact that this place was assembled as a series of vast immigrations. Here was an empty, silent valley and then you had a loud, noisy valley. And something that I would never have dreamed I would be able to say – the poverty bit was so marvellous. Because really poverty, deprivation, anguish, misery, actually create the total human being in exactly the same that the anguish of a mother creates a child in herself. I will probably retract this statement later on but still I think it is substantially true. When I ponder the jokes that we had in the valley as parts of our mythology: the family that all but held a lottery to decide which of the six brothers would have the middle cutlet of the sardine.

And, of course, there is the wonderful story of the man who went to see the remains of a friend of his. Dead. Dead. And when you are Welsh dead, you are truly dead because we make no mistake at all about this. And he went in to see the body of his friend and he looked at it very carefully, and he said to the widow – well, he looks lovely, he looks beautiful doesn't he, he's a treat isn't he. And the widow says, yes indeed that last week in Llandudno did him the world of good. And of course, this is it, I think. This is the entire Welsh myth you know. There is no life really, there is no death either. There is a simple act of mind, a simple act of sympathy, occurring beneath the sun, beneath the moon, it doesn't really matter. Simply this act of love between people.

*

Documentary narration and monologue was Gwyn at his televisual best: he could control the situation and control the language being used. But in their efforts to find work for Gwyn, TWW and HTV placed him in situations which were rather more alien, where his natural shyness and nervousness could get the better of him in live situations: as the presenter of various solo or panel talk shows. These included *As I See It*, *10.42 And All That*, and the utterly disastrous *Free House*. The BBC, too, had put Gwyn in as a presenter in its discussion programme *Show Your Hand* in 1961. *As I See It*, which launched in the spring of 1965, and was scripted by Gwyn, was intended as a 'highly personal view of life, as related to people and topics in the news.'[117] The blurb for *Television Weekly* announced that 'Gwyn Thomas won't pull his punches!' and explained to readers that the series would have 'no limits on its range of subjects' drawing attention to international, domestic, and hyperlocal matters. 'Invariably,' Gwyn was quoted as saying, 'I am moved either to wrath or to rapture.' *10.42 And All That* had more variety and was part of TWW's efforts to create a late chat show punctuated with music, drama, and audience participation. As one reviewer put it, 'Ten Forty Two's major achievement is to trap his monologue and break it up.'[118]

Those tuning in to watch could be caught out by the 'dead-pan reading' of the news, which was then punctuated by Gwyn's comedic satire and a sketch, which he scripted, starring Gwyn as patron and Ray Smith as pub landlord. A good portion of the airtime was devoted to the audience asking questions and Gwyn responding. Filmed as-live on a Wednesday evening, the programme served as a prototype for HTV's *Free House*, which was broadcast in 1968 with a young Neil Kinnock, then a tutor-organiser with the Workers' Educational Association in Merthyr

Tydfil, as co-host. *Free House* was the brainchild of Aled Vaughan, the Welsh Programme Controller, whom Gwyn knew from his time at the BBC. It was intended by Vaughan to ease Gwyn's transition into the new working ethos of HTV. Set in a pub called The Bridge, *Free House* was broadcast at eleven in the evening on a Friday, ostensibly 'just in time' for those who had been out drinking to wind down in front of the television by listening to pub chatter. It was in fact filmed in the studio in Cardiff, although the set was intended to 'place the public bar customers into a natural environment.'[119]

From the off, Gwyn was unimpressed. 'These Harlech people,' he told Nan, 'seem to be dottier than the ones who went before. When they chose that name, I had them tabbed for the straight-jacket. I've been involved briefly in a hideous programme called Free House in which drunken buffoons air their views, and the air has never been the same. I'll tell you the whole story when we meet. It's really funny … Even their advertising seems to be out of whack. They put on that Pedigree Chum advert so often I bark before I switch on.'[120] To Aled Vaughan, Gwyn was far more direct and insisted on being released from what he called an 'inscrutable shambles' adding that 'if having to perform as an undistinguished footman among the muttering rabble in that awful bar is genuinely the best thing you can think of for me, I sag with depression and blink with alarm.' He walked away from HTV not long afterwards, annoyed with the rejection of a drama serial, *The Snug*, which was to be set in a valleys club and still with the bitter aftertaste of the *Free House* debacle. The break was a sour one. Gwyn rarely appeared on HTV in subsequent years and only once as a presenter.

In the summer of 1969, he agreed to write and present *Ready For The Fanfare* as part of HTV's series of programmes to accompany the investiture of Prince Charles as Prince of Wales at Caernarfon Castle. Deliberately evoking the spirit of *Wales and the West*, as if in defiance of the character of HTV's programming, which he disliked, Gwyn provided an idiosyncratic view of the castle and its history and of the forthcoming ceremony. But try as he might to disguise his feelings, the enthusiasm for documentary making had gone, and the programme had little of the energy which had marked the earlier series. In a letter to Ron Berry sent that summer, Gwyn confessed that 'there seem to be limitations to the smooth flow of contentment in a craft as inward and wayward as writing. I am still debating whether it is any more touched with madness than any of the other professional traps one might stumble into.'[121] Gwyn was in a reflective mood, exacerbated by the drying up of his work with *Punch*. He defected once more, returning to the BBC in an entirely different televisual landscape to the one he had left seven years before. Gone was the old single channel television service, BBC TV, and in its place two channels: BBC One and BBC Two.

It was the latter, headed by David Attenborough and launched in 1964 with an emphasis on the arts and documentary making, which provided Gwyn with his route back and his rehabilitation with Auntie. As if in an act of contrition, he made the most heartfelt and honest documentary of his life, a contribution to the *One Pair Of Eyes* series launched in May 1967.[122] Directed by Gilchrist Calder, with whom Gwyn had last worked in 1962, *It's A Sad But Beautiful Joke* was broadcast 6 September 1969. It was, ostensibly, an examination of the changing face of Wales, with the autobiographical elements drawing on *A Few Selected Exits* which had been published a year earlier, but Gwyn took that idea in a direction entirely of his own, focusing on the fortunes of his career as much as his growing-up place – the Rhondda.[123] In fact, to underline his intentions, Gwyn's original title for the documentary had been

'The Nature Of My Wrath.' Filming began in Oxford on 31st March 1969. Lyn and Gwyn travelled up the previous day and stayed at the Eastgate Hotel, a short walk from St Edmund Hall. The scenes in Oxford were confined entirely to the college, with Gwyn explaining some of the difficulties he had had during his time there.

> The loneliness, the awful sense of discordance, the sense of total alienation. My father was officially unemployed when I was at Oxford. I mean there were a few thousand people whose fathers never worked but were wealthy. But my father never worked and by God we were poor. The more conservative dons took one look at me and doubled the insurance on the colleges.

From the window of what had been his third-year room, Gwyn launched into a fierce critique of contemporary society. 'I suggest only that competition in any context under the sun is a bloody farce,' he said, 'competition in the world of higher scholarship, of higher perception, is something worse. The judgements struggling to emerge in the mind of a late adolescent are hardly ever capable of being judged. There is too much blood and pain and witless arrogance on them. Everything in education tends to be about ten years before its proper time. Children in the past were sometimes executed for eating earth, but all that they were doing was looking for a bit of zinc that their bodies needed, though they didn't know it. This was what Oxford was to me, the zinc I needed, though I was unaware of it at the time. We're all of us in a crouching position waiting for deliverance.' From Oxford, the crew moved on to North Wales, where they were to film at Coleg Harlech, and from there they travelled to Chichester to record a sequence between Gwyn and his former pupil, the actor Keith Baxter. They arrived in South Wales in the second week of April travelling to the lido at Aberavon, to the Rhondda (where the crew spent several days), and to Cardiff, where they sought to capture the atmosphere at the National Stadium during the Five Nations international between Wales and England.

Behind the scenes, the documentary as originally written and cut together was not well liked by BBC executives and Calder was forced to begin a period of re-editing and re-shooting. Amongst the sequences sacrificed was that filmed in Oxford. 'Gwyn was furious about this,' Calder explained to the series executive producer, Tony de Lotbinière (1925–1995), 'but I got him to agree to it after a lot of discussion.'[124] Although short, the Oxford sequence had been an important component in the argument Gwyn intended to present, and it was clearly dropped only with a great deal of reluctance. He set about rewriting various sequences and providing new narrative commentaries to fit with the amended running order. The result was a programme of enormous emotive and reflective power which took viewers from the Rhondda to Coleg Harlech, and from the politics of water to those of social democracy and workers' education. At its heart was a rejection of 'Celtic' Wales, and the fable-driven nationalist politics which were its contemporary expression, and an assertion of the modernist tragedy of American Wales. That, Gwyn said, was 'the fomenting, real tragedy of Wales – the farce [of] the marriage of men and coal and steel and iron.' It became, he insisted, 'the same sort of bubbling polyglot cauldron as the New York of the 1900s.'

Gwyn considered, also, what he thought to be one of the great inheritances of the Welsh, the neurosis of a guilt complex.[125] He explained that 'guilt seeps through like a terrible stain, a terrible dye. Take the word for beer. Beer – it's a lovely, forthcoming word in English; it is said, and it is forgotten. But in Welsh, you see, the word is *cwrw* – *cwrw*, *cwrw* – and repeated, as it has been repeated, by the puritans in our community it achieves the quality of all the owls of the world. *Cwrw, cwrw, cwrw*. And to this very day, I cannot take a half a pint of beer without taking an owl's beak out of my ear and saying, "get away, get away, leave me in freedom."' The conclusion of the programme as originally shot took place at the Pencelli Hotel in Treorchy, where Gwyn was questioned by members of the Treorchy Male Voice Choir. It was, in the end, excised because of the similarity of the question to one posed by Keith Baxter and because Gwyn's answer to Baxter was more effective. 'Why haven't you left?' one of the choir members asked, 'you've had the opportunity to do so?' Gwyn replied:

> All my life I was magnetised by the fact that I knew I was living in a wonderful tragi-comedy situation. It was so full of magnificent absurdities. It dictated the whole course of my life as a writer and as a teacher. I saw the beginning of the tragi-comedy, and I want to see the end. In other words, I am not going to leave. I chose my coffin and it's a very pleasant view.

Despite the challenges involved in bringing the documentary to screen, the broadcast version was widely praised by critics, who thought it a bright moment in the BBC's otherwise 'dull start to autumn.'[126] Writing in the *Sun*, a few weeks before it became a tabloid and lost the intellectual rigour of what had been the *Daily Herald*, the Thomas family paper, Jon Akass observed that 'Mr Thomas, in his doom laden and occasionally hilarious view of the Welsh … thundered across with marvellous, intoxicating melodrama.'[127] The *Guardian*'s Stanley Reynolds remarked that 'the old revolutionary, playwright, novelist and humourist gave us 45 minutes of very un-bland television talk.'[128]

Gwyn's BBC comeback was a triumphant success. Cheered by its reception, the producers quickly offered more work for the second channel. For a time, he became a regular on game shows such as *Call My Bluff* and *Not A Word* and enjoyed a stint as a television reviewer for *Line-Up*. 'I consume television and cinema with the indiscriminate abandon of a goat,' he told the *Radio Times*, 'from the sublimities of Kenneth Clark isolating the radium of creative intelligence to John Wayne trumpeting the ethos of the muscled oaf, I am there at the trough saluting and chewing.'[129] And then it all started to dry up. In the 1970s, he received fewer commissions to front his own work and instead morphed into the popular and much-loved, and reliable, guest of the day. It was all he could do to keep on working. Pop-up appearances on the radio and on television programmes providing charming epigrams brought regular, modest sums of money which paid the bills and allowed a focus on writing for the theatre. But there were downsides. Some came to resent the soundbite character of Gwyn's broadcasting in the 1970s, lamenting, in the words of literary critic M. Wynn Thomas, the keenness to 'play up to an Englishman's expectation of what a picturesque Welshman should be and to play down the real thing.'[130]

In this vein, Gwyn appeared on *Parkinson* twice, in 1971 and 1976, and was a memorable guest on the *Vincent Kane Show*. There were occasional glimpses into the past including one last effort in the *Wales and the West* model. *Personally Speaking*, which was broadcast in July 1975, saw Gwyn revisit the first journey he took from South Wales to Oxford as a student four decades before. And there was a combative interview for the HTV arts programme, *Nails*, in the autumn of 1974, when Gwyn talked about the essence of what he had set out to achieve in his novels and plays. There was one last television play, *The Ghost of Adelphi Terrace*, broadcast in 1975 and published in the United States in 1993, and a special documentary in 1976, *Gazooka Summer*, to mark the fiftieth anniversary of the 1926 miners' lockout.[131] The following year

Gwyn joined his former *Punch* colleague, Alan Coren, in a quirky look at comedy and joke writing. And, of course, there was Denis Mitchell's affectionate but honest and frank portrait for Granada's *Private Lives* series in 1975. As one his oldest broadcast collaborators, Mitchell was one of the few truly able to penetrate Gwyn's defences and the documentary was the most compelling and honest third-party portrait of the writer ever committed to film.

*

The reflection evident in Gwyn's broadcasting in the last decade or so of his life, underlined the twin aspects of this part of his career: the attempt to make sense of his personal journey, on the one hand, that of the South Walian people, on the other, and the intertwining of the two. For a long time, Gwyn searched for the indicative medium to convey his ideas about American Wales, about its intellectual and political possibility, and its steady disintegration. Sometimes this was a collective image – of the family, of the patrons in a pub, of the Rhondda as a community. At other times it was a single figure, Aneurin Bevan the most potent of all. Gwyn's views about Bevan changed over time, but by the early 1960s, following the latter's death, Gwyn had firmly settled into the Bevanite politics which he was to retain for the rest of his life. For him, Bevan was the lost leader, the man who, more than anyone else, confirmed and embodied what it meant to be South Walian. Gwyn's attempt to turn reality into fiction was to bring him into direct contact with the other great figure of post-war Wales, the actor Richard Burton.

Early in 1964, Gwyn appeared on Associated-Rediffusion's chat show *Something To Say*, hosted by the writer and investigative documentary maker Daniel Farson. Known as a risk-taker and sharp inquisitor, Farson interviewed a range of public figures including Gerald Gardiner QC, counsel for the defence during the Lady Chatterley Trial in 1960, the American Beat novelist William S. Burroughs, and the singer Shirley Bassey. Maurice Wiggin wrote of Gwyn's turn in the chair that he 'came nearer to elucidating the mysterious ecology of the Welsh than anyone I have heard tackling that engrossing task.'[132] Hymie Fagan, writing in the communist literary magazine, *Comment*, for which he was television reviewer, likewise observed that Gwyn

> swamped Daniel Farson in a tidal wave of poetry, emotion, fervour, class consciousness and depth of thought. Farson did not know what had hit him! He was completely unable to comprehend this man who had won so many scholarships "that the miners in the village hinted that I ought to be nationalised, split up and distributed amongst the rest of the lads." Thomas spoke of the miners' lives, their fighting spirit, their great strikes and of their great rebel leaders – the same type of men that "that filthy obscenity McCarthy had hounded and persecuted" but whom the miners "worshipped and adored."[133]

Those leaders included Noah Ablett, Arthur Horner, and, of course, Aneurin Bevan. Fagan thought that Gwyn had expressed a certain reverence for Ablett and Horner, but that he had spoken in less enthusiastic terms about Bevan. Accordingly, Gwyn had argued that Bevan 'grew tired' of internal conflict and turned away from the Left 'over the bomb and power politics.' This was clearly Fagan's interpretation since Gwyn, by this point, only ever expressed positive views about Bevan and understood the nature of his end-of-life pragmatism. Indeed, in *Wales and the West*, broadcast just over a year earlier, Gwyn had described Bevan fulsomely as a 'statesman, orator, dreamer, [and] wit.' He was the one man who had taken the imperfections of Ebbw Vale out into the world – and Ebbw Vale was itself totemic of South Wales – as a challenge, in Gwyn's words, 'to those parts of Britain that have never been scarred by poverty or the monstrous toll that heavy industry exacts from beauty.' These thoughts were by no means accidental. Behind the scenes Gwyn had been hard at work writing his biographical play, *Return and End*, in which Bevan was the title character. It was to be a study of politics, of motivation, and of the South Wales into which Bevan and Gwyn had been born.

'I want to go right into the hinterland behind Nye,' Gwyn explained to Richard Burton, 'I would like to express the valour, wisdom, laughter of all the men and women in our part of Wales who thrust Aneurin like a lance at the spiteful boobs at Westminster who regarded us in their inmost thoughts as a kind of intolerable dirt.' *Return and End* was thus to be 'a thundering vindication of us and our kind, a salute to all the people we can recall from your boyhood and mine whose lives closed on a note of muted paths, who had loved humanity almost to their own hurt.'[134] Rather than simply narrate a life, Gwyn sought instead to find the roots of Bevan's actions, his 'strange essence,' and to do that, he felt, he needed Burton's 'immense talent.' By July 1962, the second anniversary of Bevan's death, Gwyn had completed two of the three acts and sent a copy to Burton for comment. Burton, at the time, was busy filming *Cleopatra*, the swords and sandals epic which very nearly destroyed Twentieth Century Fox and created the enduring love affair between Burton and Elizabeth Taylor. Having read the script, Burton replied by telegram from his mansion near Geneva.

Dear Gwyn, read with delight your two acts, marvellously eloquent creation and infinitely actable. Small worry about age of 51, I am 36 but booze and late nights can work wonders. Mad to see third act and you and Mrs here soon. Tiny chalet apart from the main house specially made for overworked writers. Congratulations and, to quote you, an admiring shout from Pontrhydyfen to Porth. Richard.[135]

Gwyn and Lyn flew out to Geneva in early September 1962, by which time the entire script had been completed. Burton was enthusiastic and reasserted his commitment to take on the lead role for a production the following year. The press soon took an active interest in the play, with Gwyn speaking about its development in an interview with the *Guardian* in June 1962.[136]

It was now almost impossible to secure Burton, regardless of the actor's personal relationship with the script. In early January 1963, he finished a three-year run as King Arthur in the Broadway musical *Camelot* and was committed to filming *Becket* alongside Peter O'Toole a few months later. The summer of 1963 saw Burton and Taylor committed to promoting *Cleopatra*, which was released in the United States in June and had its UK premiere on 31 July, and then *The VIPs*. Burton had promised Gwyn that he would take time out to begin rehearsals for *Return and End* in April 1963 but, as Gwyn explained to Nan, 'I think his domestic crisis has demented the boy somewhat, he planned to open in the play and then, in the middle of the run ... he would have taken a fortnight out to film "Becket" in Scotland.'[137] Having been talked out of that plan, either by Gwyn, or far more likely the producers of *Becket*, who had the financial clout to do so, Burton instead promised 'to open the play on Broadway in the autumn.' Gwyn recognised the improbability and realised that *Return and End* would slip further and further down Burton's list of priorities. 'By which time,' Gwyn observed of Burton's plan, 'Master Burton will be filming with Miss Taylor on Tahiti or the Moon and I will be wishing them the best of Welsh luck.'

Gwyn found the experience of waiting on Burton to escape his filming commitments and act in *Return and End* absurdly amusing. Although irritated, too, Gwyn valued his friendship with Burton as well as the opportunity to work with the actor and allowed his annoyance to pass. Others made their own enquiries about the play including the BBC who sought the rights to a radio adaptation, although none came off.[138] As for Elizabeth Taylor, she was the wealthiest person Gwyn ever met in his life but unlike almost every other encounter with wealth which caused him to recoil, he found himself utterly charmed. He told Nan, 'Considering her background and unbelievable wealth and amorous squalls, Miss Taylor is remarkably nice. I had an evening of magnificent refreshment and a supper of sausage and mash with them at the Dorchester.'[139] The choice of meal was almost certainly Elizabeth Taylor's, who was a noted fan of bangers and mash, often buying her favourite brands at Fortnum & Mason.[140] Indeed, around the time Gwyn met Burton and Taylor in London, the pair had been photographed in a pub near Shepperton studios with a packet of Dring's sausages on the table.

Burton and Taylor were in the city filming *The VIPs* and staying in adjacent suites at the Dorchester. Gwyn was back and forth himself attending rehearsals and performances of his play *Jackie the Jumper* which was then being performed at the Royal Court Theatre. On Gwyn's encouragement, Burton had been invited to attend the premiere in February 1963 but was unable to do so.[141] The sole occasion for which Burton's schedule and Gwyn's did not clash came as a result of TWW's invitation to both men to take part in their annual St David's Day programme, *This World of Wales*.[142] Burton undoubtedly admired Gwyn, confessing as much both privately in his diary and publicly in his obituary of Stanley Baker in the *Observer* in 1976.[143] As the historian Peter Stead, a biographer of Burton, has noted, the actor's 'published journalism was a nod in the direction of his ... hero Gwyn Thomas, the novelist whose love of American fiction and films had led him all the more to appreciate the comic potential of a South Wales where overnight a peasant labour force had stumbled into an awareness of the great social questions of the era.'[144]

Panged with regret at the failure of *Return and End*, Burton tried to make amends several times over the next few years, not least an adaptation of *All Things Betray Thee* co-starring Stanley Baker.[145] In the spring of 1965, it was widely announced (at home and abroad) that Gwyn would pen *The Greatest Train Robbery in the World*, a film intended as a Burton-Taylor showcase, with Sam Wanamaker as director.[146] Production was to commence at MGM's Elstree Studios in September following completion of the film adaptation of Edward Albee's 1962 play, *Who's Afraid of Virginia Woolf?*.[147] Gwyn's inspiration was the Great Train Robbery of 1963 which saw the theft of more than two and a half million pounds from a Royal Mail train. He worked closely with Wanamaker on the project, at one point calling on the director in London and leaving with the impression that the film was going to be 'very big indeed.'[148] But in the end it too collapsed.[149] By the time another offer from Burton arrived – this time to act in a complete televised version of 'The Keep' as part of the launch of HTV in 1968 – Gwyn looked upon it with much less excitement assuming that it too would fall by the wayside.[150] It did.

By now, these excitements and disappointments were part of the rough and tumble of working in television and radio, but they were undoubtedly frustrating – even more so early on in his career when a successful film production would have been transformative. As it was, he moved on to the next project, the next idea, and the next disappointment. All the way through Gwyn's career, filmmakers had made offers to translate his work for the cinema, none of which made it to the screen. In March 1947, Curtis Brown submitted a proposal to the prominent American film company RKO for an adaptation of *The Dark Philosophers*.[151] Although read with interest by Jack Wasserman on behalf of RKO, development of a film adaptation went no further and with good reason. During the summer and autumn of 1947, RKO came under such scrutiny from the House Un-American Activities Committee that within a year, the company's main shareholder, the industrialist Floyd Odlum (1892–1976), had resigned and sold up, eventually leaving the virulently anti-communist businessman Howard Hughes (1905–1976) in near-total control. Within weeks of the takeover in May 1948, hundreds of RKO employees had been fired and all actors, directors, and screenwriters were now carefully screened before being allowed back to work – a process which took almost six months. All films had to firmly state their anti-communist position or Hughes refused their release. RKO's once vibrant output dwindled.

It was a similar story on Broadway. In 1958, the *Empire News* reported that a New York theatre producer was keen to adapt *The Alone To The Alone*. The *Empire News* concluded enthusiastically, 'if Gwyn's lullaby of Broadway is a success the story may become a film.'[152] Gwyn told journalists that the project had 'plenty of backing ... a very good scriptwriter and a very good musician – both Americans.' Gwyn was more forthcoming and less hopeful with Nan, to whom he wrote a few weeks later to tell her all about his latest visitor, the mysterious Richard 'Dick' Frank. 'The purpose of Dick's visit here struck me as curious,' he explained, 'Dick thinks it would make a good musical. He tells me that if he can come up with a reasonably good script and lyrics he'll have no difficulty in finding the money for a production in one of the smaller theatres off Broadway.' The young composer, whose name was

never recorded, was interested in fusing 'the flavour of some of
our minor key laments' with American blues and Jewish music,
thereby providing motifs enough to take the radical edge off the
story. 'I know your book is kind of left-wing, Gwyn, but doing
it this way the music will take the curse off it,' Frank had said,
with a knowing nod towards the blacklist.

Gwyn was sceptical, 'the air is full of these wonderful ideas
of making films and musicals of this and that ... But I wish Dick
well. He's had the usual amount of bad luck from the fascist
antics of the McCarthy brigade that most intelligent Americans
have had over the last ten years.' The unnamed scriptwriter,
Gwyn told Nan, was 'a close friend of Arthur Miller.'[153] But
who was this mysterious individual? Unfortunately, no one
knows exactly who he was. Gwyn's correspondence about the
matter offered few clues and, in retrospect, those he left behind
are misleading. Frank had been, Gwyn told his sister, part of
the production team on *Somebody Up There Likes Me*, Paul
Newman's 1956 Oscar-winning biopic of Italian-American boxer
Rocky Graziano. Directed by Robert Wise, written by Ernest
Lehman, and produced by Charles Schnee, the film had no one
attached to it with the name Richard Frank.[154] It is almost
certainly the case that 'Richard Frank' was a pseudonym – akin
to Dalton Trumbo's 'Robert Rich' used for his Oscar-winning
film *The Brave One* (1956) – since the Hollywood Blacklist was
still in operation, although by 1958 very much on the wane.
The only other indication as to Frank's identity was the fact
that he had given Gwyn a copy of a 1957 recording of a Paul
Robeson concert.[155] No wonder that Gwyn told Nan he had
been 'mixed up in some very vague ventures with films and
plays latterly.'

A more concrete proposal to adapt *The Love Man* for BBC TV
came from Elaine Morgan. She had taken the initiative herself
to approach the BBC in 1958 explaining that the novel was

'Gwyn Thomas at his best and this novel has more directly liftable dialogue than most of the Welsh ones.'[156] Although Morgan was regarded as the best adapter of Gwyn's work, other than himself, the project ran aground because of concerns at the BBC about the period setting and the sense that 'in television terms' there was something 'newer and fresher and perhaps more alive in the other Gwyn Thomas novels.'[157] Morgan was convinced of the potential, however, and explained to Donald Wilson at the BBC that 'I love Gwyn's Meadow Prospect novels but apart from the fact that that background of his has been tried on t.v. and to my mind didn't jell, they don't have a plot at all, as he'd be the first to admit.'[158] Undeterred, Morgan proceeded to write a script which made its way through various producers in London and Cardiff in the summer of 1959, which was about the time Gwyn heard of the project.[159]

Most of those who read the script were enthusiastic. Donald Wilson explained to Morgan that 'I went overboard for it at once – I liked it very much. Michael Barry did too but is of course in the embarrassing position of having promised Hugh Ross Williamson to do his *The Death of Don Juan*.' The politics of the situation meant, Wilson said regretfully, that 'I think we must leave this for the time being.'[160] Producers turned, one last time, to the adaptation in January 1960, but to no avail. In a biting comment, one pondered whether anyone 'will stand more than ten minutes of this except those Welsh brought up to believe you mustn't walk out of chapel till the Doxology's done to a turn, even though your piles are giving you hell.'[161] The fault, it seemed, at least to those who had read Morgan's adapted script, was as much Gwyn's as hers. *The Love Man*, Gwyn's take on the Don Juan story, and his last novel, never made it to television. At the time, it did not seem to matter too much – at least to Gwyn. Six months after everything was set aside, Gwyn's first play opened at the Royal Court Theatre in London.

Morgan, too, was busy with the scripts for *A Matter of Degree* and her career as a scriptwriter was about to take off. She would return to adapting Welsh literature over a decade later, injecting her own sense of the veracity of the coalfield into Richard Llewellyn's *How Green Was My Valley*. The Castillo of Toledo and the figure of Don Juan was abandoned and replaced by the Morton family, the looming absence of a mother who had run off to America, and the absurdity of their Rhondda *Keep*. It was to be Gwyn's attempt to imagine 'what my family life would have been if my brothers and I had not been dispersed from our kitchen by the squalid autumn of the thirties.' The characters took their nicotine 'like captive mice,' spent hours brooding in the parlour, all the while gazing up at a portrait of 'mam,' and in so doing aligned themselves with every expanding neurosis available. The world appeared one 'of withered dreams.' And behind it all stood the urbane, bespectacled, grey-haired, pipe-smoking English theatre director: George Devine (1910–1966). 'I'm asking novelists to write plays,' Devine explained to Gwyn, in dialogue invented by Alan Plater in the early 1990s. 'So, what do you say?' The reply: 'Well I say, are you sure you're right about novelists? We are solitary, rambling, untidy animals. We never get to the point.'

---

[1] *RT*, 9 April 1948. The episode aired on 17 April 1948.

[2] *RT*, 26 August 1949. The programme aired on 31 August 1949. The *Arts Magazine* was first broadcast on the Welsh Home Service on 8 April 1949. It replaced a previous arts programme, *Music in Wales*, mixing music, literature, and the visual arts. *Merthyr Express*, 2 April 1949.

[3] BBC WAC, WA8/231/1, Talks, Gwyn Thomas, 1949–1969: Letter from Gwyn Thomas to Elwyn Evans, 2 September 1949. Elwyn Mainwaring Evans was the son of poet Wil Ifan (1883–1968). Starting out as an announcer, he moved through the ranks of the BBC, notably as a senior features producer in Wales, to become director of the Nigerian Broadcasting Corporation between 1956 and 1959. Before his retirement he served as a senior instructor at Broadcasting House in London.

[4] Letter from Elwyn Evans to Gwyn Thomas, 15 September 1949.

[5] Letter from Gwyn Thomas to Elwyn Evans, 18 September 1949.

[6] Letter from Gwyn Thomas to Hannah Thomas, 29 November 1949. The other writers interviewed (or intended to be interviewed) were Elizabeth Bowen, Rhys Davies, Richard Hughes, Emyr Humphreys, Gwyn Jones, and Dylan Thomas (although the last had to pull out eventually due to injury). 'How I Write' formed a sub-series for the *Arts Magazine*.

[7] Jones, *Dragon Has Two Tongues*, 102. A copy of the script can be found in NLW, GTP, G161.

[8] Gwyn Thomas, 'Then Came We, Singing', *Coal: The NCB Magazine* 1, no. 10 (February 1948), 24–25; 'A Mining Diary', *Coal: The NCB Magazine* 1, no. 10 (February 1948), 14.

[9] Letter from Gwyn Thomas to Hannah Thomas, 31 May 1952.

[10] BBC WAC, WA20/209/1, Gwyn Thomas File, 1951–1968: Letter from Iris Evans to Gwyn Thomas, 20 December 1951; *South Wales Gazette*, 4 January 1952.

[11] *WM*, 14 January 1952.

[12] *WM*, 8 September 1952.

[13] It was broadcast on 5 January 1953.

[14] BBC WAC, Gwyn Thomas File, Memo from Miss Ross to W.P.Ex, Cardiff, 20 January 1953.

[15] *Yorkshire Evening Post*, 26 January 1953. 'Forenoon' was repeated on 9 August 1953.

[16] On 7 January and 27 January 1953.

[17] BBC WAC. Gwyn Thomas File, Letter from Elwyn Evans to Gwyn Thomas, 21 January 1953.

[18] The broadcast was discussed by 'The Critics' on the Home Service, 1 February 1953. Lyn noted in a letter to Nan and Bill that 'they were, without exception, very enthusiastic about it. It was wonderful to listen to them.' Letter from Lyn Thomas to Hannah and Bill Thomas, 12 February 1953.

[19] BBC WAC, Letter from Chief Assistant, Talks (Home Sound) to Head of Welsh Programmes, 6 February 1953.

[20] BBC WAC, Letter from Head of Welsh Programmes to Chief Assistant, Talks (Home Sound), 11 February 1953.

[21] *The Listener*, 2 June 1949.

[22] BBC WAC, Letter from Chief Assistant, Talks (Home Sound), 12 February 1953.

[23] By happenstance, a few years later, Colin MacInnes's novel *Absolute Beginners* was likened by Keith Waterhouse as being 'a lot of [J. D.] Salinger and a little of Gwyn Thomas.' *New Statesman*, 5 September 1959.

[24] *RT*, 13 June 1954.

[25] Letter from Lyn Thomas to Hannah Thomas, 25 August 1953; *Yorkshire Evening Post*, 12 November 1953.

[26] *WM*, 13 April 1953.

[27] *WM*, 2 November 1953.

[28] NLW, GTP, G180: 'The Rich Hills'; *RT*, 8 March 1953. The documentary was broadcast on 10 March.

[29] Letter from Gwyn Thomas to Hannah Thomas, 2 April 1953.

[30] Roberta Schwartz, *How Britain Got The Blues* (Aldershot, 2007), 45.

[31] Letter from Gwyn Thomas to Hannah Thomas, 25 May 1953.

[32] A separate commission, from London, for broadcast on the North American Service came later in the year. As Lyn noted in a letter to Nan, 'The London BBC has asked him to write a special script for broadcasting to America on Wales. ... I think the show will be called "Singing in Wales" or something like that, and it should be very good.' Letter from Lyn Thomas to Hannah Thomas, 30 October 1953.

[33] Letter from Gwyn Thomas to Hannah Thomas, 30 October 1953.

[34] Letter from Gwyn Thomas to Hannah Thomas, 27 July 1953; 'Then Came We, Singing' was broadcast on 28 July 1953; 'Teilo Topliss' was broadcast on 11 August 1953. The latter was reworked and published as 'The Living Lute' in *Punch* and subsequently reprinted in *Ring Delirium, 123* (London, 1960).

[35] Letter from Lyn Thomas to Bill Thomas, 22 January 1953.

[36] Letter from Lyn Thomas to Hannah Thomas, 22 October 1953.

[37] Letter from Lyn Thomas to Hannah Thomas, 14 December 1952.

[38] Letter from Lyn Thomas to Hannah Thomas, 16 January 1953.

[39] Letter from Lyn Thomas to Hannah Thomas, 24 December 1953. Gwyn and Lyn had moved to 61 Porthkerry Road in 1948, after moving from 151 Gladstone Road to 11 Broad Street in 1945.

[40] *DH*, 24 July 1954; Letter from Lyn Thomas to Hannah Thomas, 24 June 1954.

[41] Letter from Gwyn Thomas to Hannah Thomas, 8 July 1954; *RT*, 18 July 1954.

[42] *AFSE*, 168.

[43] *Highlight*, the precursor to the more famous *Tonight* which launched in 1957, had been conceived as an emergency replacement for the aborted television debut of 'The Archers', and was part of the BBC's attempt to maintain audience loyalty against the launch of ITV in 1955. Leonard Miall, 'Obituary of Donald Baverstock', *Independent*, 18 March 1995.

[44] He wrote memorably about the experience for *Television Weekly* in 1962.

[45] *AFSE*, 171–172; Gwyn Thomas, 'A Subordinate Crumb on Television', *Lilliput*, February 1959, 24–28.

[46] Letter from Gwyn Thomas to Hannah Thomas, 8 March 1956.

[47] TNA, KV 2/3523-3524: Jacob Bronowski Personal File, 1939–1959.

[48] Ralph Desmarais, 'Jacob Bronowski: A Humanist Intellectual for an Atomic Age, 1946–1956', *The British Journal for the History of Science* 45, no 4 (2012), 573–589.

[49] NLW, GTP, G4: Present Indicative – The Literary Potential of Wales; G206: Script of Present Indicative, 2 November 1955.

[50] *RT*, 23 December 1955.

[51] Letter from Lyn Thomas to Hannah Thomas, 22 November 1956.

[52] Letter from Gwyn Thomas to Hannah Thomas, 8 March 1956.

[53] Letter from Lyn Thomas to Hannah Thomas, 22 November 1956.

[54] BBC WAC, T32/1580, Brains Trust 1946–1957: Memorandum from Kenneth Adam, Controller Programmes TV, 11 December 1957.

[55] Letter from Gwyn Thomas to Hannah Thomas, undated but summer 1959.

[56] Briggs, *History of the BBC*, volume 5, p. 162.

[57] RBA, Ron Berry Papers, WWE/1/10/2/1: Letter from Gwyn Thomas to Ron Berry, 26 June 1961.

[58] Letter from Gwyn Thomas to Hannah Thomas, undated but late July 1958. Gwyn notes that he is to read a short story on the Light Programme on Friday at 11am. This was 'The Fixers', broadcast on 1 August 1958.

[59] Maurice Wiggin, writing in the *Sunday Times*, 17 January 1960.

[60] *WM*, 11 June 1957.

[61] *WM*, 14 January, 26 January 1959.

[62] *WM*, 2 January 1959. Gwyn's copy is held at the South Wales Miners' Library.

[63] *RT*, 5 April 1959; *South Wales Gazette*, 3 April 1959.

[64] *WM*, 18 April 1959.

[65] *AWE*, 112.

[66] Harry Ransom Center, University of Texas, Constantine FitzGibbon Papers, MS-1408/24/1–6: Script and other materials relating to 'The Hungry Years', 1958–1959.

[67] *DH*, 10 February 1959; *WM*, 14 February 1959; *Belfast Telegraph*, 25 February 1959.

[68] NLW, GTP, J36: Letter from Gwyn Thomas to Constantine Fitzgibbon, 2 March 1959.

[69] *WM*, 21 July 1958.

[70] *South Wales Gazette*, 11 July 1958.

[71] *The Stage*, 9 February 1961.

[72] *TW*, 24 August 1962.

[73] Gwyn Thomas, 'Gwyn Thomas Looks Again...', *TW*, 31 August 1962.

[74] 'Letter from S. Jenkins', *TW*, 28 September 1962.

[75] 'Letter from Thomas A. Williams', *TW*, 21 September 1962.

[76] 'Letter from G. Shilton Evans', *TW*, 28 September 1962.

[77] 'Letter from Richard Williams', *TW*, 28 September 1962.

[78] 'Letter from Mrs B. Humphreys', *TW*, 21 September 1962.

[79] 'Letter from G. G. Davies', *TW*, 12 October 1962.

[80] *South Wales Echo*, 25 August 1962.

[81] Letter from Brian Evans to Gwyn Thomas, 19 August 1963.

[82] *Liverpool Echo*, 6 October 1962; NLW, GTP, G186: Rehearsal Script for 'The Slip', BBC TV, 1962.

[83] *Newcastle Journal*, 20 October 1962; Clifford Hanley, 'Television', *The Spectator*, 18 October 1962.

[84] Gwyn Thomas, 'The Slip: Tonight's play introduced by its author', *RT*, 11 October 1962.

[85] Gwyn's eulogy for Aberfan 'A Day of Mourning', broadcast on the BBC's Today programme a week after the disaster, the day of the mass funeral (28 October 1966), captured the precise mood. It was subsequently released on record by the BBC. *Daily Mirror*, 15 November 1966.

[86] Sarah Morse, 'The Black Pastures: The Significance of Landscape in the work of Gwyn Thomas and Ron Berry' (Unpublished PhD Thesis, Swansea University, 2010).

[87] Daryl Leeworthy, *Elaine Morgan: A Life Behind The Screen* (Bridgend, 2020).

[88] Sarah Morse, '"Green Always Comes Back": Ron Berry's Ecocentric Writing', in Georgia Burdett and Sarah Morse (eds), *Fight and Flight: Essays on Ron Berry* (Cardiff, 2020).

[89] Gwyn's (incomplete) manuscript for 'The Dig' is held at the National Library of Wales. NLW, GTP, D9: 'The Dig'. Unfortunately, no recording of the programme has survived.

[90] *Belfast Telegraph*, 14 December 1963; NLW, GTP, G110: 'A Meadow Prospect Christmas'. The programme was broadcast on 15 December 1963.

[91] Maurice Wiggin, 'Endings and beginnings', *Sunday Times*, 22 December 1963.

[92] Angus Wilson, *Tempo: The Impact of Television on the Arts* (London: Studio Vista, 1964).

[93] Letter from Gwyn Thomas to Hannah Thomas, 20 December 1963.

[94] Note appended to the archive recording held NLW, HTV Archive, Here Today, 23 December 1963.

[95] Letter from Gwyn Thomas to Hannah Thomas, 18 July 1963.

[96] RBA, Ron Berry Papers, WWE/1/10/2/2: Letter from Gwyn Thomas to Ron Berry, 25 August 1969.

[97] Letter from Gwyn Thomas to Hannah Thomas, 11 April 1963.

[98] *The Stage*, 8 April 1965, 24 June 1965; A full list of competition winners can be found on the Czech Television website: https://zlatapraha.ceskatelevize.cz/en/last-years/24/older [Accessed: 10 August 2019].

[99] *AFSE*, 192.

[100] *Neues Deutschland* (East Berlin), 13 June 1965. My translation from the original German.

[101] Letter from Gwyn Thomas to Hannah Thomas, 20 December 1963.

[102] Gwyn Thomas, 'Gwyn Thomas: This Is New York', *TW*, 24 April 1964.

[103] Wyn Roberts, *Right from the Start: The Memoirs of Sir Wyn Roberts* (Cardiff, 2006), 68.

[104] Gwyn Thomas, 'The Westward Fancy', *Punch*, 4 August 1965. The article was incorporated into chapter five of *A Few Selected Exits*.

[105] Gwyn Thomas, 'Into the Sunrise', *Punch*, 15 September 1965. The article was likewise incorporated into chapter five of *A Few Selected Exits*.

[106] Gwyn Thomas, 'The Growing People', *TW*, 27 October 1966.

[107] NLW, GTP, G153; 'Moscow'; G215 – 'Russia, the Growing People'. Script.

[108] Letter from Gwyn Thomas to Hannah Thomas, 30 December 1965.

[109] Russian State Archive of Socio-Political History (RGASPI), Moscow, 495.198.1911: Gwyn Thomas. The atmosphere in Moscow at that time is described by Sheila Fitzpatrick, who arrived a few years later in 1966, in her memoir *A Spy in the Archives: A Memoir of Cold War Russia* (London, 2013).

[110] Gwyn Thomas, 'Martin Luther: The New Piety', *Holiday* 25, no. 1 (1964).

[111] Gwyn Thomas, 'Gwyn Thomas in Germany', *TW*, 11 September 1964.

[112] *WM*, 16 February 1967.

[113] *The Stage*, 25 February 1965.

[114] Gwyn Thomas, 'The Ancient City Going Under', *TW,* 4 February 1965.

[115] Gwyn Thomas, 'Washington Irving Stayed Here', *Punch*, 31 May 1967. This was the third of the *Punch* articles, and the most recent, to be incorporated into chapter five of *A Few Selected Exits*.

[116] *The Stage*, 2 September 1965, 23 September 1965.

[117] *The Stage*, 1 April 1965; NLW, GTP, G103–106: 'As I See It Scripts, April–June 1965'.

[118] *Sunday Telegraph*, 30 January 1966; NLW, GTP, G92–99: '10.42 And All That Scripts, January–March 1966'.

[119] *TW*, 29 August 1968.

[120] Letter from Gwyn Thomas to Hannah Thomas, undated but December 1968.

[121] Letter from Gwyn Thomas to Ron Berry, 25 August 1969.

[122] The debut episode was James Cameron, *One Pair of Eyes: Temporary Person Passing Through* (BBC 2, 6 May 1967). The series ran until 1984.

[123] BBC WAC, T56/215/1: One Pair of Eyes: Gwyn Thomas, It's a Sad But Beautiful Joke, 6 September 1969.

[124] BBC WAC, T56/215, One Pair of Eyes, Gwyn Thomas: It's a Sad but Beautiful Joke: Letter from Gilchrist Calder to Tony de Lotbiniere, 5 June 1969.

[125] A regular theme. He had previously turned his attention to the Welsh relationship with alcohol in an article for *The Spectator* published following the Referendum on Sunday Opening held on 8 November 1961. Gwyn Thomas, 'The Opening', *The Spectator*, 2 February 1962.

[126] *Daily Express*, 8 September 1969.

[127] *The Sun*, 8 September 1969.

[128] *The Guardian*, 8 September 1969.

[129] *RT*, 4 March 1971.

[130] M. Wynn Thomas speaking on *Gwyn Thomas: A Critical Reputation* (BBC, 1986).

[131] Gwyn Thomas, 'The Ghost of Adelphi Terrace', *Shaw: The Journal of Bernard Shaw Studies* 13 (1993), 139–150.

[132] *Sunday Times*, 26 January 1964.

[133] Hymie Fagan, 'TV Notes: Revolt, Casino, Pay, Gwyn Thomas', *Comment: Communist Fortnightly*, 1 February 1964.

[134] NLW, GTP, J34: Letter from Gwyn Thomas to Richard Burton, 25 May 1962.

[135] NLW, GTP, J34: Telegram from Richard Burton to Gwyn Thomas, July 1962.

[136] *The Guardian*, 26 June 1962; RBA, Richard Burton Papers, RWB/1/2/1/17: Press Cuttings, 1962; NLW, GTP, K8-10: Press Cuttings regard Return and End, 1962; GTP, D30; GTP, E4, p. 10, p. 16.

[137] Parts of the film were also shot on location at Bamburgh Castle in Northumberland. See: http://www.yorkshirefilmarchive.com/film/becket-bamburgh [Accessed: 4 August 2019]

[138] BBC WAC, Gwyn Thomas File: Memorandum from D. L. Ross, Copyright Department, to Herbert Davies, 20 January 1964.

[139] Letter from Gwyn Thomas to Hannah Thomas, 11 April 1963.

[140] Chris Williams (ed), *The Richard Burton Diaries* (New Haven, 2013), 7 May 1965.

[141] RBA, Richard Burton Papers, RWB/1/2/2/6/4: Letter from George Devine to Richard Burton, February 1963.

[142] NLW, GTP, G107–108: This World of Wales.

[143] Burton Diaries, 16 June 1966; Richard Burton, 'Lament for a Dead Welshman', *The Observer*, 11 July 1976. Burton was not always kind about Gwyn in the diaries, however, recording on 15 June 1969 that he was 'an impersonation of a chap who would like to be big, strong and tough and who is actually fat, weak and febrile.' Although this was in the context of a list of 'all the men of talent I have ever met.' Williams, *The Richard Burton Diaries*, entry for 15 June 1969.

[144] Peter Stead, *Richard Burton: So Much, So Little* (Bridgend, 1991), 107.

[145] Smith, *Aneurin Bevan*, 6.

[146] *Sunday Telegraph*, 18 April 1965.

[147] *Daily News* (New York), 25 April 1965.

[148] Diana Devlin, *Sam Wanamaker: A Global Performer* (London, 2019), 145; Parnell, *AFSE*, 192.

[149] Boston University, Sam Wanamaker Papers, Box 28, XIV.I: File regarding the Greatest Train Robbery project, 1965–1975; NLW, GTP, J50/1-3: Letters and Telegram from Sam Wanamaker to Gwyn Thomas and reply from Gwyn Thomas to Sam Wanamaker, 3 March–24 March 1965.

[150] *The Stage*, 4 April 1968; *The Guardian*, 18 April 1968, 1 August 1969. Burton was an HTV shareholder.

[151] L. Tom Perry Special Collections, Harold B. Lee Library, Brigham Young University, Utah, Argosy Pictures Collection, MSS 1849, Box 21, Folder 1: Film Synopsis of The Dark Philosophers by Gwyn Thomas, 1947.

[152] *Empire News and Sunday Chronicle*, 22 June 1958.

[153] Letter from Gwyn Thomas to Hannah Thomas, undated but late July 1958.

[154] The credits list published by the American Film Institute is available online at: https://catalog.afi.com/Catalog/moviedetails/52009 [Accessed: 10 February 2020].

[155] Paul Robeson, *Paul Robeson's Transatlantic Concert*. London: Topic Records 10T17, 1957. The recording was of Robeson's transatlantic link concert at St Pancras Hall, London, on 26 May 1957.

[156] BBC WAC, T48/437/2, Elaine Morgan, Television Script Unit, Drama Writer's File: Memorandum regarding Elaine Morgan's Adaptation of Gwyn Thomas's The Love Man, 15 September 1958.

[157] BBC WAC, T48/437/2: Letter from Donald Wilson to Elaine Morgan, 15 October 1958.

[158] BBC WAC, T48/437/2: Letter from Elaine Morgan to Donald Wilson, undated but c. October 1958.

[159] BBC WAC, T48/437/2: Letter from Elaine Morgan to Donald Wilson, undated but c. September 1959.

[160] BBC WAC, T48/437/2: Letter from Donald Wilson to Elaine Morgan, 15 October 1959.

[161] BBC WAC, T48/437/2: Memorandum by Harry Green, The Love Man by Gwyn Thomas, 12 January 1960.

CHAPTER EIGHT

A Winning Sense of the Grotesque

'I wonder if you could find time to have lunch with me one day,' George Devine had written, in a letter sent to Gwyn in June 1956, 'as I would like to discuss with you the possibility of your writing for the theatre. As you know, it is our policy here to introduce writers to the theatre, and I would be interested to know your views on the matter.'[1] Here was the Royal Court Theatre in London, where Devine was the artistic director of the resident English Stage Company. Gwyn duly travelled to meet with Devine just before Christmas, the first opportunity he had to get away.[2] The Oxford-educated Devine had joined the ESC early in 1955, just a few months after its creation in October 1954. He used his position to develop a programme of radical theatre seeking to pull English theatre away from its interwar reliance on Shakespeare and comedies of manners. The first plays performed by the ESC at the Royal Court in the spring and summer of 1956 thus included Angus Wilson's *The Mulberry Bush*, Arthur Miller's *The Crucible* and John Osborne's *Look Back In Anger*. Devine had even persuaded Miller to travel to London to join a panel discussion on 'The Crisis in British Theatre.' An ambitious scheme to find the best of modern playwrighting talent had yielded hundreds of scripts in the first six months of 1956 – *Look Back In Anger* among them – and it was this process of discovery Devine wanted Gwyn to join.[3]

Initially, Gwyn was encouraged to think about translating and adapting the work of dramatists from the Spanish Golden Age,

340

such as Lope de Vega and Tirso de Molina – the originators of the theatrical life of Don Juan.[4] For a time, given he was writing *The Love Man*, Gwyn seems to have been attracted by the idea. He even penned a free-verse translation of Molina's great seventeenth-century religious drama *El Condenado por Desconfiado* as *The Cadence* as a trial run.[5] The themes of Molina's drama, in which the young hermit Paolo is led by his own doubts – encouraged by the devil in disguise – and finds himself in a series of absurd circumstances was typical of Gwyn's writing. In the end, the good man (Paolo) is condemned to hell, whereas his immoral shadow (Enrico, one of the worst mobsters of Naples) is taken to heaven. Some of the preparatory work on *The Cadence* and the ideas prompted by Devine's initial offer found its way into *To This One Place*, a Don Juan story, which was broadcast as a radio play on the Welsh Home Service in the autumn of 1956.[6] But in the end, Gwyn's thoughts turn back to the Rhondda and to life at 196 High Street.

Frustrated with Gwyn's slow progress, Devine persistently prodded. For several years, Gwyn picked up and put down various unfulfilled ideas. He told Nan that Devine had 'made this request to me for the last two or three summers and I still haven't come up with anything solid. I've got a lot of ideas that might come to life on a stage, but I can't really work up any considerable heat about working for live theatre. It's probably having grown up as a cinema addict. I still prefer a good film to any play. And besides, the risk of total humiliation on the stage is far greater than it would be in a novel.' Gwyn added to his portrait in a subsequent letter to his sister, sent early in 1960, explaining that:

George Devine, I think I must have told you this before, asked me a fair time back to do a play for him. I did so and took my time over it. Then I forgot about it, knowing that decisions in the theatre move like glaciers. I was quite amazed to hear that he is going to put it on this summer. It will first have a showing at what they call the club theatre which is one for Sunday night only and if the thing shows any signs of theatrical life it will be taken into the repertory. He wants me to come up to London to attend rehearsals and it should be an interesting experience. I think that one day I may write plays that will make a bit of a stir but this particular one will not perhaps have the sort of flavour that will make it popular with London audiences.

The Keep was scheduled for 7 August 1960 and was to be directed by the Scottish actor Graham Crowden, whose various performances included roles in the BBC sitcom *Porridge*, the *Doctor Who* serial 'The Horns of Nimon,' and the James Bond film *For Your Eyes Only* starring Roger Moore.[7] But disaster struck on the day of the performance: the theatre was flooded in a storm which Gwyn later used to Dickensian effect in *A Few Selected Exits*.[8] He wrote: 'the rain had stopped but everyone in the streets still looked stunned by the force of it. The doors of the Royal Court Theatre were closed tight. On the steps a considerable group of people had gathered and most of the faces I saw were gloomy. Several raised their eyes compassionately, as if to say that this was the sort of thing that would happen to them and me.'[9] The performance was rescheduled for the following week. It was 'worth waiting for,' recorded one reviewer, who thought it a funny and highly effective piece of theatre.[10] Another observed that 'I haven't heard such continuous, happy, feeling laughter in a playhouse for as long as I can remember.'[11] The *Western Mail*'s critic, Graham Samuel, thought much the same.[12] In his director's notes for the programme, Crowden observed that Gwyn's 'compassionate humour shine[s] through every line of his writing. It is hoped that this, his first play, will encourage him to write more for the Theatre.' It was a Sunday Night success and paved the way, as Gwyn had predicted, for a full run at the Royal Court just over a year later.

Opening night was 22 November 1961. A week or so before, on 13 November, the ESC gave a preview performance at the Arts Theatre in Cambridge. Devine had developed the link to take the best of the new London stage out into the provinces. *The Keep* slotted into a programme at the Arts Theatre which included Edward Albee's plays *The Death of Bessie Smith* and *The American Dream* and Max Frisch's *Biedermann und die Brandstifter* (translated into English as *The Fire Raisers*).[13] With Devine away from the theatre on sick leave – the result of a bitter conflict with Rex Harrison, who had been cast as the lead in *August for the People* earlier in the year – oversight of *The Keep* fell to Devine's close friend and co-artistic director, Tony Richardson (1928–1991).[14] The play was staged with financial backing from Laurence Olivier Productions.[15] Much of the cast, including Mervyn Johns, Glyn Owen, and Windsor Davies, were new to the roles, although Jessie Evans did return as Miriam Morton. Incidental music was written by Dudley Moore, then right at the beginning of his career but still in the glow of the 1960 revue *Beyond the Fringe* with Peter Cook, Alan Bennett and Jonathan Miller.

Critics loved what they saw. Writing in the Birmingham *Daily Post*, one went so far as to declare Gwyn the Welsh Sean O'Casey and the play 'the English Stage Company's most important find.'[16] Not everyone was quite so enthusiastic, of course. When Noel Coward saw the production in April 1962, alongside *Look Homeward, Angel* and *The School for Scandal*, he wrote in his diary that he 'couldn't bear' the play.[17] But Coward was unusual. Most of those who saw the original production shared the view of the *Sunday Mirror* critic who wrote 'what a relief to hear an audience laugh at the Royal Court! It's a rendezvous for those who, like the moody, message-sending works of young playwrights, the new wave has washed up. But Gwyn Thomas, with his witty play about a Welsh family, even had the earnest ones laughing.'[18] The Sunday tabloid, *The People*, went so far as to call the play 'the wittiest show of the season ... as sparkling as a glass of champagne.'[19] *The Tatler* added that Gwyn 'must be granted a special licence to go on rambling.'[20] He was the toast of the London theatre scene and an overnight sensation – a moment crowned in January 1962 when he was awarded, jointly with Henry Livings, who had acted in the first Carry On film, *Carry on Sergeant* in 1958, the title of most promising playwright of the year.[21] Still basking in the glow of his success, Gwyn appeared at the Cheltenham Literature Festival that year to debate 'The Living Theatre – is it alive?' alongside playwright Peter Shaffer (1926–2012) and the dramatist, novelist and playwright, John Mortimer (1923–2009).[22]

Gwyn had written a drama contained within a single household and almost entirely within a single room, something akin to the atmosphere in which he had grown up. Several of the Thomas archetypes were present: the ambitious councillor full of aspiration and on the precipice of a comeuppance, the clever, intellectual type who was always the cipher for Gwyn's own experiences, and the absent mother who, in this particular case, had faked her own death and gone to America to escape the pressures of family life. A 'Welsh death' to live an 'American life.' It was telling, from an autobiographical point of view, that the picture of Ma Morton, placed above the fireplace on set, was in the fashion 'of the 1919 period' – although the action took place specifically in 1954. 'The play is a May-day parade of our more twitching neuroses,' Gwyn wrote in his introduction to the published edition, 'The Mortons move dimly behind a veil of sardonic anguish. Their laughter is of a savage suddenness that makes the ghosts of their dreams spin around like shot goats.' In the programme, he was clearer about the roots of his ideas: 'the Morton Family ... is a unit found with remarkable frequency in South Wales. Maintained in a precarious unity by the memory of a brilliant and creative mother.'

Gwyn's influences as he was writing *The Keep* were the playwrights whose work had infused the theatre of his childhood and early adulthood: Henrik Ibsen, Anton Chekhov, George Bernard Shaw, and the Merthyr-born J. O. Francis. There was something of the flavour of J. B. Priestley, too. In the 1940s and 1950s, Gwyn had been closely involved in directing school theatre and amateur dramatics. Whilst at Cardigan he had memorably staged *The Mikado* and at Barry, he directed highbrow works such as Chekhov's *The Bear* (1888), Oliver Goldsmith's eighteenth-century classic *She Stoops To Conquer* (1771), and John Goldsworthy's wartime drama *The Little Man* (1915). It was claimed, at the time, that *The Keep* was Gwyn's first play: certainly, it was the first performed in a professional setting, but as a young man Gwyn had experimented with the form. His early efforts at writing for the stage were set down in notebooks and on scraps of paper kept when he was living and teaching in the Rhondda in the 1930s. In mid-January 1937, for instance, he wrote to Nan to tell her that he was writing a play about Spain for the League of Nations Union branch in Ynyshir and that he hoped this would spur the creation of a local Left Theatre movement.

The performance of Gwyn's Spanish 'playette' was organised by Gwyn's friend, Will Paynter, on the encouragement of Lewis Jones, ostensibly to drum up support for the International Brigades and the beleaguered Spanish Republic. There are but few fragments still in existence: only the ideas set down in pencil which were perhaps to have formed the completed drama. Yet in a notebook kept around the same time there survives a full scene of another play. The text ends abruptly with a comment by Gwyn: 'Rotten. Rotten. There's no shape at all about what I do.' In this, alas untitled, work are the germs of language, setting, and characterisation, which were to become archetypes of Gwyn's later writing. It begins with 'Steve and Mahony sitting on a wall, gazing at a house behind trees: a rich house.' The two characters, it turns out, are tramps distracting themselves from pangs of hunger by increasingly absurd discussion about becoming rag and (human) bone men.

S: Why do we have to sit on walls, I ask. I've got a right to know.
M: The wall's got a right to know why we're sitting on it. But it's unlikely that anybody will ever write out a book of answers for the wall.

S: (picking off a bit of lichen and crumbling it in his hand) This moss is soft and wet. It leaves a green mark on your hand.
M: You find entertainment in a lot of things. Could you find something to eat as well, for the sake of balance. It's one thing to be thrilled to death by moss...

S: and another to be worn down to your last bone by hunger? Should I die first my last one is yours to keep on living as long as you can.
M: That's a kindness Stephen. I won't forget. If the bone business wasn't down so low, I could keep half of it, sell that to a collector of formal specimens and lay the foundations of an abundant fortune. From cannibal to capitalist.

S: Don't be silly. No one buys human bones as fossils.
M: Why? We tramps are a type of human animal that a decent

society would have exterminated ages ago. So, we have a kind of theoretical value to a far-seeing biologist.

S: And what if he couldn't see that far?
M: I'd give him a list of battlefields past, present and needless and tell him he could find me at any of these warehouses if he should change his mind. It's a sound idea. (Patting himself on the chest and lifting his head in ironical pride). Mahony. Men's Bones. Bankrupt Stock.

S: After that, I may sound like a poor relation, but do you still feel hungry.
M: I'm still alive.

S: See that house.
M: I see the trees too.

S: The trees won't feed us.
M: No.

S: What about the house. There are lights there.
M: You remember the old Welsh woman who gave us food?

S: I can only remember those who give us food.
M: She said beware of those who live with lights. When men are afraid of the dark, they are too frightened to be kind.

S: She was drunk.
M: And wise. Do you hear somebody coming along the road?

S: I hear something. We'll wait here and see who it is. If it's a cow, don't sneer as it passes. We can't afford to sacrifice any sympathies.

Gwyn's trademark humour is unmistakeably present, for all its youthful exuberance, as is the dialogue between a pair of down-and-outs, the antipathy shown towards wealth and privilege, and the kindness of older women in the face of adversity. That this was written in 1937 alongside *Sorrow For Thy Sons* shows that Gwyn was trying to master each of the literary forms and for a purpose. The scene between Steve and Mahoney was, along with the seemingly lost Spanish play, were intended to be performed under the auspices of the Left Theatre movement. This was Gwyn endeavouring to be and working out how to be a revolutionary artist.

The Keep closed its initial run at the Royal Court Theatre after a few months. Given its success there was inevitable discussion about transferring the play to the West End. Lyn explained in a letter to Nan in February 1962, however, that 'they haven't been able to get a theatre on Shaftesbury Avenue but they are still hoping.'[23] Instead, *The Keep* returned for a second run at the Royal Court, re-opening there on 20 February 1962. Lyn and Gwyn had been in London to attend the *Evening Standard*'s theatre awards at the Savoy Hotel. 'The suite we occupied was larger than our bungalow,' Lyn wrote to Nan, still amazed at the glitz and glamour of 'the way the other half of the world lives.' She stayed to watch the opening night, but Gwyn had to travel back to Barry for the start of term: 'The audience were magnificent, very quick and appreciative, and they gave the cast so many ovations that I thought we would never get away from the theatre.'[24] Gwyn might as well have remained in London. When Lyn got home, she found him ill in bed. Antibiotics prescribed by the doctor left him dizzy and unable to work. Not long afterwards Gwyn walked away from teaching. The headmaster at Barry, Leslie Mathews, with whom Gwyn had enjoyed a fractious relationship, offered a warm testimonial in *The Barrian*:

348

At the beginning of the summer term, how grieved we all were to learn that Mr Gwyn Thomas was leaving us. As the Headmaster explained on the following Monday morning, Mr Thomas will be returning at the end of this term to make his farewells, but this was poor recompense for the gap which has been left in our school life by his departure. To attempt to refer personally to one who has gained such eminence in the literary world would be merely presumption on our part. For us, as indeed for so many many more, there is no one quite like Mr Thomas! Our only satisfaction comes from knowing that we shall, through his plays, his radio and television broadcasts, his magazine and press contributions, be constantly in touch with him.[25]

With *The Keep* now in full flow at the Royal Court, the BBC finally broadcast the long-promised excerpt on national television on 7 March and followed it up with a radio broadcast on the Light Programme on 17 March – a week before the play was due to close at the Royal Court.[26] On 22 March, sixth formers from Barry Boys travelled up to London to the play shepherded by Teifion Phillips, by then the deputy headmaster, and his colleague Alun John. John wrote the entry on the trip for that year's edition of *The Barrian*.

In the week previous to our visit a television excerpt had already sharpened our anticipation of the actual performance. We were not to be disappointed. Within seconds of the 'curtain-up' we were roaring away at the jokes of Mr Thomas' inimitable dialogue, and kept roaring almost to the end when the tone suddenly changed to carry the philosophic conclusion Mr Thomas wished to register. The performances of the case were lively and sustained, giving full measure to the play which seemed so well-tailored to them. We were able, after the performance, to go backstage, inspect the set, 'strut the boards,' and view the auditorium as if we were the players themselves. The performance of 'The Keep' made us realise more clearly the literary and dramatic distinction which Mr Gwyn Thomas has gained for himself, a distinction which we all felt we shared a little, as we sat in the audience that Thursday afternoon.[27]

After closing at the Royal Court, *The Keep* finally transferred to the Piccadilly Theatre in the West End. All sorts of predictions were made, 'I began to sniff at brochures that spoke of the sun,' Gwyn wrote sardonically, 'and to stare at estate-agents' folders that showed pictures of houses with great gables with high walls and trees.'[28] In the event, *The Keep* lasted at the Piccadilly Theatre only until 21 April – the full three weeks promised when it first opened there.[29] Gwyn later pointed to various challenges which had beset the West End transfer: 'changes of cast and the largeness of the theatre helped it into its coffin. As with sex and, they tell me, onion-growing, a transfer from a small and intimate place to a big and impersonal one rarely helps. I felt that I had satisfied any curiosity I might have felt about being a playwright.' The play was now set for its national tour in repertory, beginning in August in Birmingham, and Gwyn was in receipt of multiple commissions for new plays.[30] 'In the autumn,' Lyn told Nan, 'he has a play with music coming on the West End and he has also been commissioned to write two more.'

The first of these was *Loud Organs*, which had taken Gwyn, as he explained in the programme for the production in the *New Theatre* in Cardiff, 'about a year to write.' It received its first airing in Blackpool on 22 October 1962, although its fortunes thereafter proved to be rather bleak – the play never made it to the West End.[31] There was the ill-fated Bevan play, *Return and End*, with Richard Burton promised for the title role. There was

Sap to be written for the left-leaning Theatre Workshop based in East London. And there was a follow-up play for George Devine, *Jackie the Jumper*. George Bishop, theatre critic for the *Daily Telegraph*, noted in September 1962 that 'Gwyn Thomas looks like being the most prolific playwright of the year.'[32] Had each of these projects come to fruition, it would have been the most remarkable year of Gwyn's life since the rapid appearance of his first novels *The Dark Philosophers* and *The Alone to the Alone* twenty-five years earlier. As it was, only two of them made it to the stage, and only one to London, and neither enjoyed quite the same success as *The Keep* on its remarkable debut.

*

The freedom gained from leaving the chalkface in the wake of *The Keep* was temporary and Gwyn was soon occupied with the writing assignments which had piled up. His priority was finishing the second play for George Devine and the Royal Court Theatre. He was drawn, initially, back to Spain and an adaptation of a classic from the Golden Age, but that idea came to nothing.[33] Instead, Devine encouraged a turn towards contemporary kitchen sink drama but Gwyn had no great love of 'the words of novelists from the decayed areas of the North and Midlands,' and so resisted that idea as well.[34] They compromised on a revisit of the events of 1831 and the themes of *All Things Betray Thee*.[35] The result, finished in the summer of 1962, was *Jackie the Jumper*. Devine wrote to Gwyn congratulating him on a 'marvellous' work. But it was ambitious, perhaps overly so. Originally pencilled for December 1962, the play's run was postponed until the spring of 1963 because of casting difficulties – Rory MacDermot was replaced by Graham Crowden in the role of the sheriff, for instance –

and premiered at the Royal Court on 1 February.[36] Unfortunately, this meant a clash with the planned publication of the script in *Plays and Players* that month, giving the game away. As originally scheduled no such clash would have taken place.

Some critics loved *Jackie the Jumper*: the *Daily Mirror* declared it a delight; *The Stage* further encouraged comparisons with the Irish playwright Sean O'Casey; and the *Western Mail* thought it a triumph.[37] But there were sour notes sounded, too, not least by Bernard Levin writing in the *Daily Mail*. 'There are so many words in Mr Gwyn Thomas's new play with music,' Levin wrote, 'that it would ill become me to add unnecessarily to their number ... it is like a cross between dying of seasickness and being stoned to death with dictionaries.'[38] For Alan Brien writing in the *Sunday Telegraph*[39], the problem was not so much the number of words in *Jackie the Jumper*, but the characterisation. 'Neither in his handling of thought processes nor in his use of language does he get under the skin of the past,' Brien complained, 'he scores easy points by allowing some characters to wield latter-day enlightenment against cardboard opponents rooted in nineteenth-century prejudice. More seriously, Mr Thomas is a comic rhetorician, not a poet; here he is writing seriously, and the effect is often the kind of feverish eloquence which, on other occasions, he himself has turned to delicious parody.'[40]

Negative reviews in national newspapers dampened audience enthusiasm and the run closed a week early on 23 February 1963. George Devine wrote to explain that 'I'm afraid "Jackie" has missed it ... the public is just not coming. It is an expensive show to run – with orchestra – and we cannot afford to keep it on beyond the end of next week.'[41] In fact, the production had lost more than three thousand pounds at the box office.[42] Gwyn was clearly fed up. He sounded a bitter tone in a letter to Nan:

Jackie the Jumper, poor chap, hardly left the ground ... Too many critics from the rodent Levin upwards thought very differently and the houses diminished to a point where the people in the bars were sending out to find if there was an air-raid on. The reasons for the failure were substantially the same as for that other land-mine – Loud Organs. Both plays were ill-conceived and worse produced and I take my share of the blame. The second play had music in it as ghastly as that which helped to ruin the first. It had a Welsh flavour and background which English audiences as this fail to understand or which they bitterly resent. And more was a gaggle of supporting Welsh actors so bad they would have sunk the Titanic even without the iceberg. At the moment I feel Wales around my neck like an albatross. It is a curse, a doom. I'm convinced that the kind of material we inherited from the place, and the intelligence we distilled from that material, can never win.[43]

Compounding the 'over-Welshed' atmosphere was the score penned by Bargoed-born composer (and later Professor of Music at Cardiff) Alun Hoddinott, which consisted of adaptations and arrangements of Welsh hymns and folk music, and which Gwyn disliked.[44] He was happier with the set design by Michael Annals, who produced a remarkable rendering of the wilderness of the countryside for act one and a claustrophobic inn for the final act.[45] But all was not lost, *Jackie the Jumper* followed *The Keep* into repertory theatre where it was at last feted by critics such as J. C. Trewin. He liked the play so much that he included the script in his compendium *Plays of the Year* and therein declared Gwyn 'quite the most arresting of the new dramatists.'[46]

The experience at the Royal Court with *Jackie the Jumper* mirrored similar failures with *Loud Organs*.[47] It too suffered from a musical misreading which undid Gwyn's textual dexterity. The man initially commissioned to write the music, Dil Jones, a Carmarthenshire-born jazz pianist, emigrated to the United States before he completed the score. But the music he had already written did not seem to fit the spirit of Gwyn's play. In a letter to Nan, Gwyn explained that 'there is a feeling that his songs don't have the depth. Not to my ear, anyway, when one has been brought up on Puccini one tends to hope for that sort of talent.' Jones was replaced by Patrick Gowers (1936–2014), a young composer from Cambridge University, whose main work at that point had been for the Cambridge Footlights and a piano concerto for Dudley Moore, although he later enjoyed success as the composer of the television soundtracks to *Smiley's People* (BBC, 1982) starring Alec Guinness and the Granada adaptation of the Sherlock Holmes stories starring Jeremy Brett (1984–1994). Gwyn's opinion of Gowers was even lower than that of Jones, he was 'brash and clueless.'[48] In normal circumstances, the failure of a score would not diminish a piece of theatre too greatly; however, *Loud Organs* was an experimental musical drama. Getting the sound right was essential and Gowers failed to do so.

Set in Tiger Bay in one of the new clubs – in this case the COT Club – then springing up across South Wales, *Loud Organs* told the story of Wffie Morgan, a former boxing manager turned club owner.[49] Given the setting, one of the characters, Mollie, was originally to have been played by Shirley Bassey. However, as Gwyn explained to Nan, 'when they found that the role would need acting more than singing, they dropped her.' The role subsequently went to Roberta D'Esti, who had formerly taken on the role of Maria in the London production of *West Side Story* in 1958.[50] The removal of Bassey was one of the first indications, along with the failure to get the music right, that all would not be well with the project, although for a while Gwyn retained a degree of calm: 'the whole thing is still molten.

I've almost finished my side of the work and at the moment I have my usual serene conviction that it will either go up in smoke or, if it ever does reach the stage, will drop down dead. We'll see.' At the heart of the problem, Gwyn thought, was producer Richard Rhys, Baron Dynevor. Still in his twenties, Rhys struck Gwyn as 'charming but totally inept' an opinion that was not improved by the other figures employed to stage the play including the choreographer, John Broom.

They had Broom 'devise dances that left the cast too winded to speak their lines,' Gwyn complained to Nan. Given multiple difficulties, the play was a mess when it was first performed. Reviewers were understandably unimpressed. 'The consensus of opinion is that ... Gwyn Thomas has added fog to the well-known Celtic twilight,' remarked *The Stage*, noting that although the director, Edward Burnham, had done his best to get 'the sparkle out of the comedy punch lines' he could not 'wholly rescue the piece from a basic amorphousness.' Put simply, 'the plot and purpose seemed to escape [the] audience.'[51] After a week in Blackpool, *Loud Organs* transferred to the New Theatre in Cardiff where it spent an unhappy fortnight.[52] There was one last attempt to breathe life into the play at the Brighton Royal in November.[53] But there it died. The experience left Gwyn feeling rather bleak. 'I had the blackest doubts,' he told Nan, '[and] the doubts were justified. The production was disastrous, an expensive and unholy mess, like [the inter-continental ballistic missile project] Skybolt.' Gwyn added that 'one of the leading male parts was taken by Glyn Houston. A most likeable boy, Glyn, but even his brother, Donald, who was there on the first night, admitted that he was miles below par.'

Audiences in Blackpool and Brighton, critics aside, were sympathetic and seem to have enjoyed the play, warts and all. But in Cardiff, Gwyn's satire, and his fierce critique of

Welshness, caused a furore. Audiences felt the playwright was laughing at them. At the time, Gwyn felt that *Loud Organs* was 'one of the most significant bits of theatre since I scored a hit as the principal camel-boy in "Dan y Palmwydd" in Caersalem Vestry.' He wrote later, however, that 'groups of nationalists, temporarily deprived of detonators to blow things up, booed the piece with fervour.'[54] Not everything about the play was a disaster. Several of the actors, including Glyn Owen, Glyn Houston, and Ronald Radd, believed in what they had performed and wrote to Gwyn encouraging him to put it on once more, free of directorial and production decisions which had destroyed the playwright's original intentions. Above all, they said, the music should be relegated to its rightful place – as the support act. Unlike its contemporaries, *Loud Organs* was not published, either in part or in full, in theatre journals such as *Plays and Players*. It first appeared in print in 1990, in an edition compiled by Michael Parnell, almost three decades after its stage debut.

None of these experiences, however, could prepare Gwyn for the devastation resulting from the commission to write *Sap* as part of the relaunch of Theatre Workshop in 1962. Established in Manchester in 1945 by Joan Littlewood and Ewan MacColl, the company had its origins in the people's theatre movement of the 1930s – it was every bit Gwyn's kind of company. Following a move to London in 1953, which he did not support, MacColl left to concentrate on his music career. Littlewood left temporarily in 1961 to work on other projects and the company went into hiatus – 'she is not referred to in yesterday's announcement,' noted the *Daily Telegraph* as it reported Theatre Workshop's three new commissions in the autumn of 1962.[55] There was Alan Klein's *What a Crazy World*, which starred Harry H. Corbett and Marty Wilde and spawned a film adaptation; Brian O'Connor's *It's Got to Come Down*, a fantasia on post-war redevelopment; and Gwyn's *Sap*. The idea had struck earlier in 1962 and Gwyn began working on its development with Gerry Raffles, Littlewood's partner and the general manager of the Theatre Royal in East London where Theatre Workshop was based. As part of the research, Raffles had loaned Gwyn a copy of Charles Chilton's 1961 documentary *The Long, Long Trail*, which featured soldiers' songs from the First World War.[56]

Contracts were exchanged in July, but Gwyn was busy with other projects and slow to produce the script. 'I know you are up to your eyes with other projects,' Raffles told Gwyn in October, 'but I do hope that you are making "Sap" one of your priorities. If you remember you did promise to try and let us have it by this time.'[57] Taking the opportunity to be distracted from the mess engulfing *Loud Organs*, Gwyn finished the script for *Sap* by November 1962 and handed it to Raffles on a trip to London to deal with matters involving *Jackie the Jumper* at the Royal Court. Indeed, at some point, perhaps even at that point, Gwyn also seems to have given a copy of *Sap* to John Dexter, the director of *Jackie the Jumper*. Dexter wrote to Gwyn in mid-December telling him that *Sap* was 'potentially tremendous' and that he had given his copy of the script to George Devine. 'We ought to do it next November,' Dexter suggested to Gwyn.[58] A month later, the English Stage Company were advertising *Sap* as one of two Gwyn Thomas plays to be performed at the Royal Court in 1963.[59] A notice was also included in the programme for *Jackie the Jumper*.

Devine and his colleagues were keen to grow interest in the play, particularly given its Western Front setting and the forthcoming fiftieth anniversary of the First World War. In early January 1963, Gwyn received a letter from the press department at the Royal Court Theatre emphasising that very point:

We are very anxious that special prominence be given to the fact
that your new play 'Sap' deals with World War 1 and World War
1 songs. We have managed to get this announcement in as many
newspapers as possible. ... I would like ... to arrange for [a
journalist] to talk to you so that he can write his piece about
your deep interest in this period and the songs ... would you be
coming up to London next week?[60]

Having shown Dexter and Devine the script for *Sap* and
agreeing to a possible production at the Royal Court in 1963,
but failing to extricate himself from Theatre Workshop, Gwyn
had set in motion the process which prevented any production
of the play whatsoever that year (or, indeed, for more than a
decade). On 21 February, *The Stage* published notice of Theatre
Workshop's new musical, *Oh! What A Lovely War!* which was
to be performed at the Theatre Royal in the East End in
March.[61] No one connected with *Sap* believed this mere
coincidence, as Michael Parnell observed in his telling. 'Gwyn
could not at first believe that anyone could act in such a way
... it was his idea, his formulation, his research, that were being
used, and acknowledgement of this there was none.'[62] Derek
Paget, who studied the construction of the Theatre Workshop
production, concluded that '*Lovely War* was primarily a work
of *editorship* not authorship.'[63] The saga began when Gerry
Raffles sought a copy of Chilton's radio documentary, which he
was sent by the BBC sometime after 27 March 1962. Paget
referred to a letter from Chilton to Raffles which stated that 'I
have arranged for *The Long Long Trail* to be copied so that you
can play it to your confederates and a copy of the tape and a
script should be with you shortly.'[64]

Although Paget, at the time he was writing in 1990, was
uncertain of what happened to the tape, it is clear from
Gwyn's own papers that Raffles had passed it along in

preparation for writing *Sap*. Having handed over his script to Raffles in November 1962, it was read by Joan Littlewood and other members of Theatre Workshop before being rejected by the former as 'telling us things we already knew.'[65] Another playwright, Ted Allan, had also been asked by Raffles to write a treatment for a First World War play. This too was rejected by Littlewood, although in the aftermath of *Lovely War*'s commercial success, Allan sued Theatre Workshop for what he regarded as theft of his work. An out-of-court settlement was reached in 1964. The historian Alan Clark and Charles Chilton likewise sued for breach of copyright. Chilton later remarked that 'Joan can't do any [writing] unless someone's done it first' and that Raffles's approach to playwrights was 'to get what he could out of you, and anybody else who was willing, and give the best of it to Joan.' This appears to have been what happened to Gwyn's work, too. But he did not sue. Instead, as so often in his career, he nursed the injury behind the scenes.

In a 2014 *Guardian* interview Murray Melvin, who was involved with the Theatre Workshop at that time, recalled that 'a script was commissioned... we read the script and Joan said, "well, that's a load of rubbish", and we never looked at it again.' The script was Gwyn's own. The conclusion we can draw here is that Sap was an influence on Littlewood and the Theatre Workshop. It was then Littlewood rather than Gwyn who enjoyed the success associated with *Oh! What A Lovely War!* Had Gwyn not given the script to Raffles and instead shown it only to Dexter and Devine, who were much more loyal and honest, and committed to bringing Gwyn's work to a London audience, we might now speak of Sap in the same venerated terms. No wonder the portrait of Gwyn's London theatre experience in *A Few Selected Exits* was so bleak, he still felt the pain of having been taken so thoroughly for a ride – and by people he considered to be on the same side of politics and culture as he was. *Sap* was belatedly performed in Wales in 1974. It was regarded as new not old and compared directly with Littlewood's, by then very famous and influential, creation, and seen as not quite as good as all that.

Such experience after *The Keep* left Gwyn in considerable doubt as to whether being a playwright was an alternative to teaching and to writing long-form and short-form fiction after all. For almost a decade, he turned away from the medium, so shaken was he by what had happened with *Sap*. The exception was to be *The Loot*, a play for sixth-formers commissioned by Malcolm Stuart Fellows, which appeared in 1965.[66] *The Loot* was performed all over the world at drama festivals for schools.[67] Some student critics, however, were dismissive of a play which they felt 'presented with a considerable flatness of dialogue, and amazingly little realization of how children talk to each other.'[68] Given Gwyn's two decades of classroom teaching such an observation might seem misplaced, the kind of criticism made by the young of the old, although it was a regular observation made by critics who felt that the dialogue in Gwyn's writing was often far too rich for the characters he was presenting to the audience. His own view was simply – so what. After all, wasn't it possible that the poor could have a rich vocabulary, or children could speak as adults do? Potential mattered more to Gwyn than any sense of verisimilitude.

*

After the failure of *Jackie the Jumper* in 1963, Gwyn never returned to the London stage himself. Repertory ensured, nevertheless, that his work continued to be performed all over Britain, from the Belgrade in Coventry to the Little Theatre in Bristol, and with prominent actors in lead roles. In fact, productions of *The Keep* continued until 1970, when it was performed at the King's Theatre in Glasgow and at the Yvonne Arnaud Theatre in Guildford.[69] This run of productions began in the summer of 1962 when *The Keep* transferred from the West End to the Repertory Theatre in Birmingham, where it ran from 14 August until 1 September. Amongst the cast were Ralph Nossek, an established television actor with parts in shows such as *Hancock's Half Hour* and *The Avengers*; Georgine Anderson, then a relative newcomer but soon to become a regular presence on television; and Derek Jacobi who joined the Birmingham Repertory Theatre on graduating from Cambridge University in 1960. Jacobi took on the role of Alvin Morton, the frustrated trade union official who provided the political conscience of the play.[70] From Birmingham, the play transferred to the Grand Theatre in Swansea for its Welsh premiere. It proved so popular with Welsh audiences that it remained for a second week.[71]

In October, *The Keep* was staged at the Playhouse in Derby and at the Theatre Royal in Lincoln.[72] It then moved to Oldham, Ipswich, Nottingham, and ended the year at the Castle Theatre in Farnham under the direction of Joan Knight.[73] The closure of Cardiff's New Theatre that year prevented a production in the Welsh capital, however. At Ipswich the role of Alvin Morton was performed by Ian McKellen, who had joined the local repertory company from the Belgrade Theatre in Coventry a few months earlier. At the time, however, McKellen was not the focus of attention – that fell instead to Michael Forrest who had previously been in the Broadway production of Brendan Behan's *The Hostage* directed by Joan Littlewood.[74] The touring pattern for *The Keep* in 1963 and 1964 was much the same, taking in (amongst others) the Belgrade Theatre in Coventry, the Sheffield Playhouse, the Civic Theatre in Chesterfield, the Theatre Royal in Windsor, the Harrogate Opera House, the Bradford

Alhambra, and the Tower Theatre in Islington. The popularity of Gwyn's writing in the North of England and the Midlands was a welcome turn, but it belied a certain weakness of professional theatre in Wales.

It was the Welsh Committee of the Arts Council, the forerunner of the Arts Council for Wales, which intervened in 1962 to create the Welsh Theatre Company (WTC) under the leadership of Warren Jenkins and thereby belatedly made possible the performance of Gwyn's plays in a Welsh setting.[75] The WTC – with guest director, Hugh Goldie – took *The Keep* on a tour of the small theatres of northern and western parts of Wales in the autumn of 1963, beginning in Colwyn Bay in mid-October and ending at Llandrindod Wells in early November.[76] The play was finally staged in Cardiff, at the New Theatre, beginning on 18 November during a four-week festival which also included performances of Tolstoy's *War and Peace*, *Semi-Detached* by David Turner, and Anouilh's *Antigone*.[77] The following year, in an effort to foster relations with Northern Ireland, and with funding from both national arts councils, the WTC took *The Keep* on a three-week tour beginning and ending at the King George VI Youth Centre in Belfast.[78] The company also staged the Welsh premiere of *Jackie the Jumper* in the summer of 1965 as part of its festival of plays held at Bute Park, Cardiff. Ray Smith took the lead role.[79]

Having his plays staged in Wales was an obvious source of pride to Gwyn, who had spoken out on the 'profoundly disturbing' absence of a professional Welsh theatre a few years earlier. In 1963, similarly, this time ahead of the Welsh tour of *The Keep*, he wrote for *Plays and Players* about the relative absence of theatre and drama in Welsh life.[80] He began in typical style: 'Once, in Breconshire, in a windless dimple of the beacons, I paused to discuss life and solitude with a shepherd. I asked him if he ever found his professional apartness intolerable. He said no; he talked to himself, he said. Doesn't that get a bit tiresome? Oh, no, I'm marvellous. Top-rate. I'm never disappointed in me. I give me a theme, and believe me, I get all the juices out of it. Some shepherds talk to their sheep.' But then he moved to the point. There was no denying the performative nature of the Welsh, no denying either the historical legacies of circumstance or poverty, which had prevented the formation of a national theatre. But those times were over, Wales in the 1960s was no longer a poor country. He wrote,

I can recall preachers whose powers of gesture, voice, grimace, put them exactly between Nijinsky and John Barrymore. The trumpet voices of the louder pastors are silent now. But the trauma persists. It accounts for a certain timidity, a curious lack of resolution on this side of our talent. It is a part of the splintered past which is currently testing the stamina of the young Welsh Theatre Company, the Welsh Arts Council and such consciously Welsh actors as Clifford Evans and Meredith Edwards. As an audience we are still recuperating after the golden age of evangelism. No nation has ever listened with such constancy and rapture. The Welsh ear, subjected to the stormiest barrage of moral injunction and theological uplift since the inception of oratory, ends just inside the tympanum.

To have a reliable human basis for a theatre one needs wealth and a taste for elegance. Wales has always worn its wealth at a crooked angle. Most of our harvests are wet and furtive. Many of our farmers have tried to drive their ploughs through fields so rocky it is little wonder that so many of our most prominent citizens are quarry owners. They are farmers who decided to ignore the soil. This is why primarily agricultural counties have a reputation for meanness. If they are ever going to be persuaded to pay top price for seats in a National Theatre they will have to be put under drugs or told they can take the seat away. We've never had private patrons to put us in touch with public opulence. There never was the semblance of a joint purpose between the squires and the peasants. They were split by differences of attitude and language as decisive as those which kept the Seventh Cavalry and the Sioux at variance. The Welsh landlords were English in sympathy, otter-hunting, badger-baiting hedonists. Their tenants were earnest dedicated Radicals rationalising their bitten penury in terms of a biting puritanism.

Despite his uncertainty about financial viability and the replication of a culture of patronage by state or private enterprise capable of fostering a generation of artists able to write, perform and direct – it was the Welsh theatre which occupied Gwyn in the 1970s, all the same. And it was the Welsh theatre which gave him his final opportunities to write for the stage after he had been abandoned by London. Each of Gwyn's plays performed in the 1970s was produced by the Welsh Drama Company, the English language branch of the Welsh Theatre Company, which formed in 1973. They put on *Sap* for the first time in 1974, with funding from the Arts Council, and its success led to the commission of *The Breakers*. A lengthy and complicated work, it proved challenging for the actors who had to carry two hundred years of history and deliver Gwyn's unrelenting but nonetheless witty and sharply insightful dialogue. Ostensibly written to mark the bicentenary of the founding of the United States, the play took place at three intervals – 1776, 1876, and 1976 – and followed the Bowen family from Pennsylvania to the Rhondda. This was Gwyn's family history, albeit one stretched across centuries rather than less than a decade, and the cubist epic of the South Walian story fused together.

It was also Gwyn's theatrical response to more than a decade of rising nationalism and the increasingly self-evident and terminal decay of the American Wales which he had known as a young man. *The Breakers* was to serve as a cultural expression of that world of South Wales, and a justification of its presence in Welsh life. Contemporary audiences, however, whether in Cardiff in the south or at Theatr Clwyd in Mold in the north, failed to grasp the complexities of the writing and could not cope with the length of the play, either. It ran to three and a half hours.[81] Welsh audiences were not used to concentrating that long. Jon Holliday, writing for *The Stage*, thought that the play pointed to Gwyn's inability to discipline himself for the stage. 'The jokes are as good as ever,' Holliday explained, 'the iconoclasm spot on, but it all falls away because the plot does not interest, the characters do not convince, nothing develops.'[82] Gwyn's one-time foe, Bernard Levin, one of the few national theatre critics to view the play at the Sherman, was strikingly enthusiastic. 'It is a splendid piece of work,' he wrote, 'unhurried and profuse, but rich and sly, funny and content, inquisitive, virile, digressive and bright.'[83]

But what exactly was Gwyn trying to say? In his programme notes, he explained that the failure of post-war Wales to fulfil the promise of socialism had left a dilemma and no answers. 'One member of the family is a prophet of national rebirth,' he wrote, 'the others stir uneasily with the old, normal reflexes of defeat and evasion. What way will the Welsh cat, which now regards being scalded as a hobby, jump this time?' He concluded bluntly,

Do the fragments of our old national experience cohere sufficiently to justify the image of a single animal? ... Is there a new Philadelphia waiting within ourselves?

Bernard Levin was not the only critic to lavish praise on the production. Michael Anderson writing in *Plays and Players* thought that Gwyn had understood the centrality of America to modern experience and had made the right choice in starting the play there, keeping Wales as the distant other instead. At least, of course, until the third act when Wales came fully into view.[84] The two sides engaged in dialectical struggle in Gwyn's play were those who sought freedom and accepted history and modernity, and thus became American; and those, opposed to those American Welsh, who sought comfort and safety and fable and mythos, who rejected the ever-changing world and remained Welsh. The capitalists, proto or actual, exploit regardless, Gwyn was telling his audience, but the Welsh also found themselves split by the magnetic poles of liberty and complicity. Those who cannot reconcile themselves with the tectonic movements of history must flee. Until, that is, the final act, set in modern Wales, where shrillness of contemporary nationalism found its voice in the fanatically patriotic 'anti-heroine,' Anthea – a sociologist, one of the bands of new academics and professional Cymry for whom Gwyn had very little taste or regard.

At the end of the play, the only characters left on stage were Anthea and her father, Leroy Bowen, the latest in a long line of patriarchs who seek the safety of Wales against the rhythms of the modern world. 'What calls people,' Bowen said at the very end, 'what do they hear that I don't hear?' Gwyn was taunting the audience and those parts of society unable or unwilling to listen to the rhythms of American Wales, even as it was dying. 'They want to know the taste of defiance and the taste of submission,' he wrote, 'and they make a point of crowding both into one life.' For Anderson, the play seemed at points strangely composed, with the playwright seemingly displaying 'a sneaking sympathy for the arguments of the go-getting coal owner,' Sam

Williams. The latter was based on Andrew Carnegie, on the one hand, and D. A. Thomas on the other, and pointed to a certain acceptance of the American and modern way of life: making as much money as possible and using that money to gain material riches. Anderson concluded:

> Has Mr Thomas become so impatient with his fellow Welshmen that he's rejected even their ingrained Socialism? I don't think so: the point, emphasised again in the final act, is that in order to succeed in any recognisable way a Welshman has to abandon his very Welshness and that, naturally signals goodbye to any kind of integrity.

The Breakers was Gwyn's last new work for the stage and the highpoint of his writing in the 1970s. It brought to the fore his answer to the contemporary political debate about Wales, the Welsh, and Welshness. But there was one last theme which needed an answer, too, the failure of post-war social democracy and the avarice of local officials. Commissioned by Theatr yr Ymylon, *Testimonials* was hailed by critics as a return to form. It was nothing of the sort. In fact, Gwyn had adapted a radio play written in the early 1960s called *The Alderman*, which itself is based on the final section of Gwyn's 1956 novel, *A Point of Order*.[85] Directed by Gareth Jones, *Testimonials* received its premiere at the Forum Theatre in Wythenshawe on 30 May 1979 and then transferred to Cardiff's Sherman Theatre. No London critic saw the play. The most effective coverage was from a journalist writing for the Birmingham *Daily Post*.[86] Gwyn, the journalist concluded, was fascinated by the idea that Wales has produced so many 'superb con men – but has never produced the wealth on which they could batten, with the result that they have normally died as poor as they were born.'

There was the life-long fascination, too, with the absurdity of the evangelism which had lit up the valleys and offered a utopia which never came. 'We were deluged in a unique flood of political and religious hope,' Gwyn explained, 'the politicians promised us the Socialist Utopia. The preachers said: "Don't bother with the politicians: Die and you're there." I had more rhetoric than milk in my childhood. When you see everyone around you orating, you think that if you can't do it, you're a freak.' Above all, there was Gwyn's idea that there had been a Wales informed by the material modernity of the twentieth century, and of America. Towards the end of *Loud Organs*, one of Gwyn's characters, channelling the writer's own view, observed of this that 'we've specialised in producing people who make a mess of other people's talents. We have been ruled by two types of pest. One that saw everything from the viewpoint of heaven and denied every vestige of grace. The other is you, Wffie, and all those who see everything from the viewpoint of the gutter ... We had a vision of freedom. The light gave out. We didn't have enough knowledge, enough simple fitness in the tank to keep the vision clear.' In the nationalist clamour of the 1970s, Gwyn sought to defend that history and the culture of a capitalised South Wales and found himself pulled into an existential battle for the Welsh soul.

---

[1] NLW, GTP, J54/1: Letter from George Devine, English Stage Company, to Gwyn Thomas, 7 June 1956.

[2] Letter from Lyn Thomas to Hannah Thomas, 18 December 1956.

[3] *Newcastle Journal*, 26 June 1956.

[4] Irving Wardle, *The Theatres of George Devine* (London, 1979).

[5] NLW, GTP, D6: 'The Cadence'.

[6] *RT*, 23 November 1956; NLW, GTP, G182: Script of To This One Place, 1956; D37 – Manuscript of To This One Place.

[7] *The Stage*, 4 August 1960.

[8] *The Stage*, 18 August 1960.

[9] *AFSE*, 134.

[10] *The Stage*, 18 August 1960.

[11] *DM*, 15 August 1960.

[12] *WM*, 15 August 1960.

[13] *The Stage*, 12 October 1961, 9 November 1961.

[14] John Osborne, *Looking Back: Never Explain, Never Apologise* (London, 2004 edn), 489; Philip Roberts, *The Royal Court Theatre and the Modern Stage* (Cambridge, 1999), 87–88.

[15] British Library, Laurence Olivier Archive, Add MS 80096, ff. 33: *The Keep* by Gwyn Thomas, Royal Court, 22 November 1961.

[16] *Birmingham Daily Post*, 24 November 1961.

[17] Noel Coward, *Diaries*, 8 April 1962 (p. 502).

[18] *Sunday Mirror*, 26 November 1961.

[19] *The People*, 26 November 1961.

[20] *The Tatler*, 13 December 1961.

[21] *The Stage*, 18 January 1962.

[22] *The Spectator*, 12 October 1962. Shaffer had recently enjoyed success with the performance of his double-bill of plays, *The Private Ear/The Public Eye*, which were performed at The Globe Theatre in London in May 1962 with Maggie Smith and Kenneth Williams in the starring roles. John Mortimer's 1957 radio play, *The Dock Brief*, was adapted for the London stage in 1958 (with a Broadway run in 1961) and for cinema in 1962 with Peter Sellers, Richard Attenborough, and Beryl Reid in the lead roles.

[23] Letter from Lyn Thomas to Hannah Thomas, 13 February 1962.

[24] Letter from Lyn Thomas to Hannah Thomas, 3 March 1962.

[25] *The Barrian* 42 (1962), 3.

[26] *RT*, 1 March 1962, 15 March 1962.

[27] A.J. [i.e. Alun John], 'Theatre Visit: "The Keep"', *The Barrian* 46 (1962), 12–13.

[28] *AFSE*, 137.

[29] Victoria & Albert Museum Archives, Oscar Lewenstein Collection, THM/255/1/21: Production File for *The Keep* by Gwyn Thomas at the Piccadilly Theatre, 1962; *Sunday Telegraph*, 1 April 1962. The play commenced at the Piccadilly Theatre on 27 March 1962 and ended on 21 April. *Daily Telegraph*, 26 March 1962.

[30] *Birmingham Daily Post*, 14 August 1962.

[31] *The Stage*, 25 October 1962.

[32] *Daily Telegraph*, 10 September 1962.

[33] *AFSE*, 138.

[34] As above, 139.

[35] Wardle, *Devine*, 251.

[36] *Daily Telegraph*, 29 October 1962, 26 November 1962; *The Stage*, 31 January 1963.

[37] *Daily Mirror*, 2 February 1963; *The Stage*, 7 February 1963; *WM*, 2 February 1963.

[38] *DM*, 2 February 1963.

[39] *Sunday Telegraph*, 3 February 1963.

[40] *The Times*, 2 February 1963.

[41] NLW, GTP, J54: Letter from George Devine, English Stage Company, to Gwyn Thomas, February 1963.

[42] Terry Browne, *Playwrights' Theatre: The English Stage Company at the Royal Court* (London, 1975), 118.

[43] Letter from Gwyn Thomas to Hannah Thomas, 11 April 1963.

[44] NLW, Alun Hoddinott Papers, A8/15 contains a copy of the script of *Jackie and the Jumper*, but the incidental music is unfortunately absent.

[45] Michael Annals's designs are held at the Victoria and Albert Museum, S.262.1991 and S.263.1991.

[46] *Birmingham Daily Post*, 3 March 1964; J. C. Trewin (ed.), *Plays of the Year: Volume 26* (London, 1963), 11.

[47] NLW, Lord Dynevor Papers, LORDYN 36–37: Files relating to 'Loud Organs', 1962.

[48] Letter from Gwyn Thomas to Hannah Thomas, 21 December 1962.

[49] *Daily Telegraph*, 8 October 1962; Michael Parnell (ed), *Gwyn Thomas: Three Plays* (Bridgend, 1990), 155–219.

[50] *The Stage*, 11 October 1962.

[51] *The Stage*, 25 October 1962.

[52] *South Wales Echo*, 27 October 1962.

[53] *The Stage*, 8 November 1962.

[54] *AFSE*, 164.

[55] *Daily Telegraph*, 27 September 1962.

[56] *RT*, 21 December 1961. The original was broadcast on 27 December. A reworked documentary, presented by Bud Flanagan, was broadcast a few months later. *RT*, 15 February 1962. He asked for their return on 8 October 1962. NLW, GTP, J54: Letter from Gerry Raffles, Theatre Royal, to Gwyn Thomas, 8 October 1962.

[57] As above, Letter from Raffles, 8 October 1962.

[58] NLW, GTP, J54: Letter from John Dexter to Gwyn Thomas, 11 December 1962.

[59] *The Stage*, 10 January 1963, 7 February 1963. Similar notices were made in *Plays and Players*, too.

[60] NLW, GTP, J54: Letter from Frank Rainbow, Royal Court Theatre, to Gwyn Thomas, 11 January 1963.

[61] *The Stage,* 21 February 1963.

[62] *LFD*, 173.

[63] Derek Paget, 'Oh What a Lovely War: The Texts and Their Context', *New Theatre Quarterly* 6, no. 23 (1990), 246.

[64] As above, 247.

[65] Joan Littlewood, *Joan's Book: Joan Littlewood's Peculiar History As She Tells It* (London, 1994), 669; Paget, 'Lovely War', 248.

[66] Gwyn Thomas, *The Loot* (London, 1965).

[67] National Library of New Zealand, British Drama League Wellington Area, Eph-A-DRAMA-BDLW-1960s: Programme for Rongotai College, 'The Loot' by Gwyn Thomas; NLW, GTP, J61: Letters from Cassell & Co to Gwyn Thomas, re. 'The Loot', 1963.

[68] University College London Union Dramatic Society, *Prompt Magazine* 9 (1965), 32.

[69] *The Keep* was revived at the Theatre Royal in Bath and at Theatr Clwyd, Mold, in 1979. University of Bristol, Special Collections, Theatre Collection, PR/001784: 'Programme, The Keep at the Theatre Royal, Bath, 10 September 1979'; *The Guardian*, 24 July 1979.

[70] *Birmingham Daily Post*, 15 August 1962.

[71] *The Stage*, 4 October 1962, 6 December 1962.

[72] *The Stage*, 2 August 1962,

[73] *The Stage*, 27 September, 4 October, 18 October, 25 October, 8 November, 15 November, 29 November, 20 December 1962.

[74] *The Stage*, 22 November 1962.

[75] Minister of Welsh Affairs, *Wales and Monmouthshire: Report on Developments and Government Action, 1963* (London, 1963, Cmnd. 2284), 117.

[76] Other theatres included Aberystwyth, Pembroke, and Wrexham. Secretary of State for Wales, *Report on the Arts in Wales* (London, 1966, Cmnd. 2983), 143.

[77] *The Stage*, 3 October 1963.

[78] *Belfast Telegraph*, 30 January 1964, 3 February 1964, 15 February 1964.

[79] *The Stage*, 25 March 1965, 20 May 1965, 17 June 1965.

[80] Gwyn Thomas, 'Each Man His Own Hamlet', *Plays and Players* 11, no, 7 (1963), 16–18.

[81] The play transferred to Theatr Clwyd for a week at the end of November 1976. *Liverpool Echo*, 26 November 1976, 3 December 1976.

[82] *The Stage*, 25 November 1976.

[83] *Sunday Times*, 21 November 1976.

[84] *The Stage*, 17 June 1976; Michael Anderson, 'Theatre in Wales: A Report', *Plays and Players* 24, no. 5 (February 1977), 38–39.

[85] 'The Alderman' was initially called 'The Bungalow' and had been commissioned by the BBC in February 1964 for the Home Service. It was broadcast on the Welsh Home Service as 'The Alderman' in January 1966.

[86] *Birmingham Daily Post*, 25 May 1979.

CHAPTER NINE

This World of Wales

'I think the Welsh would have benefitted from a spell of totally mindless hedonism,' Gwyn wrote in a column for the *Western Mail* in the 1970s, reflecting on the confusions which he believed were at the heart of modern Welshness. 'A man in my town was a strong enemy of Welshness,' Gwyn continued, 'He believed that our minds had become waterlogged by the tears of a too sentimental piety and blown shapeless by too windy a political rhetoric. He had some spare cash and dreamed of becoming a Tory demagogue after the style of Joseph Chamberlain.' The man tried to set up a soccer team, thinking rugby suspect because 'rugby players tend to talk Welsh' and when that did not work turned, instead, to the electric spectacle of greyhound racing. Gwyn claimed to have attended the opening night.[1] It was a bit of a disaster:

> So on that first night at the dogs I was in a mood to break free from racial nostalgia and scientific positivism. The pro-Saxon promoter of the stadium took me to one side. 'Bet a bundle on the big, black dog in the sixth race. His name is Cromwell, after Oliver the Roundhead, who trounced the Welsh at St Fagans.' I put sixpence, my fag money for the rest of the week, on Cromwell. He would not have taken longer getting out of the trap if he had been easing out of a top security gaol. When he finally did so, he relieved himself against the railings with a disdain that took in men and running dogs.

Gwyn explained the situation to his father, who replied: 'Quite right.' Gwyn's father, Walter, was possessed of a vibrant sense of Welsh-speaking Welshness and rejected the Anglophone inheritance which, given his American birth, was the more obvious fit (in Gwyn's mind) for the modern world. 'The dawn when it comes will be green,' Walter told his son, 'its bringer will be Llewelyn Bren ... He might even give you a true sense of identity, you poor lost Anglicised loon.' It was a class jest: Llewelyn Bren had led the revolt against English rule in Glamorgan in 1316. This head-to-head between father and son was not really the purpose of the article, of course, so much as the means of conveying ideas about the rising tide of Welsh nationalism. They were as forthright then as they are now controversial, but merit quoting in full to illustrate the strength of Gwyn's feelings.

The Welsh Resurgence is in full flood and I've missed the joy-ride again. I see people around me touched by the ecstasy of new beginnings. I stand on the side-lines, baffled. I hear of areas in North Wales being made safe for pure Welshness, of traditional Welsh culture slipped like fluoride into social intercourse to prevent English caries. I am told of sub-postmasters harassed and their stamps degummed because they do not speak Welsh. And I, a product of the colossal fusion of landless peasants from West Wales and South-West England, can only marvel.

What has astonished me most about the attempted reconquest of Glamorgan and Gwent has been the barbarous division of our children on language grounds. Parents have told me with a most sinister glint of pride in their eyes, that their children are taxied and bussed five or ten miles to privileged special academies where they will not be contaminated by the children of their rough English-speaking neighbours. This is the worst wound you can inflict on a community. Welsh patriots have often boasted that with landed gentry so thin on the Jacobinical Welsh ground, we would never commit the sin of a snobbish separatism implicit in the English Public School system. Yet a growing and muttering multitude see in the Welsh Schools simulations of Eton and Harrow. A Welsh Lord Rosebery, totally insulated from the Anglophone proles, is being concocted at this moment along the banks of the Taff. God help us.

The valleys of South-East Wales had, by the beginning of World War Two, gone over totally to the English-speaking world. The attempt to degrade and replace English in the schools of those areas will do nothing but mischief in minds already plagued by every neurosis that comes with insecurity. Bilingualism, pushed to the ultimate, will complete the work of spoliation and ruin begun by the coal-owners, and the collapse into dereliction of their weird kingdom. The passionate social and academic drives of the valleys in their prime will be lost in places slumped between the stools of two imperfectly mastered tongues. The society that produced a small army of Aneurin Bevans will be lucky to come up with one darts champion and a few pennillion groups of second rank.

There can be no denying the tenor of Gwyn's views about Welshness, about the Welsh language, and about the 'American' nature of a capitalised-South Walian history. Indeed, about the entire rupture of nineteenth-century industrialisation and twentieth-century modernity which tore up the passive, rural quiescence of pre-industrial Wales and created a new, Anglophone country. Gwyn was one of the few literary voices active during the burgeoning *kulturkampf* of the 1970s willing to express so openly a deep antipathy to what he called 'separatist things' and the denial of modernity. His most trenchant use of that phrase was in an interview with Denis

Mitchell in 1975 for the series *Private Lives*. Gwyn could not help but turn towards denouncing those 'self-elevated clowns [who] are saying that the British community and the British parliament should tear themselves apart in order to provide a greater articulateness for, let us say, the Scottish and the Welsh. The Scottish and the Welsh have expressed themselves with enormous eloquence and success through the British community.' There was no disguise. At best Gwyn thought nationalism puerile and pointless, and at worst tantamount to a repeat of the mistakes which led to the political horrors of the 1930s: the ideological foundations on which Nazism, Francoism, and the holocaust were built. He explained:

> this is what makes nationalism to me, even in the most undeveloped countries, people with enormous senses of injustice ... I feel like saying to them for god's sake it's too late for this kind of nonsense, the nursery time is over, you are off rusks now, you are on man's food for god's sake, face up to it. This is a tiny orb, a tiny clinker, that's fast running out of its last juices of wealth – we've got to huddle together.

In those last years of his life, he repeated these points time and time again – sometimes with a humorous twist, other times with the twist of the knife. In 1977, he declared in a blurb that his new work was 'a book on the devolutionary splitting of the United Kingdom.' That same year, he drew direct parallels with the bloody situation in Northern Ireland telling Vincent Kane:

> Once you have become aware of the complexity of the human species – and I find it deeply hurtful to find leaders of world opinion, the men who are governing nations, taking up bigoted stands on the religious question. Because how is a man going to arrange an understanding among people when he thinks in

375

his heart of hearts, 'I'm a Baptist, he's a Muslim, he must be less well informed than I, he must be worse than I.'

Well, you know, I once lost a job. I went to Belfast to become the director of a group of social clubs. And the people facing me were sectaries of the worse description, I'm still not sure what side of the theological fence they were, but a very sharp-faced man asked me 'now Mr Thomas, the first thing we want to know is how you will accommodate yourself to the religious differences that are characteristic of our society. Now what approach would you have to this question of a society divided between Catholics and Protestants?' I said I would be totally neutral, I'm an atheist. And they were outraged. I couldn't understand this at all because it seemed so sensible to me, you know.

And in the summer of 1980, writing in the American magazine *GEO*, he observed pointedly that

half the poets in Wales, who also double as arsonists, are under lock and key and screeching in perfect rhythm and rhyme about fascist tyranny. They ache for martyrdom but threaten to sue when they find there is no cocktail cabinet in the cell. The Celts, like the adolescent, make an art form of petulance but carry the thing to a baffling conclusion by refusing to grow up. The Pan-Celtic movement must have had J. M. Barrie's Peter in mind. The founder of that movement was an uncle of Charles de Gaulle. He wasn't a Celt, but he liked us. As the impoverished chef said: all nuts are welcome to the feast.[2]

But why was Gwyn so vociferous in his opposition to Welsh nationalism, to devolution, and to the intervention of the state in support of the Welsh language? In the view of one commentator, Gwyn displayed in some of his public comments a 'total insensitivity to the feelings of those who perceived the world and lived their lives through the medium of Welsh,' and surmises that the origins of the hostility to the language (of his parents, grandparents, and older siblings) lay in the writer's complicated relationship with his mother. 'His anger with his abandoning mother landed with full ferocity on her language of preference, Welsh.'[3] This is surely inadequate as an explanation, and rather misleading – Gwyn would almost certainly find it insulting. The logical target for Gwyn's linguistic antipathy would have been his father, Walter, who was, as Gwyn's older brother Eddie put it 'quite a Welsh scholar in his weird way.' It is broadly understood, not least from Gwyn's own descriptions, that the Thomas family were broadly divided in their knowledge of Welsh between the first six children ('the top half') and the last six ('the bottom half'), although some have taken this to mean that 'numbers seven to twelve ... were explicitly taught no Welsh.' This is factually incorrect. The rupture, which was familial and social, was the result of circumstance and context, not a deliberate choice.

When Ziphorah Thomas died in 1919, the younger members of the Thomas family varied in age from fifteen to six years of age. At the 1911 census, two years before Gwyn's birth in 1913, the entire family (as composed at that time, excluding only Eddie and Gwyn) was recorded – in Walter Thomas's handwriting – as speaking *both* languages. So much for the hard and fast rule which rigidly divided the family linguistically in half.[4] The return completed by Walter is instructive as a source because three of Gwyn's brothers – the twins Gwilym and Arthur (aged seven), and John (aged six) – were then about the same age as Gwyn and Eddie (the eleventh child of the Thomas family) when their mother died. In other words, Welsh was spoken in the home, as well as at chapel, and had Ziphorah lived longer into Gwyn's childhood, he may well have retained knowledge of the language. She did not and so he did not. Nor did Eddie. Their rudimentary Welsh, along with that of their older siblings, as the 1921 census return now reveals, dissipated rapidly in an overwhelmingly Anglophone society, despite some efforts to 'revive' the language in the 1920s. 'When I was about ten,' he wrote in *Punch* in the 1960s, 'there was an effort made in the primary schools to win us back. The old language was already beleaguered and stricken. If we had been on equal terms with the defenders we would have shaken a pike and deployed our mutations with the best of them.'[5]

Children were drilled, by rote, in a series of aphorisms and idioms which sapped any life that Welsh might have had, leaving a generation able to pronounce a language which had other lost all meaning.[6] 'We were thrust,' Gwyn recalled, 'into a cosmos of moralizing and mourning conducted totally in Welsh.' Everything alive and electric and exciting and happy arrived in English. And that was long before the arrival of the Talkie. The truth of Gwyn's childhood, then, was not so much a deliberate separation of a part of the family from its cultural-linguistic inheritance, but rather a loss of knowledge commensurate with shifts taking place in wider Rhondda society. It was to this rupture Gwyn referred time and again in his writing, his radio and television appearances, and was the central node in his antipathy to those who would seek to reverse the process, artificially. Eddie and Gwyn, and their slightly older siblings including Nan, were typical of the generation which grew up in early twentieth-century Rhondda. They experienced the tail-end of the disintegration of Welsh as an everyday language and the emergence of English and later American idioms as its replacement.

Between 1901 and 1911, the number of monoglot English speakers in the Rhondda rose – to a significant degree because of immigration from Anglophone regions such as Somerset and

Gloucestershire – from about thirty-seven thousand people to more than sixty thousand; the number of those who spoke only Welsh fell from around twelve thousand to just over six thousand. The remainder of the population, just under seventy-one thousand people, claimed to be bilingual. Crucially, the largest proportions of those who spoke only English were under twenty-five years of age. For Gwyn's twin brothers, born in 1904, the ratio was more than fifty per cent monoglot English speakers compared with two and a half per cent who spoke only Welsh. The fact that Gwyn's teenage siblings lost their relatively strong grasp of Welsh, too, in the 1920s, despite having had much longer absorption in the language at home and in the chapel, shows that this was a community-based process of socialisation. The older members of the family were first-language Welsh speakers whose English was, at least at first, a secondary practicality. For the younger half, however, and especially Eddie and Gwyn, English was the mother tongue: it was the language spoken in school, in the streets with friends, and it was the language of the books and magazines which were read.

Welsh was a means of communicating with grandparents or understanding what was going on in chapel. It had a limited use in other settings, and for someone of Gwyn's generation and place of birth no practical purpose at all. This was made apparent in scenes cut from Gwyn's documentary in the *One Pair of Eyes* series in 1968. Actor Keith Baxter asked Gwyn whether he could speak Welsh, receiving a variant of the standard answer: the 'kitchen was Welsh' but the 'street was English.' Comfortable being in conversation with one of his former pupils, Gwyn went further. 'There is a resurgence of Welsh,' Baxter noted, 'are you in sympathy?' Gwyn replied: 'I see their point, why shouldn't we keep the language ... But I would flee to Argentina if Wales [was] ruled by Welsh.' He said something similar in a television interview with Wyn Roberts in 1961:

> I never wanted to become emotionally involved in the Welsh language. The story is simply that a very large family in the Rhondda valley in the early years of this century, the top half of the family spoke Welsh, the bottom half didn't, and I simply had to make the best of this. And I don't think that people in this dilemma in Wales have had quite the amount of understanding from their Welsh-speaking brethren as they should have done. Because after all, when you lose a language for say ten years if you are at all proud you are not going to try to learn it again, are you?

Gwyn's desire for indifference earned him more than a few enemies. In 1968, Gwynfor Evans, the Barry-born president of Plaid Cymru, remarked that 'Gwyn Thomas sometimes seems allergic to the Welsh Language.'[7] The older Gwyn got and the more his patience wore away, the less anyone used the qualifier 'sometimes.' In a private notebook, he complained a couple of years later that 'the Welsh language has become in both senses a club: it is a conspiracy of people seeking preferment through the speaking of an arcane tongue, it is an offensive weapon.' In a television interview with Vincent Kane broadcast in 1978, Gwyn observed that 'Welsh communities, in the long run, would lose out when they cease to be an active part of the English-speaking world because we have the spirit, we have the wit, we have the imagination to contribute something invaluable to the English-speaking world. This is central to our future happiness or future misery.' He added that 'Every active Welsh-speaking nationalist is denying the Welshman the chance to fulfil his glorious function upon this world; that is to be a man of great imagination, great compassion, in the language that would reach more people than any other.' In 1979, the year of the devolution referendum, which he had voted against, Gwyn even went so far as to suggest that Wales would have been better off had the language died its natural death. 'I have,' he said on the BBC's *Bookshelf*,

> never for one instant been tempted to compromise with my disapproval of the fact that Lazarus did not die. I think the language had been given its cue to leave the stage and I believe it would have been better for the health of the Welsh mind had it done so.

The loss of facility with Welsh in childhood, either through deliberate choice or through the natural attenuation of a second language on which there was relatively little grasp, hardly provides an adequate explanation for such an outspoken stance. In fact, there is sufficient evidence from Gwyn's own letters home in the 1930s that not only did he continue to use the language from time to time, but he could also make statements wholly compatible with the nationalism of the 1970s, or more recent times. At Oxford, especially, he expressed a variety of views about Wales, the Welsh, and the English, which were strikingly at odds with his later clarity of thought. In one letter, sent home in 1934, he told Nan that the 'English are animals, nasty little animals, rats as a word.'[8] Elsewhere in his university letters, he dropped in various phrases in Welsh. Crucially these were half-remembered lines from the dinner table at 196 High Street, or references to hymns and songs, or rote-learned phrases which lingered from school, rather than any indication of a strong grasp of the language: a hint at its secondary practicality. Gwyn was inconsistently Anglophobic at Oxford, he may have thought the middle and upper-class English he encountered were animals, but he also believed strongly in the

381

idea that 'a Welshman who does not speak Welsh belongs not to Wales, but to the world.'[9]

Gwyn's hostility was shaken from him when he went to work at the government instructional centre at Thetford. There he realised that the English working class were no less hard up than those in South Wales. He realised, too, that the antagonism he had expressed so viscerally at university had been about social class, not nation, all along, restoring his faith in universalism. Gwyn was still reeling from his final break with the Welsh language, its culture, its proponents and its self-appointed cultural guardians (the sort who became literary critics). This break occurred not in 1919, on the death of his mother, but in the autumn of 1937, when Gwyn was twenty-four. He had applied for a job as tutor-organiser with the WEA and travelled down to the Cardiff office to be interviewed. It went well until, towards the end, he was asked about his ability to teach in Welsh. He flustered. And then he got very angry. He told Nan, 'I failed to get it because I spoke no Welsh. My conceit will take several months recovering from that blow. Some imbecile on the interviewing board told me my ignorance of Welsh put me out of touch with the finest culture in Wales.'[10] It did not escape Gwyn's notice that the WEA happily employed Saunders Lewis. From that moment on, Gwyn never again used the Welsh language in his letters to Nan or to anyone else.

Little did the 'imbecile' on the interviewing panel know that, in speaking as they did, they created in an instant one of the most determined opponents of the Welsh language in the second half of the twentieth century. But that is exactly what happened. There can be no doubt that this event was the basis of the Northern Ireland story Gwyn related on the Vincent Kane Show in 1977. The religious sectarianism which demanded to know whether he was a Catholic atheist or a Protestant one was in fact about the linguistic bigotry experienced when, as a young man in desperate need of a job, he was turned away by Welsh-speaking Cardiff intellectuals and the self-appointed guardians of Wales as culturally ignorant. He never forgave this sleight of hand and in the decades afterwards privately and publicly expressed increasingly disparaging views about this cabal of Celts and their entire worldview. The softest public rendition of Gwyn's views on the Welsh language came in 1963 when he explained to viewers of TWW's *This World of Wales* that, 'We Welsh are not a united people, and I won't say we haven't enjoyed our divisions ... We have two languages and plenty to argue about in both.'

*

Gwyn's views on language and the growth of industrial South Wales shaped his sense of what he thought of as the region's American character. What he perceived was not all that different, in tone or execution, from James Baldwin's portrait of the United States. Both invoked a rupture. The South Walian rupture took Marsdens, Mustows, Billingtons, Evanses, Joneses, and Thomases, and created something entirely new. 'We were a fusion,' as he told Vincent Kane. Baldwin rendered his ideas about the American rupture most powerfully in a lecture delivered in Berkeley, California, in 1979. 'When the Italian got here, or the Greek, or whoever, there was a moment in his life when he had to start to speak English,' Baldwin said, 'when he became a guy named Joe. And that meant that he couldn't speak to his father because his father couldn't speak English. That meant a rupture. A profound rupture. So, the son did become a guy named Joe and never found out anything else about himself.'[11] Emanuel Goldenberg became Edward G. Robinson. Jacob Gershwine became George Gershwin. And Barney Fastovsky had a son called Howard Fast. According to Gwyn,

South Walians were living with the same rupture and its consequences: compelled to look outward to a global Anglophone culture because they could neither look towards, nor understand, Welsh-speaking Wales.

One early target was the National Eisteddfod, a forum which he regarded as neurotic, defensive, elitist, conspiratorial, and culturally useless. Gwyn told Wyn Roberts in 1961 that 'I can't help perceiving signs of conspiracy, even malignant conspiracy, on the part of the proud possessors of the language against the second-class citizens who don't have the language.' Deep down, the National Eisteddfod had preserved the amateurism which had been Wales' lot in times of poverty but in times of plenty had become a barrier to meaningful professionalism and cultural growth. Why not, he wondered, something 'nearer the idea of the Edinburgh Festival and a lot further away from the idea of a shoestring village cultural economy.' Adding that, 'now we can afford to forget the cultural mores that emerged from a background of poverty and we can afford to aim at a very high sophistication. Because I think that the Welsh need a bit of jolting about this: the fact they can have two quarterly magazines which die, the fact that they no longer have a theatre in Wales capable of putting plays. I mean these things are profoundly disturbing.'[12] The trouble, Gwyn concluded, much to Wyn Roberts's audible irritation, was that

> once you have the Eisteddfod as a fixed cultural norm you are simply going to insist upon an ever-spreading sea of amateurism. Because how many of the really leading instrumentalists and singers, Geraint Evans and the rest, were produced from the Eisteddfod tents? Not many. If you examine the really fine professionals, I don't think that they owe much of their beginnings to the Eisteddfod.

Gwyn had begun to court controversy about such matters in his appearances on the *Brains Trust* in the 1950s, during the failed Parliament for Wales campaign and concurrent with the Tryweryn controversy.[13] He gave short shrift to both. In 1959, a St David's Day edition of the *Brains Trust* debated national identity, language, and devolution. Gwyn's comments were reported as 'astringent' and, in the words of the *Western Mail*'s critic, seemed to have 'angered many of his kinsfolk.'[14] The journalist complained of a postbag 'loaded with protests.' A few months later, Gwyn provided the Welsh voice in BBC Northern Ireland's 'The Trouble with the English,' a series of discussion programmes designed to debate national identity and Britishness.[15] Alongside him were the Scottish novelist Compton McKenzie, the Professor of Irish history at Queen's University Belfast, J. C. Beckett, and the London-born writer Stephen Potter. One reviewer observed that 'Gwyn Thomas belabours the English with flow of language that could only come from Wales,' but his take was more universal than might have been expected given the quasi-nationalistic invitation of the programme.[16]

In *A Welsh Eye*, parts of which had been serialised in *The Spectator* in August 1964, he picked up the Tryweryn debate once more and rebuffed the mythos surrounding the construction of a reservoir in North Wales by Liverpool Corporation.[17] 'The national brain now bulges with such projects as the need to deny Welsh rainwater to the Liverpool waterboard,' Gwyn wrote.[18] One of the lines cut from *One Pair of Eyes* in 1969 similarly tackled Tryweryn. 'The Nationalists,' Gwyn put it in the original script, 'want to charge England some fantastic fee for water that just falls from the sky. The Nationalists say this is our greatest asset, as if they were producing this in some personal way.' He understood, as did Elaine Morgan in her own private correspondence with the BBC, that the controversy was a manufacture not of universal Welsh opinion, but very specifically of a nationalist movement seeking a contemporary purpose all aided and abetted by widespread ignorance of the truth and by Labour politicians wanting to give the Conservative government a bloody nose. The rise of Plaid Cymru after the Second World War was a source of deep dismay for Gwyn and he regarded the political turmoil at the end of the 1960s as an indication that the lights were beginning to go out in South Wales. 'The noise and the passion are gone,' he told the *New York Times* despairingly in 1970, 'an air of threadbare quietness hangs over the place. In the main the place is tame.'[19]

It was not just politics which had a foul air. The BBC was increasingly alien. Lyn recalled later that 'Gwyn ... found himself being less well treated... after the arrival of the new Welsh-speaking elements in the hierarchy; everything altered; going to the BBC began to be like going to a foreign country.'[20] Gwyn's own rendition of the experience was far blunter. In a letter to Nan written just before Christmas 1966, he let loose. 'I grow to dislike dealing with the Welsh BBC more and more. The reek of Plaid and the witless Gwynfor grows stronger by the day. God help us, what a choice to face – the English on the one hand and that appalling little chap, Heddi Griffiths (he's the chap who's always being photographed outside gaols and post offices demanding equal status for Welsh and a higher status for himself), son of that pompous chap, Gwyn Griffiths, who was at school with me and himself a formidable jerk.'[21] Gwyn's antipathy and his steadfast refusal even to soften the blow created many enemies and frustrated friends and sympathetic critics, not least Gwyn Jones and Glyn Jones. They found Gwyn's attitudes towards language, nationhood, and cultural institutions such as the National Eisteddfod, difficult to stomach and even harder to defend.

Writing in the late 1960s, Glyn Jones felt that where Gwyn

fell short 'of being a completely representative figure, I think, is in his attitude to Wales and Welshness. Wales has her own characteristic features and institutions ... Gwyn appears to have little sympathy with the national aspirations and indigenous culture of our country.'[22] Gwyn Jones, writing in the early 1950s, recognised his namesake's self-confessed rootlessness and his willingness, common to all 'Anglo-Welsh' artists and writers, to be 'judged as an English writer, not a Welsh one.'[23] Later literary critics have followed this path. M. Wynn Thomas, for example, has referred to Gwyn as an 'old-fashioned social humanist and spoilt Nonconformist.'[24] Others, who had once thought Gwyn a little passé, such as Alun Richards and Ron Berry, found in Gwyn's anti-nationalist sentiments a politics like their own. Richards, especially, poked fun at the nationalist turn and was uncompromising in his attitude towards the Welsh language. Hence his description of Colenso Jones, in the short story 'Bowels Jones,' as having 'got into the wrong set at one of the lesser Welsh universities and emerged a rabid Welsh nationalist with Honours Welsh and an interest in his country that amount to fetishism ... the wretch had become one of the interrupters of Her Majesty's judges, a demonstrator, a non-road-tax payer who disappeared for weeks on end to summer schools and folk festivals where they ate, slept, breathed and dreamed Welsh.'[25]

In the 1960s and 1970s, Richards enjoyed notable success as a television writer and as a playwright. He felt an antipathy to what he saw as the prevailing spirit of amateurism which cloaked (and choked) Welsh talent: easily disguised in the Welsh language where it had no meaningful competition but far harder in English where the competition included the United States of America, and Ireland, quite as much as the metropolitan call of London. Amateurism had the tendency to lead to insecurity, Richards thought; or, as Gwyn would have it, to neurosis. 'All arguments about Welshness I find to be fruitless,' Richards wrote in 1976,

> although ... I could not help but detect the security of so many writers in the Welsh language which has freed them from painful attempts to emphasize their nationality, a strain which affect the work of some of their counterparts writing in English for a time. Ironically, this freedom seems to be in danger of ending and, judging by some of the stories made available in translation, appears to have been replaced by the aim of political conversion, to the detriment, in my view, of the storyteller's art.

Gwyn's take, written at about the same time and published in a series of biographical reflections collected by Meic Stephens, was sharper. 'How much of the literary potential of Wales has found expression?' Gwyn pondered, 'About one per cent, I'd say. We lack the confidence, the professional finish and stamina that mark most English practitioners. There are still too many of us with one foot in the school magazine and the other in the Band of Hope. We are not nearly arrogant enough or arrogant in the wrong ways.' Gwyn and Alun Richards came together on the question of language and the consequent effects of a schizophrenic national psyche. 'We should by now have created a body of intelligent fiction in English of unique, tempestuous quality,' Gwyn wrote, 'something that would have had the caustic wizards of the London weeklies trembling in admiration before us.' However, he added, his frustration clear,

> they do not tremble. Nor particularly do they admire. Despite old flare-ups of enthusiasm for this bit of work or that they tend over the years to brush off what we have done as a shabby, provincial thing, devoid alike of taste or depth. A grudging

admiration, on strictly professional grounds, is offered to writers who will exploit their Welsh material in one or two books, then switch aseptically to the incidence of palsy in the Lebanon or the effects of mineral waters on nymphomania at Aix-les-Bains. That's quite a topic. If I could throw off the grinning enchantment laid upon me by the Rhondda of my childhood I'd give it a whirl.

As a result of a lack of impetus, and the consequent absence of top-flight English literature from Wales, itself an indication of intellectual and cultural decline, no one seemed to care about 'the talking places of Swansea or Cardiff'; or as Gwyn put it, the 'one acre of the Empire from which they [the metropolitan critics] can as yet conceive no possible tremor of challenge.'

Gwyn's ambition as a writer was always to break out of Welsh limitations and to place the experiences of his people into a universal format which would be read and appreciated by a much wider, indeed global audience. In that sense, he was like those American writers who did not come from major metropolitan centres such as New York, Los Angeles, or Chicago, but who came to those places, either in person or in print, and used their cultural power as a conduit to voice the experiences of another America. Early in his life, Gwyn read the works of the American novelist Thomas Wolfe, whose experience had a considerable impact on the way Gwyn thought about literature. Born in Asheville, North Carolina, Wolfe made his way first to Harvard University and then to New York City, where he taught English and began writing his epic novels *Look Homeward, Angel* (1929) and *Of Time and the River* (1935). Gwyn was a student at Oxford when he first read *Look Homeward, Angel* and wrote home to encourage Nan to read it, too. Watch out, he said, for phrases such as 'unbright cinder,' which appeared in the epigrammatic passage at the outset of the novel.[26]

A stone, a leaf, an unfound door; of a stone, a leaf, a door. And of all the forgotten faces. Naked and alone we came into exile. In her dark womb we did not know our mother's face; from the prison of her flesh we come into the unspeakable and incommunicable prison of this earth. Which of us has known his brother? Which of us has looked into his father's heart? Which of us has not remained forever prison-pent? Which of us is not forever a stranger and alone? O waste of loss, in the hot mazes, lost, among bright stars on this most wearing unbright cinder, lost! Remembering speechlessly we seek the great forgotten language, the lost lane-end into heaven, a stone, a leaf, an unfound door. Where? When? O lost, and by the wind grieved, ghost, come back again.

There can be no doubting the origins, in this passage, of the title of Gwyn's unpublished pre-war novel, 'O Lost,' written in around 1939. By coincidence, Wolfe had likewise titled the first version of the novel which evolved into *Look Homeward, Angel* as 'O Lost.' Other nods to Wolfe's work, which persisted in Gwyn's for many years, included locations such as Belmont – an echo of Wolfe's Altamont, the fictionalised version of Asheville. Like the Rhondda, Asheville had grown from a hamlet at the beginning of the nineteenth century into a bustling town by the beginning of the twentieth: the population boom between 1890 and 1910 saw Asheville grow to ten times its initial size. That boom caused a rupture between the population who lived in the city after 1910 and those who had lived in the hamlet a century earlier. Neither could know the other's real history or culture; they were so distinct. Gwyn understood, as Wolfe did, the need to create a literary culture and a history which explained that rupture and gave voice to what had happened and to the people created as a result. The writer of fiction and the historian became one and the same.

*

Aside from America, Gwyn believed, the best way of understanding Wales and all its divisions was to look at Spain. It was his other obsession, one shared with no less a writer than Ernest Hemingway. 'What lights a fire of curiosity in the mind about a country other than one's own,' Gwyn pondered on the BBC in the mid-1970s. 'With me, Spain was a thick smoulder from infancy.' Fittingly, his last major appearance on television was talking about the Spanish Civil War in John Ormond's compelling documentary *The Colliers' Crusade*.[27] Broadcast in Wales in the autumn of 1979, Gwyn provided a characteristically powerful performance which provided the narrative force of the entire documentary and served as a coda to his life's work. *The Colliers' Crusade* was largely based on doctoral research undertaken by Hywel Francis, who served as the series historical advisor, and featured many of the individuals previously interviewed by Francis including former International Brigaders Will Paynter, Morien Morgan, Edwin Greening, and Alun Menai Williams. Gwyn relished the opportunity, providing pieces to camera rich in anecdote and authoritative insight. His contribution was recorded at the South Wales Miners' Library in 1978, the transcript of which reveals a more wide-ranging discussion than the edited elements which made the final broadcast. Indeed, Gwyn seems to have been determined to impress upon Ormond his conviction that the Spanish Civil War was

> the highest act of political passion in the history of western man and when the strange smokescreen of the great banality itself, the great tribal war between England and Germany, when that has vanished, we will see this as the greatest, the most poetic of wars fought.[28]

As in his lecture to the people of the Rhondda in the early months of war in 1936, Gwyn presented a picture of Spain in the first decades of the twentieth century as a country divided between a backward-looking establishment, a forward-looking modern community of progressive artists and politicians, and a nationalist reaction. The republic which governed Spain between the abdication of Alfonso XIII in 1931 and the outbreak of the war in 1936 was almost the fulfilment of his own political hopes and dreams. Republican Spain was a country which sent artists, poets, dramatists, and musicians, out into the world to be its ambassadors; which created the University of Madrid thereby establishing an educational system 'for working, living, unbelieving people (if you like); people who wanted to try something new.'[29]

A key part of that spirit of artistic and political endeavour was expressed in the oratory of figures such as Dolores Ibárruri (better known by her affectionate sobriquet 'la Pasionaria,' the passionflower) and José Díaz, the leaders of the Communist Party of Spain; as well as in the writing of the left-wing poet and playwright, Federico García Lorca. The latter was killed shortly after the outbreak of the Spanish Civil War in 1936. In later years, including on camera for Ormond, Gwyn claimed to have heard Ibárruri speak during his time in Madrid. He likewise claimed to have spoken to Lorca in a Madrid café. These statements have been regarded with scepticism and were dismissed by Gwyn's previous biographers: he was sometimes more attached to the idea of something happening than he was the absolute truth. Thus, in Michael Parnell's view, since 'La Pasionaria's fame did not begin to spread until the Civil War made her an international celebrity, and as Lorca was at the time living in the south, a long way from Madrid, it is probable that these encounters never happened.'[30] However, sufficient evidence is now recoverable from mass digitisation of Spanish sources to vindicate Gwyn and to overturn the scepticism entirely.

Gwyn arrived in Spain in the spring of 1933. La Pasionaria, herself, was based in Madrid until November that year. She then travelled to Moscow as part of a Spanish delegation to the Comintern. On that basis, Gwyn had undoubted opportunities to hear her speak. But would he have known who she was? The answer is almost certainly, yes. Ibárruri's reputation in Spain had been established in the 1920s: together with her husband, she had broken with the Spanish Socialist Workers Party (PSOE) in 1921 on the foundation of the Spanish Communist Party (PCE).[31] By 1930, she had risen to national prominence and was elected to the PCE's central committee, the following year she was called to Madrid to work for the party's newspaper, *Mundo Obrero*. In February 1936, she was elected to the Spanish Parliament as a communist and was thrust into the international limelight. As the *Scotsman* noted at the time, Ibárruri was 'well-known in Spain under the nickname of la Pasionaria.'[32] Gwyn was an avid reader of the British *Daily Worker* in the 1930s and there is no reason (in the absence of concrete evidence either way) to suppose that he avoided the newspapers and magazines of the PCE when he lived in Madrid.

Gwyn forged political friendships when he was in Spain as a student, which he rekindled on his subsequent visits after the Second World War. Those friends would have introduced him to left-wing orators and to writers in advance of any international renown and in conjunction with his absorption of the press. Familiarity with journalism and an orator's political reputation is not the same thing as hearing them speak, of course. The most likely occasion took place in the summer of 1933, when Gwyn was journeying through the Asturias. He referred to this trip numerous times in his writing and again on air in *The Colliers' Crusade* when, in addition to the echoes of the Rhondda he found in the Asturian mining communities, he vividly recalled hearing la Pasionaria and the revelling in the response of the crowd to her oratory. The event clearly held a special place in his memory. His time in northern Spain coincided with a major open-air rally at the Torre de los Reyes football stadium in the city of Sama.[33] Organised by the PCE, the rally was addressed by prominent local communists and, more importantly, by la Pasionaria. She had travelled from Madrid for the occasion.[34]

What was probably more an encounter by chance than by design was the conversation with the poet, Lorca. Gwyn had the opportunity to meet when Lorca was in Madrid performing at the *Teatro Español* alongside Rafael Alberti and the flamenco dancer La Argentinita (Encarnación López Júlvez) in the early summer of 1933. Indeed, it seems entirely likely that Gwyn went along to what the Madrid *Herald* described as an 'incomparable fiesta of popular art' held at the theatre on 6 May.[35] It would certainly have appealed to him, aesthetically and politically. As a poet and playwright, Lorca was not widely known in Britain before the outbreak of the Spanish Civil War, and the first English translation of his poems (by Stephen Spender and Joan Gili) appeared only in 1939.[36] Gwyn had an unusual advantage. His tutor at Oxford, Dámaso Alonso, was part of the Generation of '27 movement alongside Lorca, and it may be that this common link formed part of the conversation. The other possibility, and we will never know for certain which occurred, is that Gwyn simply met Lorca by accident in a city centre café when both men were taking a break from their day's activities. Either way, the veracity of Gwyn's memory can be put beyond reasonable doubt, these things did happen as he always suggested.

As for the International Brigaders, Gwyn felt that they were fighting in 'the only war that really matters,' namely the war that begins with a thought, 'with a conviction taken, felt, on a certain day, that the world is not right, that there is going on in a part of the world a conflict that may help to solve the [world's] problems.' There was, he said, 'far more of literature than of politics in what they decided to do ... this was the heroic, the passionate thing to do.' There was something almost Romantic about this take on the involvement of Welshmen in the Spanish Civil War – almost. For the point, here, at least in Gwyn's mind, was not that these men were, like the poets and writers of Cambridge who went and fought and died, caught up in a crusade they only thinly understood. Rather, they were living out the passions which they had absorbed from their society. 'Every one of these men,' he explained,

> that went out to Spain at that time had grown up, at least in childhood, under the shadow of this enormous passion that came out of the pulpits and it had gone for nothing. Like the promises of the capitalists who said that you work in a pit or a steelworks and you will have a progressively better future. Finished. And all the promises of the pulpits had gone exactly the same way and these men were wandering the thirties in a very peculiar wilderness ... this incredible horizon, incredibly romantic horizon too, mark you; an horizon that had been broadened by the cinema, particularly by the talking cinema. To believe, you know, in these new parts of the world, where a new kind of destiny could be lived. And I'm sure the cinema had a good deal to do with the decision of these men to break away from this curiously roughshod civilisation in which they were living, because every single one of them, I would say, had had this experience of seeing homes that had been denuded of dignity, of comfort, of hope, and they went south with exactly the same exhilaration as a little later many of them went west to nowhere.

Gwyn spoke of Spain, but he had Wales in mind as well. Sadly, by the time he came to be interviewed by Ormond for *The Colliers' Crusade* at the South Wales Miners' Library in Swansea, Gwyn was visibly in decline; not that any viewers would have appreciated this, for he marshalled his full strength for the pieces to camera. Such was his enthusiasm for the project and the story being told. This, together with his failing eyesight, was probably the reason Gwyn was not asked to provide full narrative commentary for the series, rather than any partisan approach to the Spanish Civil War.[37] The programme was assuredly pro-Republican without Gwyn's direction of the narrative. In Gwyn's stead, stepped René Cutforth (1909–1984), a veteran documentary maker and journalist. *The Colliers' Crusade* was the start of a potentially fruitful friendship and Ormond was committed to making further programmes with Gwyn. A year or so after was broadcast, the two men sat down to begin another project: a six-part series of recollections for radio.

*

Ormond visited Gwyn at home in Peterston in the spring of 1981 to begin recording the series. He recalled that 'we had a drink, talked a bit, laughed, were silent for as much as five seconds and then, giving his valediction to the world, these were the words [Gwyn] spoke.'

In the ultimate moment of a life one is said to recollect the places that have had the greatest meaning, the greatest impact upon the mind: and it is very fruitful to reflect in advance on what those places might be. Certainly, in my case, the year 1940 and – the place – the west coast of Wales, Cardigan, and the road down to Gwbert, would come through the haze of terminal apprehension to give me an absolute delight.[38]

Gwyn told the story of his journey to teach at Cardigan County
School. He travelled, he said, in a rickety van driven by the
communist grocer Alun Thomas, who lived in Neath not far
from Walt.[39] 'My arrival in Cardigan was a quite splendid
affair,' he added, 'because in the context of that morbid,
varicose time, Cardigan had not been touched.' The sensation
recalled travelling to North Wales for the first time:

> I was well into my forties when I went out of South Wales for
> the first time. Now this, for a writer, for a novelist, for a
> dramatist, is very important. Because he has been writing out
> of roots of a remembrance all his life things that his mother has
> said, things that his father has said, things that he has heard
> from innumerable tongues. And then in middle life I came to
> know a part of Wales that I had never seen before – Dinas
> Mawddwy.
>
> I was travelling north in a car belonging to a friend of mine
> and the car was valiant but fallible. As we came to the top of
> that monstrous road from Dinas Mawddwy, up to the Cross
> Foxes, the car stalled and began to steam and smoke like an old-
> fashioned fish-and-chip van ... There we were stuck in this
> strange position, the car utterly stalled; and we faced what
> seemed absolute disaster. Sheep congregated around the scene,
> and ravens eyeing us up-and-down as if testing us as possible
> meals; and then all of a sudden from nowhere in this vast
> wilderness, this most beautiful place of mountains ... as we
> were trapped in this car waiting for the end, and waiting simply
> to go back into Dinas Mawddwy and ruin, there appeared about
> forty people and their one wish was to push this car in which I
> sat.

As ever with Gwyn, amid the jokes and the farce, there was the
crux:

Wales – contemporary Wales particularly – has had many moments where it has felt that all has failed: industry, finance, politics, all a completely fallible farce. Now, why shouldn't we withdraw and create another kind of Utopian community of contemplation, of loneliness?

And this, of course, is what Father Ignatius tried to do in Llanthony. Poor, deluded Ignatius. He figures often in my dreams. One of the supreme comics, I suppose, of all time. He never earned as much money as Morecambe, or Wise, or Yarwood, but a great comic in his own way. He really felt that he could revive the ideal of the Middle Ages in this strange, isolated south-eastern valley of Wales. And, of course, young men, completely dispirited, completely heartbroken about the world in which they lived, came to this monastery that Ignatius wanted to found ... and they had to try to make a living out of this terribly stony, unwelcoming terrain.

... It all happened within a few years. It's like the history of the Wild West in America. Its fascination lies in the fact that it was all over in about fifty years. ... It never reached any kind of true formal expression of any sort of idea. This, I think, in the future, is what we in Wales must try to avoid. Never start an idea of which you cannot see the end.

It was Ormond's last visit. A few weeks later, Gwyn collapsed and was rushed into hospital. The doctors recognised the final, debilitating stages of diabetes, which left Gwyn with failing eyesight, poor mobility, renal failure, and heart disease, and had already entailed lengthy stays in hospital. He lay in bed weakened and doused by pain-relieving drugs, greeting visitors as best he could. Lyn saw him for the last time on 12 April 1981. 'I'm not much use to you like this, am I,' he said to her. On their rounds in the early hours of 13 April, the ward nurses found that Gwyn had died silently in his sleep. He was just sixty-seven years old. Later that day, Radio Wales broadcast Ormond's recording in memoriam. Gwyn had delivered his own eulogy.

---

[1] This is only a slight exaggeration. The greyhound racing track at Caemawr, which was later known as Porth Stadium, originally opened on 24 October 1932. *Pontypridd Observer*, 22 October 1932. Gwyn was back in Oxford for the start of term at that time. There was, however, a greyhound who raced at various South Wales tracks in the early 1930s called Cromwell Lad. *WM*, 6 July 1931, 30 September 1931, 3 October 1931.

[2] Gwyn Thomas, 'Letter to the Editor', *GEO: A New View of Our World* (1980), 7.

[3] Prys-Williams, *Twentieth-Century Autobiography*, 105.

[4] Gwyn's regular references to a divide in his family had as much to do with the fate of the language in the Rhondda as it did in 196 High Street. It was his way of explaining a profound but near-universal cultural shift.

[5] 'Change Here for Strangeness', *Punch*, 19 April 1961.

[6] Gwyn Thomas, 'Once Again Assembled Here, Part Six: Oh, You Frabjous Asses', *Punch*, 12 August 1959.

[7] Gwynfor Evans and Ioan Rhys, 'Wales', in Owen Dudley Edwards, Gwynfor Evans, Ioan Rhys and Hugh MacDiarmid, *Celtic Nationalism* (London, 1968), 223.

[8] Letter from Gwyn Thomas to Hannah Thomas, 28 January 1934; Letter from Gwyn Thomas to Hannah Thomas, 16 February 1934.

[9] Letter from Gwyn Thomas to Hannah Thomas, 23 October 1933.

[10] Letter from Gwyn Thomas to Hannah Thomas, 13 December 1937.

[11] Cited in Ed Pavlic, *Who Can Afford to Improvise? James Baldwin and Black Music, the Lyric and the Listeners* (New York, 2016), 270.

[12] NLW, HTV Archive: 'Here Today, 27 February 1961'.

[13] *WM*, 16 January 1956, 7 March 1958; Rupert Hart-Davies (ed), *The Lyttleton Hart-Davies Letters: Correspondence of George Lyttleton and Rupert Hart-Davies, Volume Three 1958* (London, 1981), 31–33.

[14] *WM*, 9 March 1959.

[15] *RT*, 17 July 1959.

[16] *Ballymena Weekly Telegraph*, 16 July 1959.

[17] Gwyn Thomas, 'A Welsh Eye', *The Spectator*, 13 August 1964; Gwyn Thomas, 'The Way To The Sea', *The Spectator*, 20 August 1964; Gwyn Thomas, 'In Times Of Trouble', *The Spectator*, 27 August 1964.

[18] *AWE*, 103; he returned to the subject once again in *Punch* – albeit with a sideways view – in 1967. Gwyn Thomas, 'The Everlasting Noah', *Punch*, 27 September 1967.

[19] *New York Times*, 6 June 1970.

[20] NLW, GTP, M30: Interview with Lyn Thomas conducted by Michael Parnell, 3 October 1985.

[21] Letter from Gwyn Thomas to Hannah Thomas, 12 December 1966. Gwyn was referring here to John Gwyn Griffiths (1911–2004), classics scholar and academic based at Swansea University, and the husband of the German-born Egyptologist, Käthe Bosse Griffiths (1910–1998), Keeper of Swansea Museum. The son, in this instance, and misspelled by Gwyn, was the campaigner Heini Gruffudd (b. 1946).

[22] Glyn Jones, *Dragon*, 122.

[23] Gwyn Jones, 'Language, Style and the Anglo-Welsh', *Essays and Studies* (1953), 106.

[24] Thomas, *Pulpit*, 169.

[25] Alun Richards, 'Bowels Jones', in *The Former Miss Merthyr Tydfil* (London, 1979), 257.

[26] Letter from Gwyn Thomas to Hannah Thomas, 8 October 1933. The novel was first published in Britain by William Heinemann on 14 July 1930. It is clear he retained his love of Wolfe's writing. In Gwyn's surviving library is a copy of Pamela Hansford Johnson's *Thomas Wolfe: A Critical Study* (London, 1947). He also told Nan that the writers he admired were Steinbeck, Wolfe, Hemingway, and Ring Lardner. Letter from Gwyn Thomas to Hannah Thomas, 25 October 1950.

[27] *WM*, 15 November 1979.

[28] SWML, Gwyn Thomas Collection: Transcript of Interview between John Ormond and Gwyn Thomas.

[29] Gwyn Thomas, 'Contribution to *The Colliers' Crusade*, episode one'.

[30] *LFD*, 38.

[31] Paul Preston, *Comrades: Portraits from the Spanish Civil War* (London, 1999), ch. 9.

[32] *The Scotsman*, 24 February 1936.

[33] Sama is approximately ten miles south-east of Oviedo.

[34] *La Voz de Asturias*, 25 June 1933. The rally took place on 26 June 1933.

[35] *Heraldo de Madrid*, 5 May, 8 May 1933.

[36] Federico García Lorca (transl. Stephen Spender and Joan Gili), *Poems* (London, 1939). The volume was published by the Dolphin Press.

[37] Kieron Smith, *John Ormond's Organic Mosaic* (Cardiff, 2019).

[38] Gwyn Thomas, 'Torchbearers of Uneasiness', *Arcade*, 1 May 1981.

[39] Thomas was a member of Neath Rural District Council and a leading communist in the Communist Party's 'West Wales' district at that time. He stood as the communist candidate for the Neath constituency at the 1950 general election and was briefly the secretary of the South Wales District from 1951–1953.

CHAPTER TEN
Wings of Significance

The obituaries paid fulsome tribute. Gwyn was hailed as a 'true son of the Rhondda' whose 'hilarious, gab-gifted novels of proletarian life in the valleys ... were part of the wind of change that blew from the regions through the stiff house of English fiction in the late Forties and Fifties.'[1] Journalists and commentators recalled the novels, plays, broadcasting work, and a determination to put the bark back into the underdog. The *New York Times* observed Gwyn was 'an author who wove the ordinary people of his native South Wales into [his] stories.'[2] The same obituary, produced by the Associated Press, was published in Chicago and in other American cities where Gwyn's literary and broadcasting voice was once well-known.[3] For the *Daily Telegraph*, he was 'a master of epigram' whose voice had such quality that one 'could listen to him talk all day.'[4] And in the London *Times*, Dai Smith wrote that Gwyn had 'more than any other writer of the twentieth century ... captured the significance of the majority Welsh experience' adding that 'his novels and plays, so deliberately removed in style from a naturalistic mode, form a rich, often devastating, commentary on an industrial South Wales whose culture he had seen flourish and wither in his own lifetime.'[5]

Close friends, such as Jeffrey Robinson, who became a surrogate son to Lyn and Gwyn, were similarly reflective. 'We recall his surprising shyness,' wrote Robinson and Brian McCann in a compendium of Gwyn's columns for the *Western Mail* published in 1985, 'his kindness, his compassion, but above all that sharp and imaginative perception of humour, which continued to shine with unfailing enthusiasm long after his health began giving cause for concern.' Gwyn, they noted, had once written that 'in the darkest night of the spirit, laughter is the signal that we are fully and unconquerably still there. And when a fine laughter maker falls still, the night itself for a while, will be inconsolable.'[6] Only now do we fully appreciate what he meant, they added poignantly. In 1983, on the occasion of the tenth anniversary of the founding of the South Wales Miners' Library in Swansea in October 1973, Lyn donated much of her husband's library, memorabilia including his famous hat and coat, several notebooks containing penned drafts of his *Western Mail* television columns, copies of scripts, and posters from performances of his plays.[7] They were to be housed in the Gwyn Thomas Room at Hendrefoelan House. There they joined Lewis Jones's diaries and the surviving libraries of the miners' institutes about which Gwyn had been such a passionate champion. Gwyn's work was now part of a new citadel of learning devoted to the cultural memory of South Wales.

At the event in the autumn of 1983, Will Paynter, Gwyn's old friend and mentor, spoke of their shared experiences in the Rhondda of the 1930s and of the vitality of the portrait which Gwyn had embedded into his writing. The poet and documentary maker, John Ormond, who had worked closely with Gwyn on his last broadcasts for radio and television, spoke too. The audience laughed at jokes which Gwyn had made and willingly recalled a man who once told an HTV interviewer that 'I was born in 1913 and in 1914 that was an even worse year. This belongs to the cosmology of my life that – I mean I'm not modest about this at all – I believe that I was begotten with wings of significance into a certain period. Wings of terrible meaning.' Photographs from the occasion in 1983 show Lyn

Thomas flanked by Ormond, Hywel Francis, the novelist Alun Richards, and the principal of University College Swansea, Brian Clarkson. The donation of Gwyn's library was the spur to his fellow writers to donate their papers, and in subsequent years the university would become home to the literary records of Ron Berry, Elaine Morgan, Alun Richards, and Raymond Williams. Gwyn's original letters to Nan, which were passed to his nephew, David, and then to Dai Smith, and finally to me, together with other materials used and collected in writing this biography will join them, at last bringing together in Swansea both sides of Gwyn's literary career.

Of course, as befitted a broadcaster of more than three decades, testimonials to Gwyn were not only recorded in newspaper obituaries and in reflective writing by his friends. John Ormond produced a special programme for BBC Radio 4 broadcast in September 1981. *The Voice of Meadow Prospect* presented a retrospective of Gwyn's entire career on radio and television and drew on archive material together with guiding commentary from actor Ray Smith. The programme was repeated a few months later, shortly before a memorial evening at the Sherman Theatre in Cardiff. Ormond had been commissioned to write a 'compilation for theatre' drawing together the full range of Gwyn's writing, published and unpublished. Jeffrey Robinson acted as researcher. *Laughter Before Nightfall*, performed by Gerald James and Ray Smith, was staged on 18 May 1982. It was reproduced and recorded for broadcast on Radio 4 at the Bethesda Community Arts Centre in Merthyr Tydfil a year later.[8] 'There wasn't a dry eye in the house,' observed one reviewer.[9] In 1984, Gwyn's work crept back onto the radio once more. At the start of the year, Glyn Jones read several of Gwyn's *Punch* stories; at the end of the year, Ray Smith read *The Cavers*; and in the summer, *Bookshelf* discussed the first edition of Poetry Wales' *Selected*

Short Stories which had been brought together by Michael Parnell.

In 1986, *Bookshelf* turned again to Gwyn's work, this time in a programme discussing *Sorrow For Thy Sons*, then recently published by Lawrence and Wishart. With *All Things Betray Thee* also republished in 1986, Dai Smith took to Radio Wales and Radio 4 early in that summer to argue that the time had come, five years after Gwyn's untimely death, to 'assess and celebrate the writer's literary achievement.' Michael Parnell's full-length biography, *Laughter From The Dark*, added to this critical momentum albeit with a different sense of Gwyn's literary contribution. National interest soon waned, however. There had been a degree of hostility even to the new edition of *All Things Betray Thee*, which was overcome chiefly by the intervention of Dai Smith and Raymond Williams. The latter gave Lawrence and Wishart, the publisher, a positive reader's report, and a new critical introduction, thereby lending authoritative weight to the project.[10] By the early 1990s, several of Gwyn's most prominent champions had either died or were ailing. Raymond Williams passed suddenly in 1988; John Ormond two years later; Michael Parnell in 1991; and Glyn Jones in 1995. Lyn herself died in the summer of 1990; a few months shy of her eightieth birthday.[11]

Alongside the wave of publications and broadcast retrospectives in the mid-1980s, was the popular contribution to Gwyn's lasting memory by his friend and fellow graduate of the Rhondda: Glyn Houston. The one-man theatrical impersonation, *Chunks and Chips*, produced initially for the Swansea Festival in October 1986, was recorded by HTV for their *Singular Performances* series.[12] The broadcast was introduced by the Cilfynydd-born opera singer, Sir Geraint Evans. 'Gwyn Thomas,' explained Evans to a keen audience, 'was a man who lived and wrote about a world that I understood and still understand, like me he came from the Welsh valleys, well I had to leave to achieve my aims and ambitions but Gwyn, after a brief visit to Oxford and then to Spain, neither of which experiences he relished much, came back to South Wales taught in Barry and then, with the dawning of the age of television, suddenly became famous with his descriptions of valley life.' It led to a regular series of stage productions, such as at the Swansea Grand Theatre in February 1989 or at the Theatrebarn in Bretforton Grange, near Evesham in Worcestershire in September 1991.[13] 'I am a Welsh aristocrat,' Houston's character said at the start of the play, before launching into full flight of jokes and asides, 'I can trace my ancestry all the way back to my father!'

There was to be one last champion, whose reach extended across the whole of Britain: the playwright and screenwriter, Alan Plater. Early in his career, together with the singer-songwriter, Alex Glasgow, Plater had brought together the short stories of Gwyn's friend Sid Chaplin in *Close The Coalhouse Door* (1969). But it was Plater's 1988 work for Channel 4, *A Very British Coup*, an adaptation of Chris Mullins's novel about a left-wing British Prime Minister, for which he was best known. Speaking in 1993, Plater recalled that 'Gwyn was one of my role models when I started to write, and a very dangerous one because he wrote in a very ebullient Celtic way – never used one word if twenty-seven would do.'[14] The association between Gwyn and Alan Plater dated to the early 1970s. In 1972, Gwyn had penned an enthusiastic review of Plater's early teleplay *Seventeen Per Cent Said Push Off*. Then, a month after Gwyn's death in 1981, Plater paid his first tribute when he included excerpts from interviews and programmes in an episode of the Radio 4 series, *The Archive Auction*. The premise of the show was that guests could nominate recordings from the archives which they would most like to own.[15]

Over the course of the 1980s, Plater became convinced that he could bring to the screen an adaptation of Gwyn's autobiography (of sorts), *A Few Selected Exits*. Michael Chaplin (Sid Chaplin's son), then head of English language programmes for BBC Wales, agreed with Plater and commissioned the production. Lyn furnished a copy of the American edition of Gwyn's autobiography and Plater set about working on the script. By January 1993, Plater had finished writing. The adaptation was scheduled for broadcast on BBC Two on Christmas Day. In the title role Plater cast Anthony Hopkins, who was then fresh from his Oscar-winning performance as the butler, Stevens, in the motion picture adaptation of Kazuo Ishiguro's novel *Remains of the Day*. Hopkins' daughter, Abigail Harrison, took the role of Hannah Thomas; Sue Roderick starred as Lyn Thomas, and Ian McDiarmid starred as George Devine. Much of the script was true to the source material, lifting directly where necessary or adapting subtly to produce much the same effect. Hopkins, whose father was a friend of Gwyn's brother, Walt, and thus met Gwyn on family visits during the 1950s, played the role as somewhat shy, sharp-tongued, and quick-witted, with Plater's dialogue comfortably pitched in a leftist tone.[16]

'Teaching and learning were not things of beauty,' Plater had Gwyn say in full flow in the classroom, 'no, they were rope ladders, designed to help us up a lift shaft of academic grace, from a darkened and ghastly underworld to a lighted surface. And that is why I'm here, to help you boys from that underground darkness into Mr Clement Attlee's gleaming paradise.'[17] The dialogue invention was proof that Plater was the ideal translator of Gwyn's writing – and political personality – for the small screen. Critics generally agreed. At least in Britain. Plater's film won a BAFTA and a Royal Television Society Award. In *The Times*, Hilary Kingsley observed that the film was 'the best homemade present under the BBC's Christmas tree.'[18] Early promotion of the production had placed it at the heart of BBC Wales' new 'powerhouse' of drama.[19] But in the United States, where the film was shown on PBS in early October 1993, two months ahead of its UK broadcast, there was a feeling that 'as dramatic fodder, he's no Mr Chips.'[20] Plater's dramatization served, all the same, to create a renewed appetite for Gwyn's work, on radio and television. The BBC broadcast several short stories on radio between 1993 and 1995, and in 1996 came Alan Plater's fresh three-part dramatization of *All Things Betray Thee*.

Michael Chaplin was succeeded as Head of English Language Programmes for BBC Wales by Dai Smith, who seized the opportunity to bring more of Gwyn's work onto television and for a new generation. He notably commissioned a fresh production of *The Keep* for a series of programmes titled *Theatre of the Air*. Broadcast in 1996, with Glyn Houston in the title role, it was the first television production of Gwyn's theatrical masterpiece in more than thirty years. Critical essays and a BBC handbook were produced to accompany the broadcast, all with a view to generating debate and discussion of Gwyn's career and his legacy.[21] HTV, too, reached into its archives and broadcast Gwyn's sections of *Wales and the West* edited together and packaged as *Shades of Gwyn Thomas*. Although by then several of the audio tapes for *Wales and the West* had badly degraded and the lost narration was replaced with new recordings by Glyn Houston. Dai Smith had previously presented the documentary, *Wings of Significance*, for HTV in 1993, which was broadcast to mark what would have been Gwyn's eightieth birthday. A similarly evocative documentary, *A Sad But Beautiful Joke*, with interviews from Alan Plater, Anthony Hopkins, and Dai Smith, appeared on BBC One in 1993 to accompany (and partly to explain) *A Few Selected Exits*.

With the successful devolution vote in 1997, growing national self-introspection, and the complete attenuation of the industrial world of South Wales which Gwyn had known and championed, his ideas and his perspective have come to be seen as no longer a comfortable fit for a postmodern Wales – although a production of *The Dark Philosophers* by National Theatre Wales was a sell-out success at the Edinburgh Festival in 2011. The playwright Ian Rowlands observed, tellingly, in his introduction to the Library of Wales edition of *The Alone to the Alone* in 2008, that Gwyn was 'very much a man of his own testing and challenging time. But times change, and one could argue that through devolution and the renegotiation of the concept of Welshness (in whatever tongue – let us not reduce the argument to a bilingual one) our nation will finally shrug off its insecurity, and the compassion which Thomas championed will, at last, triumph.' Would Gwyn, who took wry delight in the defeat of the devolution referendum in 1979, have agreed? Given all that he said on such matters in his lifetime, the answer is surely no. The catastrophe of the 1984–5 miners' strike and the final defeat of that world of South Wales would not have surprised him, either. Nor would he have had to search for another future, as did so many on the Welsh Left in the aftermath of the strike. It was enough to spend a lifetime making sense of the catastrophe of the 1930s.

Contra the observations made by Gwyn A. Williams in a BBC radio lecture a few months after the election of Margaret Thatcher in 1979, neither that year nor 1984–5 were the years when the Welsh, as a people, stood naked in an acid rain. That was in the locust years of the Depression. Across Gwyn Thomas's life, and most especially his childhood, as he so often said, lay the great ruptures of modern Wales. There was the optimism of the Edwardian Liberal high noon, the fragility of the immediate post-First World War economy, and then the slump. Or, to pick up the metaphor of Gwyn A. Williams once more, when the rain clouds full of acid burst from the sky. In a lecture given before an audience at University College Cardiff in 1979, titled 'The Subsidence Factor,' Gwyn Thomas explained that,

> A half of the valley's population drifted away. It was a Black Death on wheels conducted with far less anguish. Some went as fruit pickers in California's San Fernando Valley, and their voices came to be heard making good harmonies and even better money in any film made in Hollywood about mining. The great mass moved South to Cardiff and east to the Midlands and London, and the permanent guard on all the trains operating the great dispersal bore the name of Thomas Malthus, who warned the migrants about humanity's way of concentrating huge battalions in tasks seeming secure for eternity, then suddenly changing the scenery, and telling the extras that they are in the wrong picture.

In such a situation, as Gwyn observed time and time again, all you can do is laugh. 'Most lives are a yearning for coherence,' he added in 1979, 'a feeling that things are good and have a look of reason about them. The sense of belonging to a firm indivisible laughing community would help. We had no such boon.' Two years later, in an interview with Dai Smith, who had come to interview his former teacher for the arts magazine *Arcade*, Gwyn said that 'somebody ought to analyse my humour.' He was convinced that it proved 'that the South Welsh did enlarge understanding. I was only a clue to the great thing that was being achieved – a mountain of achievement that has crumbled away. I think my humour shows the way in which the intellect of the Welsh working class might have developed their world.' As a young man, Gwyn often described himself, privately, as a revolutionary artist: someone who used literature and drama to further political causes and to give reality to the possibilities of the working-class intellect. To begin with, armed only with the tools immediately at his disposal, he used melodrama to tell his would-be audience what they might think. 'It's easier to make people think after you've made them cry,' Gwyn wrote in his journal at the end of December 1938, adding that 'it is wrong, profoundly wrong for a revolutionary artist to discard sentimentalism. Sentimentalism is a crime against literary dignity only when the sentimental writer weeps over it himself.'

Later, Gwyn turned to black comedy, realising that he could make readers or listeners cry with laughter instead of misery. In the novels of the 1950s and the plays of the 1960s, his comedy took on a lighter shade when 'the refulgent dreams of my dark philosophers ... turn[ed] out to be nothing.' This clarity of creative and political purpose set Gwyn apart from other Welsh writers of the twentieth century and gave him a global reach, on both sides of the Cold War divide. He was certain that this vision was tied to his origins and to the dominance of the English language. 'Places like the Rhondda,' Gwyn explained,

> were parts of America that never managed to get to the boat. In the classrooms of my childhood I sat alongside Somerset, Dorset, Gloucestershire. Our teachers were men trained in the white heat of the movement fuelled by men like Arnold, Ruskin and Rhodes, who believed that the English language was the divinely appointed adhesive that would give at least a pleasant illusion of integrity to our cracked old species.

Of all the Welshmen of the last century who achieved fame, only Aneurin Bevan and Richard Burton can be placed comfortably on the same artistic-political pedestal as Gwyn. Dylan Thomas, whose creative prowess was clear, lacked the sharp edge shared by Burton, Bevan, and Gwyn, even as the poet's creative talents were readily apparent. That trinity summed up the possibilities of twentieth-century South Wales: its politics, its creative passions, and its intellectual perspectives, as well as its social and economic limitations. Each had, to return to the abiding metaphor of their experience, an 'American' life and a 'Welsh' death. Of the three, only Richard Burton truly felt the pangs of nostalgia and a Welshness not entirely free of 'Celtic' fairy dust, as Gwyn saw it, but then he was the only one of them to live his life abroad.

The unity of art, language, and left-wing politics also explains why Gwyn's most prominent champions have so often been of a similar temperament and intellectual trajectory, and why his opponents, Welsh or otherwise, have tended to come from the opposite ends of the spectrum. There was Raymond Williams, who grew up on the border between Wales and England, between the rural and the industrial, and whose politics were more aligned with the Communist Party than with the Labour Party. Alan Plater, who was born in Jarrow and grew up in Hull, whose work attacked Britain's ruling classes and praised the endeavours of the country's workers. Elaine Morgan, Gwyn's nearest Welsh contemporary, who was born in Pontypridd and spent her professional career scripting the fictional lives of valleys folk for radio and television. The historian Eric Hobsbawm, who understood more than most the dislocation of politics and the dangers of nationalism and committed his life to studying the labour movement in all its forms. The actor, Timothy West, who laments the forgetting of Gwyn.[22] And Dai Smith, who was similarly displaced from the Rhondda to Barry, who made the same journey to Oxford and back to Wales, and whose literary and creative sensibilities have been shaped by an American imagination no less vivid than Gwyn's own. These commonalities, with due recognition of literary style and personal ambition to be a revolutionary artist, one who spoke with the humour of his people, surely vindicate the ambition and the achievement of Gwyn Thomas as a writer, one as significant, in either language, as his country has ever produced.

*

Following Gwyn's funeral in April 1981, a small group of his friends together with his surviving brother, Eddie, and Lyn, travelled to the hamlet of Llanwynno on the mountaintop separating the Rhondda and Cynon valleys.[23] Gwyn had been brought there often as a child by his father, Walter, on the premise of walking across the mountain to visit relatives in Mountain Ash. The Thomases called the plateau 'Arthur's Crown.' It was, Gwyn wrote in the poignant coda to *A Few Selected Exits*, very beautiful. In those days, 'it was bare except for a fringe of stunted trees across its top, bent and crouched by the winds that blew in from the sea.' Since the 1930s, it has been developed as a forest and is today managed by Natural Resources Wales. On that mountaintop, Gwyn found another world compared with the valleys below. 'Enchanted it was,' he wrote, 'that sea of ferns, endless to the eye of a child. A world of kind and golden light. Larks singing with a force that made it seem they were trying to burst their way into one of the local choirs. And we would sing back at them. Larks and sheep looking so gentle and intelligent one spoke to them and got answers of a kind. It was and is the land of my emotions.'

Gwyn never reached Mountain Ash. His father always stopped for refreshment. The houses at Llanwynno, which Gwyn knew as a child, have since been demolished leaving just the Victorian parish church of St Gwynno and the Brynffynon

Inn. Or, as Gwyn called it in his autobiography, *The Tavern of the Fountain*. This was rural South Wales. Quiet and calm. But for the coal tips, untouched by industry. The farms all had very old Welsh names – Daerwynno, Gelli Wrgan, Ty'nygelli, and Y Dduallt. They were the homes of the pre-industrial gentry. There was the Llewelyn family of Daerwynno, for instance. Anglicans and Conservatives, they were more interested in hunting, horses, and displaying agricultural produce, than they were in the colliery business which carried on deep beneath the fields in which their sheep grazed. At the pub, Walter Thomas would nip in for a drink leaving his children to fend for themselves in the churchyard and the fern-cleft fields. 'We never lost the sense of being in an unsmirched paradise,' Gwyn reflected many years later. On those journeys up to the plateau, Walter would tell his children stories of the local folk heroes, not least the runner Guto Nyth Bran who was buried in the churchyard opposite the pub.

It was here that Gwyn's friends and family gathered after his funeral carrying his ashes. They made their way to a small grove of trees not far away. It was a day of cloud and sunshine, and squally wind. Rain threatened at any moment. John Ormond read a poem by Edna St Vincent Millay which Gwyn had especially loved. Eddie Thomas scattered his brother's remains onto the ground as Ormond spoke. 'And when he finished the poem,' Dai Smith recalled, 'we stood silent. And then with a heavenly comment, which I think Gwyn would have approved of, the skies opened, and we were drenched with a cold burst of rain which also stuck Gwyn to the earth, back where he belonged before the wind could blow him away.' Less than fifteen years earlier, Gwyn had gone to Llanwynno himself intending to 'cross the plateau all the way to Mountain Ash and fix once and for all the location of that shrine of loveliness that had slipped furtively in and out of my father's talk and dreams so long ago.' He never made it then, either. Like his father, he took refuge in the pub. It was filled with members of the Pendyrus Male Voice Choir. They 'roared into a piece about the irrelevance of death and the certain prospect of renewal,' Gwyn wrote,

> They then eased the strain and brought all our doubts back with a very negative item called 'Ten Green Bottles.' Then, the midsummer dusk outstanding, they sang one of the loveliest of the quiet carols. The night put on a cap of gold. I was home, at my earth's warm centre. The scared monkey was back in the branches of his best loved tree. I've never had any truly passionate wish to be elsewhere.

Those were the pitch-perfect final lines of *A Few Selected Exits*. They conveyed the poignant sense of the enduring and endearing attachment which Gwyn always felt for the Rhondda and for the surrounding hillsides and neighbouring valleys. He had never travelled very far from that part of Wales. He had no wish to do so. He was never entirely comfortable on his trips outside of Glamorgan, let alone outside of Wales. As he explained to Keith Baxter in 1969, this was both a sentimental and a practical matter:

> I suppose it's rather like a sculptor opting to live near Carrara marble, my materials are there. I was born into a really stupendous jest, you know, an industry was dying, a massive popular religion was dying, and most important of all the most dynamic and passionate political belief in Britain was dying too … And as a humorous writer, of course, I've got to be near these things. I could never be the same in London, removed from them. And in any case I am a firm disbeliever in a writer going to live in a capital city like London because I find London

writers affected by a kind of dandruff of the brain, a kind of flaking away of their first integrity that they might have had in Leeds, or Halifax, or Hull. But I want to stay very near my sources and indeed I want to assure the people in Wales who would dearly love to see the back of me sometimes, I suppose, that I intend hanging around for quite a bit. It is only death that will remove me from those strange, dark pastures.

By restoring the rich scarlet-red hue of Gwyn's work, his commitment to the radical left flanks of twentieth-century politics, and the embodiment of the modernist promise of American Wales, I have endeavoured to show the complexities of a man often reduced to epigram or to cartoon villain. There is no doubting that, on certain matters constitutional, Gwyn's political fervour is out of step with the tenor of twenty-first century Wales: no one could now get away with writing, as he did in the introduction for the programme of *Loud Organs*, that 'he has never learnt his native Welsh. This has been with him a matter of principle, since he considers local national feeling to be a danger and that a wider community spirit is the only solution to present problems.'[24] Nor could they say live on radio that because he had lost 'the language of my parents ... as soon as I got to the age when I was able to lose things,' then he 'was liberated early on from any kind of obsessive nationalism.' But Gwyn did write and say such things. It is beholden on us to understand *why*, as well as to judge. There is no doubting, either, that Gwyn's literary output is less fashionable than it was several decades ago. Again, that is no less true of his contemporaries from Rhys Davies to Jack Jones to Emyr Humphreys, in the Welsh context, or Kingsley Amis, A. J. Cronin, and V. S. Naipaul in a wider British one.

And yet, because of Gwyn's involvement in the American Civil Rights Movement, alongside major figures such as Howard

Fast, Studs Terkel, Nelson Algren, Norman Rosten, Arthur Miller, and Norman Mailer; his engagement with both sides of the Cold War; and the popular interest in his work all over the world, he appears as a compelling window onto the twentieth century. He had an incredible artistic reach. Indeed, he was compelled to understand the twentieth century, to makes sense of what had happened to South Wales' social and cultural, political and economic dynamism. The world of his parents. He was not the only Welsh writer vexed by this question: Ron Berry was similarly motivated, as were, in their own ways, Elaine Morgan and Alun Richards. Nor was Gwyn the first Welsh writer who flourished because of their tremendous command of the English language: Caradoc Evans and Rhys Davies got there before him. But none of them, not even Dylan Thomas, who was Gwyn's only serious literary rival, was able to speak simultaneously to audiences in the Rhondda, London, New York, Berlin, and Moscow. That alone was Gwyn's achievement. That alone affords him primacy in the pantheon of Welsh – and British – writers.

Gwyn received the two prizes he most cherished in the late 1970s. The first, handed to him by Raymond Williams at a ceremony in 1976, was the Welsh Arts Council's lifetime achievement award. The second was a plaque from the Rhondda Presentation Committee, which had been formed by a group of civic-minded residents with a view to rewarding the achievements of those with Rhondda connections. Emblazoned with the emblem of Rhondda Borough Council, the plaque's citation read: 'Presented to Gwyn Thomas on behalf of valley residents, for his achievements in the literary world.' It was a signal to Gwyn that he had succeeded after all. At least, that is, in the eyes of the people who mattered most. There were regrets, of course. 'My books were produced from the wrong place, the wrong time, the wrong people,' he explained on

416

Women's Hour in 1964, 'I peddled hope and eloquence in a market place where a dumb, dirty despair was to become the fashion.'[25] It would have been better, he said, his irony dialled to maximum, that he had descended from a bunch of 'complacent louts' who had grown up in a Cotswold mansion. Or a similarly wealthy and bourgeois part of the country. That has so often been the fate of those from the South Wales Valleys who aspire to be artists or writers (or even historians).

In that same episode, Gwyn told listeners that he had started writing due to the 'breakdown of the pigeon post in 1927.' He added, in his typically self-effacing and jocular style, that 'we felt the need to enlarge on the rather cryptic messages we had been sending by way of the birds. So out of the South Rhondda Culture Fund I was given a grant for paper and nibs. The nibs were too sharp and the paper too thin.' It was all part of Gwyn's image of a collective society which afforded creative opportunities to those who wished them, and his defence of such a society in the face of multiple betrayals. His conveying of the fury of past time. The truth about Gwyn Thomas, the Rhondda Runyon, the Revolutionary Artist, the Joker and the Judge, in fact, is that for all the witticism; for all the droll asides and entertaining epigrams; for all the memorability of his quick and sharp tongue; for all that his political views and activities can still cause some to wince, resent and hate (as he once put it); in their totality, vibrancy, and veracity, his vast achievements on the page, the stage, and in the broadcasting studio, whether for television or for radio, were and are no less than the literary and historical record of the South Walian people. They were the hallmark of his unique genius.

[1] Norman Shrapnel, 'Welsh Jester', *The Guardian*, 14 April 1981.

[2] *New York Times*, 19 April 1981.

[3] *Chicago Tribune*, 19 April 1981.

[4] *Daily Telegraph*, 14 April 1981.

[5] *The Times*, 18 April 1981.

[6] Jeffrey Robinson and Brian McCann, *Gwyn Thomas: High on Hope* (Cowbridge, 1985), 8.

[7] The occasion was marked by Alun Richards in an article for the *WM*, 2 November 1983.

[8] *RT*, 27 April 1983; NLW, John Ormond Papers, C/2; NLW, Academi Gymraeg Papers, EER9/1: Gwyn Thomas Memorial Evening, 1982.

[9] Maureen Owen, 'Surfeit', *The Spectator*, 7 May 1983.

[10] Letter from Raymond Williams to Dai Smith, 21 February 1985.

[11] Michael Parnell, 'Mrs Lyn Thomas', *New Welsh Review* 10 (Autumn 1990), pp. 57–8.

[12] *The Stage*, 18 September 1986. A copy of the camera script (for 5 October 1986) is held at Swansea University, rare books (folios), W/DA1368.

[13] *The Stage*, 5 September 1991.

[14] Alan Plater, 'Underrated', *The Independent*, 2 February 1994.

[15] Kate Fenton made similar requests for Gwyn's work in an edition of the programme broadcast in November 1985.

[16] *The Stage*, 10 March 1994.

[17] The classroom scenes were partly filmed at Aberdare Girls' School.

[18] *The Times*, 24 December 1993.

[19] *The Stage*, 11 February 1993.

[20] *Variety*, 29 September 1993.

[21] Anna-Marie Taylor and Rob Humphreys (eds), *Opening Up "The Keep"* (BBC Wales, 1996).

[22] British Library Sound Archive, Theatre Archive Project, C1142/13: 'Interview with Timothy West conducted by Catherine Jones, 1 May 2004'.

[23] The group was Dai Smith, John Ormond, and Gwyn's first biographer Ian Michael.

[24] Gwyn Thomas, *Programme: Loud Organs* (Cardiff, 1962).

[25] 'Talking to Himself', *The Listener*, 19 May 1964.

ACKNOWLEDGEMENTS

This book started out over a pint with Dai Smith in the Llanover Arms in Pontypridd in November 2016. The idea, then, was for a gathering together of Gwyn Thomas's voluminous correspondence with editorial interventions which would help to explain both the politics and the letters. At the heart of the project was a box of treasures which Dai handed to me that day, a box containing the original letters sent by Gwyn to his sister Nan over a period of nearly four decades. He had been given the box by Nan's son – Gwyn's nephew – the late Dr David Gwyn Thomas. Here, too, were unpublished short stories, notebooks, and other materials, which suggested a far bigger project. Since my own doctoral research at Swansea between 2008 and 2011, I had been gathering notes and a sense of the archival terrain with a view to one day writing a biography of Gwyn. Over that earlier period, I had become convinced that existing biographies of Gwyn were inadequate because they missed the political heart of the writer and the writing – his true essence.

My first thanks are therefore due to David Gwyn Thomas for the archival records, to Jeffrey Robinson for the encouragement of the Gwyn Thomas Estate, and to Dai Smith who set me the challenge of making sense of a truly enigmatic subject. Unhindered work on the biography was made possible by the generosity of the Rhys Davies Trust who awarded me a once-in-a-lifetime fellowship held in conjunction with Swansea University. My gratitude to the Trustees, Sam Adams, Peter Finch, and Dai Smith, knows no bounds. Once again, I wish to thank the numerous archives and libraries, and their staff,

419

where research was undertaken – either in person or remotely, especially during the Pandemic of 2020–22. Full details can be found in the notes accompanying each chapter but especial mention must be made of the South Wales Miners' Library, the Richard Burton Archives at Swansea University, the British Library, St Edmund Hall Archive, the Norwegian Labour Movement Archives and Library in Oslo, Columbia University Special Collections, Queens University (Canada) Special Collections, Brigham Young University Special Collections, Boston University Special Collections, the BBC Written Archive Centre, and the National Library of Wales. I gratefully acknowledge, too, the support shown to the project by Gwyn's literary agent, Caroline de Wolfe (of Felix de Wolfe). Where archives required special permissions for access, I wish to thank Curtis Brown Ltd (in the United States) and Penguin Random House (in the UK).

The number of personal debts accrued and to be recognised in a multi-year project such as this are significant and, for fear of leaving anyone out accidentally, as they say, they know who they are. But a few thank you messages are in order. To the late Hywel Francis who encouraged every element of this book before his death in February 2021 and hoped that I would one day turn up the golden nugget of evidence which claimed Gwyn for the Communist Party. There was no party card but much else which delighted Hywel. To Ceinwen Statter for insights into her uncle, and Gwyn's long-running colleague, Sid Jones. To Ann Wilson, for insights into her father's absorption into communism in Cambridge, her mother's in Aberaman, and the practical implementation of 'the Party' by Alistair and Olive, and others of their circle, in the Cynon Valley. To Alexander Jackson, Duncan Stone, and David Toms, and more recently Miriam Cohen Kiel and Mohamad El Chamaa, for moral support and collective sharing in the ups and downs of lives lived by writing. And finally, of course, to my family. To my beloved grandmother, who passed away from the coronavirus aged ninety-two in February 2021; to my sister, Katrina and my niece, Kate; and above all to my father, David, to whom this book is dedicated.

INDEX

INDEX

Malayan Emergency, 211
Mallett, Richard, 251
Maltz, Albert, 202, 228
'Man Who Made Critics Laugh,
The' (*Daily Mail*), 263–264
'Man With The Chalk, The'
(*Punch*), 146–147
Marquand, Hilary, 210
Martinsville Seven, 227
Marxism, 80, 83, 107–108, 122,
163, 207, 217
Masereel, Frans, 175
Masses and Mainstream, 193,
195–196, 197, 202, 204, 214,
218–219, 224
Mathews, Leslie, 149, 348–349
Matter of Degree, A (Morgan), 303,
332
Matusow, Harvey, 201, 202
McCann, Brian, 261, 401–402
McDiarmid, Ian, 406
McDowall, Roddy, 205
McGee, Willie, 227
McGrath, Thomas, 193, 194
McKellen, Ian, 361
McKenzie, Compton, 385
'Meadow Prospect Christmas, A',
304
Meadow Prospect Revisited, 9, 252
Means Test, 78, 81–82, 115,
118, 119, 247
'Meeting, The', 63–64
Melvin, Murray, 359
Meyer, Frank Strauss, 77–78, 82–
84
Michael Joseph, 166, 169, 170–
171
Mikardo, Ian, 215
Miller, Arthur, 38n51, 191, 193–
194, 195, 213, 330, 340, 416
miners' lockouts and the General
Strike, 42, 43–44, 119, 322
Mirsky, D.S., 83–84
Mitchell, Denis, 64, 129, 278,
281–282, 323, 374–375
Modern Reading, 14, 17, 19,
163–164
Molina, Tirso de, 341
Monthly Review, 207

Montrealer, The, 254, 255–256
Moore, Dudley, 343, 354
Moore, Reginald, 14–22, 26–27,
38n43, 163–164, 171, 173
More than Somewhat (Runyon),
162–163
Morgan, Elaine, 10, 303, 330–
332, 385–386, 403, 411, 416
Morgan, Morien, 391
Morgan, Trevor, 87–88, 103n43
Morley, Robert, 150–151
Morris, William, 14
Morrison, Herbert, 222
Mortimer, John, 344
Moscow, 106, 310–311, 393
mothers, absent, 50, 119, 332,
344–345
Motion Picture Alliance for the
Preservation of American Ideals,
210–211
Muggeridge, Malcolm, 250–251,
253
Murdoch, Iris, 24, 84
music, 41–42, 50–51, 53–56,
65–68, 266, 310, 353–354,
356 (*see also* entries under
Gazooka)
'My Fist Upon the Stone', 20
My Glorious Brothers (Fast), 216–
217
My Roots on Earth, 166–169,
170, 171 (*see also All Things
Betray Thee*; *Leaves in the Wind*)
Nails, 1, 5–6, 322
Naipaul, V.S., 183, 190n83, 415
National Council of Social Service
(NCSS), 131–132
National Theatre Wales, 408 (*see
also* theatre, in Wales)
Neruda, Pablo, 219, 242n62
New Central European Observer,
181–182, 189n80
New Masses, 194, 195, 203,
204, 224, 236
New Party, 24, 77, 100n6, 101n10
New Short Stories (Singer, ed.), 20
New Statesman, 250, 256
New Theatre, Cardiff, 350, 355,
361, 362

Modern Wales by Parthian Books

The Modern Wales Series, edited by Dai Smith and supported by the Rhys Davies Trust, was launched in 2017. The Series offers an extensive list of biography, memoir, history and politics which reflect and analyse the development of Wales as a modernised society into contemporary times. It engages widely across places and people, encompasses imagery and the construction of iconography, dissects historiography and recounts plain stories, all in order to elucidate the kaleidoscopic pattern which has shaped and changed the complex culture and society of Wales and the Welsh.

The inaugural titles in the Series were *To Hear the Skylark's Song*, a haunting memoir of growing up in Aberfan by Huw Lewis, and Joe England's panoramic *Merthyr: The Crucible of Modern Wales*. The impressive list has continued with Angela John's *Rocking the Boat*, essays on Welsh women who pioneered the universal fight for equality and Daryl Leeworthy's landmark overview *Labour Country*, on the struggle through radical action and social democratic politics to ground Wales in the civics of common ownership. Myths and misapprehension, whether naïve or calculated, have been ruthlessly filleted in Martin Johnes's startling *Wales: England's Colony?* and a clutch of biographical studies will reintroduce us to the once seminal, now neglected, figures of Cyril Lakin, Minnie Pallister and Gwyn Thomas, whilst Meic Stephens's *Rhys Davies: A Writer's Life* and Dai Smith's *Raymond Williams: A Warrior's Tale* form part of an associated back catalogue from Parthian.

the RHYS DAVIES TRUST

ARTHIAN

MODERN WALES

WALES: ENGLAND'S COLONY?

Martin Johnes

From the very beginnings of Wales, its people have defined themselves against their large neighbour. This book tells the fascinating story of an uneasy and unequal relationship between two nations living side-by-side.

PB / £8.99
978-1-912681-41-9

RHYS DAVIES: A WRITER'S LIFE

Meic Stephens

Rhys Davies (1901-78) was among the most dedicated, prolific and accomplished of Welsh prose writers. This is his first full biography.

'This is a delightful book, which is itself a social history in its own right, and funny.'
– The Spectator

PB / £11.99
978-1-912109-96-8

MERTHYR, THE CRUCIBLE OF MODERN WALES

Joe England

Merthyr Tydfil was the town where the future of a country was forged: a thriving, struggling surge of people, industry, democracy and ideas. This book assesses an epic history of Merthyr from 1760 to 1912 through the focus of a fresh and thoroughly convincing perspective.

PB / £18.99
978-1-913640-05-7

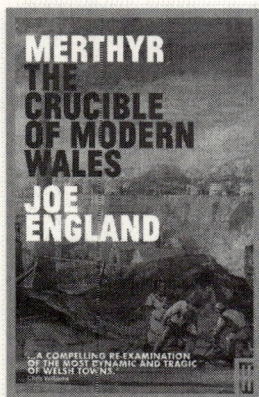

Modern Wales by Parthian Books

The Modern Wales Series, edited by Dai Smith and supported by the Rhys Davies Trust, was launched in 2017. The Series offers an extensive list of biography, memoir, history and politics which reflect and analyse the development of Wales as a modernised society into contemporary times. It engages widely across places and people, encompasses imagery and the construction of iconography, dissects historiography and recounts plain stories, all in order to elucidate the kaleidoscopic pattern which has shaped and changed the complex culture and society of Wales and the Welsh.

The inaugural titles in the Series were *To Hear the Skylark's Song*, a haunting memoir of growing up in Aberfan by Huw Lewis, and Joe England's panoramic *Merthyr: The Crucible of Modern Wales*. The impressive list has continued with Angela John's *Rocking the Boat*, essays on Welsh women who pioneered the universal fight for equality and Daryl Leeworthy's landmark overview *Labour Country*, on the struggle through radical action and social democratic politics to ground Wales in the civics of common ownership. Myths and misapprehension, whether naïve or calculated, have been ruthlessly filleted in Martin Johnes's startling *Wales: England's Colony?* and a clutch of biographical studies will reintroduce us to the once seminal, now neglected, figures of Cyril Lakin, Minnie Pallister and Gwyn Thomas, whilst Meic Stephens's *Rhys Davies: A Writer's Life* and Dai Smith's *Raymond Williams: A Warrior's Tale* form part of an associated back catalogue from Parthian.

the RHYS DAVIES TRUST

WALES: ENGLAND'S COLONY?

Martin Johnes

From the very beginnings of Wales, its people have defined themselves against their large neighbour. This book tells the fascinating story of an uneasy and unequal relationship between two nations living side-by-side.

PB / £8.99
978-1-912681-41-9

RHYS DAVIES: A WRITER'S LIFE

Meic Stephens

Rhys Davies (1901-78) was among the most dedicated, prolific and accomplished of Welsh prose writers. This is his first full biography.

'This is a delightful book, which is itself a social history in its own right, and funny.'
– The Spectator

PB / £11.99
978-1-912109-96-8

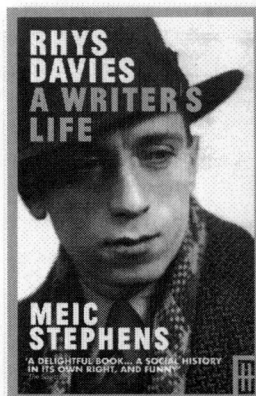

MERTHYR, THE CRUCIBLE OF MODERN WALES

Joe England

Merthyr Tydfil was the town where the future of a country was forged: a thriving, struggling surge of people, industry, democracy and ideas. This book assesses an epic history of Merthyr from 1760 to 1912 through the focus of a fresh and thoroughly convincing perspective.

PB / £18.99
978-1-913640-05-7

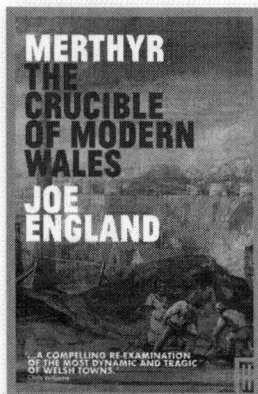